Proceedings

18th Workshop on Parallel and Distributed Simulation

Proceedings

18th Workshop on Parallel and Distributed Simulation

PADS 2004

16-19 May 2004 • Kufstein, Austria

Sponsored by

IEEE Computer Society Technical Committee on Simulation (IEEE-TCSIM)
ACM Special Interest Group on Simulation (SIGSIM)
Society for Modeling and Simulation International (SCS)

Los Alamitos, California

Washington • Brussels • Tokyo

IEEE Computer Society Order Number P2111
ACM Order Number 577040
ISBN 0-7695-2111-8
ISSN 1087-4097

Additional copies may be ordered from:

ACM Order Department
P.O. Box 11405
New York, NY 10286-1405
Tel: + 1-800-342-6626
(U.S. and Canada)
Tel: +1-212-626-0500
(all other countries)
Fax: + 1-212-944-1318
E-mail: acmhelp@acm.org

IEEE Computer Society
Customer Service Center
10662 Los Vaqueros Circle
P.O. Box 3014
Los Alamitos, CA 90720-1314
Tel: + 1-714-821-8380
Fax: + 1-714-821-4641
E-mail: cs.books@computer.org

IEEE Service Center
445 Hoes Lane
P.O. Box 1331
Piscataway, NJ 08855-1331
Tel: + 1-732-981-0060
Fax: + 1-732-981-9667
http://shop.ieee.org/store/
customer-service@ieee.org

IEEE Computer Society
Asia/Pacific Office
Watanabe Bldg., 1-4-2
Minami-Aoyama
Minato-ku, Tokyo 107-0062
JAPAN
Tel: + 81-3-3408-3118
Fax: + 81-3-3408-3553
tokyo.ofc@computer.org

Editorial production by Stephanie Kawada
Cover graphics courtesy of pro.media/jasiutyn
Cover art production by Joe Daigle/Studio Productions
Printed in the United States of America by Victor Graphics, Inc.

IEEE COMPUTER SOCIETY

IEEE

PADS 2004 Proceedings

18th Workshop on Parallel and Distributed Simulation

Table of Contents

Session 3: Optimization

Chair: ***Mineo Takai***

Session 4: Optimistic Methods

Chair: ***Adelinde Uhrmacher***

Session 5: Simulation Theory

Chair: ***Jason Liu***

Session 6: Applications

Chair: ***Carl Tropper***

Session 7: Keynote

Chair: *Axel Lehmann*

Session 8: Work In Progress

Chair: *A. L. M. Thom McLean*

Session 9: Network Simulation II

Chair: *Steve Turner*

Session 10: Emerging Methods

Chair: *David Nicol*

Message from the General Chairs

Welcome to the 2004 Workshop on Parallel and Distributed Simulation (PADS 2004), held this year in the little town Kufstein in the Austrian province Tyrol at its young University of Applied Sciences FHS KufsteinTirol.

In 788, a monk sat hunched over a paper in St. Peter's monastery in Salzburg and carefully recorded all the properties of his abbot, arch-bishop Arno of Salzburg, Austria. It was a long list because his master was the owner of many properties, among others there was also a small place called Caofstein. However, the first step is always the hardest. After the first mentioning of Kufstein, it took several centuries during which Kufstein was an unimportant hamlet. Later, the strategically advantageous position of Kufstein was reinforced by the construction of a fortress and a bridge over the River Inn, thus leading to an upward trend in the region. As a consequence, Kufstein was awarded the status of "Markt" (small town with trading rights) and later became a town (awarded by Stefan III, Duke of Bavaria). In 1504, Kufstein became part of Tirol as Emperor Maximilian I had received it as a reward for joining the "right" side in the hereditary succession conflict in Bavaria. In 1703, Kufstein was again taken by Bavarian forces. Only after the fall of Napoleon, Kufstein was given back to Tirol. The end of the 19th century was a period of enormous economic boom for the region. Within a short time, the population multiplied and important companies were founded.

On the education sector, Kufstein showed its innovativeness by establishing a kindergarten with the first kindergarten school of the Monarchy, and especially by founding a high school. The foundations for today's face of the district capital were laid. A younger contribution to the educational sector of the region is the University of Applied Sciences (FHS KufsteinTirol) founded in 1997. Today this institution offers five degree programs: International Business Studies; Facility Management; Real Estate and Facility Management; Sports, Culture and Event Management; and Business Informatics (since 2002).

A premiere of PADS 2004 is the fact that in this year we offer a workshop/tutorial combination co-located in two countries: following Kufstein's tradition as a (from a historical point of view) part-time Bavarian city, preceding the main PADS 2004 workshop, tutorials are given in Bavarian's capital at the University of the Federal Armed Forces Munich, Germany. It is our pleasure to welcome the honorary member of the PADS Steering Committee and one of the driving forces of the PADS community Richard Fujimoto (Georgia Institute of Technology, USA), presenting the tutorial "State of the Art in Parallel and Distributed Simulation." Who would be more appropriate to give that tutorial? The second tutorial entitled "PADS in the Military Domain: Training, Experimentation, and Support of Operations" is presented by Andreas Tolk (Virginia Modeling, Analysis & Simulation Center, Old Dominion University, USA).

We are also very happy to announce two excellent keynote speakers for the PADS 2004 workshop:

- Alois Ferscha (Johannes Keppler University Linz, Austria): "Beyond Time Warp: Space Warp"
- Alexander Verbraeck (Technical University Delft, The Netherlands): "Component-Based Distributed Simulations. The Way forward?"

and we look forward to hearing some exciting, challenging, and perhaps provocative talks.

I (Johannes) cannot resist making a personal comment—I am especially happy and proud to have (A)lois here since he is the person and friend who (by supervising my Diploma thesis and by a follow-up joint paper) made me interested in scientific research in the first place. Thanks for agreeing to present a keynote talk! Of course, our thanks also go to Alexander Verbraeck, Richard Fujimoto, and Andreas Tolk for presenting keynotes and tutorials, respectively. We appreciate the work of all authors who have submitted papers to PADS 2004. We would like to thank all who have helped to make PADS 2004 a success, particularly the Program Co-Chairs Ernest Page and Thom McLean, the International Program Committee, as well as the referees who worked for PADS 2004 within a very tight schedule. We would also like to thank Steve Turner and all other members of the Steering Committee for their support in planning and organizing the workshop, the people at SCS, ACM, and IEEE for their help, especially Maggie Johnson, and the editorial staff at IEEE Computer Society Press, particularly Stephanie Kawada, for their work in producing these proceedings.

Last but not least, we would like to say a very warm thank you to all who have contributed toward organizing this workshop at the local institutions, Walter J. Mayr, Norbert Witting, Isabella Haas, Hans Hetzenauer, Günter Herrmann, Daniela Mühle, Elfriede Luftensteiner, and many others whose names we cannot all list here.

We wish you a pleasant stay in Kufstein and Munich and a great PADS 2004 workshop!

Johannes Lüthi
FHS Kufstein Tirol, Austria

Axel Lehmann
Universität der Bundeswehr München, Germany

Message from the Program Chairs

Welcome to the 18th, and final, Workshop on Parallel and Distributed Simulation. The workshop is not the last in this distinguished series due to a decline in the relevance of simulation, or a decline in the quality of the research published in our proceedings. Certainly, as the systems mankind grapples with become increasingly complex, simulation continues to be a critical tool for systems design, analysis, and training. And PADS continues to be renown as a venue for the publication of high-quality research in parallel and distributed simulation. The opportunities for, and impact of, the workshop are expanding. It is in recognition of this expansion that the PADS Steering Committee has voted to change the official name of the workshop to "Principles of Advanced and Distributed Simulation" – embracing the broadening scope of our mission while preserving our beloved acronym! The new name will debut with the 2005 Workshop.

The program for 2004 is strong. We have an exceptional Program Committee and a great group of referees. Subsequent to the Call for Papers, thirty-nine papers were submitted for consideration. Utilizing a double-blind reviewing process and the WIMPE paper management system, each paper received four reviews. In most cases, three of these reviews were by members of the Program Committee. The Program Committee meeting was held on Saturday, 6 December, in New Orleans, Louisiana, in conjunction with the Winter Simulation Conference. During the meeting, sixteen papers were accepted, and five papers were conditionally accepted. These papers were assigned "shepherds" from the Program Committee who provided guidance for the revision of the paper. In the end, each of these papers was accepted resulting in a program of twenty-one papers, two keynotes, and a work-in-progress session.

Subsequent to the Program Committee meeting, a Best Paper Committee was formed consisting of the Program Co-Chairs, Fred Wieland, Greg Tackett, and Simon Taylor. The following papers were nominated:

> "Detailed OFDM Modeling in Network Simulation of Mobile Ad Hoc Networks" by Gavin Yeung, Mineo Takai, Rajive Bagrodia, Alireza Mehrnia, and Babak Daneshrad
>
> "Simulation Validation Using Direct Execution of Wireless Ad-Hoc Routing Protocols" by Jason Liu, Yougu Yuan, David M. Nicol, Robert S. Gray, and David F. Kotz
>
> "Formalization and Strictness of Simulation Event Orderings" by Yong-Meng Teo and B. S. S. Onggo
>
> "Time Parallel Simulation with Approximative State Matching" by Tobias Kiesling and Siegfried Pohl
>
> "Towards a Grid-Aware Time Warp" by Kamil Iskra, Dick van Albada, and Peter Sloot
>
> "Space-Parallel Network Simulations Using Ghosts" by George Riley, Talal Jaafar, Richard Fujimoto, and Mostafa Ammar
>
> "Optimistic Synchronization in HLA-Based Distributed Simulation" by Stephen Turner, Xiaoguang Wang, and Malcom Yoke Hean Low

We are pleased to announce that PADS has entered into an arrangement with SCS *Simulation* to generate a special issue of the journal from the workshop. The authors of articles nominated for best paper will have the opportunity to extend and revise their articles for inclusion in the special issue.

In keeping with tradition, the identity of the PADS 2004 Best Paper will be withheld until the awards ceremony at the conference.

On behalf of the PADS 2003 Program Co-Chairs, George Riley and Phil Wilsey, we are pleased to confirm that the winner of the PADS 2003 Best Paper is:

> "Large-Scale TCP Models using Optimistic Parallel Simulation" by Garrett Yaun, Christopher Carothers, and Shivkumar Kalyanaraman

We would like to express our deepest thanks to the PADS Steering Committee for their guidance, and to the Program Committee and referees for all their efforts in generating reviews within very tight timelines. We are particularly grateful to those who attended the Program Committee meeting in December.

Thanks also to our esteemed General Co-Chairs for all of their work in arranging a fantastic conference. Continued thanks to David Nicol for WIMPE. And last but not least, thanks to all those who submitted articles to the workshop. Without your efforts, there couldn't be PADS.

We hope you enjoy the program!

Ernest H. Page
The MITRE Corporation, McLean, Virginia, USA

A. L. M. Thom McLean
Georgia Institute of Technology, Atlanta, Georgia, USA

Organizing Committees

General Co-Chairs

Johannes Lüthi
Axel Lehmann

Program Co-Chairs

Ernest H. Page
A. L. M. Thom McLean

Steering Committee

Adel S. Elmaghraby
Peter S. Magnusson
Simon J. E. Taylor
Stephen J. Turner
Brian W. Unger
George Riley
Richard M. Fujimoto *(Honorary)*

Program Committee

Azzedine Boukerche
Christopher Carothers
Rick Copeland
Lorenzo Donatiello
Adel Elmaghraby
Richard Fujimoto
Risa Larsen
Maximo Lorenzo
David Nicol
Kalyan Perumalla
Francesco Quaglia
Russ Richardson
George Riley
Rob Simmonds
Greg Tackett
Mineo Takai
Carl Tropper
StephenTurner
Adelinde Uhrmacher
Brian Unger
Fred Wieland
Phil Wilsey

Reviewers

Luciano Bononi
Wentong Cai
Malolan Chetlur
Gabriele D'Angelo
Boon P. Gan
Nasser Kalantery
Cameron Kiddle
Lijun Li
Jason Liu
Malcolm Y. H. Low
Marco Roccetti
Andrea Santoro
Andreas Tolk
Junhu Wei
Qing Xu
Christopher H. Young

Session 1:
Welcome and Keynote

Virtual Space

Alois Ferscha
Institute for Pervasive Computing
University of Linz
ferscha@soft.uni-linz.ac.at

Abstract

The Parallel (and Distributed) Discrete Event Simulation (PADS) community – over it's more than 20 years of existence – has achieved remarkable results in getting the execution of simulations of discrete event systems faster, involving multiple, logically and/or physically dispersed, communicating computational resources. A solid, mature and empirically approved body of foundational concepts, models, systems, methods and algorithms are at hand and well documented in more than 50.000 pages of research papers. PADS simulation engines, model and software libraries, and operating systems have proven feasibility and applicability of these results in solving real world problems. Despite the (healthy) self-criticism of it's proponents ("Will the field survive?"), PADS was – and is – a success!

With this talk we aim at a prospect for the challenges posed by the emerging new models of computational and communication, the evolving new paradigms of interaction and coordination, the new styles of system design, and even the availability of new technologies, for which – in my opinion – no other community qualifies better than the PADS community.

Overview of the talk

From it's very roots – the pioneering *conservative* (Chandy-Misra-Bryant) and *optimistic* (Sowizral-Jefferson) thought models, PADS has attained it's most prominent achievements in the acceleration of the simulation of the dynamics of complex discrete event systems using a parallel (which governs the evolution of a system over simulated time in an iterative, synchronous way) or distributed (which decomposes the event structure underlying a system into logical space/time regions and executes those asynchronously) approach. Both the optimistic and conservative thought models have undergone extensive reshaping, enhancements, combinations, integrations and generalizations, and so have the conceptual models for virtual (or logical) time – without being conclusive up until today. Event ordering, synchronization protocols, causality preservation, speedup, time keeping and time management have had the highest research appeal in the PADS community.

In this presentation I will argue that a plethora of new challenges are waiting to be approached, possibly based on new thought (or machine) models: After Alan Turing's paper "On computable Numbers with an Application to the Entscheidungsproblem" theoretical computer science adopted the Turing machine model, and a computer science of "algorithms" emerged since the 1950s, viewing computation as the transformation of input (data) to ouptut (data) by executing algorithms. Consequently, today's computational models (like the Von Neumann machine model) explain system components in terms of "what they compute". This, however, appears less expressive than so called "interaction models" – expressing how components interact, and how these interactions are coordinated. This observation, and claim for a model able to express "interaction" is by no means new, and many approaches to extend computation beyond "algorithmics" (beyond Turing machines) have been attempted. One such concept is Robin Milner's "Elements of Interaction" originating from the CCS "concurrency" thought model, another one is Peter Wegner's "Interaction Machines" originating from an "interaction" thought model.

The observation of technological progress supports these thoughts: Most recent advances in microprocessor-, wireless communication- and sensor-/actuator technologies envision a whole new era of computing, popularly referred to as "pervasive" or "ubiquitous" computing. Autonomous, ad-hoc networked, wirelessly communicating and spontaneously interacting computing devices appearing in great number, and embedded into environments, appliances and objects of everyday use will deliver services adapted to the person, the time, the place – or most generally: the context – of their use. The nature and appearance of computing devices will change to be hidden in the fabric of everyday life, invisible networked, and augmenting environments to form a pervasive computing landscape, in which the physical world becomes merged with a "digital world". In such a world, "interaction" seems to be more powerful than "algorithms".

As for the PADS thought models, which are dominated by concepts for "virtualizing" time, the "virtualization" of space could be a promising juxtaposition.

About the Speaker

Alois Ferscha received his PhD degree from the University of Vienna, Austria, and joined the University of Linz in 2000 as a professor for computer science. He has been involved in parallel and distributed simulation for about 15 years, contributing to self-adaptive synchronization, performance evaluation and performance prediction of parallel and distributed discrete event synchronization protocols. He was general chair of PADS'97, and PC chair of PADS'98. Currently he is focused on pervasive and ubiquitous computing, new models of computation and coordination, spontaneous interaction and distributed interactive simulation.

Session 2:
Network Simulation 1

Simulation Validation Using Direct Execution of Wireless Ad-Hoc Routing Protocols *

Jason Liu, Yougu Yuan, David M. Nicol,
Robert S. Gray[†], Calvin C. Newport[†], David Kotz[†],
and Luiz Felipe Perrone[‡]

Coordinated Science Laboratory, University of Illinois at Urbana-Champaign
1308 West Main Street, Urbana, IL 61801
{jasonliu,yuanyg,nicol}@crhc.uiuc.edu

[†] Department of Computer Science, Dartmouth College
6211 Sudikoff Laboratory, Hanover, NH 03755
{robert.s.gray, calvin.c.newport}@dartmouth.edu, dfk@cs.dartmouth.edu

[‡] Department of Computer Science, Bucknell University, Lewisburg, PA 17837
perrone@bucknell.edu

Abstract

Computer simulation is the most common approach to studying wireless ad-hoc routing algorithms. The results, however, are only as good as the models the simulation uses. One should not underestimate the importance of validation, *as inaccurate models can lead to wrong conclusions. In this paper, we use direct-execution simulation to validate radio models used by ad-hoc routing protocols, against real-world experiments. This paper documents a common testbed that supports direct execution of a set of ad-hoc routing protocol implementations in a wireless network simulator. The testbed reads traces generated from real experiments, and uses them to drive direct-execution implementations of the routing protocols. Doing so we reproduce the same network conditions as in real experiments. By comparing routing behavior* measured *in real experiments with behavior* computed *by the simulation, we are able to validate the models of radio behavior upon which protocol behavior depends. We conclude that it is* possible *to have fairly accurate results using a simple radio model, but the routing behavior is quite sensitive to one of this model's parameters. The implication is that one should i) use a more complex radio model that explicitly models point-to-point path loss, or ii) use measurements from an environment typical of the one of interest, or iii) study behavior over a range of environments to identify sensitivities.*

*This work was supported in part by Dartmouth Center for Mobile Computing, DARPA (contract N66001-96-C-8530), the Department of Justice (contract 2000-CX-K001) and the Department of Defense (MURI AFOSR contract F49620-97-1-03821). Points of view in this document are those of the authors and do not necessarily represent the official position of DARPA or the United States government.

1. Introduction

Using simulation one must take the precaution that the model may not reflect the reality. Validation of a wireless network simulation is particularly difficult because not only must the implementation of the simulated protocol be validated against its design specifications, but also the model must be able to capture lower-level characteristics of the wireless environment with a proper level of abstraction [3]. The validation problem is amplified when the routing protocol deployed in a real system is implemented and maintained as a separate code base from the one used in simulation.

Direct-execution simulation alleviates the problem of maintaining separate code bases for the same routing protocol by executing the same code designed for real systems directly inside a wireless network simulator. We compile the routing protocol's source code with the simulator's source code with only moderate changes as necessary. The protocol's logic is executed inside the simulator and is driven by the simulator's time advancing mechanism. In a discrete-event simulation, the routing protocol code is invoked as a result of the simulator processing events stored in the event queue. Since each protocol instance communicates with other simulated mobile stations by sending and receiving packets through well-defined system calls, we substitute these system calls with calls to the simulator. The packets are redirected to go through the simulated wireless network—all transparent to the protocol implementation. Using direct-execution simulation is desirable for prototyping a protocol implementation, which, after initial simulation evaluation, can be deployed directly in a real network.

Our interest in direct-execution simulation is that it can help us validate the wireless network simulator using the results from real experiments. We run the same routing protocol and application traffic generator code both in simulation and in the real experiment. The difference is that in the real experiment packets are transmitted via the wireless channel and are subject to delays and losses due to signal fading and collisions during the transmission. In simulation, these packets are translated into simulation events scheduled with delays calculated by the radio channel model. Depending on the modeling details, the simulation result may or may not reflect what would happen in reality. Direct-execution simulation provides us a valuable opportunity to investigate the effect of details of a wireless network model on the fidelity of the simulation study.

This paper documents our effort in supporting direct execution of a set of wireless ad-hoc routing protocol implementations and using direct-execution simulation to validate the underlying wireless network models by comparing the results from real-world experiments. We ported five routing protocol implementations for direct execution: APRL, AODV, GPSR, ODMRP, and STARA. Versions of all five protocols were implemented as part of the ActComm project, whose goal is to provide information access through a wireless network to soldiers in the field.[1] One contribution of our research is to provide a common testbed for direct execution of these protocols in simulation. More importantly, we instrumented the testbed to enable validation of various wireless network models. We embedded the routing protocol code with various logging functions. Each laptop computer running the routing protocols in the real experiment has a Global Positioning System (GPS) device and periodically records its location information and average receiving signal quality from other laptops. We later transformed these logs into traces of node mobility and radio connectivity. We adapted the simulator to read the traces and combined them with different stochastic radio propagation models to reproduce the test scenario inside simulation. We compared the results from running these routing protocols in simulation with those collected from the real experiment. Such comparison helps us understand the effect of different wireless network models on the behavior of ad-hoc routing algorithms.

We present two set of experiments in this paper. The first one compares two implementations of the AODV routing protocol, both running in simulation. One AODV implementation was specifically designed for the simulator—the protocol sends and receives packets, and schedules timeouts using the special functions provided by the simulator. The other AODV implementation was developed by the ActComm project, designed for the real network, and was directly executed in the simulator. The goal of this experiment is to validate both protocol implementations and to identify the overhead introduced by direct-execution simulation in terms of memory usage and execution time. The second set of experiments compares the results from a real field test with those from simulation. In the real experiment, we ran the routing protocols on 40 laptop computers, each equipped with a wireless device and a GPS unit. The laptops were carried by people walking randomly in a large field. In simulation, we applied different radio propagation models together with the traces derived from the real experiment. We directly executed the routing protocol implementations in simulation and compared the behavior of these protocols in both environments. The goal of this study is to highlight the importance of modeling decisions on the validity of a wireless simulation study.

The paper is organized as follows. Section 2 provides an overview of the implementations of the ActComm routing protocols and outlines the architecture of our wireless network simulator on which we directly execute these protocol implementations. In Section 3 we briefly describe issues related to direct-execution simulation. Section 4 presents the augmented simulation testbed designed for validation purposes. We focus on the experiments and results in Section 5. Section 6 concludes the paper.

2. Background

2.1. The Routing Protocols

We ported five protocols for direct execution. Any-Path Routing without Loops (APRL) is a proactive distance-vector routing protocol [5]. Rather than using sequence numbers, APRL uses ping messages before establishing new routes to guarantee loop-free operation. Ad-hoc On-Demand Vector (AODV) is an on-demand routing algorithm—routes are created as needed at connection establishment and maintained thereafter to deal with link breakage [10]. Greedy Perimeter Stateless Routing (GPSR) uses GPS positions of the mobile stations to forward packets greedily along a path toward the target's physical location [6]. GPSR uses a perimeter-following algorithm to for-

[1] http://actcomm.thayer.dartmouth.edu/.

ward packets around the boundaries of empty regions that contain no laptops (and hence cause greedy forwarding to fail). On-Demand Multicast Routing Protocol (ODMRP) maintains a mesh, instead of a tree, for alternate and redundant routes for each multicast group [7]. It does not depend on another unicast routing protocol and, in fact, can be used for unicast routing. System and Traffic Dependent Adaptive Routing Algorithm (STARA) uses shortest-path routing [2]. The distance measure is calculated by the mean transmission delay instead of the hop count.

We implemented these protocols for the ActComm project in C++ on Linux. All five implementations perform their routing in user space using IP tunneling and UDP sockets. An IP tunnel is a virtual network device with two endpoints: one as a regular network interface, and the other as a Unix file. Packets sent to the network interface, via a standard UDP socket for example, can be read from the file by any (authorized) user process, while packets written to the file are delivered by the kernel as if they had arrived over the network interface. Each mobile station has a virtual IP address (e.g., 11.0.0.1) associated with the network interface of the tunnel, and a physical IP address (e.g., 10.0.0.1) associated with the network interface of the physical wireless device. The application communicates using virtual IP addresses. The kernel IP routing table in each mobile station is configured to forward packets with virtual destination addresses to the IP tunnel device. At the source of a transmission, the packet sent from the application is forwarded through the IP tunnel to the routing protocol reading the device file. The routing protocol then converts the virtual addresses to physical addresses and selects the next hop to forward the packet to according to its routing table. Packets are forwarded to their neighbors using UDP sockets through the physical (wireless) network device. Once the packet reaches its destination, the physical addresses are translated back into virtual addresses and the routing protocol writes the packets to the device file that represents the IP tunnel, which then deliver the packet to the application via the virtual network interface.

2.2. The Wireless Network Simulator

We developed a high-performance simulator called SWAN as an integrated, flexible, and configurable environment for evaluating different wireless ad-hoc routing protocols, especially in large network scenarios. SWAN is built based on a parallel discrete-event simulator called DaSSF, which has proved successful in simulating large-scale wired networks.[2] We ported and implemented several protocol models that are used frequently in a wireless ad-hoc network. The protocol models can be readily assembled into a protocol stack within each simulated mobile station. Using SWAN, one can dynamically configure each protocol and the underlying wireless network using a specially designed configuration language.

In this paper, we study the effect of various radio signal propagation models on the behavior of the routing algorithms in simulation. In particular, we examine three simple but frequently used stochastic radio propagation models: a Friis free-space model, a two-ray ground reflection model, and a generic propagation model. The Friis free-space model assumes an ideal radio propagation condition: the signals travel in a vacuum space without obstacles. The power loss is proportional to the square of the distance between the transmitter and the receiver. The two-ray ground reflection model adds a ground reflection path from the transmitter to the receiver. The model is more accurate than the free-space model when the distance is large and when there is no significant difference in elevation between the mobile stations. The generic propagation model describes the radio signal attenuation as a combination of two effects: small-scale fading and large-scale fading. The small-scale fading captures the characteristic of rapid fluctuation in signal power over a short period of time or a small change in the node's position—a result primarily due to the existence of multiple paths that the signals travel. The classic models that predict the small-scale fading effect include Rayleigh and Ricean distributions. Large-scale fading is mostly caused by the environmental scattering of the signals and can be further divided into two components: the distance path loss is the average signal power loss as a function of distance and is proportional to the distance raised to a specified exponent; the shadow fading effect describes the variations in signal receiving power measured in decibels and can be modeled as a log-normal distribution. Readers can refer to a textbook on wireless communications (such as Rappaport's book [11]) for a detailed discussion on the radio propagation models.

3. Direct Execution

In simulation, multiple instances of a routing protocol must run simultaneously, driven by the same event queue. Conceivably, each routing protocol can run as a separate process and interact with the simulation kernel through inter-process communication mechanisms. We only need to substitute the system calls related to either communications (i.e., sending or receiving packets) or time (e.g., querying for the current wall-clock time or potentially blocking the user process causing noticeable delays) with calls to the simulator. The replacement can be done at link time after compilation. The major attraction of this approach is that no source code modification is necessary. The drawback, however, lies in its complexity and the potential overhead introduced by the inter-process communication.

[2]http://www.cs.dartmouth.edu/research/DaSSF.

We chose an easier yet faster approach that allows multiple instances of the same routing protocol to execute in the same address space. The method involved moderate modifications to the source code. Similar approaches can be found in the literature [1, 8, 9]. We ported all five ActComm routing protocols together with related programs, such as the application traffic generator used in the real experiment. The number of lines changed accounts for only 3.8% and most changes were related to creating and configuring the routing protocols individually in each simulated mobile station, separated from the protocol's control flow.

3.1. Encapsulations

We modified the protocol code slightly to allow multiple instances of a routing protocol to run simultaneously inside the simulator. Since all these instances are executed in the same address space, we need to provide wrappers so that these instances can be identified and separated in the same execution environment.

We created a protocol session object to represent each routing protocol instance in the simulator. The protocol's interaction with the operating system, such as system calls for sending and receiving packets, was replaced by method invocations of the protocol session. These methods redirect the calls to simulator. We also replaced global variables, which are data objects specific to a routing protocol instance, with member data of the protocol session. We replaced the original `main` function in the routing protocol implementations with a method of the protocol session that configures and initializes the instance.

3.2. Communications

The routing protocol implementations use system calls for communications, such as `sendto` for sending messages through UDP sockets. As mentioned earlier, we replaced these system routines with those supplied by the simulator. Rather than replacing them manually at all places of the source code, we provided a base class that contains methods with the same names as the system routines and with the same parameters. In this way, all classes in the protocol implementations default to call the methods in the base class. The base class contains a reference to the protocol session that represents the routing protocol instance. The methods in the base class forward control through the reference to the protocol session, which passes on the messages through the simulated protocol stack.

We added support in the simulator for UDP sockets. A UDP protocol session manages the UDP sockets on top of the IP layer and its primary function is to multiplex and demultiplex UDP datagrams. We replaced system calls related to UDP sockets, such as `socket`, `bind`, `sendto`, `recvfrom`, and `setsockopt`, with methods that interact with the UDP protocol session. We also implemented the IP tunnel device in the simulator. The device is treated as a network interface below the IP layer in the protocol stack. Packets sent by the application with virtual destination addresses (via UDP sockets) are diverted to the tunnel device by the IP layer. The routing algorithm accesses the IP tunnel through a regular file descriptor. We replaced the file access functions, specifically `open`, `read`, `write`, and `close`, to distinguish the file descriptor for the tunnel device from other regular files. We did not replace operations to regular files since they are used by the directly executed code for logging purposes.

3.3. Timings

The routing protocols executed inside the simulator must be driven by simulation time rather than real time, which means that we must deal with all time-sensitive system calls carefully. We replaced `gettimeofday`, which returns the wall-clock time of the mobile station, with a call to the simulator querying for the current simulation time. We also replaced `select`, which causes the running process to be blocked until any one of the specified set of file descriptors is ready for reading or writing, or the given timeout interval has been elapsed. The ActComm protocol implementations all center on an event loop that contains one call to the `select` function. When the control returns from this function—upon timeouts or incoming messages—the algorithm invokes the corresponding event handlers to process the event. We bypassed the the event loop and directly invoked the event handlers whenever a timeout occurred or a message arrived at the protocol session.

One also has to be aware of the ramifications from the lack of a CPU work model in the wireless simulator. The simulator uses function invocations for packets to travel up and down the protocol stack, without advancing the simulation time. This bears no side-effect for a carefully designed protocol model, where the packet processing time is simulated with proper random delays, but may create problems for a directly executed protocol implementation that pays no special attention to the packet processing time. If in simulation we assume zero packet processing time, the behavior of all instances of a routing protocol could be synchronized in simulation time. This time synchrony could then lead to an unnaturally high probability of packet loss due to collisions at the radio channel. To deal with this problem, we introduced packet jitters at the interface between the simulator and the directly executed code. Each time a message goes through a UDP socket, we added a random delay to model the time needed by the operating system for processing the packet.

4. Support for Simulation Validation

In this section we discuss our support to validate a wireless simulation by comparing results from the real experiment and the direct-execution simulation. Validation of simulations in general and wireless ad-hoc network simulations in particular has been a focal point surrounding the applicability of simulation studies. Johnson first suggested using the logging information from running ad-hoc routing algorithms during the real experiment to simulate identical node movement and communication scenarios [4]. Takai et al. studied the effect of wireless physical layer and radio channel modeling on the performance evaluation of ad-hoc routing algorithms [12, 13].

Our research uses real experiments as the base for comparison. In particular, we ran the routing protocol implementations together with other applications, such as the traffic generator, directly in the simulator. We derived both mobility and radio connectivity traces from the real experiment and combined them with a stochastic propagation model in an attempt to recreate the real network conditions in simulation. We compared the results against those from the real experiment to assess the validity of the radio propagation model.

In all five ActComm routing protocol implementations we embedded a sophisticated logging mechanism, as shown in Figure 1. When the routing protocol runs, it generates an event log that includes all types of events related to the routing algorithm, such as sending or receiving a control message. We used the event log both for analyzing the performance of the routing algorithm and for debugging. We also instrumented the traffic generator with logging functions to record each packet sent and received. We later used this application log to calculate application-level statistics, such as packet delivery rate and end-to-end delay. The traffic generator executed directly in the simulator also read this log to recreate the exact traffic behavior.

In the real experiment, we ran a third program called the *service module* together with the routing protocol and the application traffic generator. The program periodically queried the attached GPS device at the mobile station to log its current position. The program also used `iwspy` to periodically record link quality information. `iwspy` allows the user to set a list of network addresses. The wireless device driver gathers the link quality information, in signal-to-noise ratio (SNR), whenever a packet is received from one of those addresses, that is, from any other laptop. The service module collected the link quality information and averaged it over the last sampling interval. Also, it periodically broadcasted beacon messages that contain position information of all known mobile stations. The original ActComm applications used them to keep every soldier in the field updated with the positions of other soldiers. We recorded the

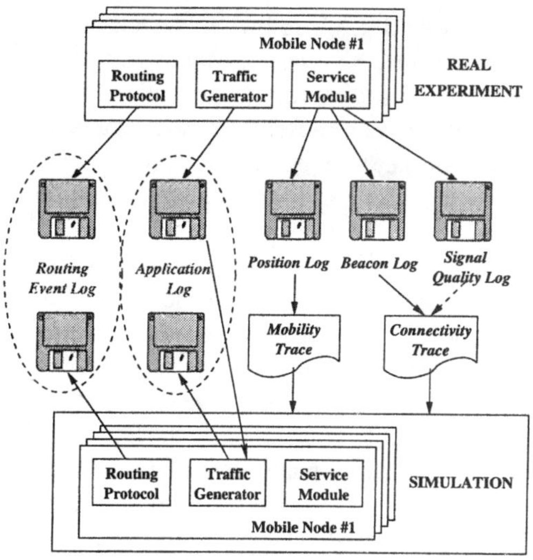

Figure 1. Logs are generated and compared for validating simulation results.

beacon messages and used them to refresh the link quality information.

In simulation, the routing protocols are running directly inside the simulator together with the application traffic generator and the service module. We chose to directly execute the service model since we need to reproduce the beacon messages and their effect on the MAC/PHY states of the wireless network.

We further processed the position log from the real experiment to produce a mobility trace, which shows how each mobile station moved during the experiment. In addition, we generated a node connectivity trace from the beacon logs recorded by the mobile stations during the real experiment. The mobility trace states whether a mobile stations can receive a packet from another mobile station over the wireless channel at a given time. The beacon log contains the times at which the beacon messages from other mobile stations were received. Receiving a beacon successfully indicates a link from the sender to the receiver, while missing several consecutive beacons indicates that the receiver may be beyond the transmission range of the sender.

The signal quality log recorded a series of averaged signal-to-noise ratios for packets received at each mobile station from other stations in the network. We did not include the signal quality log in this study. We are currently investigating the use this log to reconstruct the connectivity of the network, as it may provide a better alternative to the beacon log.

We used the radio connectivity trace as a baseline to determine whether two mobile stations could directly communicate with each other. The connectivity information, however, does not capture the state of interference—collisions could happen due to the presence of "hidden terminals." For example, if node B can hear both node A and node C situated on either side, but node A cannot talk to C and vice versa because of the distance, it is possible that node B cannot faithfully receive a packet from A if node C is transmitting another packet to node B. Although the 802.11 MAC layer protocol, which arbitrates packet transmissions over the radio medium, allocates the radio channel before each transmission, it cannot totally prevent collisions. In this case, the simulator must use an interference model to simulate what would happen when two packets arrive at the receiver—one of the packets can be accepted if its receiving power is significantly higher than the other, or both packets can be lost due to interference. Since the interference model relies on the receiving signal power to determine packet receptions, we still need a radio propagation model to simulate the signal power attenuation.

5. Performance and Validation Studies

We conducted two experiments for validation: one comparing the direct-execution simulation of the ActComm AODV protocol implementation with an AODV protocol model implemented natively in the simulator, and the other comparing a real experiment with the simulated wireless network.

5.1. AODV vs. AODV

Our first experiment compared the direct execution of the ActComm AODV protocol implementation with an AODV protocol model implemented natively in SWAN. We ran both protocol implementations in simulation under the same simulated network conditions, with the same application traffic pattern, and the same radio propagation model. Our goal is to validate both protocol implementations against each other and determine how much overhead direct-execution simulation requires.

In the simulation experiment, we tested a network of 50, 100, and 200 mobile stations, out of which we chose 20 mobile stations as traffic sources. We deployed these mobile stations in a square area, sized so that each mobile station had seven neighbors on average (796, 1126, and 1592 meters for each dimension, respectively). We used the random way-point node mobility model: each node moves to a randomly selected point in the area with a speed chosen uniformly between 1 and 10 meters/s; when reaching the point, it pauses for 60 seconds before selecting another point to move to. We chose the IEEE 802.11 protocol for the MAC and PHY layer with standard parameters according to the IEEE specification (with 11 MB/s bandwidth), and we used the generic radio propagation model (with an exponent of 2.5 and shadow fading log-normal standard deviation of 6 dB) to compute radio signal power attenuation. We used a simple application traffic generator: each source periodically sends one packet (of 1 KB in size) to a randomly selected peer with an exponentially distributed inter-arrival time.

The behaviors of the two implementations differed slightly owing to variations in treatment of the AODV specifications. In addition, the ActComm AODV protocol ran in user space using IP tunneling and UDP sockets, while SWAN AODV ran directly on top of IP. The messages from the application traffic generator, when delivered to the ActComm AODV protocol through the IP tunnel, were wrapped with UDP and IP headers. Both the data and control messages used by ActComm AODV were also augmented with UDP headers through UDP sockets. Nonetheless, we found that, with varying traffic load, the overall packet ratio—which is the total number of packets received by the application layer divided by the total number of packets sent—differed only slightly between these two implementation (less than 3%). The similarity in the behavior of the two implementations ensures that using the two implementations to assess the cost of direct execution is meaningful.

Figures 2 and 3 show the difference in total execution time and peak memory usage between the two implementations of the AODV protocol. Clearly, the ActComm AODV (direct-execution) implementation requires more computational resources, but marginally so. The greatest increase in the execution time (about 18%) is at larger network size and heavier traffic load. The increased execution time is mostly caused by the overhead of copying and serialization of real packets. The memory overhead of ActComm AODV (over 100%) is more significant. We attribute it to the additional data structures used by the direct-execution protocol session, the IP tunnel device, and the UDP socket layer, which are proportional to the number of simulated mobile stations. Moreover, in simulation, the directly executed routing protocol and the application send and receive real packets with real message headers and real payloads. The overhead grows with increasing traffic intensity as packets stay longer in the wireless network due to more contentions.

In conclusion, direct-execution simulation requires more computational resources, especially in memory usage. The benefit of directly executing a routing protocol implementation in simulation is the assurance that the protocol implementation exhibits the same behavior as in a real network. A routing protocol model implemented natively in the simulator, however, may benefit from computational optimizations such as eschewing actual message headers and payloads. Thus, a protocol model, once validated, can be used in situations where the resource requirement is critical, such as in a simulation of a large-scale wireless network. On the other hand, the extra costs of direct-execution are not so onerous that it disqualifies the technique as a means of experimen-

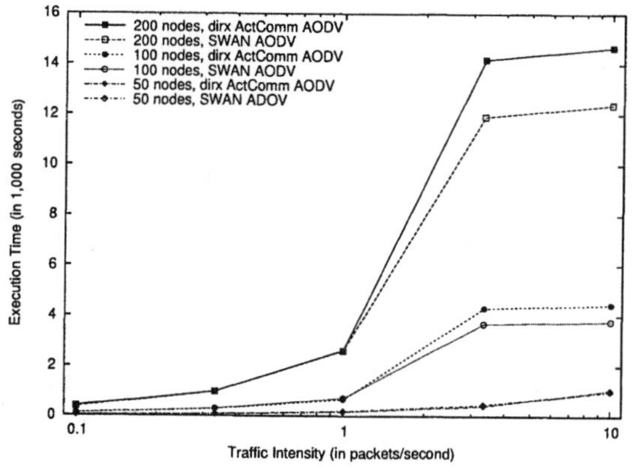

Figure 2. The simulation time for the two AODV implementations with varying traffic load (in log scale).

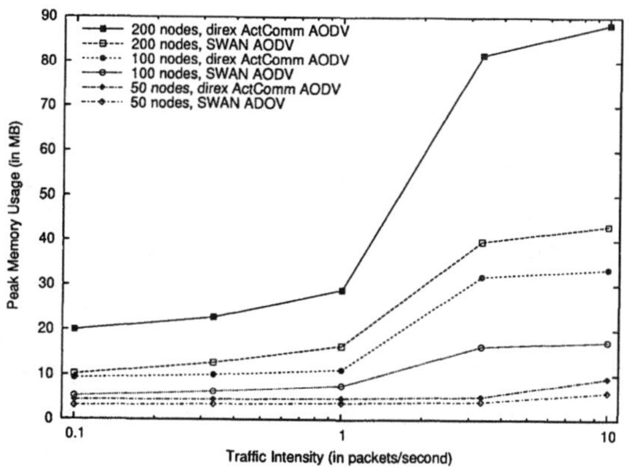

Figure 3. Peak memory usage by the two AODV implementations with varying traffic load (in log scale).

tation. There are obvious advantages to maintaining a common code base between a protocol's actual implementation, and that used to study its behavior in a simulator.

5.2. Simulation vs. Reality

As the second step in our validation, we compared the results from an outdoor routing experiment with our simulation results. In particular, we compared the results from the real experiment with the simulation results using different radio propagation models. The purpose of this study is to reveal the sensitivity of the performance of the routing protocols to the underlying wireless models.

5.2.1 The Real Experiment

The outdoor routing experiment took place on a rectangular athletic field measuring approximately 729 by 1408 feet (or 222 by 429 meters). Each of the 40 laptop computers used in this experiment had a Lucent (Orinoco) 802.11B wireless card operating in peer-to-peer mode at 2 MB/s. Each laptop had a Garmin eTrex GPS unit attached via the serial port. These GPS units did not have differential GPS capabilities, but were accurate to within 10 meters during the experiment.

For this particular outdoor experiment, we included APRL, AODV, ODMRP and STARA (GPSR was still under development). The laptops, whose clocks were set to the time reported by the GPS unit, automatically ran each routing algorithm for 15 minutes, with two minutes of network quiescence between each algorithm to handle cleanup and setup chores. After each routing algorithm had been running for one minute, providing time to reach an initial stable routing configuration, the laptops automatically started a traffic generator that generated "streams" of UDP packets. The number of packets in each stream was Gaussian distributed with mean 5 and standard deviation $\sqrt{2}$; the time between streams was exponentially distributed with mean 15 seconds; the time between packets inside a stream was exponentially distributed with mean 3 seconds; every packet contained approximately 1200 data bytes; and the target laptop for each stream was uniformly randomly selected from among the other laptops. We chose these numerical parameters to approximate the (moderate) traffic volume observed during an earlier demonstration of a military application. The routing algorithm parameters, such as the beacon interval for APRL and the forwarding group lifetime for ODMRP, were set to "standard" values taken from the literature and our own experience.

During the course of the experiment, the laptops were continuously moving. The athletic field was divided into four equal-sized quadrants, one of which was approximately eight feet lower in elevation than the rest of the field. The hills from the higher to lower elevation were steep and short, and thus did obstruct the wireless signal, increasing the frequency with which the routing algorithms needed to find a multi-hop route. At the start of the experiment, the 40 participants were divided into equal-sized groups of 10 each, each of which was instructed to randomly disburse in one of the four quadrants. The participants then walked continuously, always picking a quadrant different than the one in which they were currently located, picking a random position within that quadrant, walking to that position in a straight line, and then repeating. This approach was chosen since it was simple, but still provide continuous movement to which the routing algorithms could react, as well as similar laptop distributions across each of the four routing algorithms.

Each laptop recorded extensive logs as described in Section 4. At the end of experiment, we discovered that seven laptops failed to generate any data or routing traffic due to misconfiguration or hardware problems. Thus, the experiment, in practice, reduced to a 33-laptop experiment and the logs from these 33 laptops were used as the starting point for comparing the real-world and simulated results.

5.2.2 The Simulation

We processed the logs from the real experiments to derive the mobility and radio connectivity traces for each laptop for the duration of running each routing algorithm. We ran the simulation for each algorithm for the designated period. We directly ran the routing protocol and the service module in each simulated mobile station. We modified the application traffic generator to read the application log and generate the same packets as in the real experiment. We focused only on the 33 laptops that actually transmitted, received, and forwarded packets in the real experiments. To reproduce the traffic pattern in simulation, the application traffic generator on each of the 33 nodes still included the 7 crashed nodes as their potential packet destinations.[3]

The mobile stations in simulation followed the mobility trace generated from the real experiment. We examined three radio propagation models: a free-space model, a two-ray ground reflection model, and a generic propagation model. The simulator delivered each transmitted packet to all neighbor stations that could receive the packet with an average signal power beyond a minimum threshold. We used the propagation models to determine the power loss for each packet transmission and calculate the signal-to-noise ratio to quantify the state of interference at the receiver—whether a packet that arrived at a mobile station could be received successfully, or dropped due to significant power loss or collisions. We combined the three models with the connectivity trace derived from the beacon logs, leading to six different radio propagation models in simulation: three using the connectivity traces and the other three not. In the first three cases, we used the connectivity trace to determine whether a packet from a mobile station could reach another mobile station, and then we used the radio propagation models to determine the receiving power for the interference calculation. Comparison of models with measured connectivity with those without give us a means of determining whether the model contains accurate predictive power for connectivity.

5.2.3 The Results

We first examine the packet delivery ratio. Figure 4 shows the packet delivery ratio from the real experiment and the simulation runs with six radio propagation models (three of

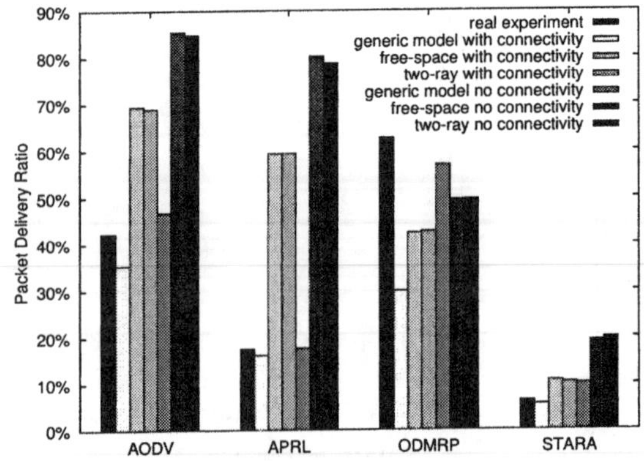

Figure 4. Comparing the data delivery ratio from the real experiment with various radio propagation models. "With connectivity" means the connectivity trace was used.

which used the connectivity trace derived from the real experiment to determine the reachability of the signals). Each simulation result is an average of five runs; the variance is insignificant and therefore not shown. The generic propagation model in the experiment used typical parameters to describe the outdoor environment of the real experiment: we used 2.8 as the path-loss exponent and 6 dB as the standard deviation for shadow fading.

We found that the simple generic propagation model offered an acceptable prediction of the performance of the routing algorithms, although different propagation models predicted vastly different protocol behaviors. The difference is significant in some cases that could result in misleading conclusions, for example, when comparing the performance of AODV and ODMRP. The inaccuracy in the model prediction introduced by the propagation model is non-uniform and can undermine a performance comparison study of different protocols.

For AODV, APRL, and STARA, the figure shows a large exaggeration of the packet delivery ratio using the free-space model and the two-ray ground reflection model. Both models overestimated the transmission range of radio signals causing shorter routes and therefore better packet delivery ratio. Even with the connectivity trace, the models overestimated the signal quality, failing to capture the lossy characteristic of the radio propagation environment. The performance of ODMRP was underestimated in simulation. ODMRP is a multicast routing algorithm that delivers packets using multiple paths to their destinations. It has a higher demand on the network bandwidth. The overestimated transmission range and signal quality in the free-space and two-ray models caused more contentions and created a negative effect on the simulated throughput.

The packet delivery ratio does not reflect the entire ex-

[3]Therefore, the packet-delivery ratios, both from the real experiment and the simulation, should be lower than expected, since those packets with unknown destinations could not be delivered.

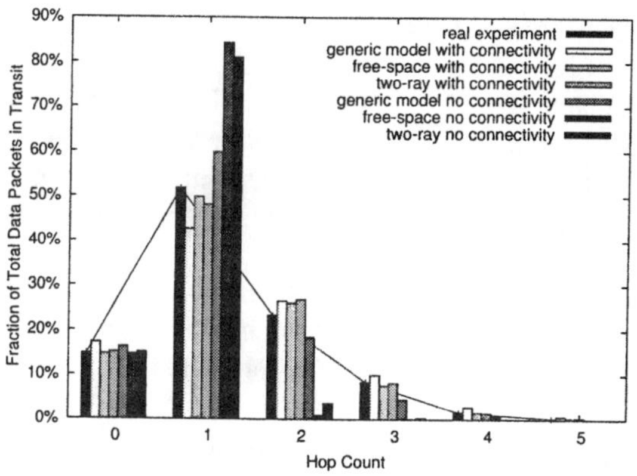

Figure 5. The hop-count histogram of AODV in real experiment and in simulation.

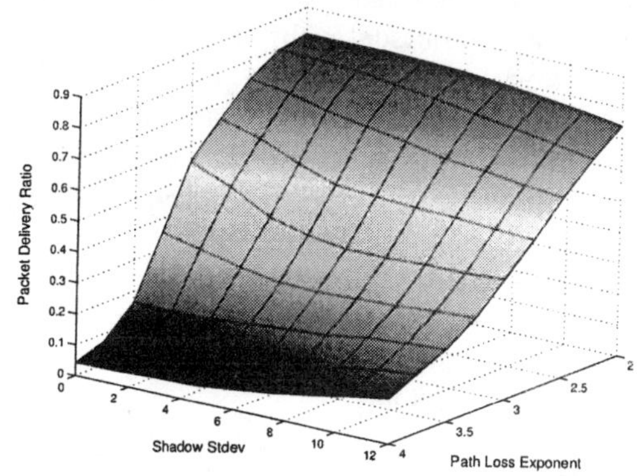

Figure 6. Sensitivity of AODV performance to parameters of large-scale fading model.

ecution environment of the routing algorithm. Figure 5 shows a histogram of the number of hops that a data packet traversed in AODV, before it either reached its destination or dropped along the path. For example, a hop count of zero means that the packet was dropped at the source node; a hop count of one means the packet went one hop: either the destination was the source's neighbor or the packet failed to reach the next hop. The figure shows the fraction of the data packets that traveled in the given number of hops. We see clearly the free-space and two-ray models resulted fewer hops by exaggerating the transmission range. We also see that the connectivity trace was helpful in predicting the route lengths, which confirms that the problem with the free-space and two-ray models using the connectivity trace was that they did not consider packet losses due to the variations in receiving signal power.

The generic propagation model with typical parameters to represent the outdoor test environment offered a relatively good prediction of the performance of the routing algorithms. However, one must carefully choose the correct parameters to reflect the wireless environment. The exponent for the distance path loss and the standard deviation in log-normal distribution for the shadow fading are heavily dependent on the environment under investigation. In the next experiment, we ran a simulation with the same number of mobile stations and with the same traffic load as in the real experiment. Figure 6 shows AODV performance in packet delivery ratio with the same network setting but varying the path-loss exponent and the shadow log-normal standard deviation.

The AODV behavior was more sensitive to the path-loss exponent than to the shadow standard deviation. That is, the signal propagation distance had a stronger effect on the algorithm's performance. A shorter transmission range means packets must travel through more hops (via longer routes) before reaching its destination, and therefore has a higher probability to be dropped. A larger shadow standard deviation caused the links to be more unstable, but the effect varied. On the one hand, when the path-loss exponent was small—the signals had a long transmission range, the small variation in the receiving signal strength did not have a significant effect on routing, causing only infrequent link breakage. On the other hand, when the exponent was large, most nodes were disconnected. A variation in the receiving signal power helped establish some routes which were impossible if not for the signal power fluctuation. Between the extremes, a larger variation in the link quality generally caused more transmission failures, and therefore resulted slightly lower packet delivery ratio.

The critical implication of this sensitivity study is that we cannot just grab a set of large-scale fading parameters, use them, and expect meaningful results for any specific environment of interest. On the one hand, pre-simulation empirical work to estimate path-loss characteristics might be called for, if the point of the experiment is to quantify behavior in a given environment. Alternatively, one may require more complex radio models (such as ray-tracing) that include complex explicit representations of the domain of interest. On the other hand, if the objective is to compare protocols, knowledge that the generic propagation model is good lets us compare protocols using a range of path-loss values. While this does not *quantify* behavior, it may allow us to make *qualitative* conclusions about the protocols over a range of environments.

To summarize, we used simple stochastic radio propagation models and the traces generated from a carefully designed real experiment. Direct-execution simulation provided a common baseline for comparing the behavior of routing protocols both in the real experiment and in simulation. We found that it is critical to choose a proper wireless model that reflects a real-world scenario for studying the performance of ad-hoc routing algorithms. In contrast to earlier studies [12], we found that using a simple stochastic radio propagation model with parameters typical to the outdoor environment can produce acceptable results. We must recognize, however, the results are sensitive to these parameters. It is for this reason we caution that the conclusions drawn from simulation studies using simple propagation models should apply only to the environment they represent. The free-space model and the two-ray model, which exaggerate the radio transmission range and ignore the variations in the receiving signal power, can largely misrepresent the network conditions.

6. Conclusions

This paper reports our effort to support direct-execution simulation of a set of wireless ad-hoc routing protocols to facilitate validation of wireless network models.

In an experiment, we compared two implementations of the AODV protocol: one with direct execution and the other implemented natively in the simulator. We found that direct-execution simulation requires more computational resources, especially in memory usage, thus making the modeled protocol more attractive in a resource-constrained situation, such as studying protocol behaviors in a large network environment. The CPU overhead of direct-execution, however, is moderate and in most case cannot keep direct-execution simulation from being a valuable means of experimentation with the obvious advantage of maintaining consistency between a protocol's actual implementation and that used in simulation.

We conducted a real experiment running the protocols on 40 laptop computers in an outdoor environment. We embedded a sophisticated logging mechanism in the protocol implementations. All activities related to the routing algorithms and the applications were recorded in files. Post-processing these files results in traces that we used in simulation to reproduce the same network condition. We found that one can use a simple stochastic radio propagation model to predict the behavior of the routing protocols with fairly good accuracy, but the results are quite sensitive to the model's parameters. We argue that choosing a proper wireless model that represents the wireless environment of interest is critical in performance evaluation of the routing algorithms.

Our future work includes further analysis to validate different wireless models under different real experimental conditions. We are currently investigating using the link quality information collected by the wireless device driver to improve the accuracy of the connectivity trace. Also, we want to translate the terrain information of the real experiment into a radio propagation gain matrix for a more realistic representation of the wireless environment, and study the effect of such modeling details on the performance evaluation of wireless ad-hoc routing protocols.

7. Acknowledgments

We thank Nikita Dubrovsky, Aaron Fiske, Chris Masone, and Michael DeRosa for implementing the routing algorithms and most of the outdoor experiment infrastructure. Piyush Gupta and Brad Karp helped with the source code of STARA and APRL. Dennis McGrath helped with the initial class structure for the routing algorithms. We thank Chip Elliott at BBN for his valuable insights and suggestions. We also thank Lisa Shay, Susan McGrath, and Eileen Entin for designing the application scenario, and the sixty Dartmouth students and staff members who participated the outdoor experiments.

References

[1] X. A. Dimitropoulos and G. F. Riley. Creating realistic BGP models. *MASCOTS'03*, October 2003.

[2] P. Gupta and P. R. Kumar. A system and traffic dependent adaptive routing algorithm for ad hoc networks. *36th IEEE Conference on Decision and Control*, pages 2375–2380, December 1997.

[3] J. Heidemann, N. Bulusu, J. Elson, C. Intanagonwiwat, K. Lan, Y. Xu, W. Ye, D. Estrin, and R. Govindan. Effects of details in wireless network simulation. *SCS Multiconference on Distributed Simulation*, pages 3–11, January 2001.

[4] D. B. Johnson. Validation of wireless and mobile network models and simulation. *DARPA/NIST Network Simulation Validation Workshop*, May 1999.

[5] B. Karp and H. T. Kung. Dynamic neighbor discovery and loopfree, multi-hop routing for wireless, mobile networks. Hardvard University, May 1998.

[6] B. Karp and H. T. Kung. Greedy perimeter stateless routing for wireless networks. *MobiCom'00*, pages 243–254, August 2000.

[7] S. J. Lee, M. Gerla, and C. C. Chiang. On-demand multicast routing protocol in multihop wireless mobile networks. *Mobile Networks and Applications*, 7(6):441–453, December 2002.

[8] J. Liu, L. F. Perrone, D. M. Nicol, M. Liljenstam, C. Elliott, and D. Pearson. Simulation modeling of large-scale ad-hoc sensor networks. *European Simulation Interoperability Workshop (Euro-SIW'01)*, June 2001.

[9] M. Neufeld, A. Jain, and D. Grunwald. Nsclick: bridging network simulation and deployment. *MSWiM'02*, pages 74–81, September 2002.

[10] C. E. Perkins and E. M. Royer. Ad hoc on-demand distance vector routing. *2nd IEEE Workshop on Mobile Computing Systems and Applications*, pages 90–100, February 1999.

[11] T. S. Rappaport. *Wireless Communications, Principles and Practice*. Prentice Hall, 1996.

[12] M. Takai, R. Bagrodia, K. Tang, and M. Gerla. Efficient wireless network simulations with detailed propagation models. *Wireless Networks*, 7(3):297–305, May 2001.

[13] M. Takai, J. Martin, and R. Bagrodia. Effects of wireless physical layer modeling in mobile ad hoc networks. *MobiHoc'01*, pages 87–94, October 2001.

Performance of a Mixed Shared/Distributed Memory Parallel Network Simulator

Cameron Kiddle, Rob Simmonds and Brian Unger
Department of Computer Science, University of Calgary
2500 University Drive N.W., Calgary, Alberta, Canada T2N 1N4
{kiddlec,simmonds,unger}@cpsc.ucalgary.ca

Abstract

Designing fast parallel discrete event simulation systems for shared-memory parallel computers is simplified by the efficient communication operations enabled by the common memory space. The difficulties involved in designing large shared-memory computers and the resulting high cost of even modest size systems has led to the proliferation of computer systems consisting of small shared-memory computers connected via low-latency message-passing interconnection networks.

This paper describes how a network simulation system using a simulation kernel optimized for high performance operation on shared-memory parallel computers has been extended to operate on computers that mix shared-memory and message-passing paradigms. Results are presented showing that the system can achieve over 60 million simulated packet transmissions per second on 32 4-processor nodes. The results demonstrate the advantage of using a mixture of shared-memory and message-passing over using only message-passing in many cases.

Keywords: *Conservative Parallel Discrete Event Simulation, Network Simulation, Scalable Network Simulation*

1 Introduction

It is possible to design very efficient parallel discrete event simulation (PDES) systems for shared-memory parallel computers. Passing events from one thread of execution to another can be achieved by simply passing a pointer to the event buffer. Also, simple variable updates can take the place of explicit message or event passing to increase the efficiency of synchronization operations. However, large shared-memory computers are very expensive and relatively few systems with more than 64 processors are available.

The trend in super computer design in recent years has been toward systems that link groups of shared-memory computers using low latency message-passing interconnection networks. These distributed-memory systems are often used to run purely message-passing programs, where communication between any pair of processors is achieved using calls to a messaging library such as MPI. With suitable software, threads running on processors on the same node can use shared-memory communications, with message-passing only used to communicate with threads running on different nodes.

This paper describes how the *Internet Protocol Traffic and Network Simulator* (IP-TN) [17] has been extended to work in an environment supporting both shared-memory and message-passing. IP-TN is a parallel Internet Protocol (IP) packet level network simulator that also provides emulation capabilities where real computer hosts are able to interact with the simulator in real-time. A primary reason for extending IP-TN to a distributed-memory environment is to improve the scalability of the emulator where maintaining real-time deadlines is crucial. This paper only reports simulation results; emulation results will appear in a later publication.

IP-TN is built on top of the *CCTKit* [18] simulation kernel that employs the *Critical Channel Traversing* (CCT) [20] algorithm. CCT is a conservative parallel discrete-event simulation algorithm based on the Chandy-Misra-Bryant (CMB) [1, 2] algorithm and was originally designed to achieve highly efficient execution on shared-memory parallel computers. CCT follows the *logical process modelling methodology* [2]. The system being modelled, referred to as a *physical system*, consists of *physical processes* that interact with each other. Each physical process is represented by a *logical process* (LP) in the simulator and interaction between physical processes is modelled by exchanging timestamped events between LPs.

All events sent from one LP to another must be passed along a uni-directional communication *channel* that will usually have been allocated prior to the start of the simulation. Each channel has a minimum *lookahead* value associated with it representing the minimum difference between the timestamp of an event sent on the channel and the timestamp of the event that generated it. Each channel also has a clock representing a lower bound on the timestamp of any event that could arrive on this channel in the future. Events are sent and received on a channel in FIFO order.

The rest of the paper is organized as follows. Section 2 describes related work. Sections 3 and 4 describe the extensions that have been made to CCTKit and IP-TN to achieve mixed shared-memory and message-passing operation. Section 5 presents the experimental methodology used for testing the performance of the distributed IP-TN system and Section 6 presents the results. Conclusions and future work are presented in Section 7.

2 Related Work

The work most closely related to that done in this paper is the extension of DaSSFNet, a network simulator built on the Dartmouth Scalable Simulation Framework (DaSSF) parallel simulation kernel, to a mixed shared/distributed-memory environment [9, 10]. In DaSSF, a multilevel synchronization mechanism combining both asynchronous and synchronous algorithms is used. Simulation processes on the same shared-memory node are coordinated using an asynchronous algorithm based on CCT. Between shared-memory nodes a global synchronization mechanism is used. This employs a global window set to the minimum lookahead among all channels for which message-passing communications are required. Locally, each node runs the CCT based algorithm until the global synchronization window is reached. At this point all messages destined for other nodes are sent after which a barrier and flushing operation with all other nodes is entered. After the barrier is completed, each node proceeds with the CCT based algorithm until the next global synchronization window is reached. This continues until the simulation completes.

The main difference between the work presented in this paper and the work above is that we use an asynchronous mechanism at both levels. Synchronous algorithms can work very well if the minimum lookahead on channels between nodes is large. They avoid the overhead in asynchronous algorithms of sending messages between nodes for each channel to indicate the time it is safe to execute up to. If the minimum lookahead is small however, the global synchronization overhead can be large. Another possible problem with synchronous systems is that they produce more tightly coupled operation. We have observed in real-time network emulation experiments that the loosely coupled execution behavior of asynchronous algorithms enables real-time deadlines to be met, even when some parts of the simulated network are lagging behind real-time due to a burst of computation.

A composite synchronization approach where both synchronous and asynchronous algorithms are used together has also been implemented in DaSSF for a shared-memory environment [11]. By using both types of algorithms the advantages of each can be exploited. Experimental results have demonstrated the success of this approach. This paper does not examine such an approach for a distributed-memory environment, but is an approach worth considering in the future.

Another difference between work on DaSSFNet and the work presented in this paper is that DaSSFNet experiments were performed on a smaller computer system. At most 16 dual processor computers were used for DaSSFNet experiments versus up to 32 quad processor computers for the experiments performed for this paper. The larger system is able to better demonstrate overall scalability and the advantages of extending a shared-memory simulator to a mixed memory environment.

Another approach that has been taken to extend a simulator to a distributed-memory environment is to federate a simulator with itself using High Level Architecture (HLA) techniques. Examples of this approach are given in [7, 13] for the *pdns* [16] and *GTNetS* [14] network simulators. A runtime infrastructure (RTI) software package called RTI-Kit [6] provides communication and synchronization between federates.

RTI-Kit uses an asynchronous algorithm to synchronize federates, but the nature of this algorithm is different from the asynchronous CCT algorithm discussed in this paper. A global asynchronous calculation is performed by RTI-Kit preventing federates from advancing more than a globally minimum lookahead amount past a *Lower Bound on Time Stamp* (LBTS) of all events in the whole system. CCT takes into account a communication topology and lookahead between simulation processes. Each simulation process locally calculates a time up to which it is safe to execute based on lookahead between neighbouring simulation processes. In this way simulation processes could advance much further in time than they could using the global asynchronous algorithm used by RTI-Kit. The algorithm used by RTI-Kit does have an advantage during periods in the simulation when there are no events as it can more quickly advance to the time of the next event. CCT has overheads due to lookahead cycles, though network simulations usually have enough events that this is not a problem.

GTNetS and *pdns* are examples where sequential simulators have been self-federated, but this technique could also be applied to a shared-memory parallel simulator. For our work we have avoided this approach since we want to keep full control of the synchronization mechanism. It should be noted that in environments where distributed nodes are shared-memory computers, GTNets and pdns still take some advantage of shared-memory. Individual federates do not share memory but communication between federates on the same shared-memory computer, for both events and LBTS computations, involves 'shared-memory' message-passing via RTI-Kit (i.e., messages must be copied from the federate into RTI-Kit and then from RTI-Kit to the destination federate) [12]. This is similar to the operation of an optimized version of MPI for use with shared-memory computers. IP-TN takes more advantage of shared-memory by using shared variables for synchronization and common event buffers between processors reducing the amount of copying. Experimental results in this paper demonstrate the advantage of using shared variables and common events buffers over message-passing libraries optimized to utilize shared-memory.

3 Extensions to CCTKit

A major task in extending IP-TN to a distributed-memory environment was implementing extensions required to CCTKit. Three different versions of the CCT algorithm have been implemented in CCTKit [18]. Only the *Simple Sender Side* CCT algorithm has been extended to operate in a distributed-memory environment. This section gives an overview of the Simple Sender Side CCT algorithm as used in shared-memory and introduces how it has been extended for use in distributed-memory.

It should be noted that in CCTKit LPs are grouped together into *objects* that are scheduled according to the CCT algorithm. The main goal of CCT is to schedule objects that are likely to have work to do. This is accomplished by having objects mark their input channel with the smallest clock as *critical* at the end of an execution session. The object cannot be scheduled again until the clock on this critical channel has advanced.

3.1 Shared-Memory CCT

When a simulation object first begins an execution session it scans all of its input channels to discover an initial *safe-time*; the time up to which it is safe to execute events without introducing causality errors. Events with timestamps less than or equal to the safe-time are executed, with the safe-time estimate being revised as necessary. The revision of the safe-time is achieved by observing the clock values on channels that are found to be empty during the execution session. Once the safe-time has been reached each output channel clock is updated. If the output channel is marked critical the destination object is scheduled. At this point, the object marks the input channel that has the lowest clock value after executing events as critical, if the clock has not already advanced. If the clock has advanced, which would happen if the source object has already updated the channel clock, the object schedules itself by placing itself in the local priority queue. Each simulation thread maintains a local priority queue for objects assigned to that thread.

The description above is for the execution of an object that has input channels. Objects that have no input channels are referred to as *source objects* and have other mechanisms for termination of execution sessions and scheduling. Mechanisms for dealing with source objects are discussed in [19].

3.2 Distributed-Memory CCT

In distributed-memory, mechanisms are required to send events from simulation objects that reside on one node to simulation objects that reside on another node. The Message-Passing Interface (MPI) standard is used for this purpose. One MPI process is created for each node in the distributed system. It is possible for each node in the distributed system to have multiple processors that communicate using shared-memory. The MPI process can create simulation threads for each processor on the node with the shared-memory version of CCT used to handle communication and synchronization of objects assigned to that node. The distributed-memory version of CCT handles communication and synchronization of objects that reside on different nodes in the system. MPI is not guaranteed to be thread safe so all calls to MPI functions must be handled in sequence. To avoid the use of locks only one of the simulation threads on a given node handles any distributed communication.

A new object called the *MPI communication object* is used to handle the distributed communication. Only one of these objects is required per node in the distributed-memory system and it is assigned to the first simulation thread on the node. The MPI communication object has a proxy LP to represent every LP residing on a different node that objects on this node have channels to or from. The proxy LP contains information to specify which node in the system its corresponding real LP resides. When creating channels between LPs that reside on different nodes, a channel is created between the LP and the proxy LP that resides on the same node. The notion of the proxy LP is similar to that of the proxy entity described in [5] except that proxy LPs are only created for LPs on other nodes that have channels to/from LPs on a given node.

The MPI communication object maintains a list of all input channels of the proxy LPs. Events received on these channels will need to be sent to the corresponding LPs on other nodes. The MPI communication object also maintains an array of all output channels of the proxy LPs. Events that arrive from other nodes will need to be inserted into the correct output channel. An MPI message containing an event from another node also includes the index of the channel that the event is to be placed in. Index information for channels is sent between nodes in the distributed-memory system during the initialization phase. MPI messages are serialized and a function must be written to pack and unpack events for each event type. Functions to create events of each type must also be registered.

When the MPI communication object executes the following occurs. First, the object checks if it has received messages from other nodes. The messages are unpacked and events are inserted in the correct output channel. Some messages are just used to update a channel clock, in which case the correct channel clock is updated. In both cases, if the output channel is marked critical, the destination object is marked for scheduling at the end of the execution session. Performing the scheduling at the end of the execution session eliminates the overhead of unnecessarily scheduling the destination object multiple times if more than one message for the channel is received. In this manner, scheduling on critical channels is performed, even between distributed nodes.

If an output channel had the lowest clock value in the previous execution session then messages must be received before the clock of the MPI communication object can be advanced. If this is the case and no messages were received the next object in the local priority queue is executed. The cycle of checking for received messages and executing the next object continues until messages have been received.

Once messages have been received, or if an input channel had the lowest clock value in the previous execution session, messages can now be sent to other nodes. The object scans all of its input channels and packs and sends all events on the channels to the corresponding nodes. After sending all events on a given channel, a channel clock update message (NULL message) is also sent if the clock value is greater than the timestamp of the last message sent. Note that unlike the CMB algorithm a NULL message is not sent every time the channel clock is updated. A NULL message is sent at most once each MPI communication object execution session and only if the channel clock is greater than the last clock or event timestamp value sent for this channel. It is possible that the channel clock was updated several times since the last MPI communication object execution.

After all events and channel clock updates have been sent the MPI communication object sets its clock value to be the minimum clock of all input and output channels (i.e., the minimum time at which any message will be received or sent by the object). The destination objects that were previously marked for scheduling are also scheduled at this time.

If an input channel has the lowest clock value, and the clock has not already advanced, then the MPI communication object marks the channel critical. If the clock has advanced, or if an output channel has the lowest clock value, the MPI communication object schedules itself by placing itself in the local priority queue. All other objects in the system operate just as in the shared-memory version of CCT and treat the MPI communication object like any other object.

Note that currently all events and NULL messages are sent as separate MPI messages. It has been noted that using message aggregation can improve the performance of distributed simulations [3]. This optimization will be tried with CCTKit at some point, though the advantage achieved using this optimization is likely far less when using the Compaq/Quadrics implementation of MPI than when using less optimized implementations.

4 Extensions to IP-TN

This section describes extensions to IP-TN, in addition to the CCTKit extensions, that were required for operation in a distributed-memory environment. These extensions included changes to initialization and addition of serialization code to pack and unpack events in the MPI communication object.

In the shared-memory version of IP-TN, initialization of the model begins by reading in files containing the model description. After reading in the model an intermediate topology graph is constructed and used to perform tasks such as IP address generation, partitioning to determine the assignment of network nodes to CCT scheduling objects and scheduling objects to simulation threads, and the generation of routing tables. Partitioning can be performed manually, in which case partitioning information is specified in the model files, or automatically using a simple algorithm based on the network hierarchy. The routing tables are generated based on shortest number of hops between network nodes. Network objects and CCT scheduling objects are then created and assigned to threads according to the partition information.

For the distributed-memory version of IP-TN an off-line pre-initialization phase has been added to create input files for each MPI process that contain only the information required by that process. This is done to reduce memory requirements for each MPI process and also allows multiple replications to be run without repeating the entire initialization process. The pre-initialization phase operates in the same manner as initialization for the shared-memory version of IP-TN. Files containing the model description are read in, with IP address generation, partitioning and routing table generation performed. Model information for each MPI process is written to separate files. Partitioning has been extended to include the MPI process on which the scheduling objects will be assigned.

With pre-initialization already performed, initialization of the distributed-memory version of IP-TN proceeds as follows. Each MPI process reads in the files containing model information required by that process. Network objects and CCT scheduling objects assigned to the MPI process are created, including the MPI communication object.

5 Experimental Methodology

This section describes the experimental methodology used to evaluate the performance of IP-TN when using both shared-memory and message-passing paradigms. Included are descriptions of the experimental environment, the network model, the experimental design, and performance metrics considered.

5.1 Experimental Environment

Simulations were conducted on an HP AlphaServer SC45 system. The system consists of 36 ES45 servers each with four 1.25 GHz Alpha Ev68 processors. At most 32 servers are used in experiments for a total of 128 processors. Each ES45 has 4 GB of RAM (1 GB per processor) and each processor has 16 MB of second level cache. The ES45s are connected using a Quadrics interconnection network. Each ES45 is running Tru64 UNIX V5.1. The Compaq C V6.4-014 and Compaq C++ V6.5-014 compilers were used with "-O3" and "-tune host" compilation flags. The Quadrics compatible version of Compaq MPI was used.

5.2 Network Model

The network model used for experiments is derived from the baseline network topology used by the DARPA NMS community [4] which was designed to demonstrate the scalability of a network simulator. At the top level, the topology is a ring consisting of N nodes, which can easily be scaled by increasing the the number of nodes in the ring. Each node is represented by a network referred to as a "campus network" (CN) which is depicted in Figure 1.

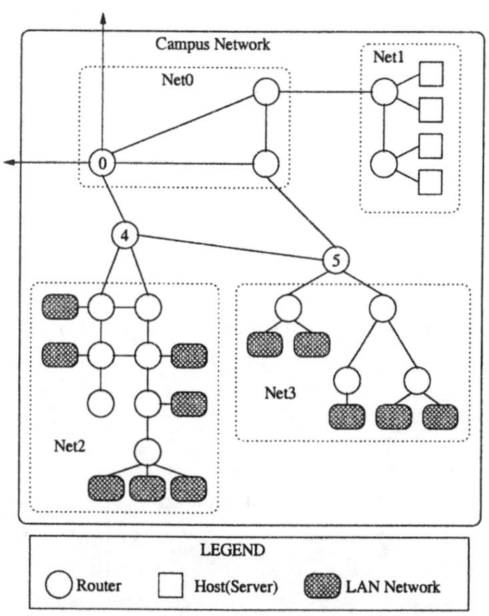

Figure 1. Campus Network Model.

The campus network consists of four subnets labeled as *Net0* to *Net4* and two routers not belonging to any of the subnets labeled as *4* and *5*. *Net0* consists of 3 routers joined by links with bandwidth of 2 Gb/s and delay of 5 ms. Router *0* of *Net0* is a border router that is connected to the border router of neighbouring campus networks in the ring by a link with bandwidth of 2 Gb/s and delay of 200 ms. Links from *Net0* to *Net1* and routers *4* and *5* have bandwidth of 2 Gb/s and delay of 5 ms. The link between routers *4* and *5* also has a bandwidth of 2 Gb/s and delay of 5 ms. Links from routers *4* and *5* to *Net2* and *Net3* have bandwidth of 1 Gb/s and delay of 5 ms.

Net1 consists of 2 routers and 4 hosts which are connected by links with bandwidth of 2 Gb/s and delay of 1 ms. Each of the 4 hosts are running a Web server.

Net2 consists of 7 routers and 7 LAN networks. A LAN network is a network representative of several LANs and consists of a router and 42 hosts. Hosts in a LAN network are connected to the LAN router with point to point links having bandwidth of 100 Mb/s and delay of 1ms. Each host runs a Web client (browser). The 7 routers and 7 LAN routers are connected by links with bandwidth of 1 Gb/s and delay of 5 ms. *Net3* consists of 4 routers and 5 LAN networks with the same connection properties as *Net2*. All together each campus network has 504 clients, 4 servers and 30 routers. Static routing tables are generated for each router based on shortest number of hops.

Two different traffic destination models called *SingleHop* and *MultiHop* are used. In the *SingleHop* model, each Web client in a campus network communicates with a randomly chosen Web server from the next campus network in the ring. In the *MultiHop* model, each Web client in a campus network communicates with a randomly chosen Web server at most $MaxHops$ campus networks ahead in the ring. Each Web client starts a TCP session with its destination server at a uniform random time between 0 and 10 simulated seconds and requests a file of size 500 million bytes. When a TCP session completes, a new file of the same size is requested. TCP Reno is used which models TCP's three-way handshake, sequence numbers, acknowledgments, sliding window flow control, slow-start, congestion avoidance, timeouts and retransmissions.

5.3 Experimental Design

Table 1 summarizes the experimental factors and levels used in the experiments. A fixed number of campus networks are used per processor (CN/CPU) such that the size of the model grows proportionately with the number of processors being used. Each network scenario is simulated using message-passing communications only (Message-Passing communication model) and using shared-memory and message-passing communications combined (Mixed communications model). In the Message-Passing communication model there is an MPI communication object for each processor such that all communication between processors is performed using MPI messages. In the Mixed communication model there is only one MPI communication object per 4 processor ES45. Shared-memory is used for communication among processors on the same ES45 with MPI only used for communication between ES45s.

Note that the Compaq MPI version used is optimized for shared-memory. Therefore the Message-Passing communication model does take some advantage of shared-memory for communication between processes on the same ES45.

Table 1. Experimental factors and levels for simulation experiments.

Factor	Levels
Processors (CPUs)	1, 2, 4, 8, 16, 32, 64, 128
CN/CPU	1, 2, 4, 8, 16
Traffic dest model	SingleHop, MultiHop
MaxHops (MultiHop)	0, 1, 2, 4
Communication model	Mixed, Message-Passing

5.4 Performance Metrics

A general measure of performance for a simulation kernel is the number of events simulated per second of wallclock time, called *events per second*. In a network simulation, another performance measure of interest is the number of packet transmissions simulated per second of wallclock time, called *packet transmissions per second*. In IP-TN only one event is required to simulate a packet transmission. However, events per second and packet transmissions per second still differ as other events are required for such things as generation of traffic and TCP timeouts.

The metric used to compare performance between the different communication models is *relative speedup*. Relative speedup of model A over model B is defined as the ratio of execution time of the simulation using model B to that of the simulation using model A.

6 Results

6.1 Results for SingleHop Traffic

The first set of simulation experiments study the scalability of IP-TN for the SingleHop traffic model. In this model, all Web clients communicate with a randomly chosen Web server in the next campus network in the ring. The number of processors is varied from 1 to 128 and the number of campus networks per processor is varied from 1 to 16. Each simulation, excluding those on 128 processors, was run five times with a simulation time of 100 seconds. Performance results were averaged over the five runs. Due to time constraints on the AlphaServer SC45 system, simulations on 128 processors were only run once.

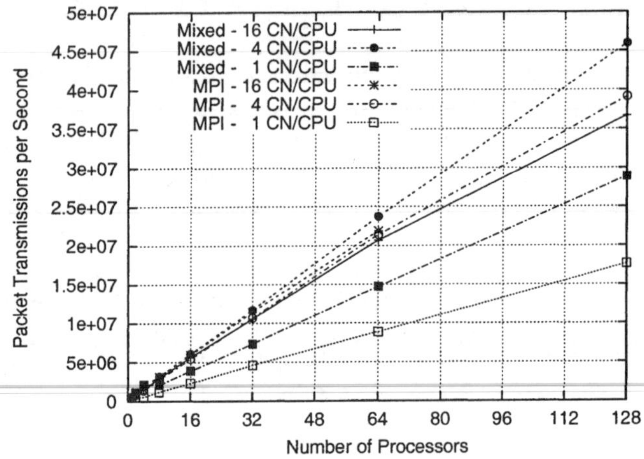

Figure 2. Plot of packet transmissions per second vs number of processors.

Figure 2 shows the number of packet transmissions per second achieved for both the Mixed and Message-Passing communication models. The results obtained show good scaling as the size of the network and the number of processors is increased. Data points for 2 CN/CPU and 8 CN/CPU are not included on the graph but exhibit similar scaling behavior.

The largest network scenario simulated had 16 CN/CPU on 128 processors for a total of over 1.1 million network nodes. 37 million packet transmissions per second (45 million events per second) was achieved by the Mixed communication model for this scenario. Data for the Message-Passing communication model is missing for this scenario as the simulation failed to complete. The best performance results were achieved by the Mixed communication model on 128 processors for 4 CN/CPU. 46 million packet transmissions per second (57 million events per second) was achieved.

Figure 3 shows the relative speedup of the Mixed communication model over the Message-Passing communication model. Tests were not run for 1 processor and 1 CN/CPU as there would have only been one campus network in the ring. For Mixed communication model runs using 2 and 4 processors, only shared-memory communication is utilized. In these cases up to 4 times speedup over the Message-Passing communication model was observed which demonstrates the advantage of using shared-memory. When the number of processors is greater than 4, the Mixed communication model involves message-passing and up to

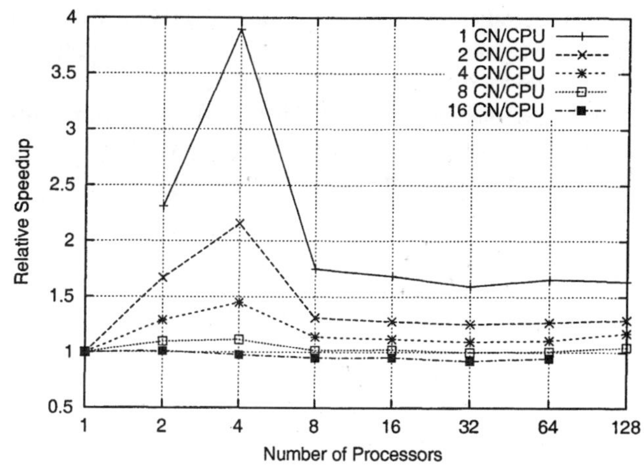

Figure 3. Plot of relative speedup of the Mixed communication model to the Message-Passing communication model.

1.75 times speedup is observed. As the number of campus networks per processor increases, the relative speedup decreases. This is because the level of message-passing communication between MPI processes remains the same while the amount of communication local to a process increases. With an increased local to message-passing communication ratio, message-passing has less impact on performance resulting in the gap between the performance of the Mixed and Message-Passing communication models decreasing.

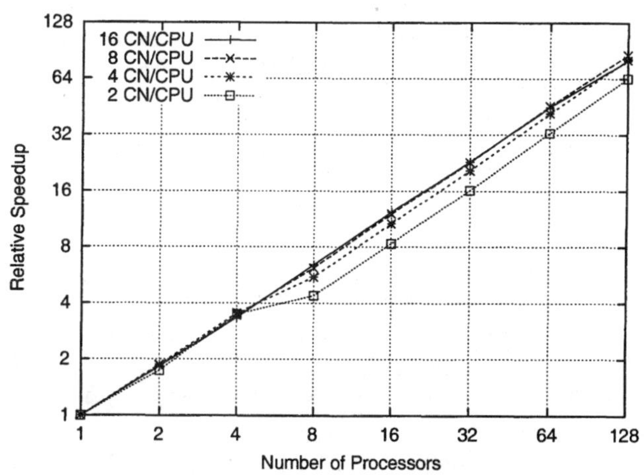

Figure 4. Plot of relative speedup of the Mixed communication model to sequential execution.

Figure 4 shows the relative speedup of the Mixed communication model over sequential execution. The Mixed communication results are compared to a model with the same number of CN/CPU running on 1 processor. Relative speedup in this case is calculated as the packet transmissions per second for the Mixed communication model divided by the packet transmissions per second for the corresponding sequential results. As the number of campus networks per processor increases the local to message-passing communication ratio per MPI process increases and the Mixed communication model scales better. Up to 86 times speedup is observed on 128 processors.

For similar NMS baseline benchmarks performed using DaSSFNet [9], GTNetS and pdns [7, 13], these performance results, in terms of the level of packet transmissions per second achieved, are some of the best for the number of processors used. Note that the benchmarks for the different simulators were performed on different computer systems making it difficult to give exact comparisons. One of the main reasons for the good performance of IP-TN is due to its excellent sequential performance. Up to 625,000 packet transmissions per second were observed sequentially. The results show that IP-TN maintains the good sequential performance in a mixed-memory environment.

Some reasons why IP-TN may have better sequential performance than GTNetS and pdns are as follows. IP-TN takes advantage of parallel simulation techniques when running sequentially, whereas GTNetS and pdns are sequential simulators with a single event queue. In IP-TN the simulated network is divided into objects with each object having its own event queue. With events divided into many smaller queues the time for event insertion/removal is less. Furthermore, objects are only scheduled (i.e., put into the local priority object queue) when there is the potential for the object clock to advance, which helps to reduce the size of the object queue. Another factor that helps to reduce the size of event queues in IP-TN is having only one event per channel (i.e., network link) in a simulation objects event queue. These mechanisms to reduce queue sizes are features of the CCT algorithm and did not require any special implementation in IP-TN. GTNetS also has an optimization where only 1 event per link is kept in the event queue [15] but it is unclear if this optimization was used for the NMS baseline benchmarks referenced to in this paper. GTNetS also models each packet transmission using 2 events, whereas IP-TN and pdns only use one event. Note that GTNetS does have an optimization to model each packet transmission using only 1 event [15] but it appears that this optimization was not used for the NMS baseline benchmarks.

DaSSFNet and IP-TN are similar in that they both implement a CCT based algorithm and both divide the system into scheduling objects (called 'timelines' in DaSSFNet). The main difference between IP-TN and DaSSFNet, with regards to sequential performance, is that DaSSFNet is process oriented, rather than using a strictly event modeling view. This adds some overhead.

6.2 Results for MultiHop Traffic

Increasing model size and number of processors for the SingleHop traffic model does not increase the amount of distributed communication per MPI process. In the MultiHop traffic model the Web clients communicate with randomly chosen Web servers at most $MaxHops$ campus networks ahead in the ring. If $MaxHops = 0$ then Web clients communicate with servers in the same campus network. If $MaxHops = 1$ then Web clients communicate with Web servers 0 to 1 campus networks ahead in the ring. By increasing the value of $MaxHops$, the amount of message-passing communication will increase.

The number of processors is varied from 4 to 128 with 1 CN/CPU and $MaxHops$ values of 0, 1, 2, and 4 are tested. The delay on the links between campus networks was reduced to 20 ms in order to better reflect the latencies between real campuses in North America. Each simulation, except for those on 128 processors, was run five times with a simulation time of 100 seconds. Performance results were averaged over the five runs. Due to time constraints on the AlphaServer SC45 system, simulations on 128 processors were only run once.

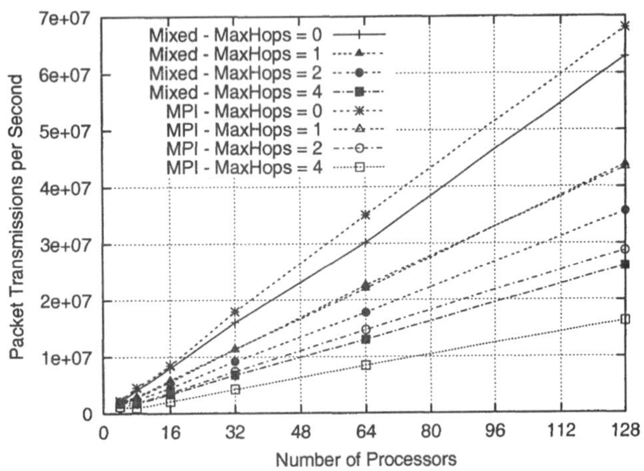

Figure 5. Plot of packet transmissions per second vs number of processors for 1 CN/CPU.

Figure 5 shows the plot of packet transmissions per second for various $MaxHops$ values. When $MaxHops$ is 0 all network communication is local. Only NULL messages are sent between MPI processes to update channel clocks. Performance results in terms of packet transmissions per second are best at $MaxHops = 0$ and decrease as distributed communication increases, as $MaxHops$ increases. The Mixed communication model achieves 63 million packet transmissions per second (71 million events per second) when $MaxHops$ is 0. The Message-Passing communication model actually performs a bit better in this case and achieves 68 million packet transmissions per second (77 million events per second). Upon closer examination, the improved performance by the Message-Passing communication model maybe a result of having fewer object execution sessions than the Mixed communication model tests for $MaxHops = 0$. The reduction in the object execution sessions is likely connected to the distributed synchronization mechanism, but further study will be required.

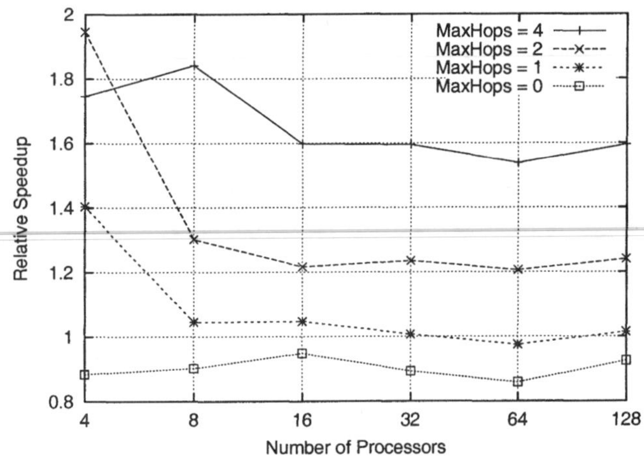

Figure 6. Plot of relative speedup of the Mixed communication model to the Message-Passing communication model for 1 CN/CPU.

Figure 6 shows the plot of relative speedup of the Mixed communication model over the Message-Passing communication model for 1 CN/CPU. Each of the graphs show that as the value of $MaxHops$ is increased, the relative speedup of the Mixed communication model increases. This is due to increased message-passing communication. The Mixed communication model is able to take advantage of shared-memory between processors on the same node and improve relative performance over the Message-Passing communication model.

As in Figure 3 (a) the graphs in Figure 6 show that the relative performance of the Mixed communication model is much higher when the number of processors is 4. This is because the Mixed communication model involves no message-passing in this case. On 128 processors the Mixed communication model shows up to 1.6 times the performance of the Message-Passing communication model.

7 Conclusions and Future Work

This paper explained how an efficient shared-memory IP packet level network simulator was extended to operate in a mixed shared-memory and distributed-memory (message-passing) environment. Processors that share memory communicate using shared-memory operations, while communications between distributed nodes are performed using message-passing. In order to achieve this the underlying parallel simulation kernel needed to be modified and the parallel synchronization algorithm it employs extended to work in this environment. Results presented demonstrate good scalability with increasing model size and number of processors. Performance of over 60 million packet transmissions per second on 32 4-processor nodes (128 processors in total) was observed. Results in this paper represent some of the best performance results achieved in the network simulation community for the number of processors used. The good sequential performance of IP-TN is one of the major reasons for this. The results demonstrate that IP-TN is able to maintain the good sequential performance in a distributed-memory environment.

The ratio of local communication using shared-memory operations, to message-passing communication per processor was shown to play an important role to the performance achieved. Increasing the amount of message-passing communication increases the relative performance of Mixed (shared-memory and message-passing) to that of Message-Passing communication (message-passing only) models, whereas increasing the amount of local communication decreases the relative performance. Up to 1.6 times relative speedup of the Mixed communication model over the Message-Passing communication model was observed on 128 processors. This demonstrates the advantage of the use of shared variables and common event buffers over message-passing libraries optimized to utilize shared-memory.

For future work, we plan to extend fluid-flow techniques previously implemented in the simulator [8] as well as emulation capabilities to work in a distributed environment. We will run experiments to determine the size of models that can be run in a real-time network emulation environment.

Acknowledgements

Financial support for this research was provided by NSERC (Natural Sciences and Engineering Research Council of Canada), iCORE (Informatics Circle of Research Excellence), ASRA (Alberta Science and Research Authority) and the University of Calgary. The HP AlphaServer SC45 system used for experiments discussed in this paper is part of WestGrid, a collaborative high performance computing project based in Western Canada. The authors wish to thank other members of the IP-TN development team, including Roger Curry, Mark Fox, Kitty Wong, Hala Taleb, Mike Bonham, and Xiao Zhong-e. The authors also wish to thank the anonymous referees for their constructive comments regarding the paper.

References

[1] R. E. Bryant. Simulation of packet communication architecture computer systems. Technical Report TR-188, MIT Labratory for Computer Science, 1977.

[2] K. M. Chandy and J. Misra. Distributed simulation: A case study in design and verification of distributed programs. *IEEE Transactions on Software Engineering*, SE-5(5):440–452, 1979.

[3] M. Chetlur, N. Abu-Ghazaleh, R. Radhakrishnan, and P. A. Wilsey. Optimizing communication in Time-Warp simulators. In *Proceedings of the 12th Workshop on Parallel and Distributed Simulation*, pages 64–71, 1998.

[4] DARPA Network Modeling and Simulation (NMS) baseline network topology. http://www.cs.dartmouth.edu/~nicol/NMS/baseline/.

[5] S. L. Ferenci, K. S. Perumalla, and R. M. Fujimoto. An approach for federating parallel simulators. In *Proceedings of the 14th Workshop on Parallel and Distributed Simulation*, pages 63–70, 2000.

[6] R. M. Fujimoto, T. McLean, K. Permualla, and I. Tacic. Design of high performance RTI software. In *Proceedings of the Fourth IEEE Workshop on Distributed Simulation and Real-Time Applications*, pages 89–96, 2000.

[7] R. M. Fujimoto, K. Perumalla, A. Park, H. Wu, M. H. Ammar, and G. F. Riley. Large-scale network simulation: How big? how fast? In *Proceedings of the 11th IEEE/ACM International Symposium on Modeling, Analysis and Simulation of Computer Telecommunications Systems*, pages 116–123, 2003.

[8] C. Kiddle, R. Simmonds, C. Williamson, and B. Unger. Hybrid packet/fluid flow network simulation. In *Proceedings of the 17th Workshop on Parallel and Distributed Simulation*, pages 143–152, 2003.

[9] J. Liu. *Improvements in Conservative Parallel Simulation of Large-Scale Models*. PhD thesis, Computer Science Department, Dartmouth College, 2003.

[10] J. Liu and D. Nicol. Learning not to share. In *Proceedings of the 15th Workshop on Parallel and Distributed Simulation*, pages 46–55, 2001.

[11] D. Nicol and J. Liu. Composite synchronization in parallel discrete-event simulation. *IEEE Transactions on Parallel and Distributed Systems*, 13(5):443–446, 2002.

[12] K. S. Perumalla. *Private electronic mail communication*, January 2004.

[13] K. S. Perumalla, A. Park, R. M. Fujimoto, and G. F. Riley. Scalable RTI-based parallel simulation of networks. In *Proceedings of the 17th Workshop on Parallel and Distributed Simulation*, pages 97–104, 2003.

[14] G. F. Riley. The Georgia Tech network simulator. In *Proceedings of the ACM SIGCOMM Workshop on Models, Methods and Tools for Reproducible Network Research*, pages 5–12, 2003.

[15] G. F. Riley. Large-scale network simulations with GTNetS. In *Proceedings of the 2003 Winter Simulation Conference*, pages 676–684, 2003.

[16] G. F. Riley, R. M. Fujimoto, and M. H. Ammar. A generic framework for parallelization of network simulations. In *Proceedings of the Seventh International Symposium on Modeling, Analysis and Simulation of Computer and Telecommunication Systems*, pages 128–135, 1999.

[17] R. Simmonds, R. Bradford, and B. Unger. Applying parallel discrete event simulation to network emulation. In *Proceedings of the 14th Workshop on Parallel and Distributed Simulation*, pages 15–22, 2000.

[18] R. Simmonds, C. Kiddle, and B. Unger. Addressing blocking and scalability in critical channel traversing. In *Proceedings of the 16th Workshop on Parallel and Distributed Simulation*, pages 17–24, 2002.

[19] R. Simmonds, C. Kiddle, K. Wong, and B. Unger. Controlling buffer usage in critical channel traversing. In *Proceedings of the 35th Annual Simulation Symposium*, pages 53–62, 2002.

[20] Z. Xiao, B. Unger, R. Simmonds, and J. Cleary. Scheduling critical channels in conservative parallel discrete event simulation. In *Proceedings of the 13th Workshop on Parallel and Distributed Simulation*, pages 20–28, 1999.

Detailed OFDM Modeling in Network Simulation of Mobile Ad Hoc Networks*

Gavin Yeung+
Display Product Business Group (DPBG)
Foxconn Technology Corp.
San Jose, CA 95112
gavin.yeung@foxconn.com

Mineo Takai, Rajive Bagrodia
University of California, Los Angeles
Computer Science Department
Los Angeles, CA 90095
{gavin, mineo, rajive}@cs.ucla.edu

Alireza Mehrnia, Babak Daneshrad
University of California, Los Angeles
Electrical Engineering Department
Los Angeles, CA 90095
{mehrnia, babak}@ee.ucla.edu

Abstract

In mobile ad hoc network (MANET) studies, it is imperative to use highly detailed device models as they provide high layer protocols with good prediction of underlying wireless communication performance. However, such studies often utilize abstract models for execution speed and simplicity. This paper first shows that physical layer variables including path loss, shadowing, multipath, Doppler have significant effects on the predicted overall networking performance. It then proposes an approach to simulate details of wireless propagation and radio characteristics in networking studies while still maintaining a reasonable simulation execution time. Through our runtime performance studies with detailed OFDM Simulink / MATLAB models and QualNet network simulator, it is shown that the proposed approach can improve the simulation runtime performance by three to four orders of magnitudes without compromising the fidelity of simulation results.

1. Introduction

Network simulation is commonly used for the evaluation of wireless network protocols. Discrete event simulators typically model the network activities on a packet-by-packet basis, in time granularity of tens of microseconds, and include a model for each layer of the entire protocol stack. Abstract models can be acceptable if they do not significantly compromise accuracy of the simulation results. However, even if abstract models may compromise the accuracy, they are often in place because detailed models are too difficult to implement and to run efficiently.

* This work is supported in part by the Office of Naval Research through the MINUTEMAN project under contract number N00014-01-C-0016.

+ This work was performed while he was at the University of California, Los Angeles.

Studies on physical layer techniques and their performance evaluation under varying channel conditions often use highly specialized mathematical tools such as MATLAB, Simulink, Maple, and Mathematica [1][2][3]. These software packages provide a rich set of built-in libraries and standard building blocks for use in rapid development of prototypes, allowing users to model channel, modulation, and demodulation with different parameters. However, this highly detailed simulation of receiving every bit transferred across the wireless channel comes at a high computing cost and a very long execution time.

An abstract model may effectively replace a detailed model if such a model does not produce inaccurate results. Such an example would be the recently proposed fluid-based analytical model to determine queue sizes for high capacity wired networks [4][5]. In other cases, detailed simulation models may be necessary to accurately predict network performance. This is especially true for the physical layer in wireless networks where slight inaccuracy may become magnified by higher layer protocols. In [6], the authors show that consideration of the physical layer is necessary to determine ad hoc routing network performance. However, even with very strong evidence at hand, current network simulators apply abstract models to simulate the propagation layer and radio device characteristics. They favor abstract, simple models for the sake of execution speed and efficiency.

There is significant information to be gained in detailed simulation of the physical layer however. In a wireless medium where channel condition changes frequently, nanosecond time granularity simulation of communication devices together with the propagation medium provides valuable insights that otherwise would be lost in abstract modeling. This paper presents an approach to develop an appropriate interface between a packet-level simulator, QualNet [7], and a MATLAB /

1087-4097/04 $20.00 © 2004 IEEE

Simulink model for an OFDM (Orthogonal Frequency Division Multiplexing) radio and associated channel, two simulators of dramatically different time scales and execution speed.

Pervious attempts to integrate heterogeneous simulators for network studies include [8][9][10]. In [8], the authors developed a backplane that enables the user to bring multiple network simulators together and harness their models in a single experiment. The split protocol stack methodology for network simulation presented in [9] allows network researchers to run different layers of the network stack on different simulators. In [10], the MAYA network modeling framework is used to emulate a distributed multimedia application. A combination of discrete event simulation, analytical modeling, and physical network emulation are tied together to form a heterogeneous modeling paradigm. The focus of these pieces of work differs from the one described in this paper in that we concentrate on the problems associated with tying a physical radio simulator with a network simulator.

Our integration of a highly detailed physical layer model and a packet-level simulator demonstrates that detailed simulation of the physical layer significantly affects the performance prediction of higher layer protocols. Specifically, it is shown that the number of MAC (Medium-Access-Control) retransmissions may significantly differ when the abstract model and the detailed model are compared at various data rates. This, in turn, causes a varying degree of impact on the packet delivery ratio.

The rest of the paper is organized as follows. Section 2 briefly describes OFDM and the IEEE 802.11 MAC followed by a discussion of the OFDM model and the network simulator, QualNet. Section 3 presents the integration technique of the OFDM model into QualNet. Simulation experiments and results are presented in Section 4. Section 5 follows with our conclusion.

2. OFDM and IEEE 802.11 Overview, OFDM Model and QualNet Network Simulator

2.1. OFDM Technology and IEEE 802.11

In order to understand the necessity of the integration effort, we briefly describe the IEEE 802.11a MAC and the OFDM (Orthogonal Frequency Division Multiplexing) PHY (Physical) layer. Readers interested in the details of the standard should refer to [11][12][13][14]. The IEEE 802.11a uses OFDM as its underlying radio technology. A combination of different modulation and coding schemes is used to give the IEEE 802.11a the wealth of data rates. Operating at the 5 GHz band, it supports rates of 6, 9, 12, 18, 24, 36, 48, and 54 Mbps.

OFDM is a modulation scheme that converts a wideband signal into a series of independent narrowband signals placed side-by-side in the frequency domain. Modulation is the process of translating an outgoing data stream into symbols for transmission by the sender. The main benefit of OFDM is that the subcarriers can actually overlap one-another. The basic idea is to split the data to be transmitted into n parallel data streams, each of which is modulated for a subcarrier. The entire allocated channel is occupied by the sum of the narrow orthogonal sub-bands. Due to implementation complexity, OFDM applications have been scarce until recently with the advances in DSP technology.

OFDM communication systems naturally alleviate the problems of multipath propagation with its low data rate per subcarrier as it is only a fraction of conventional single carrier systems having the same throughput. However, when the transmitter or receiver is moving relative to one another, Doppler shifts occur and can cause significant problems in OFDM systems as the transmission technique is inherently sensitive to carrier frequency offsets. Pilot tones are often used for channel estimation refinement. In the IEEE 802.11a, four of the 52 subcarriers are designated as pilot tones for correcting residual frequency offset errors that tend to accumulate over symbols. The PHY layer also pre-pends the physical preamble to the data frame, modulates, and codes the data frame at the MAC specified data rate. The physical preamble is used to allow the receiver to detect start of packet transmission and to synchronize to the transmitter's clock.

The IEEE 802.11 MAC is primarily responsible for avoiding collisions due to simultaneous transmissions by CSMA/CA (Carrier Sense Multiple Access/Collision Avoidance). Upon detecting a transmission by a neighboring node, a node sets a NAV (Network Allocation Vector) to yield the channel to the neighbor, avoiding the potential collision. Optionally, another medium reservation mechanism is implemented with the RTS/CTS (Request-To-Send / Clear-To-Send) [15] message exchange. Nodes that overhear an RTS or a CTS do not transmit data until the corresponding NAV expires. This can alleviate the hidden terminal problem, thus is typically used in MANETs. The timing sequence for the RTS/CTS exchange is shown in Figure 1.

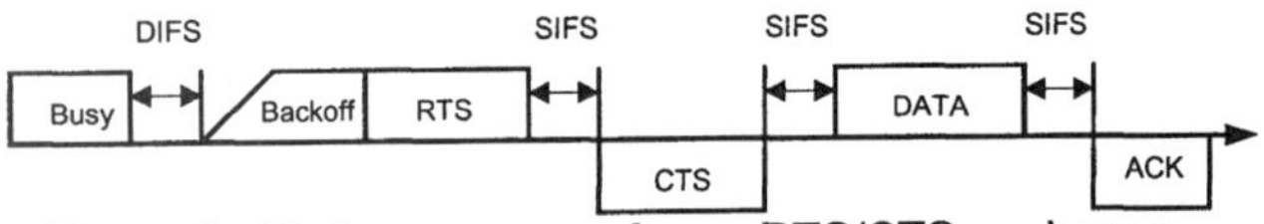

Figure 1. Timing sequence for an RTS/CTS exchange.

By integrating an OFDM model in MATLAB with the IEEE 802.11 MAC protocol implemented in QualNet, we can now predict the performance of OFDM radio technology in CSMA/CA networks with details of the physical layer and device characteristics.

2.2. OFDM Simulator

An OFDM simulator is built using MATLAB Simulink. Simulink is a simulation and prototyping environment for modeling dynamic systems [16]. The OFDM simulator contains a large set of parameters that lead to a myriad of channel conditions and, hence, BER (*B*it *E*rror *R*ate) rates. The relevant variable parameters for the purpose of this study include:

- Modulation type – BPSK, 4-QAM, 16-QAM, 64-QAM
- Multipath – up to six channel tap delays and loss
- Number of effective subcarriers – 33-1024 subcarriers
- Number of symbols in cyclic prefix and cyclic postfix
- Transmitter antenna gain, receiver antenna gain
- Mean transmit power, receiver noise figure
- SINR (*S*ignal to *I*nterference and *N*oise *R*atio)
- Frequency offset

These parameters describing channel characteristics are first fed into MATLAB. A channel is then realized in Simulink. A picture of the OFDM simulator is shown in Figure 2.

The transmitter model in Simulink, upon the start of simulation, generates a stream of bits and modulates them by the specified modulation scheme. Pilot tones are added and the last OFDM symbol is zero-padded prior to the IFFT. Guard blocks are added by cyclically pre-pending and post-pending the specified number of data samples to the beginning and end of each individual OFDM symbol. Each data symbol is 4.0 μs long. A preamble is then generated which consists of training symbols for packet detection, frequency offset, and channel estimation at the receiver.

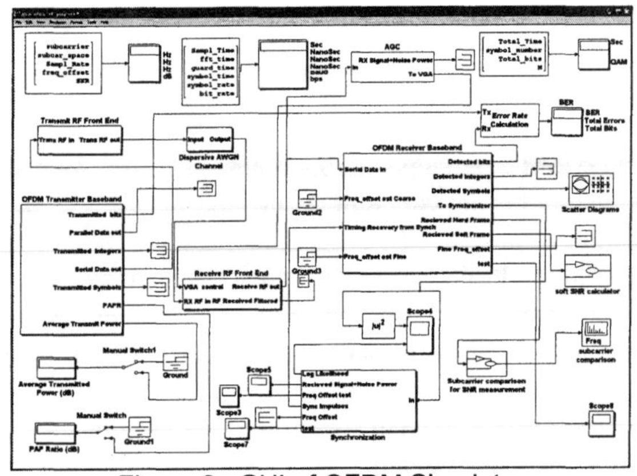

Figure 2. GUI of OFDM Simulator.

The symbols are then brought to the transmitter RF front-end and simulated across the wireless channel. In wireless communication, signals are subjected to distortions generated by the signals' interactions with obstacles and terrain conditions. Under the assumptions of multiple propagation paths to the receiver, the channel is characterized by time-varying propagation delays, attenuation factors, and Doppler shifts.

On the receiver side, the receiver must decide which of the possible digital waveforms most closely resembles the received signal, taking into account the effects of the channel. The OFDM receiver synchronizes to the incoming signal and the baseband processor demodulates the signal back to the stream of bits. The receiver first performs time synchronization and removal of cyclic prefix and postfix. After a FFT, pilot tones are removed from the data frame and the data is then reordered back to the original unscrambled sequence. The transmitted and receive bits are compared and BER is calculated based on the number of error bits and the total number of bits send. Furthermore, the receiver calculates the SINR per OFDM subcarrier seen at the receiver baseband. The average received effective SINR is calculated at the end of simulation. Simulation of 100 OFDM symbols takes about 50 seconds on 2.4 GHz Intel Xeon machine equipped with 512MB of memory.

2.3. OFDM Simulator

QualNet [7] is a discrete-event network simulator that includes a rich set of detailed models for wireless networking. QualNet is the next generation of the GloMoSim simulator [17]. GloMoSim was designed to simulate large-scale wireless networks with thousands of mobile nodes, each of which may have different communication capabilities. QualNet has extended GloMoSim's capabilities to simulate wired networks as well as mixed wired and wireless networks.

QualNet includes models of popular protocols used in each network layer. These ranges from commonly used applications like file transfer (ftp) and web browsing (http), to transport, and MAC layer protocols. QualNet defines simple APIs between neighboring layers for modular composition of protocol models developed at the different layers by different designers. A number of statistical metrics at each layer are collected automatically by the simulator and can be subsequently used by the analysts to analyze the experiment results. QualNet implements the IEEE 802.11a MAC and PHY reference standard. While the MAC layer is simulated inside the simulator, the PHY layer is abstracted to a BER based signal reception model.

The BER versus SNR performance tables were generated using the OFDM simulator from [14]. The tables were created by running the OFDM model and statistically generating the results over a number of trial runs at a specified modulation and coding rate. The abstract PHY model takes the SNR calculated by QualNet channel model and looks up the corresponding BER for that data rate. It then probabilistically determines whether each node receives a frame without errors. The error probability is then calculated using (1), where *numBits* is the number of bits simulated for the particular BER.

$$errorProbability = 1 - (1 - BER)^{numBits} \quad (1)$$

A uniformly distributed random number is then generated in QualNet. If the error probability is greater then the generated random number, that packet is presumed to have an error.

3. Integration of OFDM Model into QualNet

This section discusses implementation issues with the integration of the OFDM model with QualNet. To interface these two simulators, the time scale and execution speed differences must be carefully considered. As QualNet is developed using a layered approach, we can modify the implementation details at a particular layer without affecting other layers. To integrate the OFDM model, the physical layer in QualNet was modified to invoke the OFDM model when necessary as shown in Figure 3.

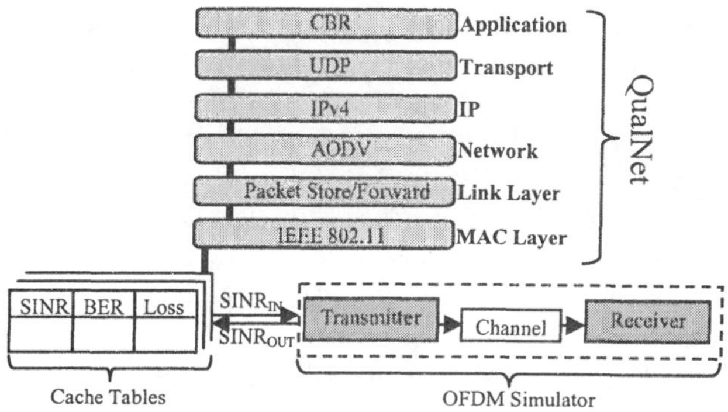

Figure 3. Integration of OFDM Simulator with QualNet.

When a QualNet node detects an incoming signal, it first determines if that signal is above the receiving threshold (RXT). If the signal is above the specified RXT value, the radio tries to receive the signal. SINR is calculated from the strength of the signal and the interference plus noise in the channel. The baseline QualNet model does not currently model Doppler, multipath, or frequency offset effects. Hence, the integration of the OFDM model is carried out as follows: the QualNet node's original SINR, $SINR_{IN}$, is fed into the detailed OFDM model. In combination with the user specified multipath, Doppler, frequency offset, and the relative speed of the nodes calculated in QualNet, a dynamic channel is generated. The OFDM model is then simulated and the resulting SINR, $SINR_{OUT}$ seen at the receiver baseband, is used to calculate the *loss* defined in (2). This *loss* value, as we will explain later, is then stored in a table inside QualNet. The new SINR result is then used to calculate weather or not the packet includes errors.

$$SINR_{out} = \frac{Signal_{in} - Loss}{Noise_{in} + Loss} \quad (2)$$

As mentioned earlier in Section 2.2, simulation of the OFDM model is time consuming. While bit level simulation in wireless environments is desirable, large-scale network simulations must trade off between simulation execution time and accuracy. Simulation time of this integrated system is considerably reduced via two methods: simulation of only a portion of the data frame and a caching mechanism to cache similar scenarios.

While evaluating the OFDM simulator, it is noticed that the simulated resulting receiver SINR value does not change significantly (within 1%) after the simulation of a certain number of OFDM symbols. This is because the transmission duration is less than the coherence time. The coherence time of the channel is a measure of the speed at which the channel characteristics change. This duration of this time is on the order of multiple frame transmissions. Using this fact, the OFDM simulation was stopped after the SINR measurement stabilized, which was after 40 OFDM symbols. This reduced simulation time as typical packet transmission length might last for 100s of OFDM symbols. For example, a 1472 byte packet modulated at 6 Mbps would transmit 503 OFDM symbols.

More significantly, a caching mechanism was developed to take advantage of scenarios with similar SINR and channel conditions. That is, after running the OFDM simulator at a given SINR and channel condition, the *loss* resulted from that run would be saved. The *loss* value is the signal strength loss; it becomes part of the noise. When a similar SINR and channel condition transmission occurs, the resulting SINR is calculated using (2) with the *loss* value previously cached. The *loss* is cached initially instead of the resulting SINR value because the granularity of the input SINR is rounded to the nearest integer; an input SINR of 11.5 dB and 12.4 dB would map to the same *loss* value, not the same SINR. Caching the original resulting SINR value would be inaccurate because of the large granularity; but using the *loss* calculated, a realistic effective SINR value that includes the effects of device and channel is obtained. With the new SINR value, the corresponding BER is retrieved. The error probability for the packet is then calculated and the packet is tested for error. Simulation runtime is sped up considerably with this caching mechanism.

4. Simulation Studies

4.1. MANET Simulation Scenarios

This section quantifies the effects of the OFDM radio and channel modeling on typical scenarios used in the performance evaluation of MANETs. Scenarios for this comparison are created as follows: each scenario is configured with a stationary 50-node network uniformly distributed over a 1000m x 1000m terrain. Twenty-five nodes are randomly chosen to be CBR (Constant Bit Rate) sources, each of which generates 512-byte data packets to a randomly chosen destination at a rate of 5, 10, 20, 40, and 60 packets per second for 180 seconds. The network uses AODV (Ad Hoc On-Demand Distance Vector Routing) [18] for each CBR source to discover a route to the destination. Each data point represents the average value from seven runs with different random number seeds. With different seeds, the node placement and CBR sessions in the network differ. Other common parameters are listed in Table 1. The transmission power and receiver sensitivity are taken from [19], an actual commercial implementation of the IEEE 802.11a.

Table 1. Parameters used in QualNet and OFDM simulation.

Parameter		Value
Channel frequency		5.2 [GHz]
Effective Subcarriers		48
Data rate		24 Mbps, ARF
Antenna gain		0 [dBi]
BPSK	**TX Power**	20.0 [dBm]
	RX Sensitivity/Threshold	-85.0 [dBm]
QPSK	**TX Power**	19.0 [dBm]
	RX Sensitivity/Threshold	-83.0 [dBm]
16-QAM	**TX Power**	18.0 [dBm]
	RX Sensitivity/Threshold	-78.0 [dBm]
64-QAM	**TX Power**	16.0 [dBm]
	RX Sensitivity/Threshold	-69.0 [dBm]

Table 2. Set of parameters used in OFDM simulation.

Parameter	Value
Fading model	Rayleigh
Doppler Spread	250.0 [Hz]
Number of Cyclic Prefix	20
Number of Cyclic Postfix	1
Path loss exponent	3

In this evaluation, two data rate types, 24 Mbps and ARF, were chosen. First, every node is set to transmit only at 24 Mbps. This corresponds to the 16-QAM modulation in the OFDM model. Second, each node uses the Auto Rate Fallback (ARF) [20] algorithm for automatic data rate adjustment to best match the varying channel conditions. The basic idea of the ARF protocol is to keep track of the number of successful transmissions, and only after a number of successful attempts, the sender sends the data packets at the next higher data rate. The sender also keeps a timer; when the timer expires, the sender tries to send the next packet at the next higher data rate. The protocol decreases the sender's transmission rate either when it misses two consecutive ACKs or when it fails to receive an ACK immediately after raising the transmission data rate. The timer value, 60 ms, is experimentally found to be optimal in [21]. In order for ARF to achieve good performance with RTS/CTS frame exchange, the sending node should count the missed CTS packet as an "ACK failure" when a node fails to receive the CTS after a RTS transmission. Thus, two missed CTS packets would lead to a subsequent data rate decrease.

Using the ARF rate-adjusting algorithm, the OFDM constellation will vary between BPSK, 4-QAM (QPSK), 16-QAM, and 64-QAM depending on the data rate.

Table 2 contains a list of parameters fed into the OFDM model by QualNet, considered as typical outdoor conditions. All the variables are chosen to mimic the IEEE 802.11a parameters.

4.2. Packet Delivery Ratio and MAC Total Retransmission with Fixed Data Rate

Figures 4 and 5 respectively show the PDR (Packet Delivery Ratio) and the number of retransmissions with the fixed data rate observed in simulation with and without the integrated OFDM model. As shown in Figure 4, The PDR performance of the integrated OFDM model simulation is significantly lower than that of the original abstract model when the transmitting data rate is fixed. As the network load increases, the PDR decreases considerably due to packet transmission errors and channel congestion. At the highest packet rate scenario, the integrated OFDM simulation produces PDR that is only two-fifths of that of the original abstract model. In Figure 5, the difference between the integrated model and abstract model is obvious. The number of retransmission attempts is significantly higher for the integrated OFDM simulation. This correlates well with the lower PDRs depicted in Figure 4. At 40 and 60 packets per second per flow, the number of MAC retransmission attempts is closer to that of the abstract model. This substantial difference in simulation results with the integrated OFDM model clearly demonstrates the need for detailed simulation of physical layer models in network system level simulation.

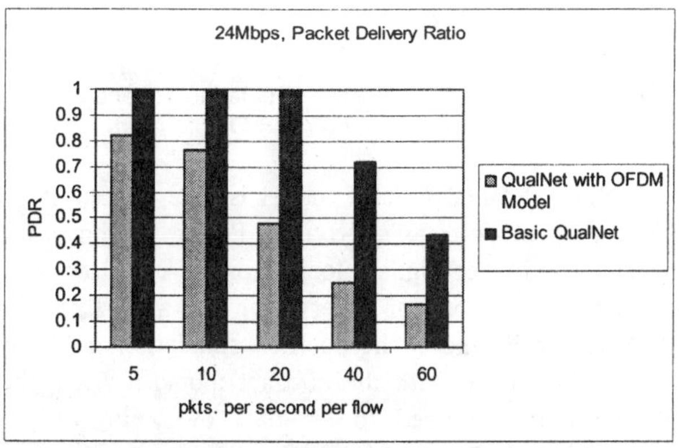

Figure 4. PDR with and without detailed OFDM model using 24 Mbps data rate transmissions.

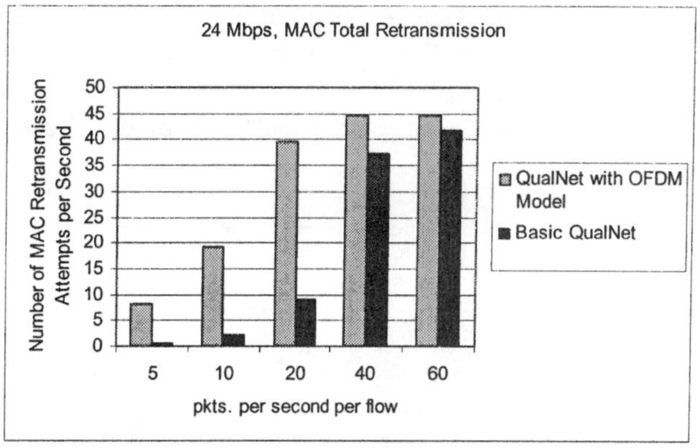

Figure 5. Number of retransmissions with and without detailed OFDM model using 24 Mbps date rate transmissions.

4.3. Packet Delivery Ratio and MAC Total Retransmission Using Auto Rate Fallback

Figures 6 and 7 show the same metrics discussed in the previous section with ARF. The results are quite different when each node uses ARF as its data rate control algorithm. For the two different simulation models, the PDR and the number of retransmission attempts match each other closely as shown in Figure 6 and Figure 7. Because ARF adjust data rates based on channel conditions, in sparse network scenarios, ARF can lower the node's transmitting data rate to ensure packet delivery without overloading the transmission medium. By comparing the PDR of Figure 4 and that of Figure 6 at 5, 10, and 20 packets per second per flow, it is easily seen that ARF takes advantage of the sparse traffic to ensure packet delivery. It is also clear that the gradual PDR decrease from the OFDM model in Figure 4 is caused by other wireless network traffic interference. ARF adapts to light load noisy environments well. However, as the packet rate increases, ARF is actually detrimental to PDR performance. Notice that the PDR performance in Figure 4 at 40 and 60 packets per second per flow is higher than that of Figure 6. By lowering the data rate, ARF, in highly congested environments, causes longer packet transmission duration and, in effect, longer delays and more queue overflows. This leads to a lower PDR ratio in congested scenarios when compared with the fixed data rate setting.

While the observation of ARF performance itself is interesting, the difference in simulation results with and without the detailed OFDM model is much smaller than that shown in the previous section. Although this particular case does not seem to require the detailed OFDM model to predict the network performance, there is no good way to determine whether the detailed physical layer model is essential, as it highly depends on the protocol characteristics. Further, the quantification of such difference in predicted performance cannot be done unless simulation results with and without the detailed model are compared.

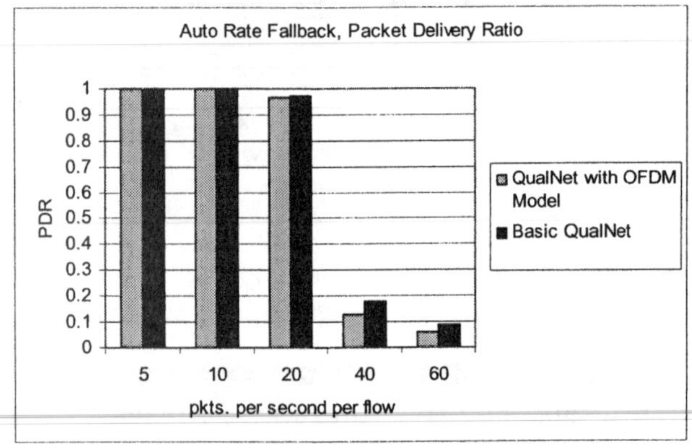

Figure 6. PDR with and without detailed OFDM model using Auto Rate Fallback.

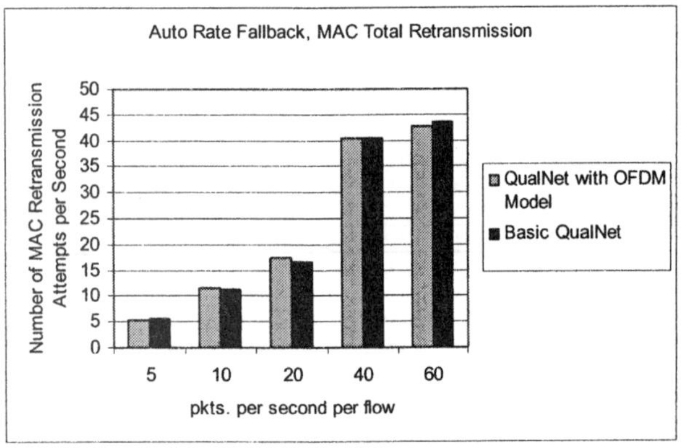

Figure 7. Number of retransmissions with and without detailed OFDM model using Auto Rate Fallback.

4.4. Runtime Performance of Caching Technique

As previously noted, link level OFDM simulation is very computationally expensive. While detailed simulation of every bit of the network is desirable, one cannot expect to use the OFDM simulator to simulate every packet in the network for large MANET scenarios. Our integration technique (described in Section 3) of caching the signal loss and partial transmission simulation alleviate the problem as it captures the interactions of the wireless channel with the radio device and yet still maintains a reasonable execution time to allow for large MANET simulations. Figure 8 and Figure 9 depicts the execution speedup benefit of using the cache detailed model method as opposed to using the OFDM model to simulate every single bit in the network. In the simulation, a stationary 25-node network is placed over a 500m x 500m terrain. Fifteen nodes are randomly chosen to be CBR sources, each of which generates 512-byte data packets to a randomly chosen destination at a rate of 1, 5, 10, 20, 40 and 60 packets per second and using AODV routing. The simulation was stopped when the execution time per simulation second stabilized. One can easily see the benefits of the caching; the improvement in execution time ranges from 2,000 times to over 75,000 times.

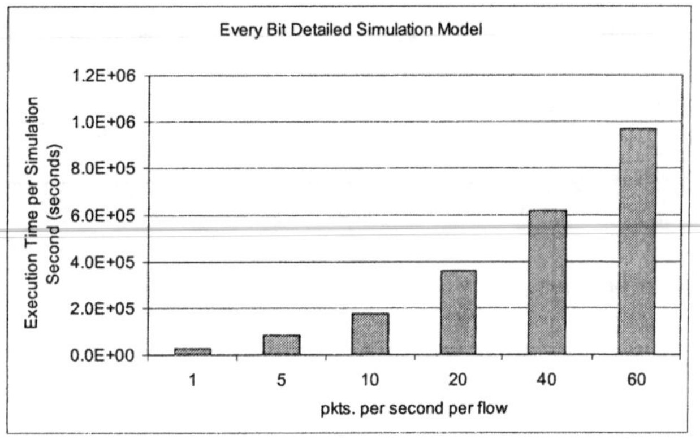

Figure 8. Execution time per simulation second, without caching results from detailed OFDM model.

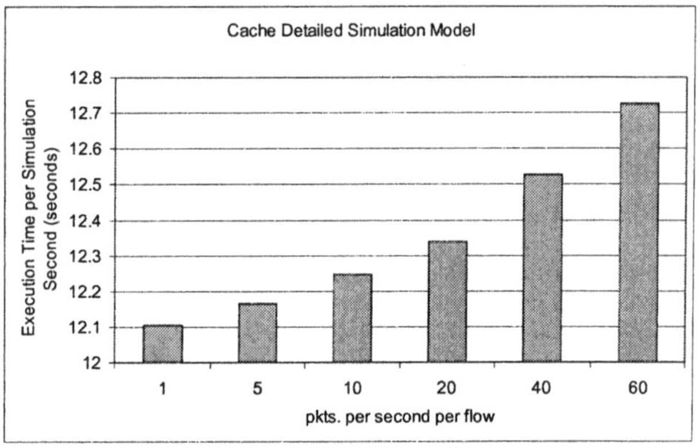

Figure 9. Execution time per simulation second, with caching results from detailed OFDM model.

Caching detailed OFDM model is able to scale with the abstract model. The X-axis in Figure 10 shows the average number of signals locked on by each receiver. Detailed simulation of every bit is infeasible for MANETs while the cache detailed simulation model is able to scale even with the abstract model. When the OFDM model is used to simulate every bit of the network, it took over 370 hours for each node to just lock on to and simulate just over 1000 radio signals.

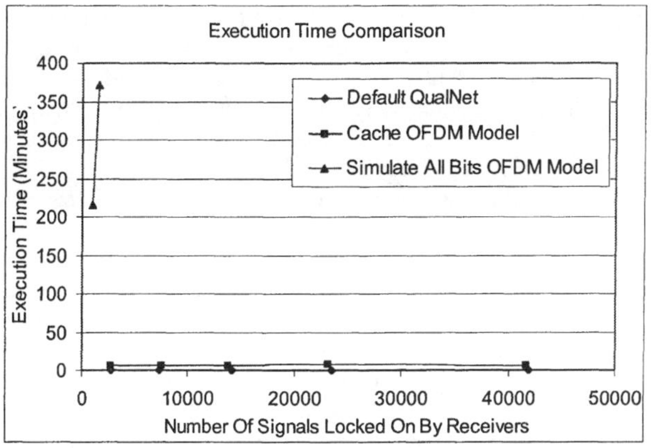

Figure 10. Comparison of execution times.

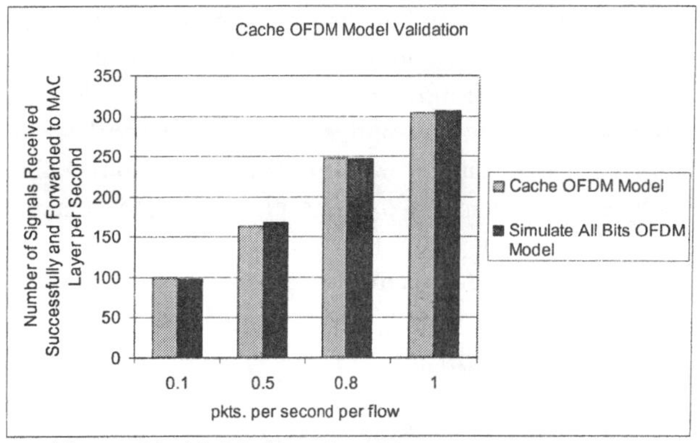

Figure 11. Validation of caching technique against simulation without caching.

4.5. Validation of Caching Technique

Caching detailed OFDM simulation is only valid if the cache saved does not compromise the accuracy of the simulation. Our next experiment validates this model with the simulation of all bits using the link level OFDM model in the network. Since simulating every bit in the network is very computationally expensive, as shown in the previous section, the experiment scenarios were limited to light network traffic situations. The same 25-node network is placed on the 500m x 500m terrain. Three nodes are randomly chosen to be CBR sources, each of which generates 512-byte data packets to a randomly chosen destination at a rate of 0.1, 0.5, 0.8, and 1 packet per second using AODV routing for 30 seconds. Even with these lighter traffic scenarios, simulating all bits with the OFDM model with just three CBR sessions and one packet per second per flow took over 32 hours on a modern Intel 2.4 GHz machine. Figure 11 shows the number of physical layer signals received successfully and forwarded to the MAC layer per second. When a physical layer frame is deemed error free by the OFDM simulator or the cache OFDM model, it passes that frame to the MAC layer for higher layer processing. The experiment shows that using the cache OFDM simulation model results in no more than 2% difference in the number of signals received successfully by the radio when compared to using the OFDM simulator to simulate every bit of the network. Hence, our cache model is well justified and we are able to speed up execution time to scale similarly to execution with the abstract model, while still preserving the fidelity and accuracy of detailed OFDM radio and wireless channel simulation.

5. Conclusion

This paper has presented on the effects of detailed OFDM and channel modeling on the performance evaluation of higher layer protocols. Our integration of an OFDM simulator with QualNet provided a realistic yet efficient model of the propagation and device layer for network performance analysis without compromising simulation accuracy. The results show that device and wireless channel can impact packet delivery ratios and even point out a deficiency of the ARF protocol. Traditionally, radio engineers have analyzed the performance of their designs against others only on point-to-point performance evaluations under various channel conditions. The integration brings an accurate physical layer model to dynamic network simulation that includes the effects of path loss, shadowing, multipath, Doppler fading, and delay spread, to allow protocol and radio designers to evaluate the effects of their designs on a full-scale system level with an eye for cross layer interactions. In addition, the integration delineates a method in which simulators of dramatically different time granularities are combined using simple APIs.

In terms of performance, our integration technique and cleanly defined interface are clearly beneficial in any MANET networking studies. Link level OFDM model to simulate every bit in the network is too computationally expensive and leads to an unacceptably long execution time. Our technique scales along with the basic abstract model and still captures the essence of the radio device and its performance characteristics in varying wireless channels. The results show that significant benefits can be obtained from our caching technique, while careful evaluation of what to cache must be properly understood.

With advances in antenna, modulation, and coding technology, it becomes increasingly important for higher-level network layers to understand their interactions with the physical device and media. It is equally important for designers to understand the innovations that are being made in each layer of the network stack and to understand how these innovations might complement or conflict with their designs. Future work on the integration method includes enhancements to the caching scheme, dynamic channel and fading characteristics utilizing detailed 3-D terrain models and movement of the nodes.

6. Acknowledgment

We would like to thank Zhengrong Ji, Junlan Zhou, and the anonymous reviewers of this paper for their insightful comments. We are also grateful to Aifeng Ren and Steve Hsu for helpful discussions on OFDM.

7. References

[1] MATLAB User's Guide, http://www.mathworks.com/.

[2] Waterloo Maple User's Guide, http://www.maplesoft.com/.

[3] Mathematica User's Guide, http://www.wolfram.com/.

[4] Vishal Misra, Weibo Gong, Don Towsley, "Fluid-based analysis of a network of AQM routers supporting TCP flows with an application to RED", in Proceedings of ACM/SIGCOMM, 2000.

[5] Tak-Kin Yung, Jay Martin, Mineo Takai, Rajive Bagrodia, "Mixed fluid flow and packet level simulation models for large scale networks", in Proceedings of SPIE, Vol 4523, August 2001.

[6] Mineo Takai, Jay Martin, Rajive Bagrodia, "Effects of wireless physical layer modeling in mobile ad hoc network," in Proceedings of MobiHoc 2001, pages 87-94, October 2001.

[7] QualNet User's Manual, http://www.scalable-networks.com/.

[8] Riley, G. F.; Ammar, M. H.; Fujimoto, R. M.; Perumalla, K.; Xu, Donghua, "Distributed Network Simulations using the Dynamic Simulation Backplane," in Proceedings of International Conference on Distributed Computing Systems, April 2001 (ICDCS'01).

[9] Xu, Donghua; Riley, G. F.; Ammar, M. H.; Fujimoto, R. M., "Split Protocol Stack Network Simulations using the Dynamic Simulation Backplane," in Proceedings of the Ninth International Symposium on Modelling, Analysis, and Simulation of Computer and Telecommunication Systems, 2001 (MASCOTS'01)

[10] Junlan Zhou, Zhengrong Ji, Mineo Takai, Rajive Bagrodia, "Maya: a Multi-Paradigm Network Modeling Framework," in Proceedings of PADS 2003.

[11] IEEE 802.11 WG, Part 11: Wireless LAN Medium Access Control (MAC) and Physical Layer (PHY) specifications, Standard, IEEE, August 1999.

[12] IEEE 802.11 WG, Part 11: Wireless LAN Medium Access Control (MAC) and Physical Layer (PHY) specifications: High-speed Physical Layer in the 5 GHz Band, Supplement to IEEE 802.11 Standard, September 1999.

[13] Richard Van Nee, Ramjee Prasad, *OFDM for Wireless Multimedia Communications*. Boston, MA: Artech House, 2000.

[14] John Terry, Juha Heiskala, *OFDM Wireless LANs: A Theoretical and Practical Guide*. Indianapolis, IN: Sams Publishing, December 2001

[15] Vaduvur Bharghavan, Alan Demers, Scott Shenker, Lixia Zhang, "MACAW: A media access protocol for wireless LAN's," in Procedings of SIGCOMM, 1994.

[16] Simulink User's Guide, http://www.mathworks.com /products/simulink/.

[17] Lokesh Bajaj, Mineo Takai, Rajat Ahuja, Rajive Bagrodia, "Simulation of large-scale heterogeneous communication systems," in Proceedings of MILCOM'99, November 1999.

[18] Charles. E. Perkins, Elizabeth. M. Royer, "Ad-hoc on-demand distance vector routing," in Proceedings of 2nd IEEE Workshop on Mobile Computing Systems and Application, pages 90-100, 1999.

[19] SMC2755W – EZ Connect 802.11a Wireless Access Point User Guide, http://www.smc.com/drivers_downloads /library/SMC2755W_MN.pdf/.

[20] A. Kamerman, L. Monteban, "WaveLAN-II: A high performance wireless LAN for the unlicensed band", Bell Labs Technical Journal, Vol. 2, No. 3, pages 118-113, Summer 1997.

[21] Gavin Holland, Nitin Vaidya, Paramvir Bahl, "A Rate-Adaptive MAC Protocol for Multi-Hop Wireless Networks," in Proceedings of MobiCom 2001, July 2001.

Session 3:
Optimization

Event Reconstruction in Time Warp

Lijun Li and Carl Tropper
School of Computer Science
McGill University
Montreal, Canada
lli22, carl@cs.mcgill.ca

Abstract

In optimistic simulations, checkpointing techniques are often used to reduce the overhead caused by state saving. In this paper, we propose event reconstruction as a technique with which to reduce the overhead caused by event saving, and compare its memory consumption and execution time to the results obtained by dynamic checkpointing. As the name implies, event reconstruction reconstructs input events and anti-events from the differences between adjacent states, and does not save input events in the event queue.

For simulations with fine event granularity and small state size, such as the logic simulation of VLSI circuitry, event reconstruction can yield an improvement in execution time as well as a significant reduction in memory utilization when compared to dynamic checkpointing. Moreover, this technique facilitates load migration because only the state queue needs to be moved from one processor to another.

1 Introduction

Modern VLSI systems are becoming increasingly complicated, posing a never-ending challenge to sequential simulation. To accommodate the growing need for increased memory as well as the need for decreased simulation time, it is becoming increasingly necessary to make use of distributed simulation[12].

Time Warp[8] is an appealing technique for the distributed logic simulation of VLSI circuitry because it can potentially uncover a high degrees of parallelism in the VLSI system being simulated. However, this benefit is at the expense of the processing time and memory required for state saving, state restoration and event saving. Several techniques[10, 3, 4, 5] have been proposed to reduce this overhead, all of which focus on reducing the overhead for state saving and state restoration.

Event saving is a significant cost in Time Warp. However, to the best of our knowledge, no research has been directed at reducing its associated cost. In optimistic simulation, every event has to be saved in case of a rollback. However, in optimistic logic simulation of VLSI circuits, the event size is larger than the state size and, as a consequence, event saving costs more in memory and processing time than does state saving. It follows that if we try to reduce the overhead of event saving, the resulting performance may well be better than that obtained by reducing the overhead associated with state saving alone. It is unclear if this improvement can be achieved for coarse-grained models.

The rest of this paper is organized as follows. Section 2 is devoted to related work. In section 3, we introduce logic simulation. Our distributed simulation environment DVS[9] is briefly described in section 4. In section 5, we present the details of our event reconstruction technique. A comparison of the memory consumption and the execution time making use of event reconstruction and dynamic checkpointing is presented in section 6. The last section contains our conclusions and thoughts about future work.

2 Related work

A number of algorithms have been proposed to reduce the memory overhead caused by state saving, including incremental saving[3], checkpointing[10, 4], reverse computation[5] and rollback relaxation[13].

[7] presents a comparative analysis of four approaches to dynamically adjusting the checkpoint interval and proposes an algorithm for dynamic checkpointing. The algorithm tries to balance the time spent saving state versus the time spent coasting forward. The goal of the algorithm is to minimize the time for state saving and coasting forward and to adjust the checkpoint interval accordingly. In our experimental section6, we compare the performance of event reconstruction and this heuristic algorithm.

Checkpointing results in a lower memory consumption

1087-4097/04 $20.00 © 2004 IEEE

value	*Purpose*	*Value Encoding*
0	Forcing zero	00
1	Forcing one	01
X	Forcing unknown	10
Z	High impedance	11

Table 1. Logic values and their purposes

and an improved execution time. However, it is difficult to achieve the optimal frequency of checkpointing. Dynamic checkpointing can be used to alleviate this problem. However, it faces the problems of choosing tuning parameters, including the initial checkpointing frequency, the average cost of event processing and the average cost of coasting forward.

Reverse computation[5] computes state variables by reversing the operation sequence applied on the variables. It uses compiler-based techniques to generate the reverse computation code automatically. As a result, its implementation is more complex, although it is able to provide a significant performance improvement over checkpointing.

In rollback relaxation[13] all LPs are classified into two categories, memoryless and LPs and LPs with memory. A memoryless LPs' output is determined by the values of its inputs. Therefore, no state is saved for memoryless LPs. Instead, the LP reconstructs any required input state from the events of the input queue. The rollback relaxation mechanism is able to reduce the state saving overhead by a considerable amount in logic simulations because most LPs(AND, OR, XOR gates) in such simulation are memoryless.

3 Logic simulation and its characteristics

3.1 The Simulation Model

In a logic simulation, the LPs represent logic gates (AND,NAND,NOR,OR). The incoming channels to an LP correspond to the fanin list of wires of a logic gate while the outgoing channels correspond to its fanout list.

The circuit model uses a finite set of values to represent the type of signal propagating throughout the circuit. The 4 values which a signal may have are portrayed in table 1.

A signal change is modeled as an update event which contains a timestamp, source and destination gate identifications and a value which corresponds to the new value of the wire. When an LP receives an update event, it sets its local clock to the timestamp of the event, and then evaluates its output and schedules the resulting output change as update events to its fanout list.

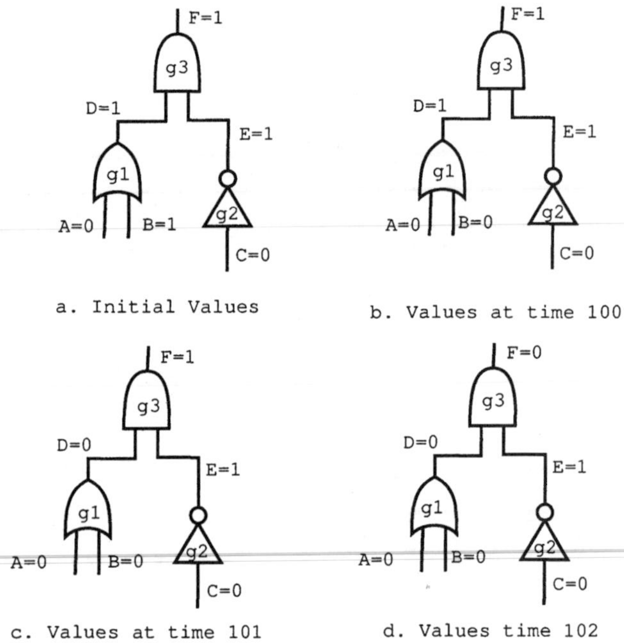

Figure 1. Logic simulation of a digital circuit

3.2 Discrete Event Logic Simulation

Figure 1 represents a simple logic circuit consisting of three gates. The circuit has three inputs(A, B and C), one output(F) and two internal wires(D and E). Assume that each gate has unit (processing) delay. At the initial point of our example, the logic gates have the values shown in Figure 1.a. An event occurs on wire B at time 100, changing it from 1 to 0 as shown in Figure 1.b. At time 100, gate g1 is evaluated to see if there's a change on its output D. Since D will change from 1 to 0, this event is scheduled for a unit delay in the future.

At time 101, gate g1s' output D will be set to 0 as indicated in Figure 1.c and this new value will be propagated to the gates on g1s' fanout, g3 in this circuit. Then g3 is evaluated to see if there will be an output change on F. As can be seen in Figure 1.d, F will change from 1 to 0.

3.3 Characteristics of logic simulation

In this section we discuss the characteristics of logic simulation which inspired our work on event reconstruction.

- Relatively small state size

  In the implementation of a logic simulator, such as DVS [9], the 4 signal values are encoded with two bits as shown in table 1. Every gate has up to four inputs and one output. Therefore, the state of a gate in Figure 2 includes ival and oval, each of which are one byte in

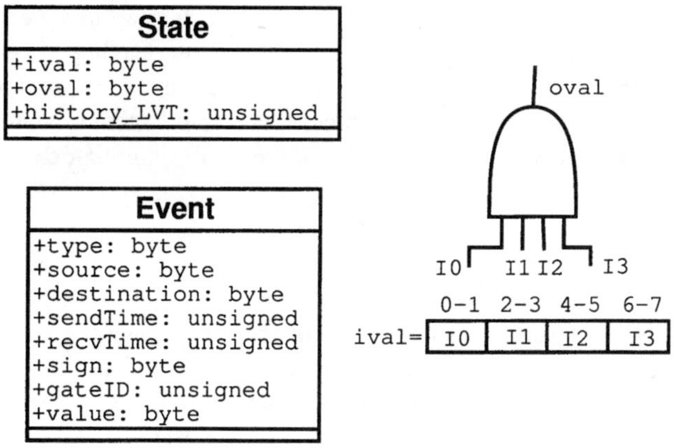

Figure 2. The size of the state and the event

length. The bits 0-1 are used to store the value of I0, bits 2 and 3 for I1, 4 and 5 for I2 and bits 6 and 7 for I3, as shown in Figure 2. For example, if ival is equal to 00001001, we know that I0 is equal to logical value 0, I1 logical value 0, I2 logical value 'x' and I3 logical value 1. This compact storage helps to save memory. The size of the state is only 16 bytes in DVS[9]. However, checkpointing has its greatest value when the size of the state is large.

- Large event size

  Figure 2 shows the structure of an event. The size of an event is 56 bytes, almost four times of the size of a state. Therefore, event saving causes at least 3.5(56/16) times more memory to be used than state saving if state saving is done for every event processed. In order to underscore this point, the amount of memory consumed in the simulation of a 16 bit multiplier is presented in our experimental section.

- Large event population

  The event population is large because of the large number of gates, each of which is mapped to an LP. For example, the event population is 8,129,815 for s38584(about 20K gates) when the clock is 500kHz and the number of random input vectors is 100. If every event has to be saved, the associated memory consumption will be very large.

- Fine event granularity

  Logic simulation is known for its fine event granularity. Thus, the performance of distributed logic simulation is especially sensitive to the overhead caused by state saving and event saving. Reducing this overhead would certainly be useful for performance improvement.

With these characteristics of logic simulation in mind, we decided to reduce the memory occupied by events instead of reducing the memory consumed by states. The following section describes our approach to event reconstruction.

4 DVS[9]: A framework for distributed Verilog[11] simulation

Before we present the implementation of event reconstruction, we give a brief introduction to DVS, a framework for distributed Verilog simulation. Event reconstruction and dynamic checkpointing are implemented in this framework.

Figure 3 portrays the architecture of DVS. The 3 layers of DVS are shown on the right side of figure 3. The bottom layer is the communication layer, which provides a common message passing interface to the upper layer. Inside this layer, the software communication platform can be PVM or MPI. Users can chose one of them without affecting the code of upper layers.

The middle layer is a parallel discrete event simulation kernel, OOCTW, which is an object-oriented version of Clustered Time Warp (CTW)[1]. It provides services such as rollback, state saving and restoration, GVT computation and fossil collection to the top layer.

The top layer is the distributed simulation engine, which includes an event process handler and an interpreter which executes instructions in the code space of a virtual thread.

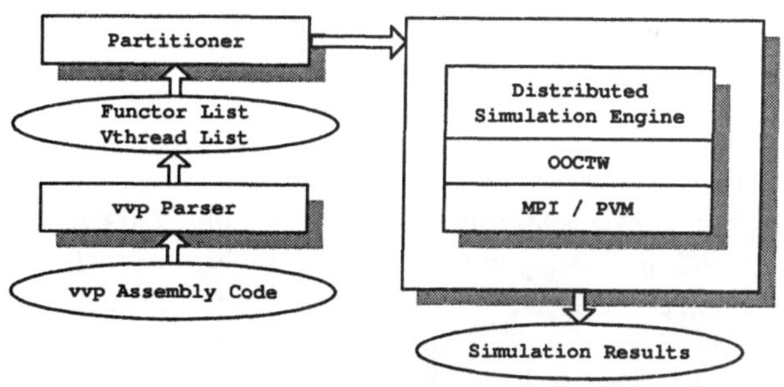

Figure 3. Architecture of DVS

A partitioner implements several partitioning algorithms including RANDOM[2], BFS(Breath-First-Search)[2], DFS(Depth-First-Search)[2] and CAKE[6]. More advanced partitioning algorithms are still under investigation as part of our research. CAKE results in a minimal inter-processor communication time and the best speed-up of the above algorithms because it takes advantage of the hierarchical design information in the Verilog source file.

5 Implementation of Event Reconstruction

In this section, we explain the implementation of event reconstruction in detail. The data structures and algorithms which comprise this approach are described below.

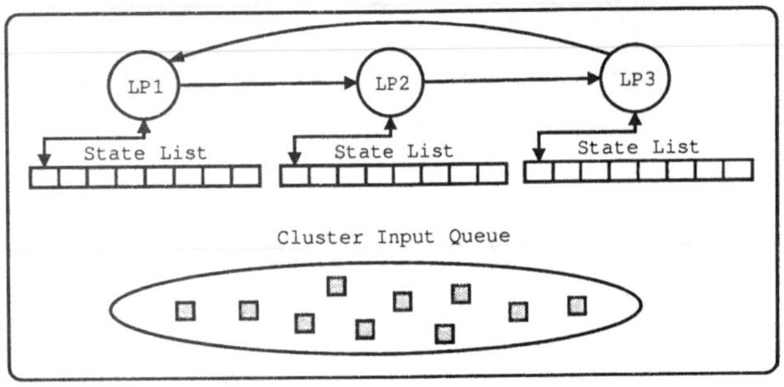

Figure 4. Cluster structure

5.1 Data structure

The data structure for event reconstruction is shown in figure 4. In DVS, the Cluster is the container and scheduler of all of the LPs. An LP maintains a state list. In event reconstruction it is necessary to store all of the states at an LP. Since we build the input events and anti-events from the state list in our approach, we don't need the input event list and output event list for every LP. The unprocessed events for all of the LPs in the same cluster are stored in a single priority queue data structure. The LP scheduling strategy is smallest timestamp first. We note in passing that the GVT computation also benefits from the single queue data structure.

5.2 Event annihilation

Time Warp uses a tuple (LPID, timestamp, eventID) to match positive events and their corresponding anti-events. The LPID is globally unique, indicating which LP will receive the event. The eventID is unique in the cluster, and is increased by one automatically whenever a new event is generated. The EventID is used, along with the timestamp to distinguish between simultaneous events. Unfortunately, the eventID is lost because we don't save input events in our approach. Instead, we use the signal value on the wire to compensate for the lost eventID information. The new tuple for event annihilation is (LPID, timestamp, signalValue). If both the timestamp and the signalValue are the same for two events, they are considered to be identical events. If there exists more than one identical event in the event queue, the anti-event will pick the first one in the queue to annihilate. This approach introduces some indeterminism. However, Verilog[11] is a concurrent language, in which there are sources of non-deterministic behavior such as arbitrary execution order in zero time and arbitrary interleaving of behavior statements. Therefore, the simulation results are not guaranteed to be deterministic. In fact, simultaneous events are executed in arbitrary order in the Verilog simulator.

5.3 Port flag

We use a different rollback strategy for LPs inside the cluster and for LPs outside of the cluster. Inside the cluster, we roll back those LPs which are descendants of the LP which receives the straggler or anti-message. Anti-messages are sent to LPs outside of the cluster.

In order to implement the two rollback algorithms, a port flag is used for each LP port in order to indicate whether it is an internal port or an external port. The port flag is set at run time. Initially, every port flag is set to be an internal flag. When the LP receives an external message, it sets the corresponding flag to external. The implementation of the rollback algorithms making use of these flags will be explained in the following section.

5.4 Event builder

Only those events which change the input signals at a gate need to be reconstructed, as it is only these events which cause a change in the state of a gate.

Let s' be the state before the execution of event e and let s be the state after the event is executed. If s is equal to s', event e is considered null and need not be reconstructed. However, if s is different from s', event e can be rebuilt according to Formula 1. The signal value is the value on the wire, as shown in Table 1.

$$\begin{aligned} e.timestamp &= s.timestamp \\ e.signalValue &= s.signalValue \end{aligned} \quad (1)$$

For example, state s' is shown in Figure 5.a and state s in Figure 5.b. It is worthwhile noting that signal values on all ports are packed into a one byte state. By comparing the value on port I1 of states s and s', the event which happened at time 200 is reconstructed with the value on port I1 of state s, which changed from '00' in state s' to '01' in state s.

5.4.1 Input event builder

In Time Warp an LP saves events after processing them because if the LP rolls back, previously processed events will have to be reprocessed. Through event reconstruction, these previously processed events will no longer have to be saved. Instead, they are reconstructed by the input event builder, depicted in Figure 6.

The algorithm loops through the state queue until the LVT of the state is less than the receive time of the event

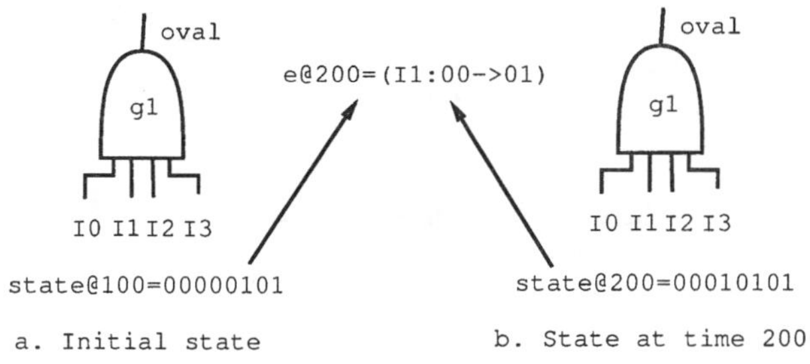

Figure 5. Event reconstruction

which causes the rollback. It picks a state s1 and its predecessor s2 from the state queue. If the input values of state s1 and s2 are different, an event e is reconstructed according to Formula 1. The input values are bound into one byte. Therefore, the comparison is executed four times, once for each input port of the LP, as shown in the Figure 6.

Moreover, due to the different rollback strategies for the internal events and external messages, we set a port flag to indicate the source of the events. For the external port, we reconstruct every event. However, we only reconstruct the events which have LVT equal to the LVT of the straggler event for the internal port. The reason for this is that the internal events which have a larger LVT than the straggler will be regenerated because of the cluster rollback strategy[1] used in DVS[9], which will rollback all LPs in the cluster. Therefore, the internal events will not be reconstructed because they will be regenerated by their source LP in the same cluster. The port flag is used to avoid unnecessary reconstruction of internal events. In fact, the algorithm of event reconstruction does not depend on the cluster rollback strategy. We are continuing to improve the rollback strategy and the event reconstruction algorithm. Further effort will focus on tree rollback instead of the cluster rollback. The tree rollback strategy only rolls back those LPs which reside in a tree whose root is the LP which receives the straggler event.

5.4.2 Anti-event builder

The anti-event builder works in the same way as the input event builder, as shown in figure 7. The anti-event is reconstructed by comparing the output values of two adjacent states, s1 and s2. After reconstruction, the anti-event is sent to those LPs which are in the fanout list of the current LP but not in the same cluster. For a cluster rollback, we don't have to use anti-events to cause a rollback in the same cluster.

5.5 Event processing loop

The basic algorithm for an optimistic LP is sketched in Figure 8. The LP removes the head event from the event

```
input_event_builder(event* rb_event)
{
  reverse_iterator iter=state_list.rbegin();

  //main loop for the event reconstruction
  while((*iter)->LVT >= rb_event->recv_time)
  {
    state* s1 = (*iter);
    state* s2 = (*iter++);

    //only reconstruct the external event
    //ignore the reconstruction of internal events

    //Event reconstruction on port 0
    if (s1->ival&3 != s2->ival&3)
      if (s1->LVT == rb_event->recv_time ||
          external_port_flag[0])

      {
        //reconstruct the event
        e->recv_time = s1->LVT;
        e->ival = s1->ival&3;

        if e->is_anti_event(rb_event)
          annihilate(e, rb_event);
        else
          schedule(e);
      }

    //Event reconstruction on port 1
    if ((s1->ival>>2)&3 != (s2->ival>>2)&3)
      if (s1->LVT == rb_event->recv_time ||
          external_port_flag[1])
      {
        //reconstruct the event
        e->recv_time = s1->LVT;
        e->ival = (s1->ival>>2)&3;

        if e->is_anti_event(rb_event)
          annihilate(e, rb_event);
        else
          schedule(e);
      }

    //Event construction on port 2 & port 3
    //compare((s1->ival>>4)&3, (s2->ival>>4)&3)
    //compare((s1->ival>>6)&3, (s2->ival>>6)&3)
  }
}
```

Figure 6. Input event reconstruction algorithm

queue and checks whether it is a normal event or a straggler or an anti- event. If it is a normal event, the LP first logs its state and processes the event. State is saved after every event. However, processed events will not be saved.

When the LP receives an anti-event or a straggler, it rolls back as in "normal" Time Warp. However, the LP reconstructs the input events and output events from the state queue. This introduces a processing overhead which is similar to the cost for coasting forward in dynamic checkpointing.

6 Experiments

All of our experiments were conducted on a network of 8 computers, each of which has dual PentiumIII processors and 256M RAM. They are interconnected by a Myrinet,

```
anti_event_builder(event* rb_event)
{
  reverse_iterator iter=state_list.rbegin();

  while((*iter)->LVT >= rb_event->recv_time)
  {
    state* s1 = (*iter);
    state* s2 = (*iter++);

    if (s1->oval&3 != s2->oval&3)
      {
        //reconstruct the anti event
        e->recv_time = s1->LVT;
        e->ival = s1->oval&3;
        e->flag = ANTI;

        for each external LP in fanout list
          send e to LP
      }
   }
}
```

Figure 7. Anti event reconstruction algorithm

```
while(GVT < FINISH_TIME)
{
  receive external events;
  pop an event from event queue;
  update LVT;
  if (event is straggler or antimessage)
    {
      input_event_builder();
      anti_event_builder();
      send_anti_events();
    }
  else
    {
      log_state();
      event_processing();
    }
}
```

Figure 8. Optimistic LP simulation algorithm

a high speed network with link capacity of 1Gbit per second. All machines run the FreeBSD operating system while MPICH-GM is used for message passing between different processors.

The Verilog source file used in the simulation describes an ISCAS'89 benchmark circuit, S38584. It includes 19253 gates, 1426 D-type flip-flops and one virtual thread which feed 20 random vectors to the circuit. The clock frequency of S38584 is 1MHz. The other Verilog source file describes a 16bit multiplier. It includes 2416 gates and one virtual thread which feeds 200 random vectors into the circuit.

We assume a unit gate delay and zero transmission delay on the wire. Each data point collected in the experiments is an average of five simulation runs. The number of machines in the figure doesn't include machine 0, which only contains vthreads[9]. The vthreads generate the events for the simulation. The simulation time for 1 machine is the running time of the DVS without partitioning.

In the experiments, we compare the performance of DVS with dynamic checkpointing and with event reconstruction to that of "pure" Time Warp. The partitioning algorithm which we use is CAKE[6]. The dynamic checkpointing algorithm is initiated every 1000 events. Our event reconstruction algorithm requires that the state is saved after each event is processed.

circuit	2	3	4	5	6
16 bits multiplier	4.49	4.50	4.78	4.68	4.73
S38584	3.60	3.68	3.54	3.53	3.55

Table 2. The memory usage ratio

6.1 Memory Usage

6.1.1 Memory consumption breakdown

The memory consumed by Time Warp is composed of the memory consumed by state saving and by event saving. Figure 9 presents the memory breakdown for the machine which has the maximum memory consumption. The data is collected for a 16 bit multiplier and for S38584 using Time Warp. The top of Figure 9 is the memory breakdown for the 16 bit multiplier with 200 random vectors while the bottom is the memory breakdown for S38584 with 30 random vectors.

We see from both of these that event saving consumes more memory than state saving. We define the *memory usage ratio* to be the ratio of the memory consumed by event saving to the memory consumed by state saving and list these ratios in table 2 for the 16 bit multiplier and for S38584. We see that event saving consumes 4.73 times the memory used by state saving when 6 machines are used. On the average, event saving consumes almost four times the memory consumed by state saving.

6.1.2 Peak memory consumption

We define the *peak memory usage* to be the maximum of all of the machines' maximal memory usages. Figure 10 shows the peak memory vs. the number of machines for the 16 bit multiplier. The memory used by one machine is only 0.45M because memory overhead is unnecessary. When two machines are used, event reconstruction uses 1.79 times less memory than dynamic checkpointing and 2.34 times less than pure Time Warp. The ratio between event reconstruction and dynamic checkpointing decreases when more machines are used. The reason for this decrease is that the average number of events processed decreases when more machines are used, and consequently the memory occupied by event saving decreases. When 6 machines are used, event

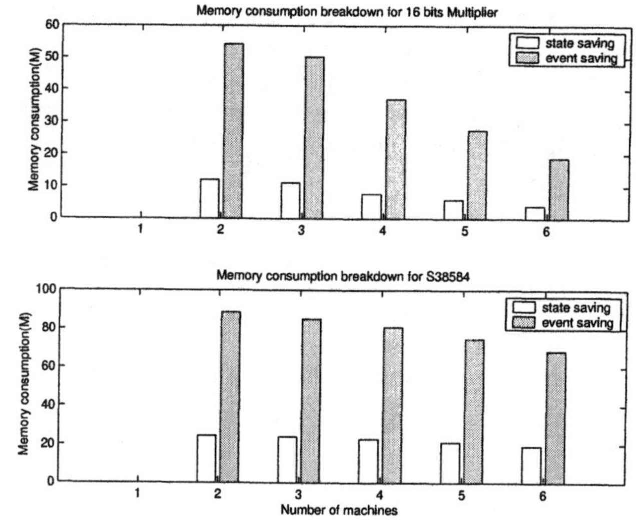

Figure 9. Memory consumption breakdown

reconstruction uses 1.29 times less memory then is used by dynamic checkpointing.

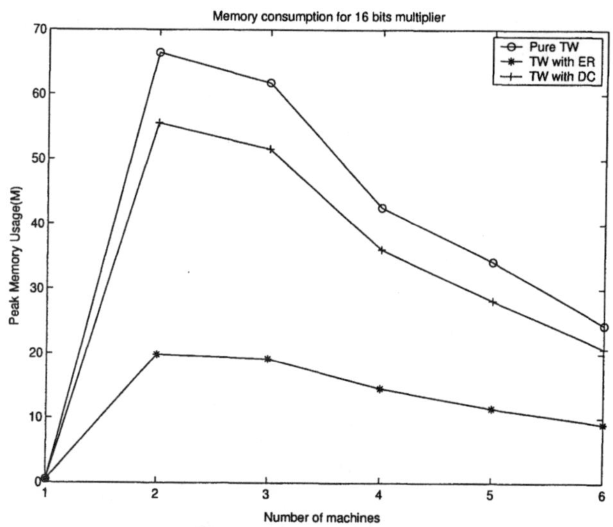

Figure 10. Memory consumption for 16 bits multiplier

Figure 11 presents the peak memory vs. the number of machines for S38584. Time Warp uses 119.06M when 2 machines are used. This leads to memory swapping and bad performance, as shown in Figure 13. Event reconstruction uses 54.21M when two machines are used, versus 99.18M by dynamic checkpointing.

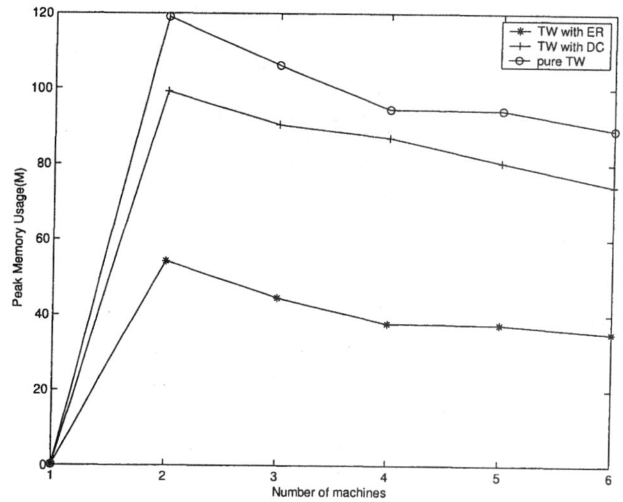

Figure 11. Memory consumption for S38584

6.2 Simulation Time

The simulation time vs. the number of machines for the 16 bit multiplier is presented in figure 12.

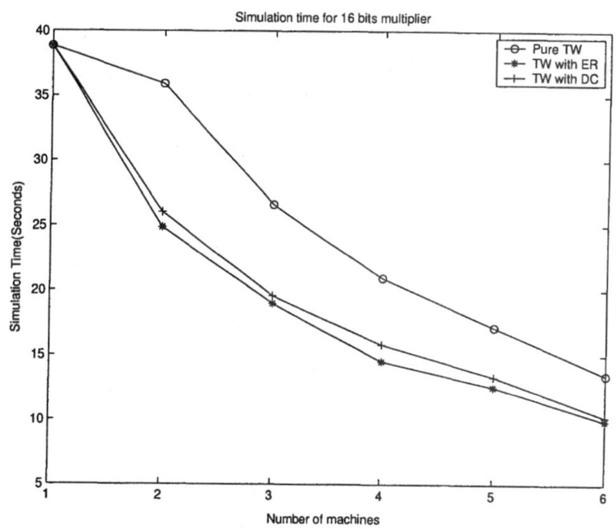

Figure 12. Simulation Time for 16 bits multiplier

We observe from figure 12 that event reconstruction results in a 10% execution time improvement over dynamic checkpointing and a 40% improvement over Time Warp when 2 machines are used. The speedup decreases when more machines are used for the same reason that the improvement in memory consumption diminishes when more machines are used. The speedup obtained using event reconstruction is 3% better then dynamic checkpointing and

35% better then Time Warp when 6 machines are used.

Figure 13 presents the simulation time vs. the number of machines for S38584. The simulation time of pure Time Warp is 25.55 because of memory swapping. Both dynamic checkpointing and event reconstruction eliminate memory swapping. However, event reconstruction is 11% faster than dynamic checkpointing.

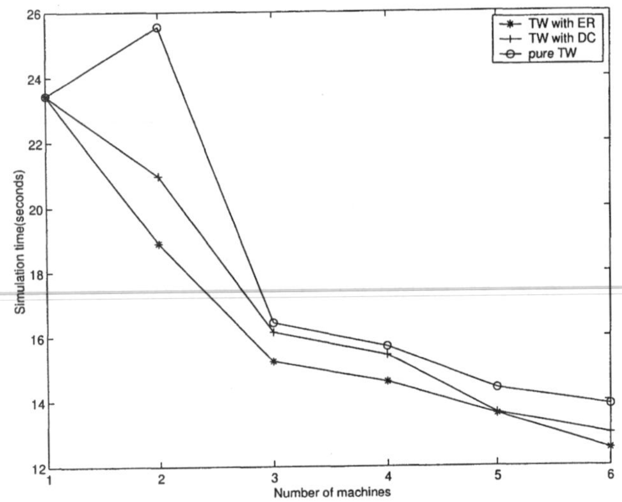

Figure 13. Simulation Time for S38584

7 Conclusions and work in progress

Time Warp is known to use a great deal of memory. In this paper, we observe that event saving is a significant factor in memory consumption for optimistic VLSI simulation. Our proposed technique of event reconstruction eliminates event saving by reconstructing events from the state queue. For simulations with fine event granularity and small state size such as the VLSI logic simulation, event reconstruction yields a significant reduction in memory utilization compared to checkpointing. This reduction leads to a faster execution time. Finally, event reconstruction facilitates load balancing because only the state queue of an LP needs to be moved between processors. We plan to implement dynamic load balancing in DVS[9].

References

[1] Herve Avril and Carl Tropper. Scalable clustered time warp and logic simulation. *VLSI design*, 00:1–23, 1998.

[2] M. Bailey, J. Briner, and R. Chamberlain. Parallel logic simulation of vlsi systems. *ACM Computing Surveys*, 26(03):255–295, Sept. 1994.

[3] H. Bauer and Sporrer C. Reducing rollback overhead in time-warp based distributed simulation with optimized incremental state saving. In *Proc. of the 26th Annual Simulation Symposium*, pages 12–20. Socity for Computer Simulation, April 1993.

[4] S. Bellenot. State skipping performance with the time warp operating system. In *6th Workshop on Parallel and Distributed Simulation*, pages 53–61. Socity for Computer Simulation, January 1992.

[5] Christopher D. Carothers, Kalyan S. Perumalla, and Richard Fujimoto. Efficient optimistic parallel simulations using reverse computation. In *Workshop on Parallel and Distributed Simulation*, pages 126–135, 1999.

[6] Hai Huang. A partitioning framework for distributed verilog simulation. Master's thesis, School of Computer Science, McGill University, 2003.

[7] P.A. Wilsey J. Fleischmann. Comparative analysis of periodic state saving techniques in time warp simulators. In *Ninth Workshop on Parallel and Distributed Simulation (PADS'95)*, pages 50–58, June 1995.

[8] D. Jefferson. Virtual time. *ACM Transactions on Programming Lauguages and Systems*, 7(3):405–425, 1985.

[9] Lijun Li, Hai Huang, and Carl Tropper. Dvs: an object-oriented framework for distributed verilog simulation. In *Parallel and Distributed Simulation, 2003. (PADS 2003)*, pages 173–180, June 2003.

[10] Yi-Bing Lin, Bruno R. Preiss, Wayne M. Loucks, and Edward D. Lazowska. Selecting the checkpoint interval in time warp parallel simulation. In *Proc. 1993 Workshop on Parallel and Distributed Simulation*, pages 3–10. Institute of Electrical and Electronics Engineers, May 1993.

[11] Donald E. Thomas and Philip R. Moorby. *The Verilog Hardware Description Language Fourth Edition*. KLUWER Academic Publisher, 1992.

[12] Carl Tropper. Parallel Discrete-Event Simulation Applications. *Journal of Parallel and Distributed Computing*, 62:327–335, 2002.

[13] P. Wilsey and A. Palaniswamy. Rollback relaxation: A technique for reducing rollback costs in an optimistically synchronized simulation. In *International Conference on Simulation and Hardware Description Languages, Society for Computer Simulation*, pages 143–148, January 1994.

Just-In-Time Cloning

Maria Hybinette

Computer Science Department
University of Georgia
Athens, GA 30602-7404, USA

maria@cs.uga.edu

Abstract

In this work we focus on a new technique for making cloning of parallel simulations more efficient. Cloning provides a means for running multiple similar simulations in parallel where many computations are shared rather than repeated [12]. A simulation is cloned on an event for a particular set of logical processes, creating new LP clones. The clones diverge as messages from the new LPs arrive at uncloned LPs. Until replication, all the computations for a particular LP are shared between the clones. Simulation kernels using cloning achieve efficiency by incrementally replicating logical processes as necessary. This enables regions of the simulation that have not been affected to use the same computations for both the new and old clone. Clearly, the longer replication can be delayed, the more efficient the simulation. We hypothesize that in many cases replication takes place before it is strictly necessary. We propose **just-in-time cloning** *that addresses this issue by relaxing the constraints of simulation cloning to further benefit from shared computations.*

1. Introduction

In this work we focus on a new technique for making cloning of parallel simulations more efficient. We briefly review the cloning approach here. For a full description please see [12]. We report on a significant efficiency improvement to the algorithm for simulation cloning.

Simulation cloning in Time Warp simulations enables efficient exploration of multiple simulated futures based on policy decisions made at decision points. Time Warp simulations are composed of multiple logical processes (LP) that exchange messages to advance the simulation. In the standard approach to cloning, a simulation is duplicated a portion at a time by replicating LPs as necessary. Our improvement concerns the timing of LP replication. In particular, we are able to delay many replications and to avoid some replications altogether.

As an example of how simulation cloning might be applied, consider an air traffic control scenario where inclement weather may force a change in policy for one or more airports. One might use simulation to compare alternate strategies for managing the flow of aircraft in this portion of the air space. Many strategies are available to controllers to address such problems, but their impact on the situation may be difficult to predict. Simulation cloning can provide a means for efficiently evaluating many policies at once.

Continuing with the example, the simulation can be initialized with the current state of the airspace, then executed forward until reaching the point where new policies are to be imposed. The simulation can then be cloned (replicated), with each clone simulating the traffic space with a different control policy. The point where the simulation is cloned is referred to as a *decision point*. The cloned simulations execute concurrently, and will produce results identical to a traditional replicated simulation where the entire simulation is executed from the beginning using different policies.

Simulation cloning assumes a message-based computation paradigm like that commonly used in parallel discrete event simulations. Specifically, the simulation is composed of a collection of *logical processes* (LPs) that communicate exclusively by exchanging time stamped events or messages. A synchronization algorithm is used to ensure that each LP processes its events in time stamp order, or in the case of *optimistic* simulation protocols, the net effect of each LP's computation is as if its events were processed in time stamp order. Simulation cloning can be used with either conservative or optimistic synchronization techniques.

Simulation cloning improves performance because it allows computations to be shared between the clones. Up to the decision point the simulations are identical and a single computation suffices for the cloned simulations. After the decision point the simulations slowly diverge as aircraft

1087-4097/04 $20.00 © 2004 IEEE

emanating from the airport of interest begin to affect other airports in the simulation. In air traffic simulations airports are typically mapped to LPs[19]. As an airport (LP) accepts an incoming aircraft from an airport (LP) that diverged, it too diverges (or replicates). Eventually, the entire simulation is fully replicated and the simulations are doing all the computations as two replicated simulations plus some small overhead.

We envision two general schemes for improving the performance of cloning: (1) By **delaying** the replication of a cloned logical process until it is absolutely necessary, thus allowing LPs to continue to share computations and (2) by **merging** cloned simulations so that replicated simulations that have re-converged to the same state can resume sharing computations. This paper focuses on a discussion of delaying replication.

As an example of how delaying replication may be beneficial, consider a single flight from a replicated LP representing the Atlanta (ATL) airport to Stockholm (ARN) that is forced to land one hour late. Further assume that this late arrival has no additional effect on the state of the Stockholm airport. In standard simulation cloning, the Stockholm airport is replicated by the delayed flight since now there are two different simulations. The cloning of the Stockholm's airport is illustrated in Figure 1, where a new physical clone 2 is created and virtual clone 2 is remapped to Stockholm's physical clone 2. As aircraft depart from the *new* Stockholm airport clones destined to other European airports, those airports will also be cloned, even if the two copies of the Stockholm airport are equivalent. In Figure 1 a flight from Stockholm's clone 2, destined to Vienna, has an identical flight in clone 1 and will cause Vienna to clone. The two physical copies of Vienna will be the same after receiving both copies of the flights from Stockholm. The problem here is that by virtue of an interaction from a diverged clone, airports become unnecessarily replicated.

In this work we propose a *just-in-time cloning* as an approach to delaying replication of cloned logical processes. We evaluate the approach in two benchmark simulation applications: PCS and P-Hold.

2. Related work

Simulation cloning has been shown to improve performance of interactive applications such as simulations of the ground transportation [16, 17] and air-traffic control [12]. Cloning has been implemented both in conservative [2, 16, 17] and optimistic [12] simulation executives.

With respect to cloning in general, related work in interactive parallel simulation include [7] and [6]. The approach of [7] allows for the testing of what-if scenarios provided they are interjected before a deadline. Alternatives are examined sequentially using a rollback mechanism to erase

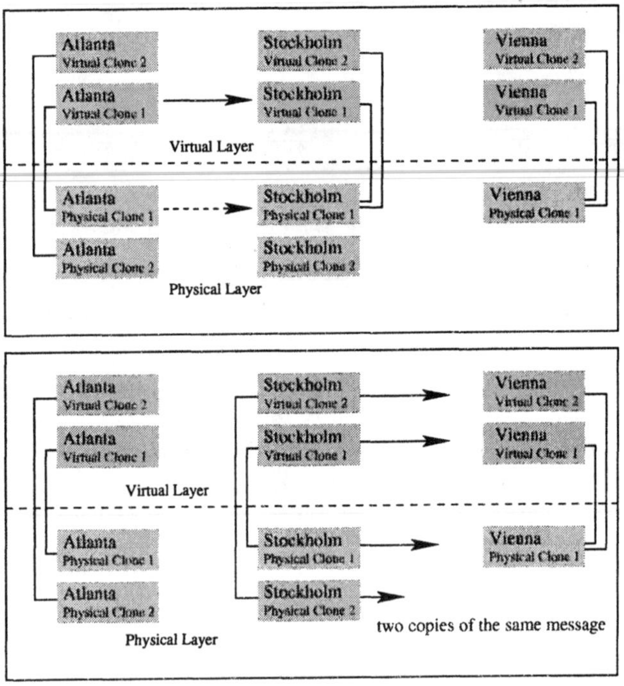

Figure 1. Sequence of Events in Standard Simulation Cloning: *Top:* **A delayed flight from Atlanta arriving at Stockholm forces Stockholm to clone physical clone 2;** *Bottom:* **A flight, from Stockholm's clone 1 has an identical flight in clone 2, causes Vienna to clone.**

exploration of one path in order to begin exploration of another. [6] create a new simulation from a previous base-line simulation by executing forward. They can determine if a computation can be reused by using a predicate function that is tested on the baseline simulation, however as in [7] only the testing of one alternative at a time is allowed. A drawback of this latter approach is that one must manage the entire state-space of the baseline simulation.

Cloning has been used to improve accuracy of simulation results, i.e., to run multiple independent replications then average their results at the end of the runs. For example, in [10] research focuses on how to achieve statistical efficiency of replications spread on different machines. In [18] replications are synchronized via a shared clock. In this way the same event occurs at the same time at all replicas.

Cloning is also used in sequential simulations to propagate faults in digital circuits [14], modeling of flexible manufacturing systems [4] or to fork transactions in simulation languages [11]. Sequential simulation languages typically clone dummies ("shadows") to do time-based waiting [15].

Our approach that delays replication is similar to techniques that reduce the cost of rollbacks: Lazy cancellation [9], the aggressive no-risk (ANR) [5] protocol and exploiting "lookback" [3] for example. Lazy cancellation delays sending anti-messages until the event that originally scheduled them is guaranteed not to be re-generated. ANR delays delivering messages until the event that created them is guaranteed not to be rolled back (the sender event), this technique avoids cascading rollbacks. Lookback is a techniques that identifies situations where one can avoid rollback.

Our approach is applicable both to optimistic and conservative protocols. It uses message comparison as in the lazy cancellation protocol, but does not suffer from the same performance penalty since it only compares messages if the LP is subject to replication.

3. Problem statement

A Time Warp simulation is composed of multiple *logical processes* that communicate by exchanging messages. To support multiple parallel clones of a simulation, the concepts of *physical logical process*, *virtual logical process* and *virtual messages* were introduced in [12]. Virtual LPs and messages do not have a physical realization. Instead, each virtual LP maps to one *physical logical process* that does have a physical realization in the parallel simulation system. Similarly, each virtual message maps to a single physical message.

Computations common between two or more clones are completed by a physical LP and shared by the virtual LPs in the clones that are mapped to the physical LP. Similarly, virtual messages among different clones are mapped to a single physical message to avoid duplication. Sharing of common computations may proceed until the state of one of the virtual LPs diverges from the others. At this point the LP must be replicated and it becomes a physical LP.

We know that a virtual LP cannot diverge from the others until it receives a message from a replicated LP. It is possible at this point that the information in a message from a replicated LP sender will cause the state in the receiver to diverge from the others. An earlier implementation of cloning took a conservative approach, and replicated the receiving LP when this occurs [12]. However, if replication can be delayed we may be able to gain even more efficiency.

Observe that some replicated LPs generate messages identical to their un-replicated (pre-cloned) counterparts. In these cases it is not necessary to replicate LPs that receive such messages. If we account for these situations and delay replication there may be a significant advantage, especially considering that if we did clone identical logical processes they in turn would send out identical messages causing further unnecessary cloning and so on. This observation is the basis of our new approach, *just-in-time cloning*.

The two problems we must address then, are:

- How long can we delay replication? and
- How can we implement just-in-time cloning so that the resulting simulation outcome is correct?

4. Implementation

As long as messages for a virtual LP from a replicated LP are identically matched by messages from the other corresponding replicated LPs there is no need to replicate the receiver. Thus our implementation of just-in-time cloning relies on message checking to detect situations where replication is necessary.

Message comparison is expensive. If we do too much comparing, performance will suffer. However, it is not necessary that all messages be tested, it is only necessary for certain virtual LPs to conduct this comparison. We hypothesize that the set of LPs that must inspect messages is usually a small fraction of those in the entire simulation.

Consider the fact that simulations are cloned on an event at a specific LP. So, initially, only one LP is replicated. From that point, changes spread across the simulation outward, much like the ripples from a pebble dropped in a pond. It is at the boundary, the leading edge of the ripple, where messages must be checked. Now consider an LP on this boundary. It has received a message from a replicated LP. Must it replicate itself? Perhaps not. If it receives an identical message from all the other corresponding senders, it does not have to replicate. But how long should it wait to receive these messages?

We implemented just-in-time cloning in an optimistic simulator. In this case we know that it is probable that the corresponding messages have been received by the time GVT matches the timestamp of the first message, however this is not guaranteed[1]. So, at this time we check to see if all the messages have arrived; if not, the receiving LP is replicated. The net effect is that the LPs on the boundary execute events conservatively, while the rest of the simulation proceeds optimistically.

Just-in-time cloning was implemented within an optimistic Time Warp simulation kernel [13]. Below we provide pseudocode for the portions relevant to the JIT algorithm.

```
Data structures:
   // Each LP has an associated array of queues;
   // one queue for each simulation clone.  Queues
   // are sorted in timestamp order.
   delay_queue[LP][clone]

Event processing:
   // get next message
   message = dequeuePendingQueue();

   if( message might cause replication )
         {
         rcvt = message.receive_time

         // block messages after rcvt;
         // handled by TimeWarp executive
         sendBlockingMessage( self,rcvt,putInJITList )

         // queue message in delay queue
         enqueue( delayQueue[self][message.clone] );
         }
   else
         {
         process message normally
         }

Cancellation: // if there is a rollback
   remove message from delay queue
   if message scheduled a blocking message,
cancel it
```

We add a data structure, `delay_queue[][]`, which contains an array of queues for each LP. For each LP, the array contains one queue for each simulation clone. The queues are used to store incoming messages that might force replication.

When a new message arrives, it is inspected to see if it might cause replication. Specifically, if it is from a replicated LP, and the receiving LP has not yet been replicated, the message may cause a replication. If the message might cause replication the LP sends a `BlockingMessage` to itself (more on that in a moment), and adds the message to the appropriate `delay_queue`. If the message cannot cause replication it is processed normally.

[1] this only affects the performance and not the correctness of the simulation

The sending of a `BlockingMessage` with a timestamp of the incoming message sets the following chain of events in motion. First, the optimistic executive will block processing on all messages with a timestamp after the time of the `BlockingMessage`. This ensures that the messages equal to or larger than GVT and less than the time stamp of the `BlockingMessage` are available for processing and allows our software to capture the messages that need to be inspected.

Next, our callback function `PutInJITList` (see below) will be called automatically when GVT reaches the timestamp. `PutInJITList` and `ProcessJITLIST` accomplish evaluation of the `delay_queues` to see if the LP must be replicated. Code for `PutInJITList` and `ProcessJITLIST` is included below.

Note that it is possible for one or more messages to still be in transit when the `delay_queue` is processed. Therefore, an LP may be unnecessarily replicated. This may lead to inefficient, duplicated processing by the new LP, but the simulation will still produce correct results.

```
PutInJITList() // called when GVT reaches blocktime
   JITList = NULL;
   Put LPs that sent blocking messages scheduled
   at GVT onto JITList
   ProcessJITList( GVT )

ProcessJITList( GVT )
 while( ((readyLP = next from JITList ) != NULL) )
    merged_message = NULL;
    for( clone = 0; clone < num_clones; clone ++ )
      {
      message = dequeueAtTime( GVT,
                     delayQueue[readyLP][clone] )
      if( message != NULL)
         if( merged_element == NULL )
            merged_message = message;
         else
           if( checkEqual( merged_message, message ) )
              mergeMessage( merged_message, message )
           else
                queue message in Pending Queue
      } /* for all clones */
    process merged_message
```

`dequeueAtTime()` will only return a pointer to a message if one or more exist at the specified time; in our case GVT.

We require `checkEqual()` to be provided by the application programmer. `checkEqual()` evaluates its two message arguments to determine if they are equivalent. We do this for two reasons. First, it may be the case that two messages are not bit-wise identical, but still equivalent. The kernel cannot determine this without help from the application level. Second, the user may consider that two very slightly differing messages may be considered identical. By relaxing the constraint on how similar messages must be to be considered identical, we may achieve more efficiency.

(The performance of this aspect of just-in-time cloning has not been evaluated yet.)

If the two messages are equivalent, they are merged by `mergeMessage()`. Our cloning implementation adds additional information to messages in order to determine the origin of the message (i.e. if it came from a replicated LP). `mergeMessage()` ensures that the data structure is appropriately updated when the messages are combined.

5. Performance

We evaluated the performance just-in-time cloning using two benchmark applications: P-Hold and PCS [8, 1]. For each application we constructed best case and worst case scenarios. In the best case scenarios, a single LP is replicated, but it continues identically to the original LP, thus additional replications do not usually occur. Unnecessary replications are possible due to the race condition outlined in Section 3, but they cause inefficiency at worst; not incorrect results. In the worst case scenarios, every message from a replicated LP to an un-replicated LP forces replication. The worst case was implemented by revising the application-level function `checkEqual()` to always return `false`.

The best and worst case scenarios help us explore the upper and lower performance bounds of just-in-time cloning for a particular application. For reference we also include results of traditional replication (two fully physically replicated simulations) and a single simulation. By "single simulation" we mean the original simulation has not been cloned.

P-Hold provides synthetic workloads using a fixed message population. Each LP is instantiated by an event. Upon instantiation, the LP schedules a new event with a specified time-stamp increment and destination LP (for more details on P-Hold see [8]). P-Hold is instrumented by varying the rate at which a clone causes the replication of other LPs. This is done by adjusting the selection of the destination LP of a message (logical processes are instantiated by receiving messages).

We instrumented to variations of P-Hold. In the first case the spreading is slowed by having an LP send messages only to itself or to its neighbor (slow spreading). In the second case the spreading is not constrained and the destination is selected from a uniform distribution of all logical processes in the simulated system (fast spreading). The time stamp increment to schedule a new event is 1.0 in the slow spreading case and is selected from an exponential distribution between 0.0 and 1.0 in the fast spreading case. In our experiments the P-Hold simulations use a message population of 8096 and 1024 logical processes.

PCS is a benchmark which simulates a personal communication services network. The network is wireless (radio receivers and transmitters) and provides services to mobile PCS subscribers. The radio ports are structured in a grid with one port per sector. Each cell services *portables* or mobile phone units that each occupy a cell for a period of time before proceeding to one of the four neighboring cells. Call arrival, call completion, and move are example behaviors or types of portables which are modeled by events in the simulation. Cells are modeled by LPs. Here we use a PCS network of 1024 cells (a $32X32$ grid) and 8192 portables. Most of the communication, typically 90%, is between LPs residing on the same processor. Many of those messages are self-initiating, or sent between the same logical process. More details of PCS are described in [1].

Evaluation of just-in-time cloning was conducted on an SGI Origin 2000 with sixteen 195 MHz MIPS R10,000 processors. The first level instruction and data caches are each 32 KB. The unified secondary cache is 4 MB. The main memory size is 4 GB. All experiments use 4 processors

The independent variable for this experiment is execution time and the metric is simulation progress (virtual time). Larger values indicate better performance. Simulated time is also referred as the virtual time to distinguish it from wall-clock time. For all P-Hold simulations the decision point (cloning) occurs at one logical process (LP_0) at simulated time 1000. In PCS the decision point is at simulated time $500,000$.

Figure 2 shows the simulation progress (virtual time) of P-Hold where the destination address is selected from a uniform distribution (the fast spreading case) versus wall clock time.

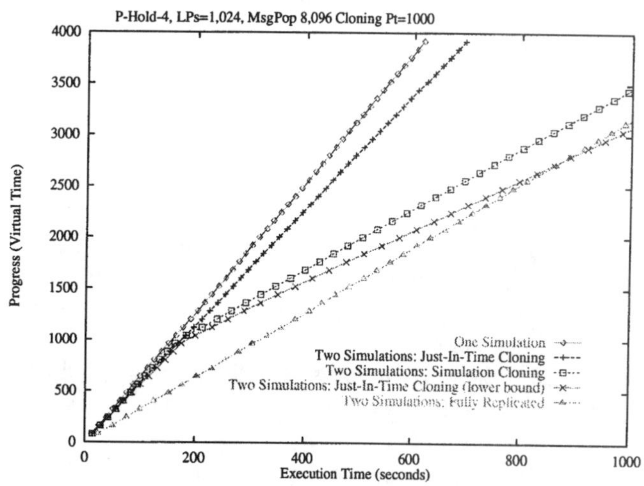

Figure 2. Performance of P-Hold Where destination LP Is Selected from a Uniform Distribution of All LPs in the Simulation. Larger numbers indicate better performance.

Figure 3 shows the performance of P-Hold in the slow

spreading cases. In both plots a larger number indicates better performance.

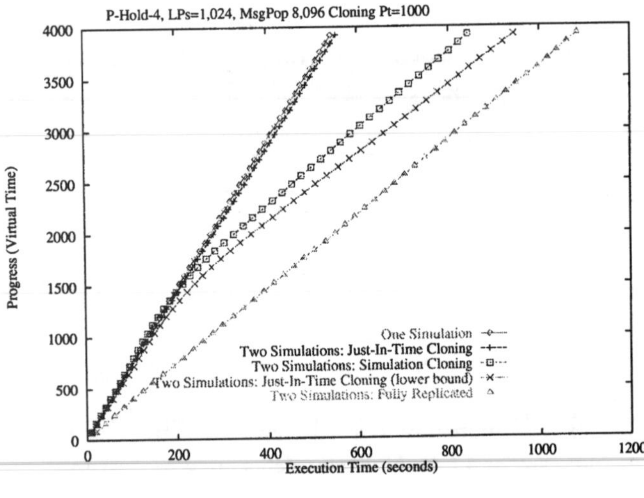

Figure 3. Performance of P-Hold Where destination LP Is Either Self or Nearest Neighbor. Larger numbers indicate better performance.

The performance for traditional cloning, in the fast spreading scenario, initially degrades upon the instantiation of a new clone, but then later continues linearly. The execution time for the best case of just-in-time cloning slows down but is closer to the performance of a single simulation. Just-in-time cloning, in the best case, improves on simulation cloning by 39%, and is about 12% slower than a single simulation. Its worst case performance is about 14% slower than simulation cloning.

In simulation cloning the slow spreading scenario shows a more dramatic slow-down but then proceeds linearly as well. The slow-spread case performs significantly faster than the fast-spread case, once the performance stabilizes. In this scenario, the performance of just-in-time cloning is tight to the performance of a single simulation, there is about about 2% difference. It improves on simulation cloning by about 34% and at its worst it is about 12% slower than simulation cloning.

The best case is tighter to a single simulation in the slow spread scenarios since fewer logical processes interact with a cloned logical process, causing them to wait conservatively for "corresponding" messages until they can progress further. In contrast in the fast spread scenario, there is a larger set of *neighboring* logical processes and hence more logical processes progress in conservative mode. The worst case of just-in-time cloning perform worse than simulation cloning because just about every logical process is likely to interact with the cloned logical process, causing all logical process to progress in conservative mode.

Our results, shown in Figure4 from the experiments using the PCS benchmark show similar performance as P-Hold, except in the worst case. The worst case, that always replicates a logical process when it receives a message from a cloned logical process initially behaves similar to the performance of simulation cloning but then at simulated time 1,750,000 it degrades more toward the performance of the fully replicated PCS simulation. The performance of the fully replicated PCS eventually surpasses the worst case performance of just-in-time cloning. In the best-case however, just-in-time cloning is closer to the performance of a single simulation.

Figure 4 shows the performance of PCS. These performance improvements of both PCS and P-Hold indicate that there may be a significant performance improvement of just-in-time cloning over simulation cloning which makes a difference for an interactive simulation, where alternatives need to be compared and instantiated dynamically.

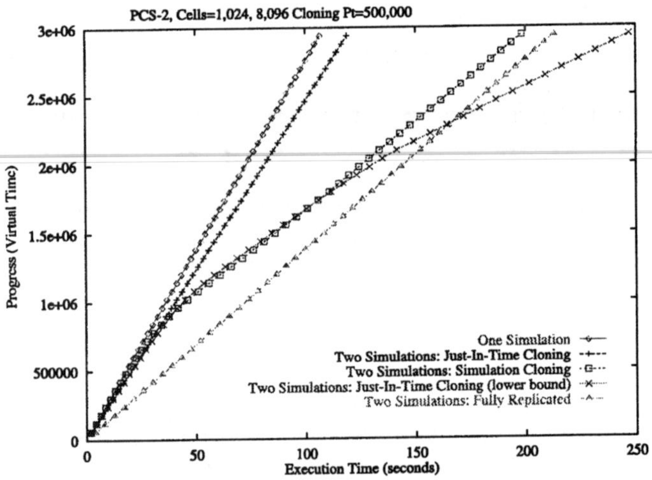

Figure 4. Performance of PCS. Larger numbers indicate better performance.

6. Conclusion

Just-in-time cloning enables cloned simulations to avoid replication of receiver LPs, thus enabling computations to be shared longer. The potential benefit of just-in-time cloning is demonstrated using two benchmarks, P-Hold and PCS. Results indicate that just-in-time cloning can improve the performance of simulation cloning by a factor of 1.7. It is especially efficient when the influence of a message introduced by a logical process does not spread to other processes in the simulation at a high rate. At best it runs only 2% slower than a *a single simulation* run. These initial performance results indicate that just-in-time cloning may significantly reduce the time required to compute multiple simulations.

At present we have only evaluated the approach in synthetic best and worst case scenarios. In future work we will investigate performance in typical simulation tasks. Additionally, we assume that the cost of message comparison is low. This may be reasonable since we only need to to compare messages when an LP receives messages from a cloned LP. In future work we will examine the impact of message size and also explore realistic applications for just-in-time cloning.

References

[1] C. D. Carothers, R. Fujimoto, Y.-B. Lin, and P. England. Distributed simulation of large-scale PCS networks. In *MASCOTS*, pages 2–6, 1994.

[2] D. Chen, S. J. Turner, B. P. Gan, W. Cai, J. Wei, and N. Julka. Alternative solutions for distributed simulation cloning. *Simulation: Transactions of The Society for Modeling and Simulation International*, 79:299–315, 2003.

[3] G. Chen and B. K. Szymanski. Four types of lookback. In *Proceedings of the seventeenth workshop on Parallel and distributed simulation*, page 3. IEEE Computer Society, 2003.

[4] W. J. Davis. On-line simulation: Need and evolving research requirements. In J. Banks, editor, *Handbook of simulation: Principles, methodology, advances, applications, and practice*. John Wiley & Sons, August 1998. Co-published by Engineering and Management Press.

[5] P. Dickens and P. Reynolds. SRADS with Local Rollback. In *Proceedings of the SCS Multiconference on Distributed Simulation*, pages 161–164, 1990.

[6] S. L. Ferenci, R. M. Fujimoto, M. H. Ammar, and K. Perumalla. Updateable simulation of communication networks. In *Proceedings of the* 16th *Workshop on Parallel and Distributed Simulation (PADS-2002)*, pages 107–114, May 2002.

[7] S. Franks, F. Gomes, B. Unger, and J. Cleary. State saving for interactive optimistic simulation. In *Proceedings of the* 11th *Workshop on Parallel and Distributed Simulation (PADS-97)*, pages 72–79, 1997.

[8] R. M. Fujimoto. Performance of Time Warp under synthetic workloads. In *Proceedings of the SCS Multiconference on Distributed Simulation*, volume 22, pages 23–28. SCS Simulation Series, January 1990.

[9] A. Gafni. Rollback mechanisms for optimistic distributed simulation systems. In *SCS Multiconference on Distributed Simulation*, volume 19, pages 61–67, February 1988.

[10] P. W. Glynn and P. Heidelberger. Analysis of parallel replicated simulations under a completion time constraint. *ACM Transactions on Modeling and Computer Simulation (TOMACS)*, 1(1):3–23, 1991.

[11] J. O. Henriksen. An introduction to SLX. In *Proceedings of the 1997 Winter Simulation Conference*, pages 559–566, December 1997.

[12] M. Hybinette and R. M. Fujimoto. Cloning parallel simulations. *ACM Transactions on Modeling and Computer Simulation (TOMACS)*, 11(4):378–407, 2001.

[13] D. R. Jefferson and H. Sowizral. Fast concurrent simulation using the Time Warp mechanism, part I: Local control. Technical Report N-1906-AF, RAND Corporation, December 1982.

[14] K. P. Lentz, E. S. Manolakos, E. Czeck, and J. Heller. Multiple experiment environments for testing. *Journal of Electronic Testing: Theory and Applications*, 11(3):247–262, December 1999.

[15] T. J. Schriber and D. T. Brunner. Inside discrete-event simulation software: How it works and why it matters. In *Proceedings of the 1997 Winter Simulation Conference*, pages 14–22, December 1997.

[16] T. Schulze, S. Strassburger, and U. Klein. On-line data processing in simulation models: New approaches and possibilities through hla. In *Proceedings of the 1999 Winter Simulation Conference*, pages 1602–1609, December 1999.

[17] T. Schulze, S. Strassburger, and U. Klein. Hla-federate reproduction procedures in public transportation federations. In *Proceedings of the 2000 Summer Computer Simulation Conference*, July 2000.

[18] P. Vakili. Massively parallel and distributed simulation of a class of discrete event systems: a different perspective. *ACM Transactions on Modeling and Computer Simulation (TOMACS)*, 2(3):214–238, 1992.

[19] F. Wieland. Parallel simulation for aviation applications. In *Proceedings of the IEEE Winter Simulation Conference*, pages 1191–1198, December 1998.

High-Speed, Scalable, Real-Time Simulation Using DSP Arrays

Roy Crosbie[a], John Zenor[a], Richard Bednar[a], Dale Word[a],
Narain Hingorani[b], and Terry Ericsen[c]
[a]*McLeod Institute of Simulation Sciences, California State University, Chico, CA, USA*
[b]*Consultant, Los Altos Hills, CA, USA,* [c]*Office of Naval Research, Arlington, VA, USA*
E-mail: rcrosbie@csuchico.edu

Abstract

Real-time simulation is a familiar technique for testing hardware and software in the loop and for operator training. An important parameter of these simulations is the frame-time necessary to capture the dynamics of the system being simulated. Modern power electronic systems, using higher frequency pulse-width modulation (PWM) converter control demand frame times that are significantly shorter than those found in most real-time simulators. The paper describes an approach to real-time simulation that is capable of achieving the frame times of 10μS and less required for this application. It is a scalable technique that uses arrays of digital signal processors on commercially available boards plugged into a conventional desktop computer. Analog and digital interfaces provide for the connection of real hardware to the simulation. Although the technique has so far been applied only to power electronic systems, it is capable of being used in a wide range of applications in which frame times of less than 10μS are required.

1. Why High-Speed Real-Time Simulation?

Real-time simulation has been used for many years for operator training and design or testing of hardware and software in situations in which it is inconvenient to use the real system. Examples include flight simulators for pilot training, plant simulators for operator training, and a wide range of applications in which the simulator is used to test hardware and embedded software in the loop.

One of the key parameters of a real-time simulator is the frame rate at which its outputs are updated. Many real-time simulators, including those used for operator training, perform satisfactorily with frame times in the range 10 to 100ms. All the calculations needed to advance the simulation by one frame must be completed, along with all necessary data transfers within one frame.

In some applications real-time simulation is used as a test environment for real hardware or embedded software, referred to as the system under test (SUT). In some cases much shorter frame times (<10μs) are required because of the high-frequency dynamics of both the simulated system and the SUT. Such applications are found, for example, in aerospace, automotive and power electronic systems. The techniques described here focus on power electronic systems, but they are equally relevant to other applications requiring similar frame times. Modern power electronic systems are used to provide flexible alternating and direct current (ac and dc) power, as well to improve power quality. They generally consist of combinations of electronic switches (converters) that convert ac to dc (rectification) or dc to ac (inversion). Feedback controllers control switch timing to maintain demanded current, voltage or power levels. These converters are often based on pulse-width modulation (PWM) techniques.

Reduction of harmonics of the ac line frequency is important in maintaining power quality. This is achieved in a number of ways including careful choice of the switch configuration, the use of harmonic filters and higher switching frequencies for the PWM controllers, which can vary from a few hundred Hz to as much as 20 KHz for converters in the range of hundreds of KW to hundreds of MW. Converters of this kind are important, for example, in the design of the new generation of all-electric Navy ships. Studies of non-real time models of these systems indicate that for PWM switching frequencies in this range, frame times of 10μS and less are required. For PWM frequencies of 20 KHz frame times may need to be as low as 2 to 3μS.

Real-time models of power electronic systems are referred to as Real Time Power System (RTPS) simulations. Although the technique described below has been applied initially in the field of power electronics, it is applicable in other fields in which similarly short frame times are required. In general, therefore, we refer to high-speed, real-time (HSRT) simulation.

1.1. Approaches to HSRT Simulation

A computing platform that can support HSRT simulation should not only be capable of completing the

1087-4097/04 $20.00 © 2004 IEEE

necessary computations and I/O within the allowable frame time, it also needs to synchronize accurately with a real-time clock that ticks at the start of each frame. The shorter the frame time, the more precise must be the clock. It is also desirable to use a processing system that is scalable so that it can support more complex models without compromising frame time. As the required frame time becomes shorter, the choices for suitable computing platforms become more and more restricted. Linux-based systems are a popular choice for real-time systems using longer frame times, such as training simulators. Fully supported extensions such as are found in the standard 2.5 Linux kernel have been thoroughly tested [1] and found to be useable for frame times down to the 10 ms range.

Achieving frame times in the tens of microseconds requires equipment that is specifically designed for the purpose. There are a few companies that specialize in systems that meet these needs. Most of them base their designs on clusters of Pentium, PowerPC or similar high-performance microprocessors combined with real-time kernels. At the present time these systems are not capable of the sub 10μS performance required for higher frequency PWM-based power electronic systems. For example, Opal-RT Technologies Inc. offer a system that has achieved a frame time of 35μS using a cluster of Pentium processors and its own RT-Lab real-time software [2]. The dSPACE company specializes in applications to automotive electronics and offers a simulator [3] based on the AMD Opteron processor that claims frame times of "under 150μS". RTDS Technologies Inc. offers customized power system simulators using arrays of RISC processors of different types [4]. These simulators are focused on public utility applications and can execute with frame times as low as 50μS.

None of the above systems currently meets the requirement for frame times of less than 5μs needed for advanced power electronics applications. An alternative approach is to use arrays of digital signal processors (DSPs). Boards are commercially available that contain one or more DSPs that plug into the PCI bus of a desktop computer. They also offer the ability to interconnect several boards, which increases the total number of DSPs engaged and offers a scalable approach to HSRT simulation. This is the approach adopted for the application described in the next section.

1.2. Real-Time Power Electronic Simulation

We now look in more detail at the simulation of power electronic systems, and the approach adopted at CSU, Chico. It needs to be made clear at this point that this task and its solution are not claimed to represent the results of new research. Rather they represent an engineering solution to a difficult task that has required careful design in integrating hardware, software and numerical analysis components to meet the design goals. The result has been to produce real-time simulations that are believed to use the shortest frame times so far achieved in power electronic simulation and, possibly, in any real-time simulation application. The paper is written with the intention of promoting discussion of HSRT simulation and particularly interaction between users of HSRT simulation in different fields of application.

Power electronics involves the conversion of electrical power from ac to dc (rectification), dc to ac (inversion), converting ac power from one frequency to another, and maintaining power quality free from unwanted variations in voltage, current, frequency etc. Among the key components are the converters that change ac to dc and dc to ac. These contain combinations of electronic switches that can be turned on and off by means of electrical control pulses. Although there is a wide variety of three-phase converter configurations, the most common combination contains six switches (Fig. 1).

RTPS has concentrated on systems consisting of two three-phase ac systems connected back-to-back through converters that are connected to opposite ends of a dc line. The two ac systems may operate at different voltages and frequencies. Figure 2 contains a schematic of such a system by means of a screen produced by the Virtual Test Bed (VTB) simulation environment described in Section 2.1. A mathematical model for a typical system of this kind would consist of 20 to 30 differential equations, additional algebraic relationships and logic equations representing the operation of the switches.

Feedback controllers are used to maintain voltage, current and power at the required levels. These controllers typically use pulse-width modulation (PWM) techniques to determine the appropriate timing for turning the converter switches on and off. The dc line is often represented by a large capacitance but in some cases, involving long lines, a distributed-line model of some kind is required. The switching frequency for the PWM controller is chosen to be an odd multiple of 3 times the line frequency to ensure elimination of even harmonics and reduced odd harmonic content. With a line frequency of 60 Hz the PWM switching speed will be at least 9*60 or 540 Hz. Much higher multiples are common, once again with the intention of reducing or eliminating lower frequency harmonics. 540 Hz yields a period of 1850 μS. Faithful reproduction of the waveforms by the simulation in these cases requires integration time-steps of 10 μS or less. More demanding applications with higher frequency PWM controllers require that the frame time be reduced to less than 5 μS. Solutions of the 20 to 30 differential and other equations and changes in the states of the switches (12 in the example) must be calculated and all I/O completed within the time allowed for each frame

2. Digital Signal Processors for RTPS

RTPS uses off-the-shelf DSP boards that plug into the PCI bus of a conventional desktop computer. These boards offer acceptable real-time performance, and are potentially scalable because additional processors and boards can be added to handle more complex computational tasks.

DSP chips are produced by several semiconductor manufacturers such as Motorola, Texas Instruments, and Analog Devices, and are inexpensive. OEM companies integrate these DSPs into complete boards that can be plugged directly into the PCI bus of a desktop computer. These boards include one or more processors, external memory, bus controller, DMA controllers, real-time clock, software, and all the electronic glue required to provide a working system. They are moderately expensive, typically costing from \$3,000 to \$8,000 depending on the number and type of processors and the amount of on-chip and external memory.

The RTPS project uses DSP boards based on the Analog Devices SHARC family [7] of digital signal processors. Current results are based on a board housing four Analog Devices 21160 processors which have an 80 MHz clock and dual floating-point multipliers and adders giving a peak theoretical computing speed of 320 MFlops. Actual performance is, of course, much less than this peak figure. More powerful (TigerSHARC) processors are now available, and a system containing 4*TS101 (300MHz) processors will shortly be available to the project.

SHARC or **S**uper **H**arvard **ARC**hitecture processors contain dual-ported memory with separate instruction and data areas. The pipelined architecture supports the fetching of an instruction and an operand in each cycle. If the required instruction is already in the instruction cache, with one required operand in data memory and one in instruction memory, both operands can be fetched in the same cycle. The arithmetic processor contains a floating-point multiplier and adder. These are pipelined each with a 3-stage pipeline. The arithmetic unit is theoretically capable of completing one floating-point multiply and one floating-point addition in each clock cycle. Floating-point division is performed by software.

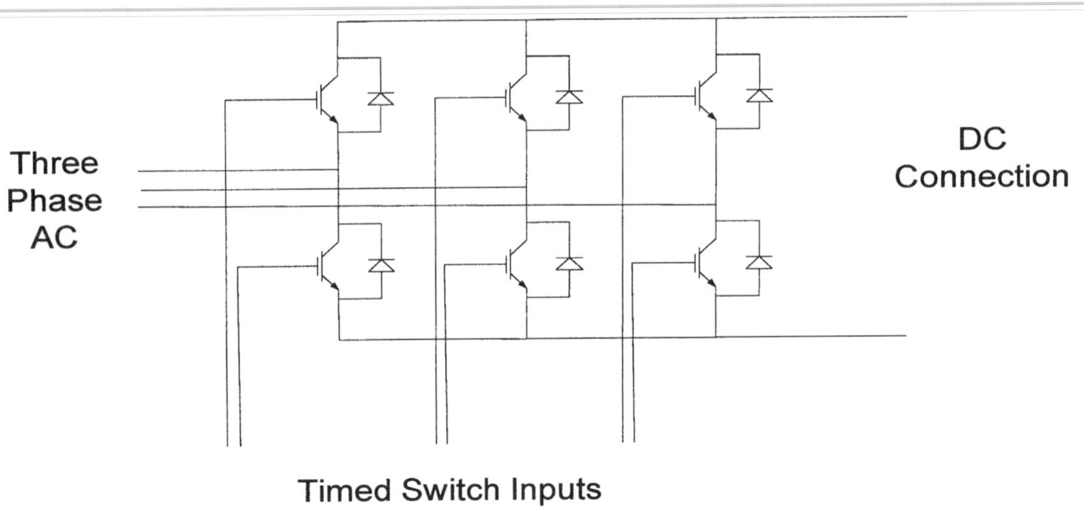

Figure 1. Switch connections for a 3-phase voltage-sourced converter.
Each switch consists of a turn-off device and a diode in parallel. For high-voltage/high-power converters each switch may contain many devices in series and/or parallel.

2.1. The user interface

Any simulation must be provided with a user interface that allows the user to enter system parameters, control the simulation and generate output data in a suitable form. The choices facing a simulation developer are either to design a special-purpose interface from scratch or to incorporate the simulation into an existing user interface. In the case of RTPS it was decided to integrate the models within a powerful existing simulation environment, the Virtual Test Bed (VTB), developed at the University of South Carolina [8] with support from the Office of Naval Research (ONR). The VTB provides a simulation environment that supports the development of models of electrical, mechanical and thermal systems using either internal model components within the VTB libraries or user supplied model components written in the user's choice of language including C++, Matlab, SPICE, ACSL and others. The VTB has an associated advanced graphics package, the VXE, that supports graph plotting and animated 3-D graphical representations of

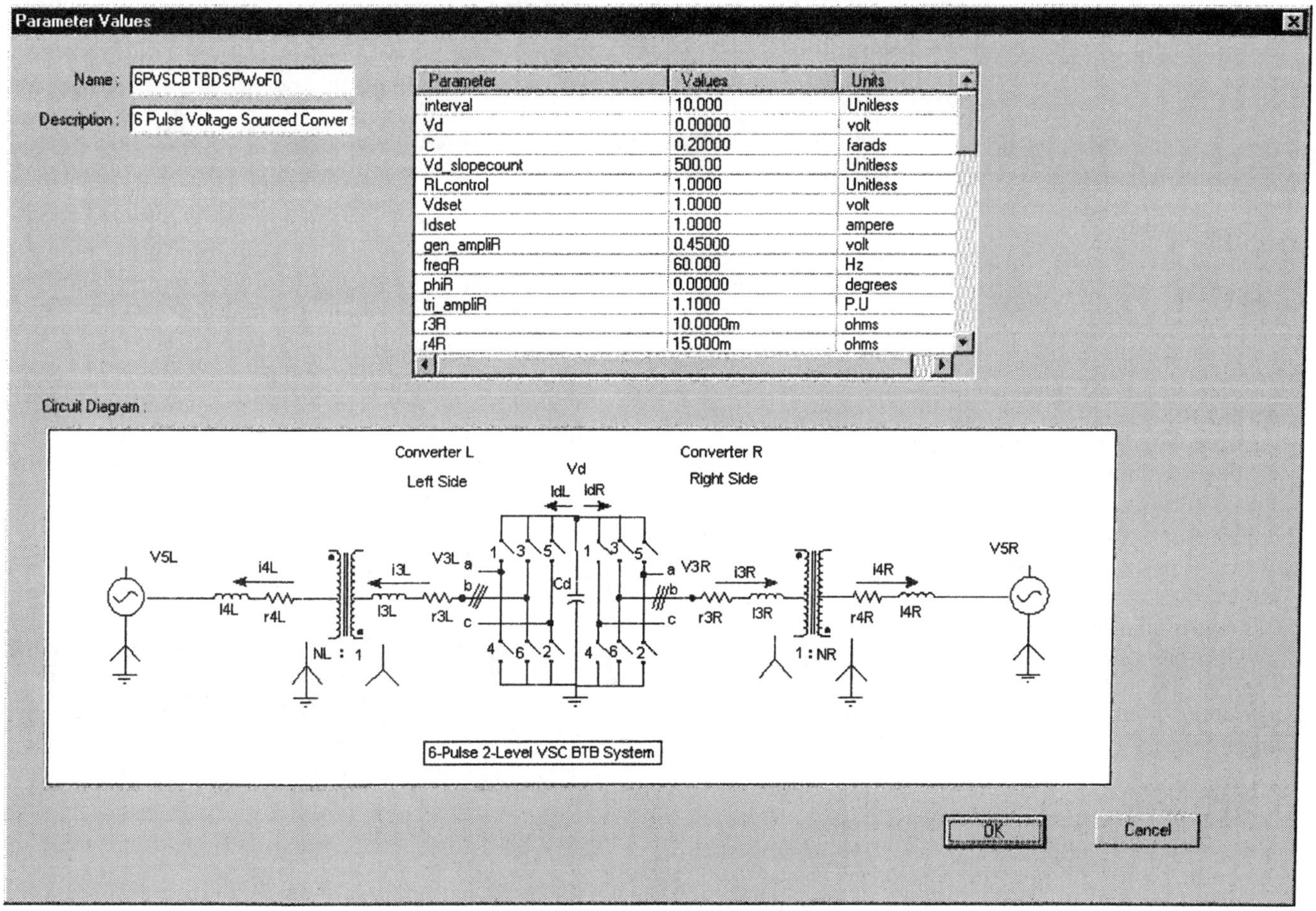

Figure 2. A typical RTPS system.

The figure shows a VTB screen that includes a diagram of the system. The back-to-back converter switches are in the center coupled via a capacitor, Cd. The ac systems at either end are three-phase systems with series inductance and resistance and three-phase transformers. The system illustrated is a basic system that contains no additional components to filter out unwanted harmonics.

the system being modeled. The original RTPS models used a simple interface developed in house, but the user interface and graphical output features of the VTB/VXE are much more powerful and user friendly and the effort involved in integrating RTPS models within the VTB has proved well worth while.

Integrating the models into the VTB simply to utilize the user interface and graphical output of the VTB/VXE represents a first step towards more complete integration. Models operating in this way do not invoke the internal solver of the VTB that is normally used to execute VTB models. The next level of integration would couple the real-time models directly with model components solved using the VTB solver. There is, of course, no question of the real-time models communicating with the VTB at the end of every integration step while maintaining real-time operation. Rather, it is anticipated that the VTB models would represent slowly varying subsystems that would require communication with the real-time models at a much slower rate. With the recent development of a real-time VTB solver [9], such combined models should soon be feasible.

2.2. The mathematical model

The development of a new RTPS model begins with a circuit diagram showing the components of the system, generators, transformers, impedances, switches etc. together with a specification of the controller. Circuit theory is then used to produce a set of differential equations that describe the dynamic behavior of the system. A simplified model (with the switches frozen in one typical configuration) is tested using a conventional continuous simulation product such as the VTB, Matlab/Simulink, or the circuit simulator SPICE, and the results assessed for authenticity. The model is then programmed in C++ and run on a conventional PC and again the results are compared with the earlier test results. At this stage a power electronics expert evaluates the prototype model to validate its behavior.

Once validated, the model is then completed on the PC with an interface to the VTB. This allows the user of the model to enter values of system parameters, set up output graph specifications, and to control the execution of the simulation. Graphical output is generated by the VXE.

The high-switching speeds that occur in these systems mandate short, fixed-step integration methods to avoid excessive timing errors. More sophisticated methods of handling discontinuities, which are used in many non-real-time applications, are not an option because they can significantly extend the time needed to calculate one frame. The necessary short step sizes mean that simple integration algorithms are capable of meeting the accuracy requirements, which helps to ensure that the required computation is completed within the time available. Care must be taken, however, to ensure that stability is maintained over the range of valid parameter values and stability analysis receives a great deal of attention.

3. RTPS configurations

All the RTPS models have been implemented on both real-time and non-real-time platforms. All models are first implemented on a conventional desktop PC running in non-real-time under various versions of the Windows operating system. Models are coded in C++ and these PC versions allow the model to be thoroughly checked by a power electronics expert to ensure that it behaves as expected. In this case the PC runs both the VTB/VXE environment and the simulation itself. The execution speed of the simulation on a PC is affected significantly by the amount of work demanded of the VXE. If, for example, graph plots of several variables are plotted every few integration steps then the simulation is much slower than if only one or two variables are plotted every few hundred integration steps.

The current real-time platform consists of a 4-processor, AD 21160 (80 MHz) board from Bittware interfaced to the PC host through a 66 MHz, 64-bit PCI bus. The Bittware board supports a mezzanine board containing A/D and D/A converters, which can be used to interface hardware to the simulation. The DSP array is used as the simulation engine that solves the model equations in real-time. The host PC runs the VTB/VXE and is responsible for the user interface and processing and display of graphical results. Nothing that occurs on the PC is allowed to impact the execution of the real-time model.

Real-time simulations are used to interface system models to external hardware or human operators. The RTPS models are intended to be interfaced to real controllers and to external ac system components such as generators and motors. The current RTPS models incorporate simulations of system controls and PWM converter controls, but eventually real controllers will replace these parts of the simulation. The first step has been to remove one of the simulated controllers from the RTPS platform and implement it on a second platform from another manufacturer (also using a DSP board executing in real time). The interface between the RTPS model and the controller is digital and the DSP link ports are used for this purpose. Future plans call for a real controller to be interfaced through the DSP link ports.

Interfacing real hardware, such as a motor/generator, in the loop would require powerful amplifiers to drive the machines. However, for ease of demonstration, this hardware is currently represented by a separate PC platform running Linux with real-time extensions that is used to emulate the external ac system components. The dynamics of these components is such that the Linux platform can use longer frame-times. The Linux platform uses an analog interface to represent the analog inputs and outputs of the real hardware, and these signals are connected to the analog interface on the RTPS platform.

3.1. Performance issues

The requirement for real-time operation is that the code that represents the model should execute in less than the required frame time. The three most important factors affecting the execution speed of the array of DSPs are model partitioning, code efficiency, and data transfer. These three factors are now be dealt with in turn.

The models that have been implemented so far lend themselves to a simple partitioning between processors. The left side converter and its associated transformer and impedances are assigned to one processor and those for the right side to a second. The controllers for both sides are assigned to a third processor and the remaining DSP is used to handle synchronization and communication with the host processor. Ideally, partitioning should be done naturally, with each processor representing a natural subdivision of the entire system. This is particularly true of the controller model since it is to combine the simulation of the power system with a real controller. Separation of the controller model into a processor dedicated to that purpose facilitates replacement by a real controller. At the same time it is important to equalize the computing loads so that no single processor unduly delays the completion of each frame. Ultimately, the trade off between natural partitioning and load equalization between processors is a matter of judgment.

The SHARC processors used in these simulations offer architectural features that promise enhanced execution speeds but this promise is only realized if the executable code uses these features effectively. The programming approach adopted for RTPS is to rely as much as possible on C++ programming. The efficiency of the available C++ compiler therefore becomes very crucial in achieving optimum performance. Experience with the available SHARC C++ compiler has, however, been disappointing. Although the processor is capable of executing complex instructions that allow simultaneous data transfers and floating point arithmetic including, in some situations, two data transfers in parallel with a floating point multiply and a floating point add, the code produced by the compiler is largely made up of linear sequences of single operations. Furthermore, careful comparison of compiled code with the source code from which it is generated has shown that different ways of coding the same process in C++ can lead to significant differences in execution speed. The reasons for these differences are not intuitively obvious and considerable effort is required to produce guidelines for efficient C++ programming. One way of improving the efficiency of the code in the critical loops of the program is to use careful hand coding. This is not regarded as an acceptable option for this work. Hand-coded assembly language is notoriously prone to errors, difficult to document and almost impossible to maintain satisfactorily.

A more satisfactory approach is to use optimized routines in the available software libraries. Fortunately it has been possible to adapt a fast matrix multiply routine of this kind for use in the RTPS models. This has the further advantage of providing greater uniformity of code from model to model, since each has a main loop that consists largely of a set of matrix difference equations.

The choice of data transfer method between partitions is critical to achieving optimum performance. Initially it was planned to use the common memory available in multi-DSP configurations to exchange information between processors. During a frame, each processor updates its portion of the system state based on the information available at the beginning of the frame. Some of this new data must be passed to other processors. Common memory seems to offer a natural mechanism for achieving this. Access to the off-chip, common memory proved, however, to be much slower than expected.

Fortunately, the processors offer a number of alternatives for inter-processor communication. Multiple DMA channels provide for both inter-processor data transfers and transfers between the DSP board and the host PC. Each processor is also equipped with four link-ports that support inter-processor communication. These link-ports can be used to connect DSPs together in large arrays.

Detailed evaluation of the data-transfer options has produced a combination of link-port and DMA based transfers that minimize the data transfer overhead. The use of common memory is now limited to transfers that are less time critical.

3.2. Hardware-in-the-loop (HIL)

The primary motivation for real-time power electronic simulation is the need to include hardware in the loop. One use of HIL is to test new controller designs within a simulated environment before introducing it into a real system. The controllers consist of embedded systems with digital control software typically running on DSP processors. Introducing a real controller into the simulation requires a compatible digital interface that presents the simulation to the controller as if it were a real system. Pending the procurement of a real controller a simulated controller, implemented on a second DSP board and host platform has been used to test this mode of operation of the RTPS system. This board is interfaced using the DSP link ports. Because the controller board uses AD 20161 processors, which have a different link-port design to the AD 21160 processors on the RTPS board, a link-port converter was designed to support this configuration. The RTPS simulation was modified so that the controller for one side of the back-to-back system was ported to the external platform to function more like a real controller. This has the effect of increasing the frame time of the combined system slightly, but the basic system still operates within the 10 μS limit.

A second use of HIL is to interface a simulated system to real generators, motors, loads etc. Unlike the control interface, the interface to a power system component of this kind requires the transfer of large amounts of power. This kind of power hardware-in-the-loop (PHIL) interface is outside the scope of the current project, so simulated power system components are connected through analog interfaces to the RTPS simulation. A separate real-time Linux platform is used for this purpose. Generally speaking the frame times required for the external equipment are significantly longer than those for the RTPS simulator and are well within the capability of the Linux system.

3.3. Scalability issues

HSRT simulations need to be scalable if they are to be applied to more complex systems. The potential for scalability was a key factor in choosing the DSP approach to implementing RTPS simulations. There are two aspects to this question. First is the ability of the DSPs to be connected in increasingly large multiprocessor combinations. The second is the way in which the simulation program and its inter-processor communication needs grow.

The selected DSPs are designed to be connected together in large arrays using their link ports. Each DSP has four link ports which lends itself to the construction of rectangular arrays of DSPs. The boards currently being used are limited to a maximum of four processors/board but multiple boards can be installed in the PCI slots of a given host and multiple host PCs can be used to produce larger arrays. Inter-processor communication is, however, limited in that each processor can only communicate directly with its four nearest neighbors; communication with other processors must be done indirectly via intermediate processors. This is a potentially serious obstacle to scaling the simulations. Fortunately, the nature of power electronic systems, and many other engineering systems, is such that coupling between variables in different parts of the system is relatively sparse. Such systems tend to consist of a loosely connected sequence of subsystems with each subsystem coupled only to a few near neighbors. From a mathematical point of view, the system equations can be ordered into a form in which the system matrix presents a largely banded structure with few non-zero elements that are distant from the leading diagonal. This structure maps well on to a multiprocessor array in which each processor is connected to only a few near neighbors. Large power electronic systems, such as might be found in all-electric ships are likely to consist of almost independent systems with a very few key connection points. These should scale relatively easily on to DSP arrays.

4. The role of real-time simulation

We have discussed a specific initiative to achieve new performance goals for real-time power electronic simulations. No single aspect of the techniques adopted is original. DSP arrays have been used for power electronic simulations in the past. What is new is the emphasis on achieving the shortest possible frame times consistent with accurate, stable simulations. It is the combination of hardware, numerical methods, and software design that pushes the envelope of what can be achieved.

The quest for speed in real-time simulation is not confined to the power electronics field. As stated earlier, high-speed real-time simulations are of increasing importance in, for example, the aerospace and automotive fields. Furthermore, the need for reliable high-speed real-time simulations is increasing. Systems of many kinds use embedded digital control to improve their performance. As the dynamic range of both the systems and their controllers continue to increase, the need for faster real-time simulations to perform hardware-in-the-loop test also increases. At the same time system complexity is increasing. This is certainly true in the power electronic field and it presents particular problems for the validation of new hardware components intended for use in the new generation of all-electric ships.

Today, modeling and simulation is widely used in the power electronics field as an analysis tool. However, systems with many power electronic components are emerging – driven by the need for power quality, availability, security, and efficiency. The complexity of these systems exceeds the capability of today's rule-based design methods. Tomorrow's systems will require a relational and rational design process using modeling and simulation. The model becomes the specification. Paper documents cannot address the complexity of the next generation power electronic systems.

Furthermore, two types of models are envisioned: requirement models and product models. Requirement models can be behavioral, empirical, and relational. Product models must be physics based to include the nature of the constituent materials and the methods of manufacture. Physics-based models enable one to predict the physics of failure, quantify risk as a function of known and unknown physics, and quantify cost as a function of materials and manufacturing.

A key part of physics-based design is validation and incremental prototyping. Today's power electronic systems require a completed and commissioned system to validate the design. New power electronic concepts such as Power Electronic Building Blocks (PEBB) [10] enable designers to avoid re-commissioning elements that have been proven in previous designs. A new design of power electronics that uses the same PEBB elements as a previous design need only validate the new application stresses and design elements. A physics-based design process can provide confidence levels and quantified risk to any degree of certainty. However, there is still a great cost to build and test the new elements and to characterize the system under new application stresses. If most of the elements in a system are new, as in a new class of electric ship, the cost of validation can be enormous.

Real-time simulation is designed to interface with real hardware in hardware-in-the-loop (HIL) simulations. HSRT simulation enables parts of a converter (switches, phase-legs, and bridges) to be run with the rest of the converter in a HSRT simulation. Consequently, the whole converter does not need to be built to validate the design – only the elements that are new. In the same way, new converters could be simulated with an entire system emulated in a HSRT simulation. A process of incremental prototyping can be developed that proceeds by calculating a minimum significant HIL experiment for a given design problem. Based on the results obtained, a new HIL experiment would be configured for the next minimum significant hardware validation. The process continues until an acceptable level of confidence is obtained from the incremental prototyping steps performed. In the case of entirely new systems, these steps can be used to build one-of-a-kind prototypes that can be validated based on physics in a process where the building steps are quantified and confidence is established prior to each prototyping step.

5. Summary

Commercial boards containing small arrays of digital signal processors have been used to implement RTPS models with frame times of 10μs and less. Newer, higher-performance processors promise to reduce frame times nearer to the 2-3μs goal. The approach promises a flexible, cost-effective, scalable answer to the need for high-speed, real-time (HSRT) simulations. Work still needs to be done on incorporating hardware-in-the-loop, and optimizing the efficiency of executable code. Successful integration of a number of power electronics models into the VTB environment has been accomplished.

The technique is flexible, scalable and has potential for further improvement. It should prove capable of being adapted to other fields in which HSRT simulation is required. It has an important role to play in new approaches to system design and validation based on incremental prototyping.

6. Acknowledgements

The work described in this paper is the result of a team effort. The authors wish to thank Professor Ralph Hilzer and numerous graduate students for their contributions, and Dean Kenneth Derucher and Dr. Larry Wear for their support and encouragement. The research described in this paper is supported by the US Office of Naval Research (ONR) through Grants N00014-01-1-0394 and N00014-03-1-0950.

7. References

[1] R.E. Murray, "Real Time with a Red Hat: Analysis of Standard Linux for Real-Time Simulation" Proceedings of I/ITSEC conference, Orlando, Florida, Dec. 2003. Available on CD ROM from www.iitsec.org/proceedings.cfm

[2] C. Dufour, J. Bélanger, and S. Abourida, "Accurate Simulation of a 6-Pulse Inverter with Real-Time Event Compensation in ARTEMIS", Electrimacs 2002, Montreal. Available from www.opal-rt.com/downloads/pdfs/331C_Dufour.pdf

[3] dSPACE Inc., "dSPACE Sets the Pace in HIL Simulation Again", Feb. 2004. www.dspaceinc.com/ww/en/inc/company/press/pr_0402001.htm

[4] RTDS Technologies Inc. Information available at www.rtds.com/hardware.htm

[5] M. Kezunovic, "Advanced Modeling Approaches and Simulation Tools for Power Engineering Research and Development," *SCI 2000/ISS 2000*, Orlando, July 2000

[6] M. Kezunovic, J. Domaszewicz, V. Skendzic, M. Aganagic, J.K. Bladow, S.M. McKenna, D.M. Hamai, "Design, Implementation and Validation of a Real-Time Digital Simulator for Protection Relay Testing," *IEEE Transactions on Power Delivery*, Vol. 11, No. 1, pp. 158-164, January 1996

[7] Analog Devices Inc. "Tiger SHARC Processor", www.analog.com/processors/processors/tigersharc/

[8] R.A. Dougal, S. Liu, L. Gao, M. Blackwelder, "Virtual Test Bed for Advanced Power Sources", J. of Power Sources, Vol. 110, No. 2, pp. 285-294, 09/02.

[9] B. Lu, W. McKay, S. Lentijo, A. Monti, X. Wu, and R. Dougal, "The Real Time Extension of the Virtual Test Bed", Proceedings of the Huntsville Simulation Conference, Society for Modeling and Simulation International, October 2003, Huntsville, AL., www.scs.org/hsc

[10] G.S. Thandi, R. Zhang, K. Xing, F.C. Lee, and D. Boroyevich. "Modeling, control and stability analysis of a PEBB based DC DPS" IEEE Transactions on Power Delivery, April 1999, 14(2): 497-505.

Session 4:
Optimistic Methods

Towards Grid-aware Time Warp

K. A. Iskra G. D. van Albada P. M. A. Sloot

Computing, System Architecture and Programming Laboratory
Universiteit van Amsterdam
Kruislaan 403, 1098 SJ Amsterdam, The Netherlands
E-mail: {kamil,dick,sloot}@science.uva.nl

Abstract

We study the adaptation of an optimistic Time Warp kernel to cross-cluster computing on the Grid. Wide area communication, the primary source of overhead, is off-loaded onto dedicated routing processes. This allows the simulation processes to run at full speed and it thus significantly decreases the performance gap caused by the wide area distribution. Further improvements are obtained by employing message aggregation on the wide area links. We achieve many of our objectives for lazy cancellation and moderate communication, but high communication rates with aggressive cancellation remains a challenge.

1 Introduction

Time Warp [1] is the best known optimistic Parallel Discrete Event Simulation [2] protocol. The events are executed without considering their causal relationship, and, should a causality error occur, a rollback takes place, which moves back the simulation time. Communication in Time Warp tends to be intensive, with a large number of typically rather small messages. To keep the whole system stable, it is advised to run it on a tightly coupled parallel machine with a low-latency interconnection infrastructure.

However, some problems could conceivably be too large to run efficiently on a single machine. Larger computing and memory power, while generally available, tends to be distributed. A significant effort is underway [3] to create an ubiquitous computing infrastructure: the Grid – where large, distributed resources should be easily available in a uniform fashion. The Globus toolkit provides a set of services to make Grid computing viable, employing in the latest, third version, web services for increased interoperability [4]. Useful as it is, Globus does not solve the fundamental problems associated with the distributed, cross-cluster computing (which is an essential part of the Grid computing). These problems include: network latency across the wide area links, potential inhomogeneity of co-allocated resources, and the lack of their guaranteed availability.

In the field of parallel simulation, lack of homogeneity can be alleviated with the help of load balancing [5, 6], which helps to keep the logical processes synchronised. Fault tolerance [7, 8] can be used to allow the simulation to continue when some of the resources become unavailable.

The effort described in this work focuses on the first of the problems mentioned above: performance in the face of latency stemming from the wide area, cross-cluster distribution. APSIS, a locally developed Time Warp kernel [9], has been modified to make it more resistant to the conditions resulting from an inhomogeneous network infrastructure. First results have been described in [10], where special attention has been given to cancellation optimisations.

Related work has recently been described in [11]. A locally optimistic simulation distributed over loosely coupled domains can adjust its behaviour to the changing network conditions. However, no experiments on a real-world system have been performed, instead wide area network has been emulated by inducing artificial delays in the communication channels. [12] presents another experimental study of the communication overhead and its effects on the performance of Time Warp. Neither paper focuses on optimising the process topology for cross-cluster communication or on the message aggregation for more optimal wide-area communication, which are the focus of the work described in this paper.

The application of MPI to Grid/Metacomputing environments has been summarised in [13]. Some of the major efforts include PACX-MPI [14] and Stampi [15]. Typically, extra nodes, transparent to user MPI code, are employed for wide area communication, depending on the technology used and the authors' imagination called gateways, proxies, daemons etc. Also in the work described here extra nodes, called routing processes, are introduced. Compared to the aforementioned more generic solutions, this work is domain specific, as it is implemented on top of an existing Grid capable MPI version (MPICH-G2 [16] based on the second

1087-4097/04 $20.00 © 2004 IEEE

version of the Globus toolkit), in a way most suitable for the functionality needed by a Time Warp kernel. For example, it allows to implement extra optimisations such as the message type specific aggregation.

Message aggregation in Time Warp has been studied in [17]. Messages are aggregated for an age window, which is either constant, or changes depending on the current message rate. [18] compares several different aggregation schemes for conservative simulations, in particular the traditional sender-initiated vs. receiver-initiated. In a related field of Distributed Interactive Simulation, [19] describes the experiences of using message aggregation while preserving real-time constraints.

The remainder of this paper is organised as follows. Section 2 presents a more in-depth introduction in the form of a motivating example. Section 3 introduces new mechanisms implemented in the kernel: the routing processes and the message aggregation. Section 4 provides the results of the experiments performed. Finally, Sec. 5 summarises the work and outlines possible future directions.

2 Motivating Example

In order to properly describe the experiment that is to serve as the motivating example, the environment that the experiment has been executed in must be introduced.

DAS-II is a 200-node cluster distributed across 5 locations in the Netherlands. The sub-clusters are interconnected using a wide area gigabit backbone. Within each cluster, Myrinet 2000 and Fast Ethernet are used. Each node is a dual Pentium-III 1 GHz machine running a Linux kernel 2.4.x. MPICH 1.2.5-1a is used for communication. Communication is highly non-homogeneous, performance depends on the particular flavour of MPICH used and the distance. For example, sending a short message between two processes running on the same node takes slightly over 2 μs with the Myrinet flavour, while it takes over 1400 μs between two sub-clusters with a WAN-capable MPICH flavour.

With this knowledge, the example in Fig. 1 can now be analysed. This example is an extended version of the experiments discussed in [10]. Here, the run times of a simulation parallelised for 24 processors (12 nodes thus) have been measured using various available combinations of communication channels and MPICH flavours. Lazy cancellation was used, as it tends to minimise the amount of communication. Still, the communication was quite intensive: during each run, every process received on average 380 thousand of externally-scheduled positive events. Divided by the run time, this amounts to some 750 to 5000 messages/sec for each of the 24 processors. For more information on the simulated application, see Sec. 4.1.

As can be seen in Fig. 1, the best results are obtained with

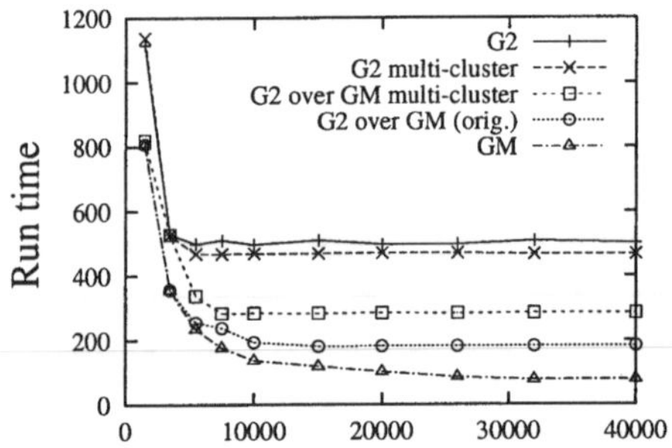

Figure 1. The influence of various communication layers on the run times for different Virtual Time Window sizes (*x* axis).

MPICH-*GM*, which uses the low-latency Myrinet network. Myrinet is a local area network, hence these runs have been performed on a single cluster. On the other hand, the worst results have been obtained with MPICH-*G2*, a Grid-enabled flavour which uses TCP/IP for all its communication. Given that the performance of MPICH-G2 for small messages is some 30–45 times worse than that of MPICH-GM, a six times longer run time is not that dramatic. Surprisingly, *multi-cluster* runs of MPICH-G2 (with processes evenly divided between two DAS-II sub-clusters) actually perform slightly better than the single-cluster MPICH-G2 runs, in spite of the fact that the latency of the inter-cluster links is twice that of the intra-cluster ones. The cause of this phenomenon is unclear, but it is in fact not that relevant given the availability of better options described below.

Between those two extremes one can find the results of the runs obtained with MPICH-*G2 over GM*, a version of MPICH-G2 configured to use MPICH-GM for communication within the cluster, and the regular TCP/IP links of MPICH-G2 for inter-cluster communication. The *multi-cluster* runs of MPICH-G2 over GM perform visibly better than any of the "pure" MPICH-G2 runs, but there is still a performance gap of a factor of four compared to MPICH-GM. Surprisingly, a single-cluster run of MPICH-G2 over GM (marked in Fig. 1 as *(orig.)*), while clearly an improvement over the multi-cluster run, fails to close the performance gap. That is because this MPICH flavour regularly queries both MPICH-GM and TCP/IP links for messages. Querying TCP/IP sockets is rather expensive, even if they are empty, as is always the case for single-cluster runs. If one modifies MPICH-G2 not to perform such redundant polls, the performance gap to MPICH-GM is almost completely closed (the relevant plot is missing in Fig. 1, as it would be indistinguishable from MPICH-GM on this scale).

Therefore, a significant part of the slowdown with MPICH-G2 over GM can be attributed to the overhead of polling TCP/IP sockets, and not just to the inherent network

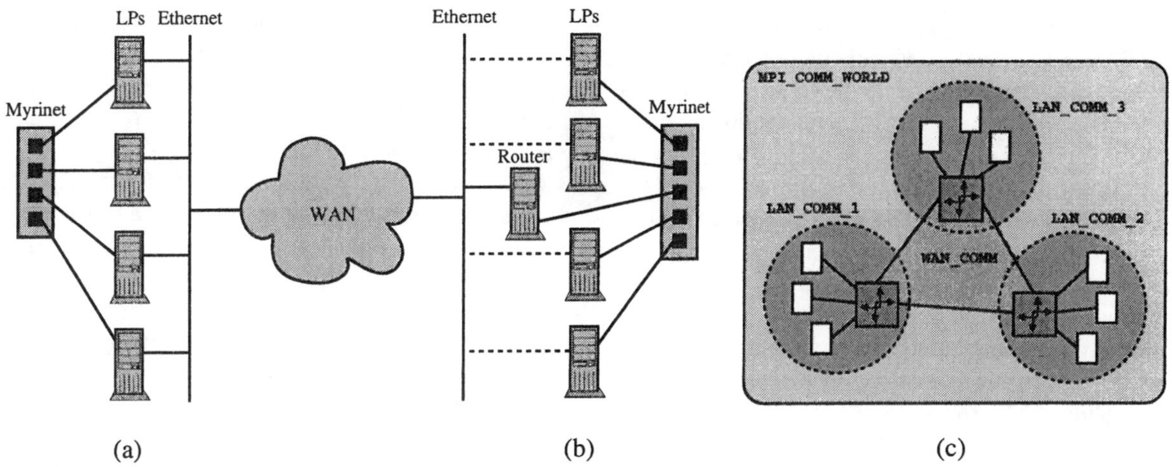

Figure 2. Process topology: original (a) and grid-aware (b). MPI communicators used (c).

properties. While eliminating the queries of TCP/IP sockets is not an option for multi-cluster runs, performing them more smartly could result in a substantial speedup.

3 Grid-awareness

3.1 Topology

Multi-cluster runs presented in Sec. 2 have been distributed using an approach that could best be described as naive. A simulation kernel with no notion of network topology has been compiled with a Grid-enabled version of MPICH and executed in a highly heterogeneous networking environment. Yet, the kernel was able to execute the simulations in a stable (albeit slow) fashion.

Figure 2 (a) depicts a single sub-cluster of such a simulation. Logical processes in the sub-cluster communicate with each other via Myrinet. A subset of logical processes will also want to communicate with the logical processes on other sub-cluster(s). These messages are sent using TCP/IP via Fast Ethernet to the local switch/router (not shown), which has a gigabit uplink to the wide area network. The situation at the remote sub-cluster(s) is identical. Because all logical processes are allowed to communicate with each other, they must all poll both Myrinet and Fast Ethernet for any messages that might have arrived. This has a detrimental effect on the performance, as shown in Sec. 2.

A solution to this problem is shown in Fig. 2 (b). A *routing process* is reserved on every sub-cluster, that is responsible for the wide area communication. Routing processes, while part of the MPI job, are not part of the simulation, no logical processes are assigned to them. Simulation processes are relieved of the wide area communication: whenever a message needs to be sent to a process at a remote sub-cluster, it is sent (via Myrinet) to the local routing process instead. The local routing process obtains the intended destination process identifier from the message header, consults its routing table and forwards the message to the appropriate remote routing process, using TCP/IP. The remote routing process sends the message (via Myrinet) to the intended destination.

To emphasize, no physical modifications to the cluster are made: every node is still capable of direct wide area communication, this ability simply is not used by the resident processes anymore (hence the dashed lines in Fig. 2 (b)).

3.2 Routing Processes

On initialisation, the simulation uses the topology discovery extensions offered by MPICH-G2 [16] to find out how it is distributed. On every sub-cluster, one process is selected to be the routing process (see Fig. 2 (c)). The global MPI communicator `MPI_COMM_WORLD` is split into sub-communicators local for every sub-cluster (`LAN_COMM_`*i*). Simulation processes only use those local communicators to exchange messages, which allows them to avoid the expensive TCP/IP socket polls (if the modified version of MPICH-G2 is used). In addition to that, a sub-communicator is created that consists of the routing processes only (`WAN_COMM`). This communicator should only poll the TCP/IP sockets when queried. However, because the calling process itself was accessible via Myrinet, MPICH-G2 would still consult the Myrinet, receive any pending messages from the local simulation processes and store them in a rapidly growing internal queue. This would result in a considerable slowdown, but could easily be fixed by adapting MPICH-G2 sources.

Currently, each routing process acts as follows: as long as there are pending messages from the local simulation processes, they are received and forwarded to the remote routing processes. Then, an analogous procedure is performed for pending messages from the remote routing processes. Both subroutines are executed in an infinite loop.

Given that each subroutine only terminates when no more messages of a particular origin are left to be forwarded, the process might be expected to be prone to starvation under high loads. This is indeed the case, as will be shown in Sec. 4.2. However, putting a limit on the number of messages forwarded per subroutine invocation, which in general prevents starvation, was in fact experimentally found to be more prone to unstable behaviour than not enforcing any limit at all. The reason is that, for the simulation model tested, the beginning phase of the simulation appears to be critical, because very intensive communication takes place then for a short time period. If a limit on forwarding is in place, a routing process attempts to satisfy both LAN and WAN traffic. In reality, under high loads, it fails to satisfy either, as the queues on both sides just keep on growing. With no artificial limits, the peak throughput of the routing process is maximised. Provided that the high communication load is only temporary, such a process is more likely to handle the load in near real time. This comes at the expense of temporarily neglecting the opposite forwarding direction. If the communication is too intensive for a longer period, the queue in the opposite forwarding direction to the currently handled one will grow too long to be handled in near real time. This unstable behaviour gets worse with every iteration and quickly destabilises the simulation processes.

3.3 Message Aggregation

The existence of separate processes concerned only with the wide area communication makes it easy to implement message aggregation. Instead of performing the time consuming send operation separately for every little message, the messages can be stored in a buffer, which is sent when it gets full or once a timeout expires.

The effectiveness of the scheme is increased by the fact that the routing processes concentrate messages from multiple sources and for multiple destinations, which would not be possible if message aggregation was implemented in the simulation processes themselves. The concentration improves the efficiency by increasing the average size of the wide area messages sent.

While message aggregation undoubtedly increases the latency by storing the messages in the buffers instead of sending them immediately, it increases the maximum wide area bandwidth available by performing TCP/IP communication more efficiently. This should help simulations that have excessive communication requirements.

The implemented aggregation mechanism is highly tunable. First, it can be turned off completely. The aggregation buffer size (which is separate for every remote routing process) can be changed, with the default value at 4 KB. It was experimentally found, using a dedicated ping-pong benchmark, that the travel time of a 4 KB message across the available wide area link is less than 20% higher than that of a non-aggregated APSIS message of 156 bytes, while at the same time the throughput increases by a factor of 22 (from 115 KB/s to 2.5 MB/s). Increasing the buffer size further was experimentally found to have negligible effect on the performance, so all the experiments presented below have been performed with the default buffer size. The aggregation timeout is also tunable. A value of 0 is not quite the same as no aggregation at all: it will still receive and aggregate the pending messages from the local simulation processes, but they will be sent out as soon as a non-blocking receive attempt returns without a message. Finally, the aggregation behaviour can be influenced by the message type. Currently, the only implemented mechanism of this sort is the special treatment of anti-messages: adding an anti-message to an aggregation buffer can force the buffer to be sent immediately. The influence of this aggregation strategy is shown in Sec. 4.3.

4 Experiments

4.1 Software

The simulation kernel used, APSIS, is a locally developed implementation of the optimistic parallel discrete event simulation protocol Time Warp. It is targeted at distributed memory architectures, in particular clusters [9]. The intended application field is complex systems simulation. The kernel features incremental state saving, optimism throttling via a tunable moving virtual time window, aggressive or lazy cancellation, and individual or bulk anti-messages. Virtual Time Window (VTW) specifies the maximum distance allowed between the local and global virtual time: once a process reaches it, processing the next input event is suspended until a new GVT value is received (which takes place 20 times per second). Bulk anti-messages is an optimisation where, instead of sending individual anti-messages for every erroneous positive event, remote processes receive a single *bulk* anti-message that annihilates all the erroneous events [10, 20].

The simulation model employed is Ising spin, a cellular automata model of magnetism. It is essentially used as a benchmark, as it is easily scalable and parallelisable. The cellular automata lattice is spatially decomposed and mapped onto the simulation processes arranged in a torus topology. The borders of the individual sub-lattices are duplicated at the neighbours (for the configurations used in the experiments, some 5–9% of sites were at the border). When a state of a site at the border changes, the copy at

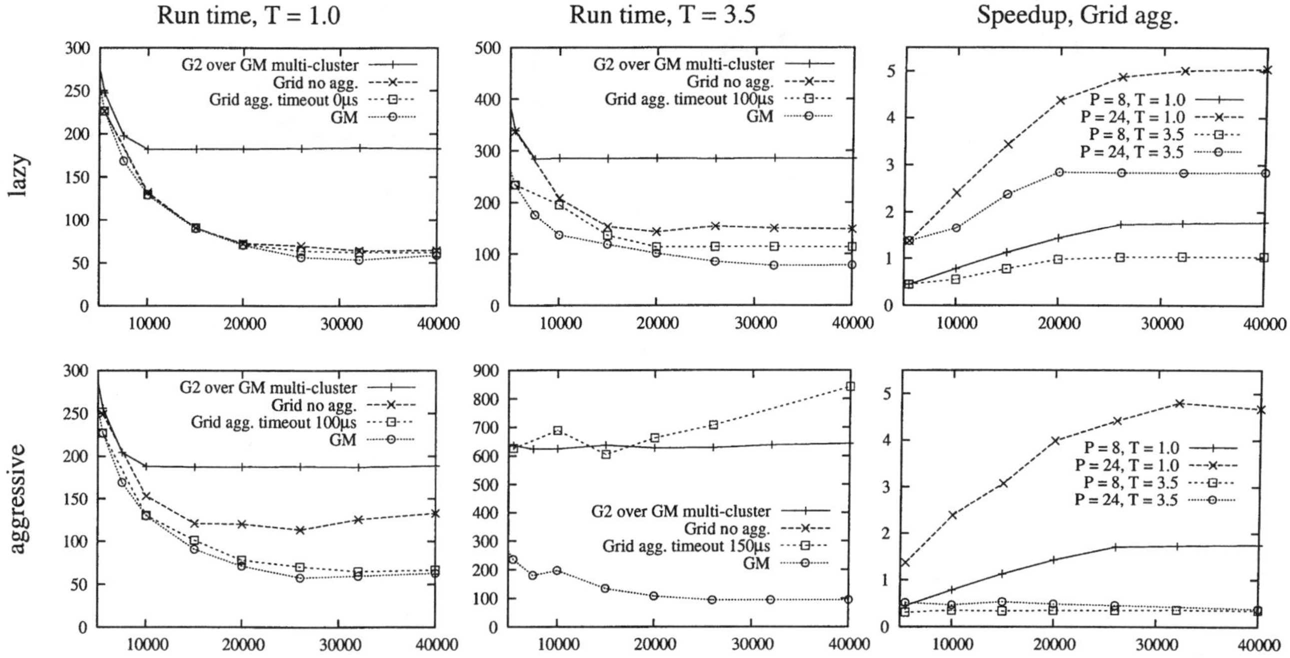

Figure 3. Performance of the Ising spin simulation when running on different communication layers for different VTW sizes (*x* axis), for 24 processes. Run times in sec. (left, center) and speedup (right).

the neighbour is updated by scheduling an external update event. These are the only external events scheduled, apart from them each process executes a self-sustaining stream of locally scheduled events that attempt to change the state of randomly chosen sites. A model parameter called the *temperature* determines the probability of these attempts being successful, and thus indirectly influences the amount of the inter-process communication. There is a difference of two orders of magnitude in the communication volume between the temperatures of 1.0 and 3.5 used in the experiments. Because the spatial correlations in cellular automata are limited, lazy cancellation is generally an advantage for this model, as the events are largely independent.

More details on these implementations of the simulation kernel and the model can be found in [9, 10, 21, 22].

4.2 Communication Layers

Figure 3 presents an overview of the performance measured during the experiments. In fact, the top-middle plot presents some of the same data as Fig. 1. The results for lazy and aggressive cancellation are shown (both with individual anti-messages), for different model temperatures, for 24 processes (the results for 8 processes were quite similar). Measurements were taken over a range of the virtual time window sizes. Four curves are present in each of the run time plots (Fig. 3 left and center). *GM* and *G2 over GM multi-cluster* are already known from Fig. 1: they refer respectively to single-cluster runs using only Myrinet and two-cluster runs using both Myrinet and TCP/IP. The two new *Grid* curves use the new mechanisms described in Sec. 3. *Grid no agg.* uses routing processes, but no message aggregation. *Grid agg. timeout* xμs uses both routing processes and message aggregation, the timeout shown is the one giving the best results from a series of experiments, see Sec. 4.3.

Both of the *Grid* runs perform visibly better than *G2 over GM multi-cluster.* Especially for lazy cancellation, they tend to achieve results quite close to those of the single-cluster *GM* runs, especially for the temperature of 1.0. This is not surprising given that both lazy cancellation and low temperature decrease the amount of communication in the system. Still, also for the temperature of 3.5 the results are quite good, while the communication is a lot more intensive then. Also aggressive cancellation runs perform quite well for low temperature if aggregation is used. High temperature presents a challenge, though: the *Grid* versions actually perform worse than the basic multi-cluster version. *Grid* runs with no or little aggregation are unstable and cannot finish the simulation in any reasonable time. Such results are an indication of rollback thrashing: the communication layer stops coping with the message traffic in real time, so messages are forwarded with large delays. Handling of such delayed messages at the receiver's side re-

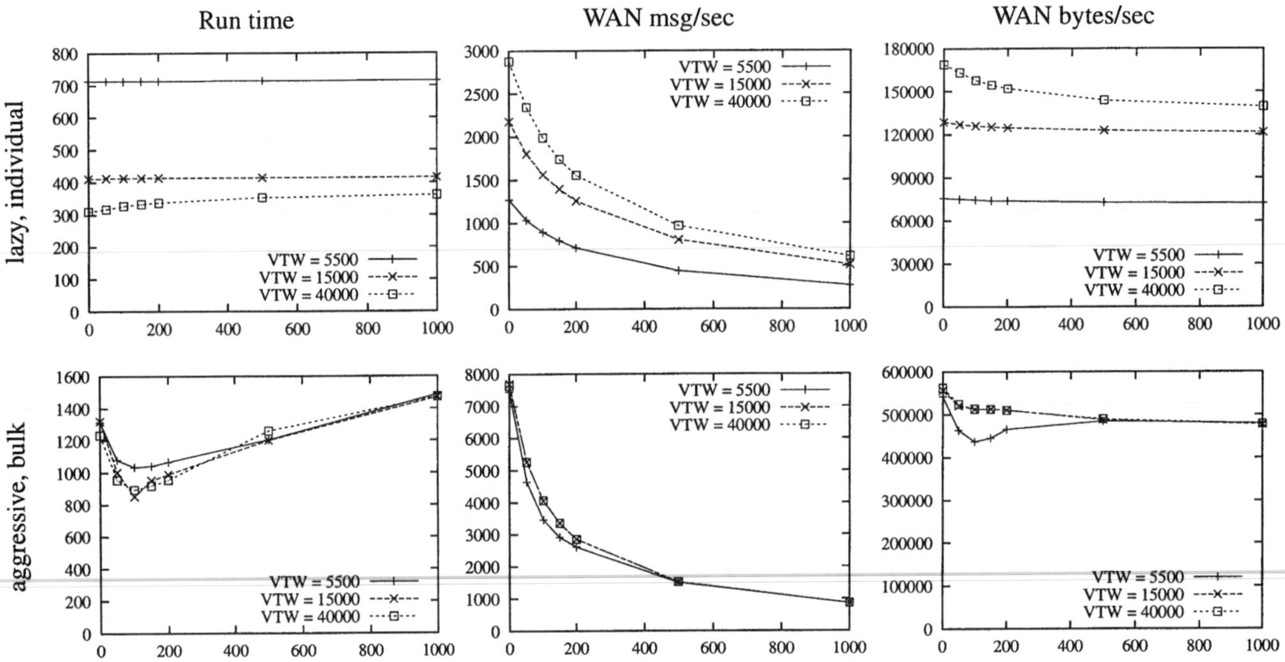

Figure 4. The influence of the different aggregation timeouts (*x* axis) on the behaviour of the APSIS kernel for 8 processes and T = 3.5: elapsed run time (first column), average number of messages (second column) and bytes (third column) sent by a single routing process via the wide area link.

quires huge rollbacks. Not only is this expensive, but it further destabilises the system, since anti-messages generated while rolling back cause secondary rollbacks at other processes resulting in rollback cascades. In the end, the processes almost permanently roll back without making any real progress. It is very difficult for the system to regain stability once this starts taking place.

Figure 3 right presents the speedup obtained during these experiments. In order to obtain the sequential run times, the same parallel implementation of the Ising spin model was used, configured to run on a single process only. While this is not optimal, the simulation kernel has been optimised to skip the operations causing most overhead (maintaining output and state queues, GVT calculation and garbage collection of past events, communication layer polls). Given the low computational weight of Ising spin events, this overhead significantly affects the performance for the parallel runs. That translates into low speedup for the runs with 8 processes: between 1 and 2 for the runs with lazy cancellation. However, good locality of the model makes it scalable, so for 24 processes one can observe a significant improvement in speedup, quite in line with the increased number of processes. Speedups for the runs with aggressive cancellation and high temperature are below 1: these are the unstable runs as discussed above, and addressing them clearly requires further improvements to the infrastructure.

4.3 Aggregation

One more observation to be made from Fig. 3 is that *Grid* runs without message aggregation are never better than with aggregation. Aggregation is thus generally an advantage.

Figure 4 focuses on the influence of the aggregation timeout on the behaviour of the kernel. Measurements have been taken for a range of timeout values, with a special focus on 0–200 μs region. Results are presented for three virtual time window sizes (of those, *VTW = 40000* is the most relevant one, as the run times are shortest for it). The influence of timeout on both the simulation run time and the communication are presented. The experiments presented are for the case of 8 processes and temperature of 3.5 (intensive communication thus), for two cancellation strategies: lazy with individual anti-messages and aggressive with bulk anti-messages. The latter tends to take less bandwidth and is somewhat more stable than the aggressive cancellation with individual anti-messages (as presented in Fig. 3), but apart from that the results are quite similar.

The results presented in the top row of Fig. 4, for lazy cancellation, are typical for the majority of the experiments made. Run time is only slightly influenced by the aggregation timeout, with small timeouts, often the timeout of 0, performing best (see Sec. 3.3 for the semantics of timeout 0). The effect of the timeout is far more pronounced on

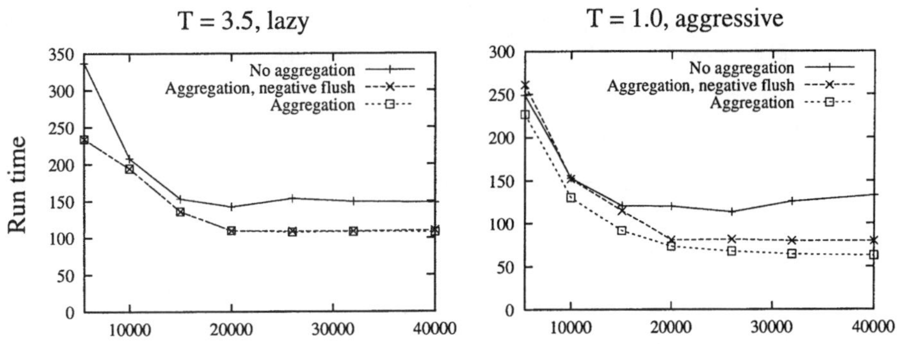

Figure 5. Performance of the Ising spin simulation with different configurations of the message aggregation for different VTW sizes (*x* axis), for 24 simulation processes.

the number of messages sent via the wide area link. Quite naturally, the smaller the timeout, the larger the number of messages sent. Also the throughput increases with the decreasing timeout, but only to a limited degree. A better method to decrease the bandwidth requirements, should that be needed, is to decrease the VTW size (but that does increase the run time).

The result in the bottom row of Fig. 4, for aggressive cancellation, is sort of an exception. The system appears to be saturated, as the differences in results between different VTW sizes are largely gone. There is also a far more pronounced minimum in the run time than before. The steep increase for low aggregation timeouts can easily be explained by excessive number of the wide area messages exchanged (close to 8000 per second). However, no clear explanation is available for the run time rise in the region of 200–1000 μs, or for the minimum in the wide area communication for VTW equal to 5500 (bottom right plot). No such phenomena can be observed with lazy cancellation. However, the communication throughput on the wide area link is much higher with aggressive cancellation. It crosses a respectable value of 0.5 MB/sec (in each direction), but it is still far from the (not shown) more unstable runs with 24 processes, which for aggressive cancellation achieve 1.6 (bulk anti-messages) to 2.4 (individual anti-messages) MB/sec.

A general conclusion is that the aggregation timeouts should be small. Often, a timeout of 0 μs gives the best results, in some cases values around 100 μs are better, but values above 150 μs always perform sub-optimally.

Finally, Fig. 5 presents a comparison between three different aggregation strategies: no aggregation (only routing processes), ordinary aggregation and aggregation where receiving a negative message causes an immediate flushing of the aggregation buffer (both aggregations with 0 μs timeout). The results are somewhat disappointing: forcing the premature sending has either no effect (as shown for lazy cancellation with high communication intensity) or it makes the performance worse (as shown for aggressive cancellation with low communication intensity). In the former case, too few anti-messages are sent to make a difference, whereas in the latter case the significant increase in the number of expensive wide area messages apparently outweighs the benefit of faster delivery of anti-messages.

5 Conclusion and Future Directions

This paper discussed the issues of adapting a Time Warp kernel to the Grid, focusing on overcoming the performance gap caused by high latency networks.

A significant reason for this gap was found to be the local overhead of maintaining TCP/IP sockets in the simulation processes, and not the inherent properties of the networks. Therefore, an infrastructure has been built to off-load wide area links onto dedicated routing processes. Subsequently, routing processes have been extended with message aggregation to further optimise the wide area communication.

Experiments performed with the Ising spin model confirm the effectiveness of the approach taken. The performance gap is very significantly reduced with the introduction of the routing processes. For low communication cases, the performance is very close to that of the single-cluster runs. In case of moderate communication, the introduction of message aggregation with a small timeout proves advantageous. While the influence of aggregation on throughput is limited, the number of messages exchanged is significantly reduced.

Nevertheless, for the cases of highest communication rate, the approach shows its weaknesses. The simulations become unstable and are only able to terminate if message aggregation with timeout is used. Even then, the results are far from the single-cluster ones, and can even get worse than that of multi-cluster runs without the routing processes.

The exact reason for that remains to be identified. Apparently, the routing processes simply cannot cope with the load and become the bottlenecks. Perhaps increasing their number (beginning with splitting the sending and receiving operations into separate processes), or simply using several TCP/IP links in parallel (which is easy to do in MPICH-G2) will help. Without the routing processes, the simulation processes would be slowed down as a side effect of the wide area communication under such circumstances, but with routing processes in place there is nothing to stop them. Clearly, optimism control is insufficient if the simulation processes keep on sending new messages while the routing processes are already overloaded. In fact, the currently used GVT algorithm is still located inside one of the simulation processes and does not take the topology into account. It needs to be moved to the routing processes instead and be made distributed.

Finally, the results must be verified with other PDES applications. An effort is underway to make use of the established PHOLD benchmark for that purpose.

Acknowledgments: This work was partially supported by the ICES/KIS-II: Virtual Lab project.

References

[1] D.R. Jefferson, Virtual Time, *ACM Transactions on Programming Languages and Systems*, vol. 7, no. 3, pp. 404–425, July 1985.

[2] R.M. Fujimoto, *Parallel and Distributed Simulation Systems*, Wiley, 2000.

[3] I. Foster, and C. Kesselman (eds.), *The Grid: Blueprint for a Future Computing Infrastructure*, Morgan-Kaufmann, 1999.

[4] I. Foster, C. Kesselman, J. Nick, and S. Tuecke, The Physiology of the Grid: An Open Grid Services Architecture for Distributed Systems Integration, *Open Grid Service Infrastructure WG, Global Grid Forum*, June 2002.

[5] C.D. Carothers, and R.M. Fujimoto, Efficient Execution of Time Warp Programs on Heterogeneous, NOW Platforms, *IEEE Transactions on Parallel and Distributed Systems*, vol. 11, no. 3, pp. 299–317, March 2000.

[6] D.W. Glazer, and C. Tropper, On Process Migration and Load Balancing in Time Warp, *IEEE Transactions on Parallel and Distributed Systems*, vol. 4, no. 3, pp. 318–327, March 1993.

[7] D. Agrawal, and J.R. Agre, Replicated Objects in Time Warp Simulations, In *Proc. 1992 Winter Simulation Conference*, Arlington, VA, USA, pp. 657–664, December 1992.

[8] O.P. Damani, and V.K. Garg, Fault-Tolerant Distributed Simulation, In *Proc. 12th Workshop on Parallel and Distributed Simulation*, Banff, AB, Canada, pp. 38–45, May 1998.

[9] B.J. Overeinder, *Distributed Event-driven Simulation – Scheduling Strategies and Resource Management*, Ph.D. thesis, Universiteit van Amsterdam, The Netherlands, November 2000.

[10] K.A. Iskra, G.D. van Albada, and P.M.A. Sloot, Time Warp Cancellation Optimisations on High Latency Networks, In *Proc. 7th Int. Symposium on Distributed Simulation and Real Time Applications*, Delft, The Netherlands, pp. 128–135, October 2003.

[11] A. Boukerche, A. Fabbri, and A.R. Mikler, Distributed Simulation over Loosely Coupled Domains, In *Proc. 4th Int. Workshop on Distributed Simulation and Real-Time Applications*, San Francisco, CA, USA, pp. 18–25, August 2000.

[12] C.D. Carothers, R.M. Fujimoto, and P. England, The Effect of Communication Overheads on Time Warp Performance: An Experimental Study, In *Proc. 8th Workshop on Parallel and Distributed Simulation*, Edinburgh, Scotland, UK, pp. 118–125, July 1994.

[13] M. Müller, M. Hess, and E. Gabriel, Grid Enabled MPI Solutions for Clusters, In *Proc. 3rd Int. Symposium on Cluster Computing and the Grid*, Tokyo, Japan, pp. 18–25, May 2003.

[14] E. Gabriel, M. Resch, and Roland Rühle, Implementing MPI with Optimized Algorithms for Metacomputing, In *Proc. 3rd MPI Developers' and Users' Conference*, Starkville, MS, USA, pp. 31–42, March 1999.

[15] T. Kimura, and H. Takemiya, Local Area Metacomputing for Multidisciplinary Problems: A Case Study for Fluid/-Structure Coupled Simulation, In *Proc. 12th Int. Conference on Supercomputing* Melbourne, Australia, pp. 149–156, July 1998.

[16] N. Karonis, B. Toonen, and I. Foster, MPICH-G2: A Grid-Enabled Implementation of the Message Passing Interface, *Journal of Parallel and Distributed Computing*, vol. 63, no. 5, pp. 551–563, May 2003.

[17] M. Chetlur, N. Abu-Ghazaleh, R. Radhakrishnan, and P.A. Wilsey, Optimizing Communication in Time-Warp Simulators, In *Proc. 12th Workshop on Parallel and Distributed Simulation*, Banff, AB, Canada, pp. 64–71, May 1998.

[18] C.D. Pham, Comparison of Message Aggregation Strategies for Parallel Simulations on a High Performance Cluster, In *Proc. 8th Int. Symposium on Modeling, Analysis and Simulation of Computer and Telecommunication Systems*, San Francisco, CA, USA, pp. 358–365, August-September 2000.

[19] L.A.H. Liang, W. Cai, B.-S. Lee, and S.J. Turner, Performance Analysis of Packet Bundling Techniques in DIS, In *Proc. 3rd Int. Workshop on Distributed Interactive Simulation and Real-Time Applications*, College Park, MD, USA, pp. 75–82, March 1999.

[20] M.S. Balsamo, and C. Manconi, Rollback Overhead Reduction Methods for Time Warp Distributed Simulation, *Simulation Practice and Theory*, vol. 6, no. 8, pp. 689–702, December 1998.

[21] B.J. Overeinder, A. Schoneveld, and P.M.A. Sloot, Spatio-Temporal Correlations and Rollback Distributions in Optimistic Simulations, In *Proc. 15th Workshop on Parallel and Distributed Simulation*, Lake Arrowhead, CA, USA, pp. 145–152, May 2001.

[22] P.M.A. Sloot, B.J. Overeinder, and A. Schoneveld, Self-organized Criticality in Simulated Correlated Systems, *Computer Physics Communications*, vol. 142, no. 1–3, pp. 76–81, December 2001.

Time Warp - Connection Oriented

Nasser Kalantery
Cavendish school of Computer Science
University of Westminster
115 New Cavendish St., London W1M 8JS
E-mail: kalantn@wmin.ac.uk

Abstract

Conservative parallel discrete event simulation takes a connection-oriented approach to inter-process communication. Conservative processes modeling physical entities are connected via channels that represent physical links in the target system. By contrast, optimistic strategy and its implementation in Time Warp machine, take a connectionless approach where a process can communicate freely with any other process without prior connection. This paper presents the case for a connection-oriented optimistic approach and provides a data structure for the event set of Time Warp processes that significantly reduces the cost of event scheduling and cancellation under connection-oriented operation. Detailed description of the proposed implementation is given and performance of the structure in forward event scheduling and backward event cancellation is tested and the results are discussed.

1. Introduction

In a Time Warp system [5] processes are allowed to push ahead with asynchronous parallel execution. Provisions are made to detect and rectify event ordering errors as and when they occur. A periodic check-pointing scheme is maintained whereby a process can be rolled back to a previously saved state whenever an ordering error is discovered. In the event of an error-detection, anti-messages are sent out to cancel the erroneous or unsafe output of the process. Forward execution along the corrected execution path can then be restarted. All these procedures are carried out by the Time Warp operating system and are hidden from the user.

Performance of Time Warp has been subject of a number of studies. A well known review paper by Fujimoto [4] is an essential read for the understanding of the subject area. Recent research into optimization or enhancement of the local control mechanism include the work of Zhang and Tropper[8] who study the impact of dependence list construction. Also considering local control structure, Carothers et. al.[1] propose and evaluate 'reverse computation' as part of the error correction mechanism. In [2] Chetlur and Wisely report on the performance of a proposed method that avoids cascading rollbacks in simulation of models with FIFO communication channels. Within that broader context, our work is focused on enhancement of the event set structure within the local control mechanism.

The impact of event set structure in Time Warp is two folds: it influences the pace of forward execution and it determines the time spent in a rollback. In both cases the event set must be searched. In forward execution the objective of the search is to find the correct position where a scheduled event can be inserted. In rollback, the objective of the search is to find the event entry that must be deleted (cancelled).

The cost of searching an event set depends on its implementation. If a linear list is used, the overall event handling costs increase proportionally to the event set size [6]. This is also true for the sequential simulation, where the need for more complex structures has been well documented. However, in the context of optimistic simulation, there is yet another, more significant side effect. The dependency of the event ordering costs on the size of each local event set implies that the slowest process (in simulated time), tending to accumulate a larger backlog of pending events, is made progressively slower. Thus the work load imbalance is further aggravated, which in turn leads to a greater number of rollbacks within the system. This effect was empirically demonstrated by

1087-4097/04 $20.00 © 2004 IEEE

Ronngren et al [7], where it was shown that the impact of event set implementation on the performance of the optimistic simulation can far exceed the improvement accounted for by simple reduction in event search cost. Particularly for asymmetric workloads, by more efficient input queue implementation the number and extent of rollbacks were reduced such that, as a result, a speedup improvement of an order of magnitude over linear list implementation was demonstrated. In this paper we show that by adopting a connection oriented approach the need for searching the event set during rollbacks can be eliminated. And search costs during forward execution can be significantly reduced.

2. Connection Oriented Time Warp

Connection oriented implementation of Time Warp is based on the two assumptions that underpin the dead-lock avoidance algorithm [3]. These assumptions are expressed below:

i) A message-passing process-oriented environment, wherein communication among processes takes place by exchange of messages over inter-process communication channels. Messages sent over a channel are delivered in the same order as they are transmitted.

ii) At the model implementation level, multiple links between two physical processes of a simulated system are represented by an equivalent number of logical channels.

Provided assumptions (i) and (ii) are satisfied *simulation messages* sent over a logical channel *within* each forward execution period (consecutive forward execution periods are separated by rollback operations) will have non-decreasing time-stamps. Given that messages arriving over a channel are maintained in separate queues, each separate queue takes a First-In-First-Out (FIFO) characteristic. FIFO queuing of messages received over a given channel corresponds to their queuing in increasing time-stamp order. This is a key point in our synthesis of a connection-oriented event set structure: we aim to take full advantage of the FIFO characteristic of channel queues. FIFO queues provide an extremely efficient direct access route to any required event that may need to be annihilated.

At each process messages, arriving over a given channel, are appended to the 'back' of the corresponding FIFO queue. During the simulation messages are selected from the front of the queue. At each queue the entry at the 'front' always contains the smallest time-stamp. Thus at each event selection point, instead of the entire set of unprocessed messages, only the front entry of each queue needs to be examined as a possible candidate. Hence the event search space is significantly reduced. Likewise when an anti message arrives over a channel, it finds its match directly at the back of the corresponding FIFO queue. Again search of the event set and associated costs are avoided.

Handling of FIFO queues in a Time Warp environment requires careful organization. The next section describes how this is achieved in our implementation. The source code for the described implementation is available on request from the author.

2.1. Event handling structure of a connection oriented Time Warp

In the event repository of every Time Warp process two types of events can be distinguished: unprocessed events and events that have been processed (at least once) and have not yet been deleted. After arriving on a specific input channel, an unprocessed event is appended to the 'back' of the respective FIFO queue. However when that event is eventually selected for processing , it is not removed from the FIFO queue. Only the queue 'front' pointer is advanced past the selected event. Therefore a FIFO queue consists of two sections: a 'future' section that contains the unprocessed events and another 'past' section where links to processed events remain intact. In our implementation these links are maintained for the sole purpose of providing a direct cancellation route to the processed as well as unprocessed events.

Once an event is processed it is entered into a so called Combined Input History (CIH). CIH is another FIFO queue, where at-least-once-processed messages from all input queues are maintained in their timestamp (VRT) order. When a roll back occurs the CIH queue provides the mechanism whereby once processed and now rolled back events can be reprocessed.

A process would typically have multiple input channels and hence multiple FIFO queues. At each 'next-event' selection point, any of the events residing at the front of each input queue may have the smallest time stamp. The number of input channels (but not the number of events in them!) constitutes the search space in this implementation of Time Warp. To that end FIFO queues of the process are maintained in a priority list such that the queue with smallest time-stamp at its front event can be always found at the head of the list. It is worth noting that while this is a necessary condition for the correct selection of the next-event, it is not however the sufficient one. The linked list contains only the events that have never been processed. Once processed events are kept in the CIH as described above. Therefore at each event selection

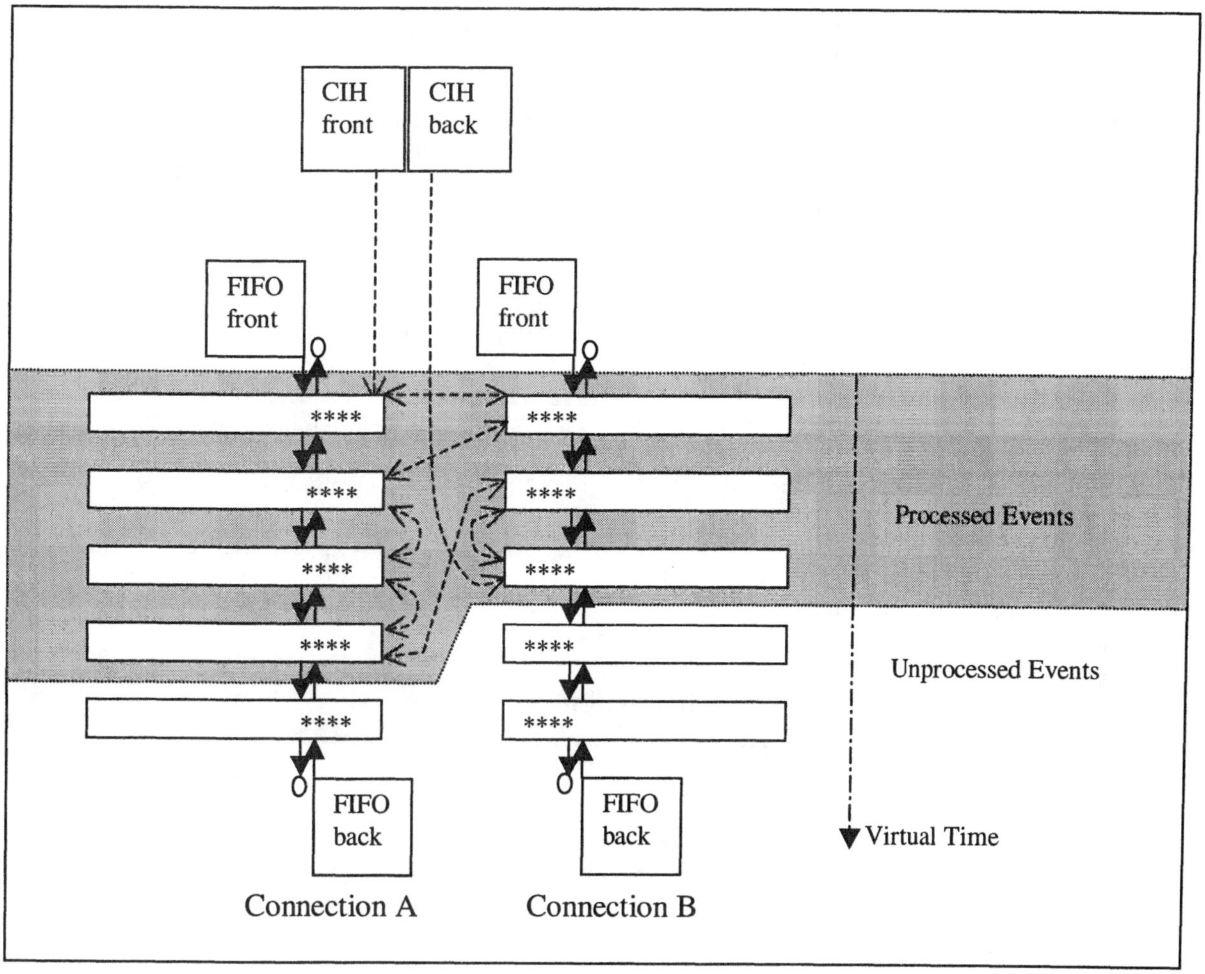

Figure 2.1. Combined input history in a simple process with two inward connections A & B.

point timestamp of the event at the head of CIH must be compared to the one at the head of the FIFO list. The event with the smallest timestamp can then be safely selected.

As mentioned earlier, links to processed messages also remain intact in the FIFO queues but are not used for reprocessing purposes. They are only used when cancellation messages arrive to annihilate these past events. Then they find them directly at the back of the 'past section' of the respective FIFO queue. Such messages are then directly delinked from the CIH as well as the FIFO queue. To facilitate direct delinking of random CIH entries, CIH entries are bi-directionally linked. Fig 2.1 provides an illustration of CIH and its relation to FIFO buffers. For simplicity here a process with two inward connections is depicted. CIH also serves as a direct and efficient route for fossil collection.

3. Empirical measurements

To measure the performance of the proposed data structure, the algorithm was implemented in C and the benchmarking experiments were carried out on a Dell PowerEdge 1400SC computing node with 1 GHz single Pentium III processor and 512MB of RAM running Red Hat Linux 7.0 operating system. The same tests were carried out on a linear list and a splay tree implementation. Linear list is a commonly used event set implementation that is known to perform well when the event set is small. Its performance however rapidly deteriorates as the event set grows in size. By contrast splay tree is one of the best performing data structures available that could possibly be adapted for optimistic simulation. It provides a benchmark for efficient search of large event sets.

The connection-based implementation includes all the features that were discussed above and thus represents all the associated overheads of the mechanism.

In each one of the experiments the pending event set was allowed to grow to the required size S (by inserting S events into the event list). The time-stamp of each event was sampled from a uniformly distributed random number generator. For connection-oriented structure a random input channel was also sampled from the same distribution. To maintain identical random number streams for both sets of experiments, 'channel selection' was performed for the other two benchmark structure as well (although it was not used). Once the initial event set was constructed in this manner, the performance measurement started. The measurements indicate the execution time spent in repeated insert/select (fig 1) and insert/cancel (fig 2). For each experimental point operations (insert/select or insert/cancel) were repeated 1000 times.

3.1. Event scheduling and selection

Figure 3.1 shows the relative event holding times for the linear list and splay tree as well as connection based structure. The event set size is shown in logarithmic scale. As expected, the figure indicates that the linear list performs best in situations where the event set size remains under 20 but its performance rapidly degrades as that size grows. The cost of splay tree scheduling also increases, moderately but surely, with the growing size of the event set.

Performance of our connection-based structure is represented in three distinct scenarios. At each scenario a different number of input channels (200, 32 or 8) is assumed. When the number of input channels is large (200 here) then as the number of pending events increases, more event-holding channels enter the fray and need to be ordered. Hence the cost grows proportionally. As the figure indicates when the number of channels is high, the cost of event

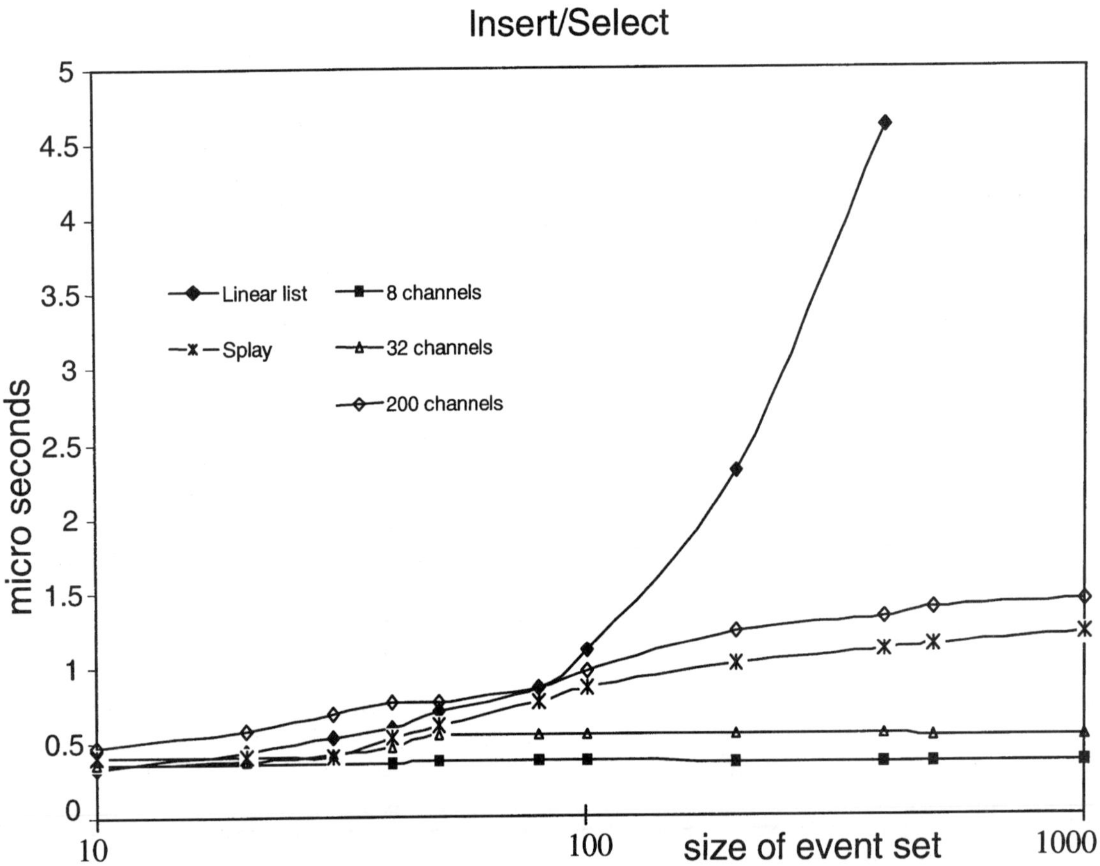

Figure 3.1. Comparison of event scheduling (insert/select) costs

scheduling in our structure can be greater than the splay tree. However, in our experience of modeling realistic systems (e.g. telecommunication, road traffic or biological networks) such a large number of interconnection channels between model entities (processes) is not encountered. For more realistic, small and moderate number of channels (8 and 32 in Fig 3.1) connection-based structure out-performs both of the two benchmarks. Its performance is largely independent of event set size and its costs remain constantly at a low level.

3.2. Event cancellation cost

Figure 3.2 represents the *insert/cancel* cost with the three data structures. As the figure indicates, the cost of event cancellation in linear list and Splay tree is related to the size of the event set which must be searched before the target event is found. Also it can be seen that in these two structures *insert/cancel* costs more than *insert /select* that was reported in Fig 3.1. This is due to the fact that *select* is concerned with the event at the head of the list (or the tree) and does not involve list or tree traversal while *cancel* requires a search comparable to *insert*. In a cancellation the search space may be either the set of the future events, which have not yet been processed, or the set of the past events (but not the sum of the two). The past events are searched when the cancellation time refers to the time in the past of the process. Otherwise the future events are searched. The size of the past event set may differ in various applications implementations. For instance, search through the state queue may reduce the set of the past events that are to be visited. However, for the set of unprocessed events the need for the traversal of the linear list and/or splay tree remains independent of the state queue. And in a slow process it is the backlog of unprocessed events that is expected to grow large.

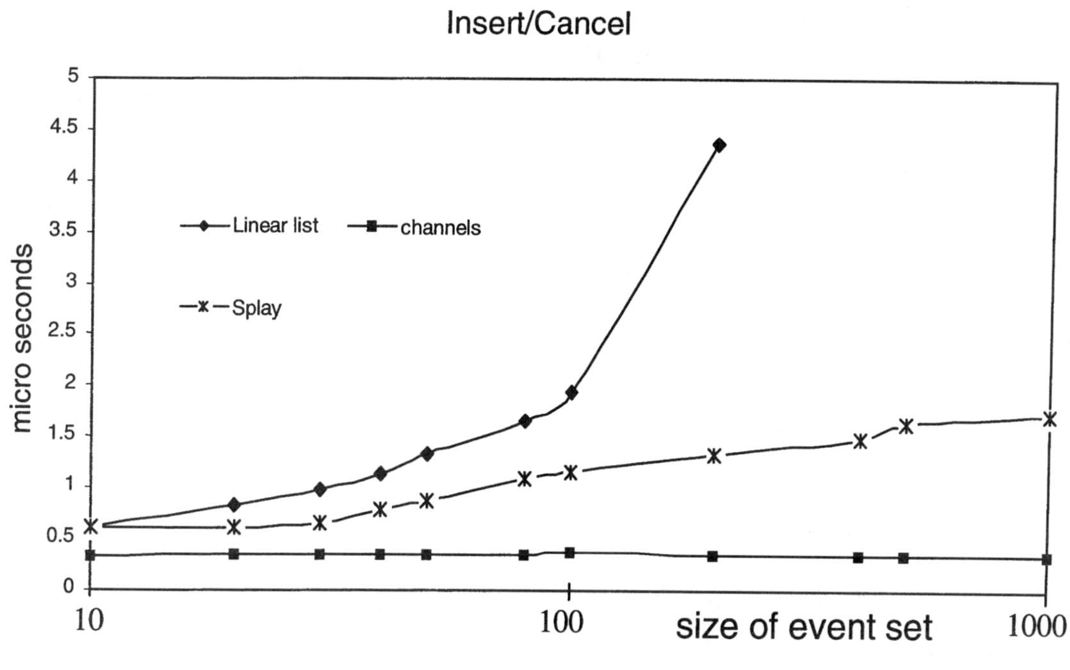

Figure 3.2. Comparison of event cancellation (insert/cancel) costs

As the figure shows, the event cancellation time in connection oriented structure remains constant and at all times smaller than that of the two benchmarks. This is due to the fact that neither *insert* nor *cancel* requires a search in our connection-oriented structure. FIFO queues provide a direct access in both operations.

Connection-based structure outperforms both the linear list and the Splay tree in all cases and the margin grows as the size of the event set increases. Even at a modest event set size of 40, a cancellation in linear list cost three times, and in splay two times that of the connection based structure.

3.3. Discussion

Generally in any discrete event simulation most of the processing time is spent on operations on the event set structure. But the impact on Time Warp performance is expected to be even more pronounced: the structure dictates the pace of the forward execution and it also determines the time spent in each rollback. This two-fold dependency on the event set structure is further exacerbated by the fact that in an optimistic execution slower processes tend to accumulate a larger backlog of pending events. When event ordering costs increase as a function of the number of pending events, a slow process is made progressively slower. This increases the workload imbalance, which in turn leads to a higher number of rollbacks. And if the cost of event cancellation is dependent on the size of the event set, each rollback constitutes a progressively greater overhead. The overall system performance is bound to suffer as a result. Experimental results reported above show that in our proposed structure event cancellation costs are extremely low and entirely independent of the size of the event set. Forward event scheduling costs are also independent of the event set size and are only influenced by the number of inward connections (input channels) at each process, a number that, in most practical applications, remains small and stable (if not constant) throughout the execution.

The advantages of connection-oriented approach are therefore clear. The approach provides a mechanism whereby dramatic reductions in processing time of both forward event scheduling and backward event cancellations can be achieved. The experiments reported above demonstrated that for an event set size of 1000 in a process with inward connections of 8, connection-based structure is over an order of magnitude (12 times) faster in forward event scheduling than the linear list, and 45 times (%4500) faster in event cancellation. Compared to splay tree, one of the best performing structures known, our structure performs over 3 times (%350) faster in forward execution and over 5 times (%560) faster in rollbacks.

4. Group Cancellation

Under connection-oriented approach, a group of messages sent over a connection can be easily annihilated by a single *group cancellation* message. Figure 4.1 illustrates the group cancellation of messages over a given connection. Messages are depicted as boxes with time-stamps: cancellation-messages are depicted as crossed out boxes. As the figure indicates the same result can be achieved either by transmission of multiple individual anti-messages or one single group cancellation message. In the figure the time-stamp of the group cancellation message is 9.2. This indicates that all messages with timestamp

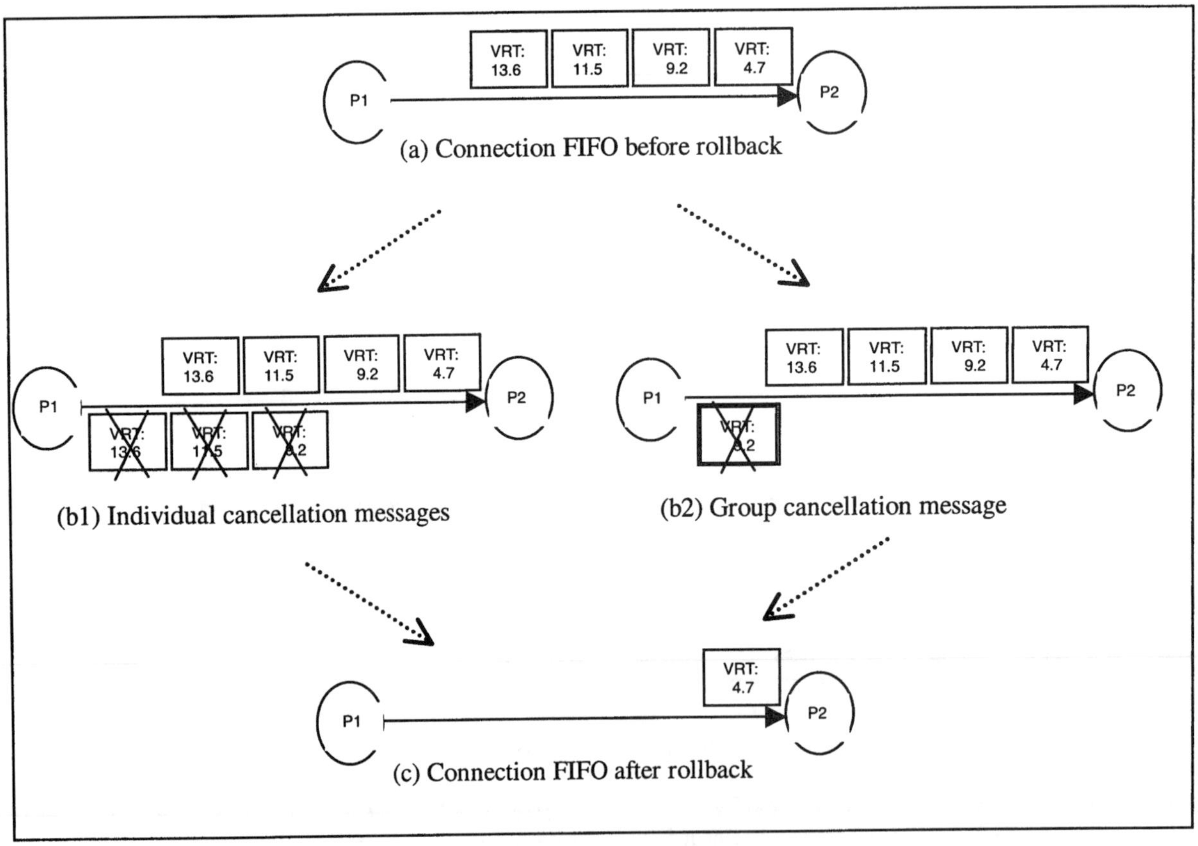

Figure 4.1. Group cancellation in a connection oriented setting

9.2 or greater, sent over this connection, are invalid and must be annihilated. Group cancellation saves on the required number of cancellation messages and is expected to provide further significant reductions in rollback overheads.

5. Conclusion

Connection oriented approach to inter-process communication provides the opportunity for a significantly improved input handling mechanism in Time Warp environment. In this paper we presented a structure that outperforms two of the best-known alternatives available to connectionless implementations: linear linked list and splay tree. The proposed connection based approach is based on similar assumptions that operate in the conservative deadlock avoidance algorithm. Most physical systems such as information, transportation and biological networks are naturally modeled as a set of processes with pre-defined inter-process communication channels. For such applications our proposed approach is a natural fit that promises a significantly improved performance too. In addition to cost saving in event set structure, connection oriented approach allows a simple method of group cancellation whereby communication costs of rollbacks can be reduced. We are currently working on an implementation of Time Warp operating system that will incorporate the structure introduced in this paper.

6. References

1. Carothers C D, Perumalla K, Fujimoto R M, "Efficient Optimistic Parallel Simulation using Reverse Computation, ACM TOMACS, 2000.

2. Chetlur M and Wilsey P A, Causality Representation and Cancellation Mechanism in Time Warp Simulations, Proceedings of the 15th workshop on Parallel and Distributed Simulation(PADS'2001), IEEE, May 2001.

3. Chandy, K. M. and Misra, J. Asynchronous distributed simulation via a sequence of parallel computations. Commun. ACM 24, 11 (November 1981), 198-205.

4. Fujimoto, R. M. Parallel Discrete Event Simulation, Communications of the ACM, vol. 33, No. 10, October 1990.

5. Jefferson, D. R. Virtual time. ACM Trans. Prog. Lang. and Syst. 7, 3 (July 1985), 404-425.

6. Jones, D. W. An empirical comparison of priority queue and event-set implementations. Commun. ACM 29, 4 (April 1986), 300-311.

7. Ronngren, R. Ayani, R. Fujimoto, R. M. and Das, S. R. Efficient implementation of event sets in Time Warp. In Proceedings of 7th Workshop on Parallel and distributed simulation PADS93, (May 1993).

8. Zhang J L and Tropper C, The Dependence List in Time Warp", Proceedings of the 15th workshop on Parallel and Distributed Simulation(PADS'2001), IEEE, May 2001.

Batch Based Cancellation: A Rollback Optimal Cancellation Scheme in Time Warp Simulations

Yi Zeng Wentong Cai Stephen J Turner
School of Computer Engineering
Nanyang Technological University
Singapore 639798
{pg00847560, aswtcai, assjturner}@ntu.edu.sg

Abstract

An efficient cancellation scheme is essential to the performance of Time Warp simulations. The pitfalls of rollback echoes, chasing hazards and cascading rollbacks can be identified as being attributable to the inefficiency of the conventional per-event based cancellation scheme. Instead of capturing the happen-before relation between events, which is used by the range based cancellation scheme, the batch based cancellation scheme proposed in this paper utilizes a modified paradigm of vector time, namely, state vector, to capture the dependence of events. We prove that with conformance to specific rules regulating the advancement of LPs*, the events to be cancelled by a straggler message can be determined using a range of the state vector. Thus, knowledge of the range enables any* LP *to recover from the receipt of a straggler message at the cost of at most one rollback (i.e., rollback optimal). The results of preliminary experiments conducted using a manufacturing model show that the proposed scheme is successful in reducing the number of anti-messages and increasing the ratio of the number of committed events to the number of processed events.*

1 Introduction

In Time Warp simulations, the dependence of events can be expressed using state dependence or scheduling dependence or a transitive closure of both [4]. For any two processed but not yet rolled back events at the same *LP*, the later event is defined to be state dependent on the earlier event due to the order of their accesses to the *LP*'s state variables; for an event scheduling another event, the latter is defined to be scheduling dependent on the former. To remove the wrong computations based on an event when it is rolled back, all events that depend on it have to be cancelled [1].

The conventional way of cancelling events is solely carried out on a per-event basis. When an *LP* decides to cancel an external event which was previously scheduled by an outgoing positive message, it proceeds by constructing its counterpart, namely, an anti-message, and sending it to the same destinations. Upon receipt of the positive message and its anti-message, the receiving *LP* cancels the scheduled event and performs necessary rollbacks if that event has been processed.

The above cancellation scheme empirically proves to be simple and feasible in Time Warp simulations. But it still leaves performance concerns behind and has drawn researchers' attention. Given that *LPs* proceed aggressively in a Time Warp simulation, during the period between processing an incoming positive message and receiving its anti-message, a certain amount of events may have been scheduled by an *LP*. Without loss of generality, these events are dependent on the cancelled event, hence need to be rolled back by means of sending further anti-messages. For the cancellations triggered by a straggler message, it is apparent that the cost is mainly dominated by the way *LPs* process and cancel events. In the presence of dynamic CPU workload and varying channel speed in a parallel or a distributed simulation, the cost is hardly predictable.

Several pitfalls in Time Warp simulations which can be attributable to the cost of cancellations have been figured out by researchers. Rollback echoes and chasing hazards have been identified [4] in particular circumstances which could severely impact or even destroy the simulation. Multiple rollbacks, an inherent performance pitfall of the conventional cancellation scheme, has been investigated in [2], which argues that anti-messages may result in unwanted multiple rollbacks at a single *LP* and trigger a cascading rollback situation,

[1] In this paper, "cancel" means not only a rollback of a processed event but also a cancellation of an unprocessed event.

1087-4097/04 $20.00 © 2004 IEEE

where the rollback cycles back to the original LP where the straggler message was received.

There are many approaches that have been proposed to reduce the cost of cancellations. As opposed to aggressive cancellation, lazy cancellation [5] reduces the number of anti-messages by delaying the sending of anti-messages till reprocessing of the event produces a different positive message. Unfortunately, the performance comparison shows that lazy cancellation can arbitrarily outperform aggressive cancellation and vice versa [11]. Lazy re-evaluation [14] lets an LP directly jump back to the state prior to when the rollback occurred if the straggler message does not affect its state. To avoid chasing hazards, wolf calls [9] expedite the propagation of the knowledge of cancellations by sending protocol messages with higher-priority over positive messages in their transmission. However, all these approaches do not address the inefficiency of the conventional per-event based cancellation scheme itself.

Chetlur and Wilsey addressed this issue and proposed the range based cancellation scheme [2] by taking advantage of vector time [12, 10], a well-understood mechanism to capture the happen-before relation (denoted as $\rightarrow$) [7] between events in distributed systems. A new type of message, namely, *CANCEL_MESSAGE*, was introduced as a replacement of anti-messages in Time Warp simulations. By exploiting the happen-before relation among messages, the range information carried by a single *CANCEL_MESSAGE* is capable of cancelling multiple events at an LP, thus the number of messages sent among LPs can be reduced and many unwanted rollbacks can be avoided.

However, further study reveals that Chetlur and Wilsey's approach cannot guarantee the removal of all unwanted rollbacks. In other words, some LPs still suffer from multiple rollbacks to cancel events incurred by a straggler message (so the scheme is not rollback optimal). In this paper, the batch based cancellation scheme is proposed to address this problem.

The remainder of this paper is organized as follows. Section 2 presents several concerns in Chetlur and Wilsey's approach which motivate our further investigation. Section 3 presents the basic mechanism, state vector, which is employed to capture the dependence of events in Time Warp simulations. Based on this machanism, Section 4 gives supporting theories which prove the possibility of a rollback optimal cancellation scheme. This results in our implementation, the batch based cancellation scheme, which is elaborated in Section 5. Section 6 presents the experimental results obtained from the comparison of the conventional cancellation scheme and our batch based cancellation scheme running on a manufacturing model [8]. Section 7 concludes the paper.

2 Motivation

In discrete event simulations (DES), the delivery order of scheduled events at an LP is mandatorily determined by their simulation time, a virtual representation of the real time in the physical system being modelled. This rule is also referred to as the local causality constraint (LCC). LCC is prone to being violated in Time Warp simulations because the optimistic advancement of LPs gives rise to the possibility of receiving a straggler message, a positive message scheduling a "past" event, at an LP. Once this happens, LPs have to cancel wrong computations accordingly. Figure 1 shows a common cancellation scenario found in Time Warp simulations, where the events are denoted as black dots and scheduling of the events through positive messages and cancellation of the events through anti-messages are represented as solid arrows and dashed arrows respectively. In addition, the straggler message is labelled with S.

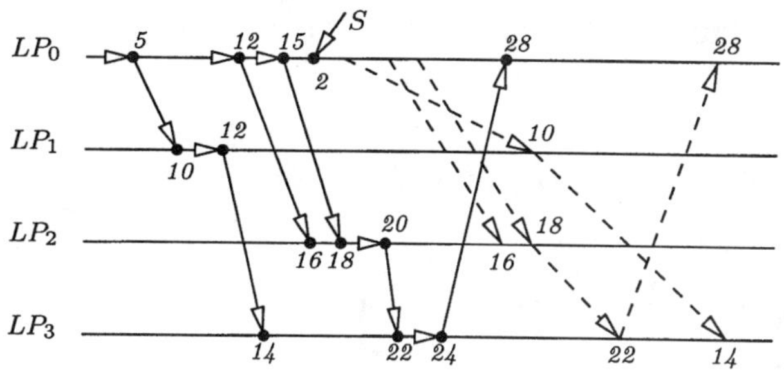

Figure 1. Per-event based cancellations triggered by a straggler message

The performance concern of the conventional scheme can be explained using Figure 1. (1) When LP_0 receives the anti-message for event $e_{0,28}$[2], LP_0 may have already advanced to a certain time in the future and scheduled considerable events. Further efforts are therefore needed to cancel these wrong computations. (2) Because the anti-messages for events $e_{3,14}$ and $e_{3,22}$ are sent from different LPs, LP_3 may suffer from more rollbacks if the anti-message for $e_{3,14}$ arrives later.

The mechanism of Chetlur and Wilsey's approach is shown in Figure 2, where the dashed arrows represent the *CANCEL_MESSAGEs*. The combination of simulation time (the first component) and vector time (the remaining N components) forms the Total Clock, where N is the number of LPs in the simulation (N = 4 here). Total Clock is always sent along

[2]To simplify the representation, $e_{i,t}$ denotes the event scheduled at LP_i with time-stamp t.

with messages (not shown in the figure). The updating rules of simulation time and vector time are independent from each other and correspond to those defined in [2, 6, 7]. Each *CANCEL_MESSAGE* carries a range, denoted by $[a, b]_i$, which indicates that the set of events that have been cancelled at LP_i are those whose i^{th} component of vector time lies in between a and b. Based on a received range, the receiving LP cancels events by checking their vector time. A new range for the cancelled events is then deduced and sent out via new *CANCEL_MESSAGEs* (if the range is not empty).

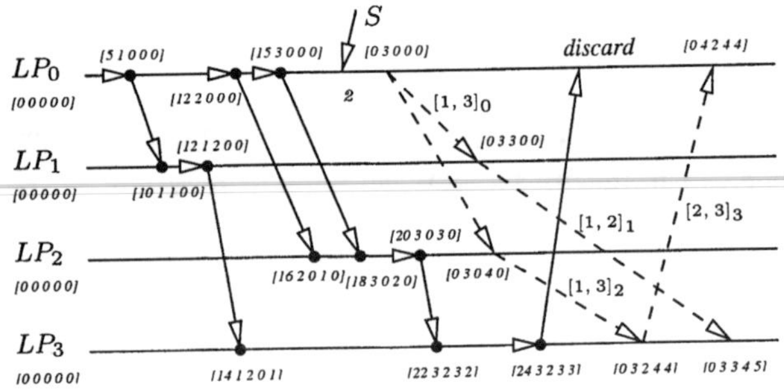

Figure 2. The range based cancellations triggered by a straggler message

Comparing Figure 2 with Figure 1, it can be seen that Chetlur and Wilsey's approach has several advantages. (1) A *CANCEL_MESSAGE* is capable of cancelling multiple events. Upon receipt of range $[1, 3]_0$, LP_2 is able to cancel events $e_{2,16}$, $e_{2,18}$ and $e_{2,20}$. This results in a new range $[1, 3]_2$ being sent to LP_3. (2) Because the received ranges are recorded at LPs, an LP has intelligence to discard some incoming messages which are to be eventually cancelled so as to prevent wrong computations from being further propagated. For example, LP_3 schedules an event at LP_0 at simulation time 24. Because event $e_{0,15} \rightarrow e_{3,24}$ and $e_{0,15}$ has already been cancelled, the event scheduled by $e_{3,24}$ is simply discarded based on the range $[1, 3]_0$ recorded at LP_0.

Regarding the number of rollbacks from which an LP may suffer to thoroughly remove the wrong computations incurred by a certain straggler message, we define a cancellation scheme to be rollback optimal if any affected LP is guaranteed to be recovered at the cost of at most one rollback. Chetlur and Wilsey's approach has reduced rollbacks to some extent, however, it is not rollback optimal (in Figure 2, LP_3 rolls back twice). A rollback optimal cancellation scheme requires some kind of mechanism to identify all the events which are destined to be cancelled upon receipt of a straggler message.

3 State Vector

The happen-before relation proves to be the most basic but universal partial order relation in distributed systems and vector time proves to be the simplest means to characterize it [1, 12]. However, vector time (as shown in [2]) is not an ideal candidate to capture dependence of events. This is illustrated in Figure 3. LP_i schedules e_{j,t_2} and later on cancels it due to the rollback caused by a straggler message. For events e' and e'' scheduled by LP_j, where e' is scheduled after e_{j,t_2} but before the cancellation and e'' is scheduled after the cancellation, both $e_{i,t_1} \rightarrow e'$ and $e_{i,t_1} \rightarrow e''$ hold. But, in fact, e'' does not depend on e_{i,t_1}.

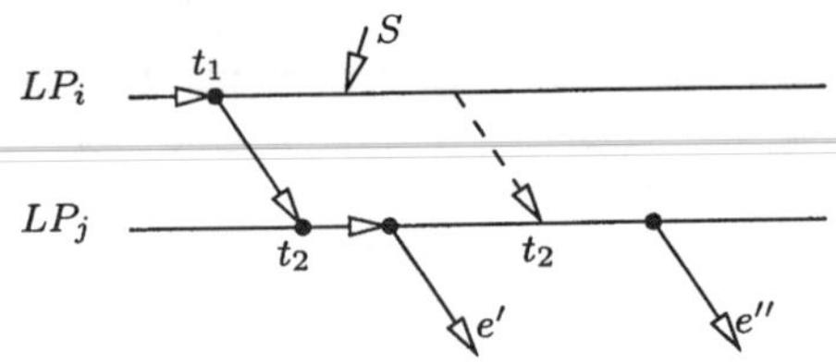

Figure 3. Happen-before relation between events

Suppose that every LP changes its state whenever it processes an event. A monotonically increasing scalar, namely, state counter, is introduced into each LP to uniquely identify its state. A vector of state counters, namely, state vector, is constructed at each LP as well. For LP_i's state vector, denoted as $SV(LP_i)$, $SV(LP_i)[j]$, $j \neq i$ reflects LP_i's current knowledge of LP_j's latest state counter, while $SV(LP_i)[i]$ is just the placeholder of its own state counter.

The propagating and updating rules of LP_i's state vector are shown in Figure 4. It can be seen that the last rule makes state vector different from vector time.

With the rules in Figure 4, $SV(LP_i)[i]$ uniquely identifies an event processed at LP_i. Given an event e processed by an LP with state vector $SV(e)$, the latest event in LP_i on which e depends can, therefore, be determined by $SV(e)[i]$ (formally stated in Theorem 4.4). Looking back to Figure 3 again, the link is broken because $SV(e'')[i]$ is restored from an earlier state. $SV(e'')[i] < SV(e_{i,t_1})[i]$ indicates that e'' does not depend on e_{1,t_1}. Other properties of state vector and dependence are exploited in Section 4.

4 Characterization of Cancelled Events

A widely accepted model [12] is adopted and modified in the proof of the following theorems. A Time Warp simulation is viewed as consisting of N sequential LPs, communicating solely by exchanging two

1. Let N be the number of *LPs* in the simulation. Initially, $SV(LP_i)[k] = 0$, $0 \leq i, k < N$.
2. Let $SV_m(e)$ be the state vector of e which is piggybacked on its scheduling message m and let $SV(e)$ be the state vector of e at the time e is processed. When LP_i processes e, these updates are performed: $SV(LP_i)[i]$ first increases by one; then $SV(LP_i) = sup(SV(LP_i), SV_m(e))$, where *sup* performs component-wise maximum operation; then $SV(e) = SV(LP_i)$.
3. At the time LP_i schedules event e, either for itself or for another *LP*, $SV(LP_i)$ is piggybacked on the scheduling message, i.e., $SV_m(e) = SV(LP_i)$.
4. Except for $SV(LP_i)[i]$, other components of SV are state saved. At the time a rollback occurs at LP_i, $SV(LP_i)[i]$ increases by one and other components are restored from the state to which LP_i rolls back.

Figure 4. The propagating and updating rules of state vector at LP_i

kinds of messages, namely, positive messages and *CANCEL_MESSAGEs*. Each *LP* changes its state whenever it processes the event scheduled by a positive message or performs a rollback. The transmission channels are assumed reliable and FIFO.

Let E_i denote the set of events processed at LP_i, and let $E = \bigcup_{i=0}^{N-1} E_i$ denote the set of all events processed in the simulation. As we assume that each LP_i is strictly sequential, we can index the events of LP_i in their processing order: $E_i = \{e_{i1}, e_{i2}, \ldots, e_{in}, \ldots\}$. This processing order is referred to as the *standard enumeration* of E_i. Given E_i, the local successor set of event e_{in}, denoted as $\mathcal{S}_l(e_{in})$, represents all the events locally processed after e_{in}, $\mathcal{S}_l(e_{in}) = \{e_{ik} | k > n\}$.

Theorem 4.1 through Theorem 4.5 state the properties of state vector and the dependence of events. They are obvious by applying the rules shown in Figure 4 and are listed below without proving.

Theorem 4.1. *Let $e \Rightarrow e'$ denote that event e' depends on e. Dependence is transitive, i.e., for three events e, e' and e'', if $e \Rightarrow e'$ and $e' \Rightarrow e''$, it also holds that $e \Rightarrow e''$.*

Theorem 4.2. *$SV(LP_i)[i]$ increases monotonically throughout a simulation.*

Theorem 4.3. *For any event $e_{ik} \in E_i$, $SV(e_{ik})[i] = k$.*

Theorem 4.4. *For event $e' \in E_j$, suppose that $SV(e')[i] = k$, then $e_{ik} \Rightarrow e'$.*

Theorem 4.5. *For events $e_{ik} \in E_i$ and $e' \in E_j$, if $e_{ik} \Rightarrow e'$, then $SV(e')[i] >= k$.*

Observing that receiving straggler messages is the root cause of rollbacks in *LPs*, let m_s denote a straggler message received at LP_o. LP_o is thus named as rollback originator. During the cancellations triggered by m_s (for the ease of discussion, assume there is no other intervening cancellations triggered by other straggler messages), let $C_i(m_s)$ denote the set of events cancelled at LP_i and $C(m_s)$ denote all the events cancelled in the simulation. Thus, $C(m_s) = \bigcup_{i=0}^{N-1} C_i(m_s)$. Note that for $i \neq o$, $C_i(m_s)$ is essentially the set of events that have dependence on the events in $C_o(m_s)$, i.e., $\{e' | e' \in E_i \wedge \exists e \in C_o(m_s), e \Rightarrow e'\}$.

Although $C(m_s)$ can be expressed in terms of $C_o(m_s)$, $C_o(m_s)$ or $C(m_s)$ is still unpredictable without any regulation of the advancement of *LPs*. To be able to identify $C_o(m_s)$, which is expressed as a range (shown in Theorem 4.7), and furthermore, identify $C(m_s)$ using this range (shown in Theorem 4.8), the rules of event processing at LP_i are given in Figure 5. In the first rule, if event e is processed, it would be rolled back unnecessarily because e' will be eventually cancelled. In the second and the third rules, event e can be discarded immediately as it is known to be dependent on a cancelled event.

At the time LP_i processes event e, where $SV_m(e) = \{x_0, x_1, \ldots, x_{N-1}\}$,

1. If a processed (but not yet committed) event e' at LP_i depends on a cancelled event e_{jk}, $j \neq i$, $k \leq x_j$ on which e does not depend, processing of e is blocked until e' has been cancelled;
2. If e_{ix_i} has been cancelled locally, e is discarded without processing.
3. If e depends on a cancelled event e_{jk}, $j \neq i$, $k \leq SV(LP_i)[j]$, e is discarded without processing.

Figure 5. The rules of event processing at LP_i

Theorem 4.6. *Suppose that the rollback originator LP_o receives straggler message m_s and events e_{oa} and e_{ob} are the earliest and latest events among those being cancelled by LP_o. It holds that,*

$$C_o(m_s) = \{e_{oa}\} + \mathcal{S}_l(e_{oa}) - \mathcal{S}_l(e_{ob}).$$

Proof. The event set $\{e_{oa}\} + \mathcal{S}_l(e_{oa}) - \mathcal{S}_l(e_{ob})$ represents all the events cancelled by LP_o upon receipt of straggler message m_s. The second rule in Figure 5 prohibits their effects from further spreading at LP_o, hence this set essentially equals $C_o(m_s)$. □

Theorem 4.7. *The oth component of the state vector of events in $C_o(m_s)$ forms a continuous range $[a,b]_o$, that is,*

1. $\forall k \in [a,b]_o,\ e_{ok} \in C_o(m_s)$;
2. $\forall e_{ok} \in E_o$ *and* $e_{ok} \notin C_o(m_s),\ k \notin [a,b]_o$.

Proof. From Theorem 4.3, $SV(e_{oa})[o] = a$ and $SV(e_{ob})[o] = b$. According to Theorem 4.2 and Theorem 4.6, the correctness is obvious. □

Theorem 4.7 offers an efficient way to convey the set of events being cancelled at a rollback originator to other *LPs* (recall the similar way in which *CANCEL_MESSAGEs* work in the range based cancellation scheme). As shown in the next section, our proposed scheme also employs *CANCEL_MESSAGEs* to carry these ranges.

Theorem 4.8. *Given range $[a,b]_o$ representing $C_o(m_s)$, $\forall e \in E_i$, $i \neq o$,*
$e \in C_i(m_s)$ *iff* $SV(e)[o] \in [a,b]_o$.

Proof. (1) Necessity. On one hand, for any event $e \in C_i(m_s)$, it holds that $\exists k \in [a,b]_o$, $e_{ok} \Rightarrow e$. Applying Theorem 4.5, $SV(e)[o] \geq k \geq a$. On the other hand, it must hold that $SV(e)[o] \leq b$. Otherwise, assume $SV(e)[o] = k' > b$, then $e_{ok'} \Rightarrow e$ according to Theorem 4.4. $e_{ok'}$ does not depend on any event in $C_o(m_s)$, or it should have been discarded according to the second rule in Figure 5. Therefore, e must have dependence on other events as shown in Figure 6, where dependence of events is denoted as curved arrows. There must be two events e'' and e' which were processed in this order at LP_i, $i \neq o$: e depends on e'' and e'' depends on an event $e_{ok''}$ in $C_o(m_s)$ as $e \in C_i(m_s)$; e is identical to or depends on e' and e' depends on $e_{ok'}$ as the knowledge of k' was propagated to e; e'' was processed before e' (otherwise, e'' was discarded by LP_i according to the third rule in Figure 5). This violates the first rule in Figure 5 at the time LP_i processed e' because processing of e' should have been blocked until e'' was cancelled. (2) Sufficiency. Let $SV(e)[o] = k$, $k \in [a,b]_o$. Applying Theorem 4.4, $e_{ok} \Rightarrow e$. Because $e_{ok} \in C_o(m_s)$, $e \in C_i(m_s)$. □

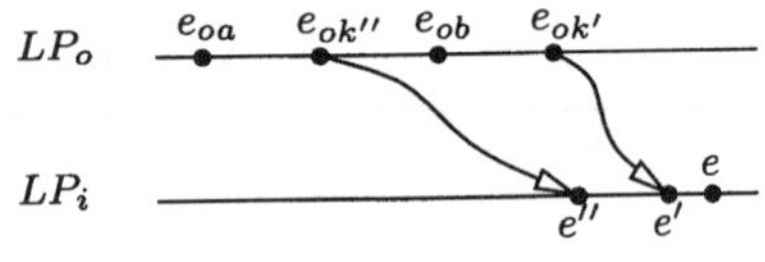

Figure 6. The dependence of event e

The rules in Figure 5 and Theorem 4.6 through Theorem 4.8 form the basis for a rollback optimal cancellation scheme. The essential difference from the range based scheme is that instead of continuously constructing ranges along the propagation path of *CANCEL_MESSAGEs*, which could gradually limit their abilities to determine events in $C_i(m_s)$, $i \neq o$ (see ranges $[1,3]_0$ and $[1,3]_2$ in Figure 2), a rollback optimal cancellation scheme comes to the conclusion that LP_i is able to directly deduce what $C_i(m_s)$ is like based on the received $[a,b]_o$ from the rollback originator LP_o. For any processed events in $C_i(m_s)$, LP_i performs a single rollback to cancel all of them; For any received but not yet processed events or any events arriving in future, LP_i simply discards them if they are identified to be in $C_i(m_s)$. This ensures that any *LP* will discard all those events to be cancelled by a straggler message in a batch manner and at the cost of at most one rollback (rollback optimal).

5 Batch based Cancellation Scheme

5.1 Rollback History

From Section 4, it can be seen that the rules in Figure 5 are essential for the correctness of the scheme. Empirically, these rules can be fulfilled by employing the concept of rollback history. We have shown in Theorem 4.7 and Theorem 4.8 that range $[a,b]_o$ identifies all the events in $C(m_s)$. The rollback history of an *LP*, denoted as $RH(LP)$, is actually defined as a list of those ranges that were locally generated or learnt from other *LPs* through message passing.

Piggybacking its current rollback history on any event scheduled by an *LP* makes it possible for other *LPs* to process the event in the way that satisfies the first rule in Figure 5. Particularly, at the time an *LP* processes event e, it first looks into those events that have been processed but not yet committed. If an event that is to be cancelled by a certain range in the rollback history carried by e is found, processing of e is blocked until that event is cancelled.

The greatest challenge to the above approach is the increasing size of rollback histories carried by events, which could incur significant communication cost and storage cost, and render the approach itself empirically useless. Thanks to the FIFO property of communication channels, communication cost can be reduced by sending rollback histories incrementally and reconstructing them at the receiving *LPs*. To do this, a similar technique to that of compressing vector time described in [13] is employed together with more sophisticated data structures.

LP_i locally maintains a rollback history table, denoted as $RHT(LP_i)$. For $0 \leq j < N$, $j \neq i$, $RHT(LP_i)[j]$ records LP_i's latest knowledge of

$RH(LP_j)$. $RHT(LP_i)[i]$ is the placeholder of LP_i, but in addition, each range inside is tagged with a scalar, and denoted as $[a,b]_o^s$, where s was the current value of LP_i's state counter when the range was recorded. LP_i keeps a "last scheduling" vector, denoted as $LS(LP_i)$, as well. $LS(LP_i)[j]$, $0 \le j < N$, $j \ne i$, tracks the latest value of LP_i's state counter when an event was scheduled at LP_j.

Let $\Delta RH(e)$ denote the increment of the sender LP's rollback history piggybacked on e, and let $RH(e)$ denote its reconstructed rollback history at the receiving LP. The updating rules of $RHT(LP_i)$ are shown in Figure 7.

1. Initially, $RHT(LP_i)[j]$, $0 \le j < N$, is set empty, and $LS(LP_i)[j] = 0$, $0 \le j < N$.
2. At the time LP_i receives event e from LP_j, $\Delta RH(e)$ is appended to the end of $RHT(LP_i)[j]$ and then emptied. The reconstructed $RH(e)$ is the current value of $RHT(LP_i)[j]$, represented by a pointer to the current end of the latter.
3. At the time LP_i processes an event e from LP_j, $\forall [a,b]_o \in RH(e)$, $[a,b]_o^{SV(LP_i)[i]}$ is merged (without any duplication) into $RHT(LP_i)[i]$, and then $[a,b]_o$ is removed from $RHT(LP_i)[j]$.
4. At the time LP_i schedules an event e to LP_j, $\Delta RH(e)$ is first set to the list of ranges in $\{[a,b]_o | [a,b]_o^s \in RHT(LP_i)[i] \wedge s > LS(LP_i)[j]\}$. $LS(LP_i)[j]$ is then updated with the current $SV(LP_i)[i]$.

Figure 7. Updating rollback history table in FIFO environments

Note that in the third rule, removal of ranges from $RHT(LP_i)[j]$ means that it is not an exact reconstructed $RH(e)$ in the strict sense. However, its correctness is obvious.

The rollback history table is also subject to fossil collection. After a GVT calculation cycle, let x_j, $0 \le j < N$, be the maximum state counter fossil collected at LP_j. Because it holds that there are no events (including transient events) dependent on any cancelled event e_{jk}, $k < x_j$, $\forall [a,b]_j \in RHT(LP_i)$, $[a,b]_j$ is discarded if $b \le x_j$.

5.2 Routines

An LP is assumed to have a similar architecture to that depicted in [3], which routinely maintains three queues, namely, the input queue (IQ), the output queue (OQ) and the state queue (SQ). Because *CANCEL_MESSAGEs* are processed at the time they are received and will not be rolled back for reprocessing, an IQ only queues positive messages. Let E_{IQ_i} denote the currently buffered processed events, i.e., neither having been rolled back nor fossil collected, at IQ_i. It is obvious that $E_{IQ_i} \subseteq E_i$ and empirically only events in $E_{IQ_i} \cap C_i(m_s)$ are considered to be rolled back by the straggler message m_s.

Let $ST(e)$ and $ST(LP_i)$ denote the simulation time of event e and LP_i respectively, and let $m.e$ denote the event scheduled by message m. The major routines of the batch based cancellation scheme are presented in Figure 8 through Figure 11.

```
PROCESS(m) {
  /* Rule 1 in Figure 5 */
  IF (∀[a,b]ₒ ∈RH(m.e), ∄e' ∈ E_IQi ,SV(e')[o]∈[a,b]) {
    ST(LPi)=ST(m.e);
    SV(LPi)[i]++;
    SV(LPi)=sup(SV(LPi),SVm(m.e));
    /* Rule 3 in Figure 7 */
    merge RH(m.e) into RHT(LPi)[i];
    execute m.e;
  }
}
```

Figure 8. Processing a scheduled event at LP_i

```
SCHEDULE(e) {
  construct message m scheduling e;
  set ST(m.e);
  SVm(m.e)=SV(LPi);
  /* Rule 4 in Figure 7 */
  set ΔRH(m.e);
  queue m into OQi and send m to its destinations;
}
```

Figure 9. Scheduling an event at LP_i

Figure 8 shows the steps for LP_i to process a positive message from IQ_i. LP_i first checks if it is safe to proceed. If yes, LP_i continues with updating its simulation time, state vector and rollback history table, and then executing the scheduled event, which involves saving LP_i's current state in SQ_i, updating the current state and probable scheduling of new events (Figure 9). Note that since possible receipt of straggler messages has been detected and handled at an earlier stage (see Figure 10), the messages to be delivered here can be processed without further checking for causality violations.

Figure 10 demonstrates the handling of a message when it is received from the communication channel. Basically there are four different ways according to the criteria the message meets. (1) Message m is a *CANCEL_MESSAGE* carrying a range. LP_i first checks if any processed event falls within the range. If there is,

```
RECEIVE(m) { /* m from LPj */
  IF (m is a CANCEL_MESSAGE) {
    IF (∃ min k, eik ∈ EIQi ∧ eik in m's range) {
      ROLLBACK(eik, m);
    }
    merge m's range into RHT(LPi)[i];
    ∀m' ∈ IQi, discard m' if m' in m's range;
  } ELSE {
    /* Rule 2 in Figure 7 */
    reconstruct RH(m.e);
    IF (∃[a,b]^s_o ∈RHT(LPi)[i], SV(m.e)[o]∈[a,b]) {
      /* Rule 2 and Rule 3 in Figure 5 */
      discard m;
    } ELSE IF (m is a straggler message) {
      find earliest eik to be rolled back by m;
      construct a new range [k,SV(LPi)[i]]i;
      construct CANCEL_MESSAGE m'' carrying the range;
      ROLLBACK(eik, m'');
      merge the range into RHT(LPi)[i];
      LS(LPi)[i]=SV(LPi)[i];
      ∀m' ∈ IQi, discard m' if m' in the range;
      insert m into IQi;
    } ELSE {
      insert m into IQi;
    }
  }
}
```

Figure 10. Receiving a message from communication channels at LP_i

LP_i performs a rollback action (see Figure 11). Then LP_i merges this range into its rollback history to identify any events for cancellation arriving in the future. Finally, LP_i looks into its IQ_i to discard those events that have been received but are now identified to be cancelled. (2) Message m is a positive message but identified as to be cancelled by a received range. It means that LP_i is already free from the rolled back state on which m depends. Thus, m is simply discarded. (3) Message m is a straggler message, so LP_i becomes a rollback originator. Except for the need to create a new *CANCEL_MESSAGE*, similar actions to

```
ROLLBACK(e, m) {
  SV(LPi)[i]++;
  restore the proper state from SQi;
  unprocess messages being rolled back in IQi;
  IF (cancelled messages in OQi) {
    send m to their destinations;
  }
}
```

Figure 11. Rollback to the state prior to executing e at LP_i

those in (1) are carried out. Finally, message m is inserted into IQ_i and expected to be the next message to be processed. (4) Message m is a positive message identified as neither to be discarded nor a straggler. It is simply inserted into IQ_i for future processing.

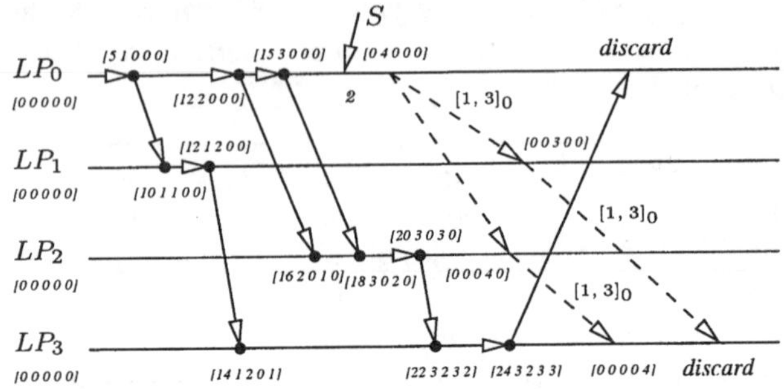

Figure 12. The batch based cancellations triggered by a straggler message

Figure 12 shows a possible scenario applying the batch based cancellation scheme to the scenario in Figure 1. Upon receipt of the straggler message at LP_0, the set of events to be cancelled at LP_0 is determined as $C_0(m_s) = \{e_{01}, e_{02}, e_{03}\}$ (or $\{e_{0,5}, e_{0,12}, e_{0,15}\}$). Range $[1,3]_0$ is sent along with a multicast *CANCEL_MESSAGE* to LP_1 and LP_2. Upon receipt of the range, $C_1(m_s) = \{e_{11}, e_{12}\}$ (or $\{e_{1,10}, e_{1,12}\}$) and $C_2(m_s) = \{e_{21}, e_{22}, e_{23}\}$ (or $\{e_{2,16}, e_{2,18}, e_{2,20}\}$) are determined respectively and the range is further forwarded to LP_3 independently by LP_1 and LP_2. The earlier range received by LP_3 triggers the cancellation of $C_3(m_s) = \{e_{31}, e_{32}, e_{33}\}$ (or $\{e_{3,14}, e_{3,22}, e_{3,24}\}$). The later received one is found to be a duplicate and is discarded.

6 Experiments

Our experiments were carried out on a Dell 2650 Server, a cluster of 11 nodes (dual 2.6GHz Xeon CPUs, 1GB RAM) interconnected through myrinet and running MPI-GM.

A generic manufacturing model [8] was used to evaluate the proposed scheme. According to the model, a manufacturing process is viewed as a sequence of production, assembling and testing stages. The production stage consists of a number of parallel production lines, each producing a different quality-guaranteed component through a sequence of processing stations (PS) and control stations (CS) (See Figure 13). Note that PS and CS are always paired. Once a flaw is found by a CS, having been introduced by its previous PS, the component is sent for reprocessing immediately. Each component is also tested at the end of its production line. In case of malfunction, the defective component is wholly reworked. Figure 14 shows the procedure of the assembling and testing stages, in which constituent components collected from the production lines are assembled to a product at any assembling station (AS) and tested at one of the testing stations (TS). For the sake of clarity, three different kinds of connectors are used for the interconnection. A forker (F) routes an input to several output links with configurable probability. A merger (M) generates an output when it receives inputs from all its input links. A collector (C), however, generates an output on any input. Note that connectors do not increase simulation time.

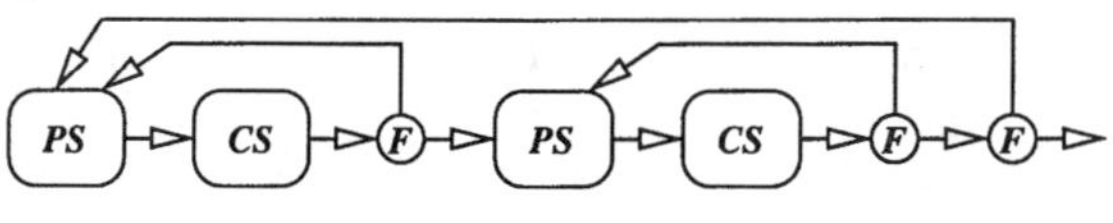

Figure 13. Production line

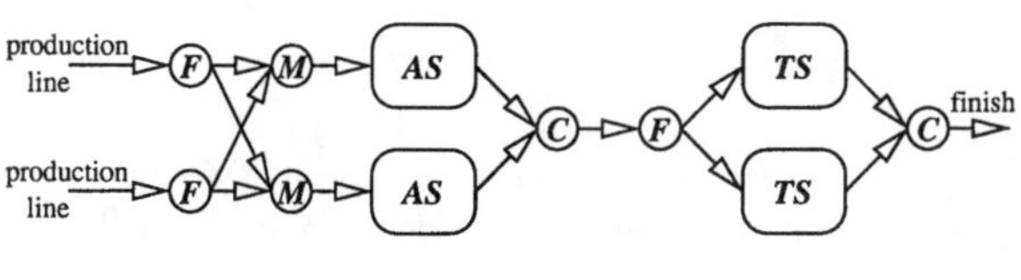

Figure 14. The assembling and testing stages

Without loss of generality, our running model is configured with a moderate number of *LPs*. The production stage is configured with two production lines and each line has one pair of PS and CS installed. There are two ASs and two TSs at the assembling and testing stages. All the units (eight stations plus 11 connectors), i.e., 19 *LPs*, are one-to-one mapped on 19 CPUs.

Two sets of experiments were carried out with different settings of event granularity and each set reports the comparison between the conventional per-event based cancellation scheme and the batch based cancellation scheme. In each run, 10000 components are fed to each production line. Table 1 and Table 2 show the measurements obtained using fine and coarse event granularity respectively. Note in each case the number of events and messages are the sums of those collected from all the *LPs*.

Studying the measurements reported from the experiments, the properties of the batch based cancellation scheme can be better understood. (1) Due to the ability to cancel multiple messages, the reduction of the number of anti-messages was significant. (2) In the batch based scheme, a smaller total number of processed events and straggler messages were always achieved. This can be explained by the rules in Figure 5 and Theorem 4.8. Once a potential wrong computation is identified by a range at an *LP*, it is always prevented from happening or being further propagated. (3) In order to evaluate the effectiveness of the batch based cancellation scheme, the concept of efficiency, which is defined as the ratio of the number of committed events and the total number of processed events, is introduced. Although both schemes committed similar amount of events, which meant similar behavior in the simulations, counting the total number of processed events, the batch based scheme had better results. (4) Based on the execution time obtained from both schemes, the speedups of the batch based scheme compared to the per-event based scheme were calculated. It can be seen that the batch based scheme has only slight performance gain over the per-event based scheme. This is understandable when we look into the running model more closely. The manufacturing model lacks the necessary long range forward links to expedite propagation of ranges. Due to reworking of components in the production stage, PSs have higher probabilities of receiving straggler messages. Once such a straggler message is received by a PS and the range identifying cancelled events is generated, the range has to follow a unique propagation path defined by the model and subsequent units have no means of early detection of potential wrong computations. Therefore in this case, units in the assembling and testing stages still suffer from excessive rollbacks. However, the batch based cancellation scheme may be modified to enable the detection of potential wrong computations at an earlier time, this is addressed in Section 7.

7 Conclusions

In this paper, a rollback optimal cancellation scheme, the batch based scheme, is presented. Rollback optimal means that any *LP* is able to recover from the receipt of a straggler message at the cost of at most one rollback. To do this, a state vector is used to capture the dependence of events and a rollback history is utilized to regulate the advancement of *LPs* and discover at an earlier stage any possible events to be eventually cancelled. We prove that in the batch based cancellation scheme, the set of events to be cancelled by a straggler message is fully deterministic in terms of the range generated by the rollback originator.

The proposed scheme is feasible in most Time Warp simulations. Given specific knowledge about the communication pattern of the running model, better performance can be expected. With the knowledge of the critical path in a simulation, an *LP* can send a range to those *LPs* on the path even if there is no event exchange among them. For the manufacturing model discussed previously, PSs can directly send their generated

	total events	committed events	efficiency	straggler messages	anti-messages/ cancel_messages	execution time	speedup
per-event based	406729	206521	50.78%	16987	96484	130883ms	1.00
batch based	300371	206315	68.69%	9962	38462	109961ms	1.19

Table 1. comparison of schemes with setting of fine event granularity

	total events	committed events	efficiency	straggler messages	anti-messages/ cancel_messages	execution time	speedup
per-event based	524513	237952	45.37%	22218	136016	446927ms	1.00
batch based	429634	237581	55.30%	20448	68432	408732ms	1.09

Table 2. comparison of schemes with setting of coarse event granularity

ranges to ASs and TSs to intercept any wrong events issued earlier. The extreme case is to broadcast CANCEL_MESSAGEs. Since each *LP* is guaranteed to be informed about the range and capable of cancelling all the events that need to be cancelled, the receiving *LPs* need not forward the range.

The most noteworthy overheads introduced by the batch based cancellation scheme include the communication cost of the additional state vector and increment of rollback histories carried by positive messages, the storage cost of maintaining rollback history tables and the computing cost of looking up and fossil collecting rollback history tables. With the assumption of FIFO channels, the compression approach for the rollback history is also applicable to the state vector. Observing that an *LP* in a simulation normally only communicates with a small number of *LPs*, the rollback history table at the *LP* can be maintained within a reasonable amount of space. Currently, the rollback history is simply implemented as a linear list of ranges, and each time an *LP* receives or processes an event, the list has to be fully scanned. This is believed to be one of the performance hindrances in our experiments. The next challenge to the proposed scheme is to organize rollback histories more efficiently so as to provide an optimized lookup time.

References

[1] B. Charron-Bost. Concerning the size of logical clocks in distributed systems. *Information Processing Letters*, 39:11–16, July 1991.

[2] M. Chetlur and P. A. Wilsey. Causality representation and cancellation mechanism in time warp simulations. In *Workshop on Parallel and Distributed Simulation*, pages 165–172, May 2001.

[3] A. Ferscha. *Handbook of Parallel and Distributed Computing*, chapter Parallel and Distributed Simulation of Discrete Event Systems, pages 1003–1041. McGraw-Hill, 1996.

[4] R. M. Fujimoto. *Parallel and Distributed Simulation Systems*. Wiley Book Series on Parallel and Distributed Computing. Wiley, New York, NY 10158, USA, 1999.

[5] A. Gafni. Rollback mechanisms for optimistic distributed simulation systems. In *Proceedings of the SCS Multiconference on Distributed Simulation*, pages 61–67, 1988.

[6] D. R. Jefferson. Virtual time. *ACM Transactions on Programming Languages and Systems*, 7(3):404–425, July 1985.

[7] L. Lamport. Time, clocks, and the ordering of events in a distributed system. *Communications of the ACM*, 21(7):558–565, July 1978.

[8] Chu-Cheow Lim, Yoke-Hean Low, Wentong Cai, Wen-Jing Hsu, Shell-Ying Huang, and Stephen J. Turner. An empirical comparison of runtime systems for conservative parallel simulation. In *IPPS/SPDP Workshops*, pages 123–134, 1998.

[9] V. Madisetti, J. Walrand, and D. Messerschmitt. WOLF: A rollback algorithm for optimistic distributed simulation systems. In *Proceedings of the Winter Simulation Conference*, pages 296–305, San Diego, California, 1988.

[10] M. Raynal and M. Singhal. Logical time: A way to capture causality in distributed systems. Technical Report RR-2472, INRIA - Rennes, March 1995.

[11] R. L. Reiher, R. M. Fujimoto, S. Bellenot, and D. R. Jefferson. Cancellation strategies in optimistic execution systems. In *Proceedings of the SCS Multiconference on Distributed Simulation*, pages 112–121, 1990.

[12] R. Schwarz and F. Mattern. Detecting causal relationships in distributed computations: In search of the holy grail. *Distributed Computing*, 7(3):149–174, 1994.

[13] M. Singhal and A. Kshemkalyani. An efficient implementation of vector clocks. *Information Processing Letters*, 43:47–52, August 1992.

[14] D. West. Optimizing time warp: Lazy rollback and lazy re-evaluation. Master's thesis, University of Calgary, Calgary, Alberta, 1988.

Session 5:
Simulation Theory

Formalization and Strictness of Simulation Event Orderings

Y.M. Teo[1,2] and B.S.S. Onggo[1]
[1]*Department of Computer Science, National University of Singapore*
3 Science Drive 2, Singapore 117543
[2]*Singapore – MIT Alliance*
National University of Singapore, Singapore 117576
email: teoym@comp.nus.edu.sg

Abstract

This paper advocates the use of a formal framework for analyzing simulation performance. Simulation performance is characterized based on the three simulation development process boundaries: physical system, simulation model, and simulator implementation. Firstly, we formalize simulation event ordering using partially ordered set theory. A simulator implements a simulation event ordering, and incurs implementation overheads when enforcing event ordering at runtime. Secondly, we apply our formalism to extract and formalize the simulation event orderings of both sequential and parallel simulations. Thirdly, we propose the relation stricter and a measure called strictness for comparing and quantifying the degree of event dependency of simulation event orderings respectively.

1. Introduction

As the size and complexity of simulations grow, the computational demand required is fast becoming a limited factor in solving large and complex real-world problems. Consequently, understanding simulation performance becomes increasingly important. Parallel simulation speeds up simulation execution by distributing the simulation across a number of processors. In parallel simulation, a physical system is viewed as a number of physical processes that interacts in some fashion [11]. In the Virtual Time simulation modeling paradigm, each physical process is modeled by a logical process (LP) [12]. The interactions between physical processes are modeled by exchanging timestamped events between the corresponding logical processes. Parallelism is exploited by simulating LPs concurrently.

Research in parallel simulation in the last decade has resulted in a number of synchronization protocols [11]. These protocols, introduced in an algorithm fashion, are frequently evaluated by comparing its performance among protocols [11]. Moreover, the performance metrics and benchmarks used vary among the different studies. A serious drawback is the lack of performance comparison framework. We proposed a time and space performance evaluation framework based on the concept of event ordering [17][20]. Event ordering in simulation refers to a set of rules that is used to order a set of events. The framework characterizes simulation performance along the three natural boundaries in simulation modeling and analysis (see Table 1) [17]. The physical system layer corresponds to real world systems, the simulation model layer corresponds to different simulation event orderings that can be used to simulate a real world system, and the simulator layer corresponds to the simulator implemented to enforce a simulation event ordering. The layered approach provides a framework to study the factors affecting simulation performance from the physical system to its simulator implementation.

Layers	Types of Event	Event Ordering
Physical System	Real events	One
Simulation Model	Real events	Many
Simulator	Real events + Overhead	One or more implementations for a given event ordering

Table 1. Layered Simulation Performance Framework

Event ordering (or message ordering) has been studied in the time management component of High Level Architecture (HLA) [11]. The simulation of a physical system in HLA is distributed across a number of federates. Message ordering in HLA time management dictates the ordering of messages within each federate. Fujimoto et al. introduces five message orderings which form a spectrum of orderings where at one extreme, messages are not ordered; and at the other extreme, messages are totally ordered based on their timestamps [9]. To exploit the temporal uncertainty in a simulation model, Fujimoto proposes Approximate Time (AT) and Approximate Time Causal (ATC) orders [10]. Recently, Zhou et al. investigate the causality issue in distributed simulation and propose the causal receive ordering [23]. In parallel simulation, event ordering dictates the ordering of events within each LP and across LPs. To produce

1087-4097/04 $20.00 © 2004 IEEE

correct simulation result, events in the same LP are executed in non decreasing timestamp order [11]. This constraint is referred to as local causality constraint (*lcc*).

This paper discusses the formalization of simulation event orderings based on partially ordered set (poset). This formalization provides a theoretical foundation for carrying out performance analysis of simulation. If events with the same timestamp are grouped as a set or there is a priority function that can differentiate those events, there will only be one event ordering in a physical system. Simulation can use different event orderings to exploit parallelism in the physical system. This paper shows that a simulator implements a specific event ordering. Two major benefits may be derived from the separation of simulation event ordering from its implementation. First, this facilitates the understanding of the relationship of different event orderings. We propose the relation *stricter* to compare different event orderings. Second, the performance of different event orderings can be evaluated independent of implementation overheads [17][20]. The separation between event ordering and its implementation is motivated by research in memory operation orderings in memory consistency model [6] and message ordering in broadcast services in distributed system [1]. Our work is different from Critical Path Analysis (CPA) that is also used to analyze the performance of parallel simulation [2]. CPA uses an event dependency graph that is based on *happened before* event ordering [13]. Hence, CPA is a subset of our event ordering analysis.

The rest of this paper is organized as follows. Section 2 formalizes the concept of simulation event ordering. We apply this formalism to extract and formalize simulation event orderings in both sequential and parallel simulation. In section 3, we propose the stricter relation and apply this concept to analyze a number of event orderings. We show the empirical result in section 4. Our concluding remark is in section 5.

2. Formalization of Event Orderings

In this section, we propose to formalize simulation event ordering based on partially ordered set (poset). Research in poset theory was triggered by Dushnik and Miller's publication in 1941 [7]. They propose the definition of partial order as given in Definition 1.

Definition 1. *An order R over S (where S is a set) is called a* ***partial order*** *if R is anti-reflexive (i.e.* $(x, x) \notin R$*), anti-symmetric (i.e. either* $(x, y) \in R$ *or* $(y, x) \in R$*), and transitive.*

For example, an order "descendant of" for a given set of people is of partial order. However, an order "friend of" for a given set of people may not be a partial order depending on the given set of people. This leads to the concept of *partially ordered set* [7].

Definition 2. *A* ***partially ordered set (poset)*** *is a tuple (S, R) where S is a set and R is a partial order on the set S.*

Definition 3. *A* ***simulation event ordering*** *(or event ordering in short) is a tuple* (E, S_R) *where E is a set of events and* S_R *is a set of comparable events based on event order R. Event order R must be anti-reflexive, anti-symmetric and transitive.*

Based on the definition of poset, we formalize event ordering in Definition 3. Just as a poset that has two components, an event ordering also comprises two main components: a set of events E and an event order R. An event order R refers to a set of rules that is used to order events. A pair of events $(x, y) \in S_R$ denotes event x is ordered before event y in event order R. Two events x and y are *comparable* if either $(x, y) \in S_R$ or $(y, x) \in S_R$, otherwise x and y are non-comparable (or *concurrent)*.

2.1 Physical System

An event order in the physical system corresponds to how events in the physical system are ordered. Based on the physical time, there is only one event order for any physical system, i.e. an event with a smaller physical time is ordered before an event with a larger physical time (Definition 4). The definition of predecessor and antecedent (Definition 5 and 6) will be used throughout this paper.

Definition 4. *Let x be an event in a physical system and x.ts the physical time when event x happens. The event order in any physical system dictates that for all x and y (where* $x \neq y$*), x is ordered before y if and only if* $x.ts < y.ts$.

Definition 5. *Event x is the* ***predecessor*** *of y (denoted by* $y.pred = x$*), if x and y are at the same service center and there is no other event z that is also at the same service center such that* $x.ts < z.ts < y.ts$.

Definition 6. *Event x is the* ***antecedent*** *of y (denoted by* $y.ante = x$*), if x spawns y.*

2.2 Simulation Model

Based on the virtual time paradigm, a simulation model emulates a physical system and the interaction among physical processes in the physical system (see Figure 1). Each physical process in the physical system is mapped onto a logical process (LP) in the simulation model. Each event in the simulation model models an event in the physical system. The simulation time of an event in the simulation model models the physical time of the corresponding event in the physical system. The event ordering in a physical system can be modeled and simulated using different event orderings to exploit different degrees of event parallelism.

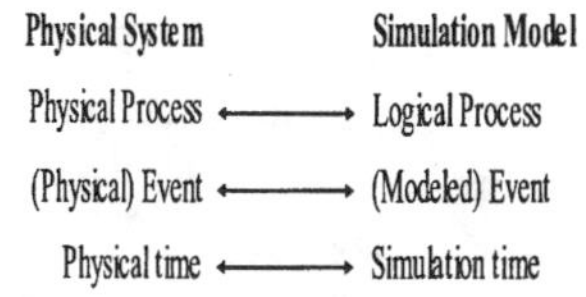

Figure 1. Physical System and Simulation Model

Lamport defined happened before partial order and total order [13]. He proved that both orders are anti-reflexive, anti-symmetric and transitive which match our definition of simulation event order (Definition 3). Hence, we refer to these event orders as partial event order and total event order respectively (see Definition 7 and 8). The priority function in total event order is used to decide which event should be processed when two or more events have the same timestamp. Based on interval order in poset [16], we formalize timestamp event order and time-interval event order [17][20].

Definition 7. ***Partial event order*** *imposes that event x is ordered before event y in if (y.pred = x) or (y.ante = x).*

Definition 8. ***Total event order*** *imposes that event x is ordered before event y in iff (x.ts < y.ts) or (x.ts = y.ts and priority(x) < priority(y)).*

Definition 9. ***Timestamp event ordering*** *imposes that event x is ordered before event y in iff x.ts < y.ts.*

Definition 10. ***Time-interval event ordering*** *imposes that event x is ordered before event y in if: (y.pred = x) or (y.ante = x) or (x.ts + W < y.ts), where W is a constant window size.*

2.3 Simulator

A simulator, written as a sequential program or a parallel program, is an implementation of a simulation model. In parallel simulation, a synchronization algorithm (or simulation protocol) is required for maintaining correct event ordering across processors. Enforcing event ordering at runtime incurs implementation overhead such as null messages in CMB protocol and rollback in TW protocol that results in performance loss.

To show that each simulator implements a certain event order, we extract and formalize the ordering rules of a number of simulator implementations. These include sequential simulation and parallel simulation protocols such as CMB [5], Bounded Lag [14], Time Warp [12] and Bounded Time Warp [21].

2.3.1 Sequential Simulation

The sequential simulation algorithm is presented in Figure 2. Events in sequential simulation are totally ordered (only one event is executed at any time). To enforce this ordering, sequential simulation maintains a future event list (FEL) where events are sorted in chronological timestamp order. In line 2, the function *f* returns the event with the smallest timestamp in the future event list. FEL enables sequential simulation to execute an event with the smallest timestamp (line 12). In case of a tie (i.e. $M \neq \varnothing$ in line 14), an event with the highest priority will be chosen (*z* in line 15). Issues and examples on implementing the priority function have been studied in [18][22]. Lemma 1 formalizes the event ordering in sequential simulation.

```
SEQUENTIAL SIMULATION
1.  initialize
2.  while (~stop) {
3.     e ← f(FEL)
4.     local_clock ← e.ts
5.     FEL ← FEL - {e}
6.     E ← execute (e)
7.     FEL ← FEL ∪ E
8.     stop ← g()
9.  }
10.
11. f(L):event {
12.    x ← head(L)
13.    M ← {y | ∀y∈L • y.ts = x.ts}
14.    if (M = ∅) return x
15.    else return {z | ∀y∈M ∃!z∈M y≠z •
              priority(z)>priority(y)}
16. }
```

Figure 2. Algorithm of Sequential Simulation

Lemma 1. *Sequential simulation implements total event order.*

Proof. Sequential simulation employs a global event list that is sorted by the smallest timestamp first. This guarantees that event *x* is ordered before event *y* if and only if *x.ts* < *y.ts*. The use of a priority function when more than one event have the smallest timestamp guarantees that if *x.ts* = *y.ts* event *x* is ordered before event *y* if and only if *priority(x)* < *priority(y)*. ❑

2.3.2 CMB Protocol

The algorithm of CMB protocol [5] is given in Figure 3. Each LP maintains a list of LPs that may send events to it (for LP *x*, it is denoted by *SENDER*(*x*)). The ordering rule of CMB protocol imposes that only safe events are executed. An event in LP *x* is safe for execution if no other LP ∈ *SENDER*(*x*) will send any event with a smaller timestamp to LP *x*. Therefore, to maintain this ordering, LP *x* must wait to receive events from all other LPs (see line 4). This could lead to deadline as all LPs are blocked. To avoid deadline, null messages are introduced. Each null message is stamped with a timestamp *ts* which equal to LP's local simulation clock plus a lookahead value (line 12) to indicate that the sending LP will never transmit any events with a smaller timestamp than *ts*.

Each LP maintains an event list (EL), a set of input buffers (IB) and a set of output buffers (OB). IB[*i*] of an LP *x* stores the incoming message from LP_i ∈ *SENDER*(*x*). OB[*i*] stores the messages that will schedule events in LP_i. An LP is blocked if at least one of its IBs is empty (line 4). In lines 5-6, an event with the smallest timestamp is chosen from its IBs and EL for execution. Line 7 removes the chosen event from the corresponding list (one of the IBs or EL). The local clock is updated in line 8. In line 9, an event execution may schedule a set of *internal events* (IE) and a set of *external events* (EE). The internal events (i.e. scheduled to happen in the same LP) are saved to EL (line 10) and external events (i.e. scheduled to happen in other LPs) are saved to their respective OB (line 11). Line 12 sets a null message with a timestamp equal to the local clock plus a lookahead value. Line 13 adds a null message to any empty OB. Line 14 sends all the external events and null messages in OBs. Finally line 16 checks the stopping condition.

```
CMB PROTOCOL
1. initialization
2. run all LPs

LOGICAL PROCESS
3. while (~stop) {
4.     while (∃i IB[i] = ∅) {}
5.     L ← EL ∪ {∀i IB[i]}
6.     e ← f(L)
7.     if (∃i e∈IB[i]) IB[i] ← IB[i]-{e}
       else EL ← EL-{e}
8.     local_clock ← e.ts
9.     {IE, EE} ← execute (e)
10.    EL ← EL ∪ IE
11.    ∀i OB[i] ← OB[i] ∪ {z|z∈EE • z.lp=i}
12.    nullMsg.ts ← local_clock + lookahead
13.    ∀i if (OB[i] = ∅) OB[i] ← OB[i] ∪
           {nullMsg}
14.    ∀i send (OB[i])
15.    stop ← g()
16.}
```

Figure 3. Algorithm of CMB Protocol

Lemma 2. *CMB protocol implements an event order whereby event x is ordered before event y if:*

1. *y.pred = x, or*
2. *x.ts + la < y.ts.*

Proof. The conditional statement in line 4 (Figure 3) ensures that an LP has to wait until all LPs in its SENDER list have sent their events. This ensures that an LP always executes events scheduled in it in timestamp order. Hence, for all events in the same LP, if *y.pred* = *x* then *x* is ordered before *y*. Further, event *y* in LP_j is executed only if it has the smallest timestamp among the unprocessed events of all LP ∈ *SENDER*(LP_j). Therefore, event *x* in any LP ∈ *SENDER*(LP_j) is ordered before event *y* only if *x.ts* + *la* < *y.ts* where *la* is the lookahead value. ❑

Researchers have proposed various optimizations such as demand driven protocol [3], and carrier null message protocol [4] to reduce the null-message overhead,. These optimizations do not alter the event ordering in the original CMB protocol, but rather, they can be seen as different implementations of the same event order.

2.3.3 Bounded Lag Protocol

Lubachevsky proposed the Bounded Lag (BL) protocol which combines two main rules: bounded lag restriction and minimum propagation delay [14]. Bounded lag restriction imposes that events can be executed concurrently if they are within the same time window. Minimum propagation delay between LPs is used to determine whether an event is safe to execute. The latter is similar to the rule in CMB protocol; however in the implementation BL protocol uses a distance matrix instead of using null messages. To maintain its ordering, BL protocol uses barrier synchronization because the global clock (for imposing bounded lag restriction) and the minimum propagation delay must be broadcasted to all LPs. The algorithm is given in Figure 4.

```
BL PROTOCOL
1.  initialization
2.  run all LPs

LOGICAL PROCESS
3.  while (~stop) {
4.     β ← min {∀lp∈LP, e = head(lp.EL) •
           e.ts + d(lp, this)}
       γ ← min{∀lp∈LP, e = head(EL) •
           e.ts+d(this,lp) + d(lp,this)}
       α ← min {β, γ}
5.     barrier synchronization
6.     E ← {∀e∈EL • e.ts ≤ min(α,
           global_clock + W)}
7.     EL ← EL - E
8.     while (E ≠ ∅) {
9.        e ← head(E)
10.       E ← E - {e}
11.       {IE, EE} ← execute (e)
12.       local_clock ← e.ts
13.       EL ← EL ∪ IE
14.       Send(EE)
15.    }
16.    stop ← g()
17.    barrier synchronization
18.    global_clock ← min {∀lp∈LP •
         lp.local_clock}
19.    barrier synchronization
20. }
```

Figure 4. Algorithm of Bounded-lag Protocol

There are two main processes: the nomination of safe events (lines 4-7) and the execution of safe events (lines 8-15). The lookahead between any two LPs is stored in a distance matrix *d*. Based on the distance matrix, an LP (denoted by *this* in Figure 4) determines α, i.e. the earliest time when its system state can be affected by other LP (line 4). The barrier synchronization (line 5) ensures that all LPs receive α before continuing to the next line. Each LP identifies its safe events based on this rule: events with a timestamp less than α and within a time window of *W* are safe to process (line 6). *W* is termed as BL size in [14]. Line 7 removes all safe events from EL for execution. Next, safe events are executed in lines 8-15.

The barrier synchronization in line 17 is used to ensure that all LPs have processed their safe events before the time window is moved. Line 18 computes the global clock as the minimum of all LPs' local clock. This process is repeated until the stopping condition is met.

Lemma 3. *BL protocol implements an event order whereby event x is ordered before event y if:*

1. *y.pred = x, or*
2. *x.ts + la < y.ts, or*
3. $\lfloor x.ts/W \rfloor < \lfloor y.ts/W \rfloor$.

Proof. In line 7, α returns the smallest timestamp of an unprocessed event *x* (plus lookahead) that may be sent to a particular LP (Figure 4 line 4). Line 9 shows that if event *y* in LP_i can be executed in parallel with event *x* from another LP, then $y.ts \leq \alpha$ (i.e. $x.ts + la$) and both *x* and *y* must be in the same time window of size *W*. Therefore, event *x* is executed before event *y* only if $x.ts + la < y.ts$ or events *x* and *y* are in two different time windows of size *W* is true (of course the time window of *x* should be earlier than the time window of *y*). ❑

2.3.4 Time Warp Protocol

Jefferson proposed Time Warp (TW) protocol imposes that if event *x* causes event *y*, then the execution of event *x* must be completed before the execution of event *y* starts [12]. The definition of "*x* causes y" follows the relation *happened before* in [13]. To implement this ordering, TW protocol uses what is called local control mechanism (rollback and state saving) and global control mechanism (global clock calculation and fossil collection).

```
TIME WARP PROTOCOL
1. initialization
2. run all LPs

LOGICAL PROCESS
3. while (~stop) {
4.    do {
5.       m ← head(IB)
6.       if (m.ts < local_clock) {
7.          if (((m ≠ anti_message) and
            dual(m)∉ IQ) or
            ((m = anti_message) and
            dual(m)∈ IQ)) RollBack()
8.       }
9.       if (dual(m) ∈ IQ) Annihilate(m)
         else IQ ← IQ ∪ {m}
10.      IB ← IB - {m}
11.   } while ((m = anti_message) and
      (IB ≠ ∅))
12.   if (m = anti_message) e ← head(EL)
13.   else {
14.      if (m.ts < head(EL).ts) e ← m
15.      else {e ← head(FEL);
         EL ← EL - (e}; EL ← EL ∪ {m}}
16.   }
17.   {IE, EE} ← execute (e)
18.   local_clock ← e.ts
19.   EL ← EL ∪ IE
20.   StateSaving()
21.   Update(global_clock)
22.   FossilCollection()
23.   Send(EE)
24.   stop ← g()
25.}
```

Figure 5. Algorithm of Time Warp Protocol

Each LP stores all incoming events in an input buffer (IB) which is sorted based on the timestamp of the incoming events. Lines 4-11 find the first real event *m*. Line 5 retrieves an event *m* with the smallest timestamp for execution. Line 6 checks if *lcc* is violated. Line 7 detects whether rollback has to be done. If *m* is an anti-message, line 9 will annihilate the associated event that has to be cancelled; otherwise, it will add *m* to a list called input queue (IQ). IQ is used to store the history of all incoming messages (processed and unprocessed). Line 10 removes *m* from IB. Lines 12-15 retrieve an event *e* which has the smallest timestamp from the EL and choose the event with a smaller timestamp, between *m* and *e*. Line 17 executes the chosen event. This execution may produce a set of internal events (IE) and a set of external events (EE). Line 18 updates the local clock and line 19 updates the event list (EL). Line 20 saves the state of an LP. The global clock is updated in line 21. Events with timestamp less than the global clock will never be rollbacked. These events are called *committed events*. Hence, memory allocated to committed events can be reclaimed with the fossil collection process in line 22. Line 23 sends out the external events. Lastly, line 24 checks the stopping condition.

Lemma 4. *Time Warp protocol implements a partial event order.*

Proof. The rollback process ensures that all events in the same LP are executed in timestamp order. This implies that event *x* is ordered before event *y* if *y.pred* = *x*. The insertion of internal events to EL and transmission of external events are done after the event execution in line 17. This ensures that event *x* is ordered before event *y*, if *y.ante* = *x*. ❑

2.3.5 Bounded Time Warp Protocol

The Bounded Time Warp (BTW) protocol [21] is proposed to limit the degree of optimism in TW protocol by setting a bound on how far an LP can advance ahead of other LPs. This is accomplished by setting a time window (*W*). LPs are allowed to optimistically process events ahead of the global clock (*GVT*) but bounded by the time window *GVT+W*. No LP can advance beyond *GVT+W* before all LPs have reached this boundary.

Lemma 5. ***BTW protocol*** *imposes that event x is ordered before event y in if:*

1. *y.pred = x, or*
2. *y.ante = x, or*
3. $\lfloor x.ts/W \rfloor < \lfloor y.ts/W \rfloor$

Proof. Without time window, BTW protocol is the same as TW protocol hence the ordering rules of partial event order hold, i.e. event x is ordered before event y if $y.pred = x$ or $y.ante = x$. The additional time window synchronization imposes that the partial event order is applied to a set of events that occur within the time window. Therefore, if event x occurs within a time window that is earlier than the time window of event y, event x will be executed before event y. ❑

We summarize the formalization of the event orderings discussed in Figure 6. The ordering rules of each event order are shown in the form of x is ordered before y (denoted by $x \Rightarrow y$) if a list of conditions hold. A simulator implements a certain event order. The arrow from event ordering R in simulation model to simulator S denotes that S implements R.

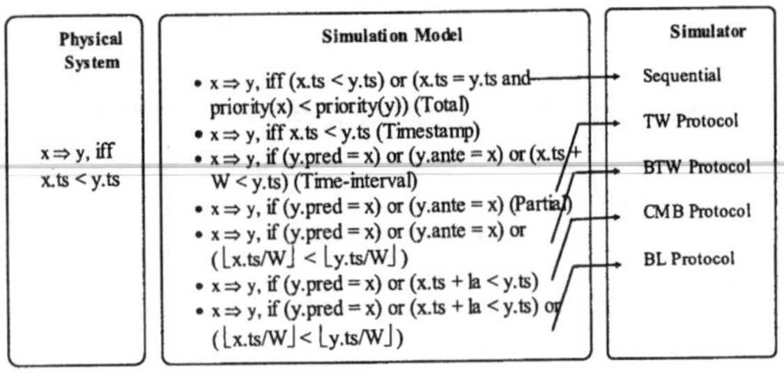

Figure 6. Summary on Event Ordering Formalization

3. Strictness of Event Ordering

To compare the degree of event dependencies among different event orders, we propose a relation *stricter*. The term stricter is borrowed from memory consistency model [6]. In memory consistency model, stricter relation is used to compare different models by considering the set of possible outcomes that is allowed by each model for a given set of instructions. In simulation event ordering, we consider the set of events that have to be executed one after another due to the ordering rules imposed by an event order for a given set of events.

Definition 11. *An event order R_1 is **stricter** than event order R_2 if for any set of events E, $R_2 \subseteq R_1$. An event order R_1 is **incomparable** to event order R_2 if we can find two sets of events E_1 and E_2, such $R_2 \subseteq R_1$ is true for E_1 but $R_2 \subseteq R_1$ is not true for E_2.*

Two events are concurrent in an event order if the event order does not impose any ordering on them. Definition 11 implies that a stricter event order produces less number of concurrent events than a less strict event order (or at most the same number of concurrent events). Since concurrent events can be executed in parallel, a stricter event order produces less event parallelism. To quantify the degree of event dependency, we propose the measure of *strictness*. Since relation stricter is built based on set inclusion, the strictness of event order R is quantified based on the number of elements in S_R as shown in Definition 12.

Definition 12. *The strictness of an event order R (ς_R) is defined as $\| S_R \| / \| S_{tot} \|$ where $\| S_R \|$ and $\| S_{tot} \|$ is the size of the set of comparable (or non-concurrent) events ordered by R and the total event order respectively.*

Since total event order is the strictest event order, we normalize the number of elements in S_R with the number of comparable elements in total event order (S_{tot}). Hence, the strictness of an event order ranges from zero when $S_R = \emptyset$ and one when R is the total event order. To measure $\| S_R \|$ for a given set of events E, we have to determine for any two events x and $y \in E$ whether $(x, y) \in S_R$ based on the ordering rules of the event order. This process is computationally expensive especially for a large number of events. Since $(x, y) \in S_R$ implies that event y cannot be executed before the execution of event x completes, in our experiments we measure the number of events that are ready for execution but cannot be executed because of the ordering rules imposed by the event order.

3.1 Strictness Analysis

Event order R_2 is stricter than event order R_1 implies that for any two distinct events x and y, if x is ordered before y in R_1 then x is also ordered before y in R_2, but not vice-versa. Therefore, to prove whether an event order is stricter than another event order, we show that the ordering rule of one event order is a subset of the other event order. If the ordering rule of event order R_1 is a subset of event order R_2, then definitely if x is ordered before y in R_1 then x is also ordered before y in R_2. Using this approach, in the following theorems, we establish the relationship of the simulation event orderings summarized in Figure 7.

Theorem 1.

a) *Total event order is stricter than TS event order.*
b) *The event order of BL protocol is stricter than the event order of CMB protocol*
c) *The event order of BTW protocol is stricter than partial event order.*

Proof. The proofs are derived by comparing their properties in Figure 6. If the property of an event order R_1 is a subset of the property of event order R_2, then R_2 is stricter than R_1. ❑

Theorem 2. *TS event order is stricter than BL event order.*

Proof. In TS event order, $x \Rightarrow y$, iff $x.ts < y.ts$. On the other hand, in BL protocol, $x \Rightarrow y$, if ($y.pred = x$) or ($x.ts + la < y.ts$) or ($\lfloor x.ts/W \rfloor < \lfloor y.ts/W \rfloor$). These rules can only be true if $x.ts < y.ts$. Therefore, if $x \Rightarrow y$ in BL protocol, then $x \Rightarrow y$ is true in TS event order, but not the converse. Hence, timestamp event order is stricter than the event order of BL protocol. ❑

Lemma 6. $\forall x, y \in E$, $\{y.ante = x\} \subseteq \{x.ts + la \le y.ts$ and $x.lp \in SENDER(y.lp)\}$.

Proof. From the definition of *SENDER* list and lookahead, if $y.ante = x$ then $x.lp$ must be in the *SENDER* list (i.e. $x.lp \in SENDER(y.lp)$) and the timestamp difference between x and y must be greater than the lookahead la (i.e. $x.ts + la < y.ts$). However, it is possible that $x.lp \in SENDER(y.lp)$ and $x.ts + la < y.ts$ is true but $y.ante \neq x$. ❑

Theorem 3. *The event order of CMB protocol is stricter than partial event order.*
Proof. Both have two ordering rules (Figure 8). The first rule is the same, i.e. $x \Rightarrow y$ if $y.pred = x$. In the second rule, partial event order imposes $x \Rightarrow y$ if $y.ante = x$ whereas CMB protocol imposes that $x \Rightarrow y$ if $x.ts + la < y.ts$. Lemma 6 shows that the second rule of partial event order is a subset of the second rule of CMB protocol, therefore, the event order of CMB protocol is stricter than partial event order. ❑

Theorem 4. *The event order of BL protocol is stricter than the event order of BTW protocol.*
Proof. Both have three ordering rules (Figure 8) and two of them are the same, i.e. $x \Rightarrow y$ if $y.pred = x$ or $\lfloor x.ts/W \rfloor < \lfloor y.ts/W \rfloor$. The other rule is different, BTW protocol imposes $x \Rightarrow y$ if $y.ante = x$ whereas BL protocol imposes that $x \Rightarrow y$ if $x.ts + la < y.ts$. Based on Lemma 6, BL protocol imposes a stricter event order than BTW protocol for the same window size W. ❑

Figure 7 shows the spectrum of event orders based on our proposed stricter relation. BL, BTW and CMB refers to the event ordering of BL protocol, BTW protocol and CMB protocol respectively. An arrow from event order R_1 to event order R_2 denotes that R_1 is stricter than R_2. Stricter relation is transitive and the arrows can be traversed transitively as well. Sequential simulation implements total event order and the remaining event orders belong mainly to parallel and distributed simulation.

Depending on its window size, the relative position of TI event order can be anywhere between timestamp event order and partial event order. If TI event ordering uses a window size of zero, then it becomes a timestamp event ordering. Similarly, there is a constant c such that $0 < c < W$ where time-interval event ordering becomes partial event ordering (W is the window size) as shown in Theorem 5. This property is useful in strictness analysis because we can create different points (representing different event orderings) between timestamp event ordering and partial event ordering by changing the value of W.

Theorem 5. *For a given set of events E, there is a constant c such that $0 < c < W$, where a TI event order will become a partial event order.*

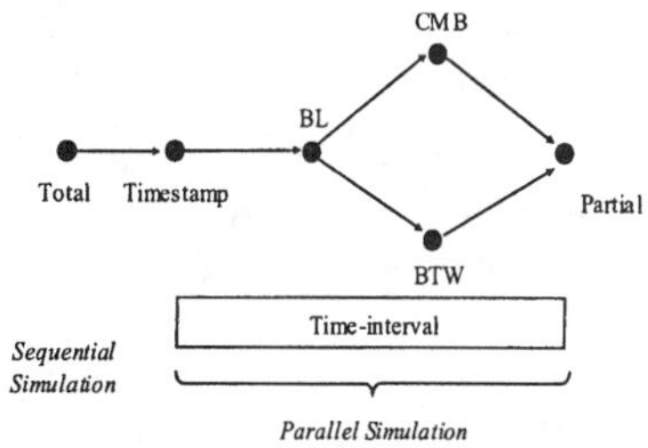

Figure 7. Spectrum of Event Orders and its Strictness

Proof. To prove this, we show that if $0 < c < W$, the third rule of time-interval event order (i.e. $x.ts + W < y.ts$) is redundant. Let a and b be two distinct events in E where $b.pred \neq a$ and $b.ante \neq a$ and $b.ts - a.ts = c$ is the largest. If $W > c$, then the rule $x.ts + W < y.ts$ will produce an empty set. Hence, only the first two rules ($y.pred = x$ *and* $y.ante = x$) determines the ordering, resulting in TI event order with $W > c$ and partial event order producing exactly the same event ordering. ❑

4. Empirical Result

We measure the strictness of five event orders (i.e. total, timestamp, time-interval, CMB and partial) using two benchmarks:

a) Multistage Interconnected Network (MIN) represents an *open system* [19]. It is parameterized by the number of service centers (n), and traffic intensity (ρ).
b) Parallel Hold (PHOLD) represents a *closed system* with multiple *feedbacks* [8]. It is parameterized by the number of service centers (n) and job density (m).

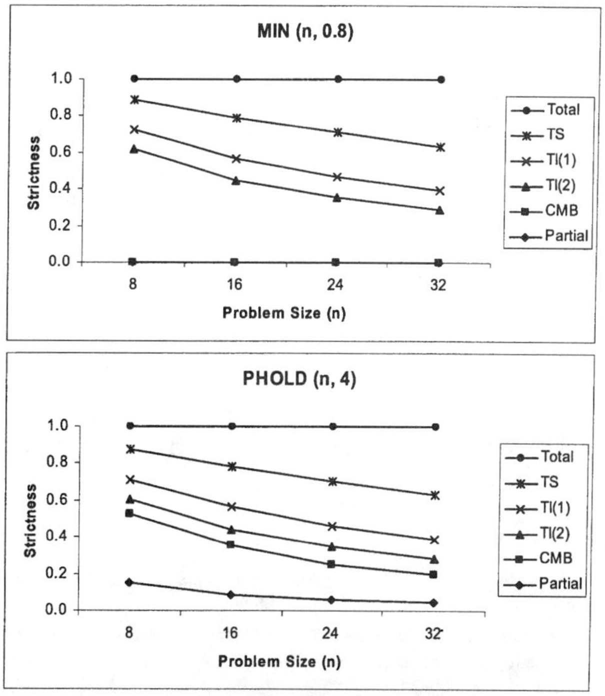

Figure 8. Strictness of Event Orderings

We measure the strictness of the event orderings using TSA [17]. The simulation duration is set at 100,000 timestamp units. Figure 8 shows the strictness of event orderings as problem size increases. First, the result shows that the strictness value is between 0 and 1, where total event order is the strictest event order. Second, the figure reveals that partial event order, CMB event order, timestamp event order and total event order are in increasing order of strictness. This confirms their positions on the event orders spectrum in Figure 7. The time-interval event order with window size of 1 and 2 represent two event orderings with different degrees of strictness. As we reduce the window size, the curve for time-interval event order moves towards timestamp event order and conversely, when we increase the window size, it moves towards the partial event order.

As problem size increases and consequently the number of events, strictness reduces. This is due to the higher probability of concurrent (non-comparable) events in the benchmarks. The strictness measure shown also reflects that the degree of event dependency in closed system is higher than in open system. Misra reported that CMB protocol can achieve optimum performance for a tandem topology and any acyclic topology [15]. Our result confirms this, i.e., strictness of the CMB (and partial) protocols for the open MIN(n, 0.8) system is lower than in the closed PHOLD(n, 4) system with multiple feedbacks.

5. Conclusions

The main contribution of this paper is the formalization of simulation event ordering based on partially ordered set theory. First, we characterized simulation performance along the three natural boundaries in simulation modeling and analysis namely: *physical system*, *simulation model* and *simulator*; and formalized the event orderings in each of the layers. Events in a physical system are ordered based on their time of occurrences. In simulation, different event orderings can be used to simulate the physical system. In the implementation, the simulator ensures that the chosen event ordering is maintained throughout a simulation run. We extract and formalize the event orderings of both sequential and parallel simulation. To compare the event dependency among different event ordering, we propose the stricter relation and to quantify the degree of event dependency a new strictness measure is proposed.

References

[1] H. Attiya, and J. Welch, *Distributed Computing: Fundamentals, Simulations and Advanced Topics*, McGraw-Hill, 1998.

[2] O. Berry, and D. Jefferson, "Critical Path Analysis of Distributed Simulation", *Proceedings of the SCS Multiconference on Distributed Simulation*, 1985, pp. 57-60.

[3] W.L. Bain, and D.S. Scott, "An Algorithm for Time Synchronization in Distributed Discrete-Event Simulation", *Proceedings of the SCS Multiconference on Distributed Simulation*, 19, 3 (Feb), 1988, pp. 30-33.

[4] W.T. Cai, and S.J. Turner, "An Algorithm for Distributed Discrete-Event Simulation – The Carrier Null Message Approach", *Proceedings of the SCS Multiconference on Distributed Simulation*, 1990, pp. 3-8.

[5] K.M. Chandy, and J. Misra, "Distributed Simulation: a Case Study in Design and Verification of Distributed Programs", *IEEE Transaction on Software Engineering*, 5, 5 (Sep), 1979, pp. 440-452.

[6] D.E. Culler, J.P. Singh, and A. Gupta, *Parallel Computer Architecture: A Hardware/Software Approach*, Morgan Kaufmann, 1999.

[7] B. Dushnik and E.W. Miller, "Partially Ordered Sets", *American Journal of Mathematics*, 63, 1941, pp. 600-610.

[8] R.M. Fujimoto, "Performance of Time Warp under Synthetic Workloads", *Proceedings of SCS Multiconference on Distributed Simulation, 22(1)*, 1990, pp. 23-28.

[9] R.M. Fujimoto, and R.M. Weatherly, "Time Management in the DoD High Level Architecture", *Proceedings of the 10th Workshop on Parallel and Distributed Simulation*, 1996, pp. 60-67.

[10] R.M. Fujimoto, "Exploiting Temporal Uncertainty in Parallel and Distributed Simulations", *Proceedings of the 13th Workshop on Parallel and Distributed Simulation*, 1999, pp. 46-53.

[11] R.M. Fujimoto, *Parallel and Distributed Simulation Systems*, John Wiley & Sons, Inc., 2000.

[12] D.A. Jefferson, "Virtual Time", *ACM Transaction on Programming Language System*, 7, 3 (July), 1985, pp. 404-425.

[13] L. Lamport, "Time, Clocks, and the Ordering of Events in a Distributed System", *Communication ACM*, 21, 7 (July), 1978, pp. 558-565.

[14] B.D. Lubachesky, "Efficient Distributed Event-driven Simulations of Multiple-loop Networks", *Communications of the ACM*, 32(1), 1989, pp. 111-123.

[15] J. Misra, "Distributed Discrete-event Simulation", *ACM Computing Surveys*, 18 (1), 1986, pp. 39-65.

[16] J. Neggers, and H.S. Kim, *Basic Posets*, World Scientific Publishing, 1998.

[17] B.S.S. Onggo, and Y.M. Teo, "Performance Trade-off in Distributed Simulation", *Proceedings of the 6th IEEE International Workshop on Distributed Simulation and Real Time Applications*, pp. 77-84, IEEE Computer Society Press, 2002.

[18] R. Ronngren, and M. Liljenstam, "On Event Ordering in Parallel Discrete-Event Simulation", *Proceedings of the 13th Workshop on Parallel and Distributed Simulation*, 1999, pp. 38-45.

[19] Y.M. Teo, and S.C. Tay, "Modeling an Efficient Distributed Simulation of Multistage Interconnection Network", *Proceedings of International Conference on Algorithms and Architectures for Parallel Processing*, IEEE Computer Society Press, pp. 83-92, 1995.

[20] Y.M. Teo, B.S.S. Onggo, and S.C. Tay, "Effect of Event Orderings on Memory Requirement in Parallel Simulation", *Proceedings of the 9th International Symposium on Modeling, Analysis and Simulation of Computer and Telecommunication Systems*, IEEE Computer Society Press, pp. 41-48, 2001.

[21] S.J. Turner, and M. Xu, "Performance Evaluation of the Bounded Time Warp Algorithm", *Proceedings of the 6th Workshop on Parallel and Distributed Simulation*, 1992, pp. 117-126.

[22] F. Wieland, "The Threshold of Event Simultaneity", *Proceedings of the 11th Workshop on Parallel and Distributed Simulation*, 1997, pp. 56-59.

[23] S.P. Zhou, W.T. Cai, S.J. Turner, and B.S. Lee, "Critical Causality in Distributed Environment", *Proceedings of the 16th Workshop on Parallel and Distributed Simulation*, 2002, pp. 53-59.

The Effect of Detail on Ethernet Simulation*

Alefiya Hussain, Aman Kapoor and John Heidemann
USC/Information Sciences Institute
{hussain, kapoor, johnh} @isi.edu

Abstract

An important question for network simulation is what level of detail is required to obtain a desired level of accuracy. While in some networks, the level of detail is an open research issue (for example, radio propagation models in wireless networks), it has long been assumed that wired networks could be accurately modeled by fairly simple queues with a bandwidth limit and propagation delay. To our knowledge this assumption has not been widely tested. In this paper we evaluate different levels of detail for an Ethernet simulation. We consider two models for Ethernet simulation; a detailed, CSMA/CD protocol based model and a more abstract model using a DropTail, shared queue. Using web traffic with two different TCP simulation models, we evaluated the accuracy of these Ethernet models as compared to testbed measurements. We observed the DropTail Ethernet model requires significantly less execution time and can accurately model performance using a bandwidth normalization factor.

1. Introduction

Network simulation is widely used to develop new protocols for the Internet. Even with the existence of public testbeds, simulation remains the only way to study very large models, and as software-only, simulation is much more accessible to researchers and students than a physical testbed. When designing simulations to study a protocol, a researcher needs to make choices regarding details in the protocol that should be exercised or implemented. Although there are a number of network simulation packages available, the onus of choosing the right level of detail for simulation still lies on the researcher.

Network protocols can be simulated at many levels of detail (or, alternatively, the level of abstraction)—from the physics of electromagnetic propagation, to bit-, packet-, and flow-level simulations. In some domains such as wireless networking, identifying appropriate levels of detail remain an open research challenge [13], and recent work suggests that radio propagation vagaries can greatly influence network protocol operation [6, 38], demonstrating a complexity beyond traditional analytic models (see for example [25]) that affects protocol operation.

In *wired* networks, however, fairly simple abstractions have long been assumed to be appropriate. For example, wide-area links are usually simulated as a queue, with some amount of fixed propagation delay, and a fixed bandwidth or bit-rate. Internet-like networks are then formed from collections of these abstract links. We know that networks in reality are much more complex, with multi-link routers with complex internal structure, often meeting at exchange points joined by local-area networks such as Ethernet or FDDI. While these abstractions are readily accepted, we are not aware of any systematic study about their validity—do these abstractions affect the accuracy of network simulations?

This paper begins that kind of systematic study, to understand what level of detail is needed in simulation models of wired networking protocols. In addition to common use at exchange points, Ethernet networks are often present as the last hop of most networks on the Internet today. With the fast growing Internet it has become important to revisit these lower layers and understand their behavior with respect to the changing traffic patterns and to understand network dynamics when a new protocol is deployed. We can only begin to explore such questions in this paper because ultimately the answer depends on the design question being investigated through simulation. Studies of capture effect might require a detailed model of Ethernet, while a trivial model is probably sufficient to simulate the Ethernet connecting a single home computer to a DSL modem.

Although Ethernet networks have been extensively studied in the past, yet little is known about their behavior. Several analytical models for throughput have been formulated [1, 3, 5, 8, 9, 11, 16, 17, 21, 32, 34, 33, 31, 30]. However due to the complexity of the CSMA/CD protocol, analytical approaches often make many simplifying assumptions about different parameters, for example packet size, load distribution, population size, to make the problem

*The research is based on work supported by DARPA via the Space and Naval Warfare Systems Center San Diego under Contract No. N66001-00-C-8066 ("SAMAN"), by NSF under grant number ANI-9986208 ("CONSER").

1087-4097/04 $20.00 © 2004 IEEE

tractable. These assumptions sometimes lead to contradictory results. For example, research has shown maximum achievable CSMA/CD utilization of 60% with one set of assumptions [30], while later work showed utilization up to 97% with large packet sizes [4].

To complement analysis, several simulation models of Ethernet have been presented [1, 14, 19, 23, 22, 24, 36]. Many of the simulation models represent the Ethernet as a point-to-point link with special characteristics. It is not clear if abstractions in these networks are appropriate for different simulation scenarios. Simulation of the Ethernet with accurate representation of the CSMA/CD mechanisms such as binary exponential backoff, inter-frame spacing and transmission of a jamming signal after a collision are expensive in computational power and memory requirements. The complexity added to the simulation model by these mechanisms may or may not be justified during the investigation of a particular protocol. In particular it may not be worth the extra effort to model the physical layer interactions with the MAC protocol or the computational overhead at the interface. Increasing the level of detail in a simulation model makes it difficult to quickly explore alternate network scenarios and protocol interactions.

To overcome the limitation posed by computational power and memory, some simulation models use parallel and distributed Ethernet simulations [37]. This technique however requires extensive coordination among a set of machines and at times requires specialized hardware that may not be available. Hence a more viable option is to reduce the level of detail in the simulation model. Accessing the appropriate level of detail required to accurately simulate the Ethernet networks is a difficult problem and varies depending on the network scenario. A high level of detail in the model allows accurate simulation of the Ethernet, but increases the time required to implement and debug the design as well as takes longer to run simulations on different network scenarios. Making use of detailed simulations do not allow quick evaluation of network scenarios to see which ones are most interesting. On the other hand low level of detail may produce distorted and misleading results.

In this paper, we present an abstract model of the Ethernet that replaces the complex CSMA/CD mechanisms by a drop tail queue. Reducing the level of detail in the model allows quick implementation, debugging and testing cycles within the simulation framework and has lower runtime and comparable memory costs permitting quick studies of the Ethernet and its interactions with other components of the network. The abstract model can be normalized to achieve the accuracy of the detailed model.

The contribution of this paper is to study the effects of detail in Ethernet simulations on application performance. We compare qualitatively the Ethernet specification against two simulation models (Section 3). We then examine the quantitative performance difference on a web traffic workload, comparing testbed experiments against these models for both 10Mb/s and 100Mb/s networks (Section 5). We also consider the run-time simulation costs of these models (Section 5.3). We will show that, in this case, abstraction provides runtime performance improvements, and that it can provide high accuracy provided that bandwidth is normalized by a scaling factor.

2. Related Work

Ethernet behavior has been extensively studied both analytically [1, 5, 8, 9, 11, 16, 17, 3, 21, 32, 34, 33, 31, 30] and through simulation models [1, 14, 19, 23, 22, 24, 36]. Most analytical models developed, make assumptions about one or more parameters: packet size, cable length, population size etc. to make their calculations tractable. Metcalfe provided the first detailed measurement analysis of a 3Mbit/s Ethernet calculating throughput as a function of packet length [21]. Their results showed a near 100% throughput for large sized packets and a drop to about 37% for smaller packets. Almes studied the Ethernet in terms of response time as a function of offered load [1]. They showed that the response time stays under 1msec for an offered load of about 75% and grows asymptotically with any further increase in load. They developed a simulation model to evaluate their analytical results. The simulation results matched with their analysis for fixed packet sizes but were worse in case of variable packet sizes. Many researcher groups [30, 34, 33] analyzed CSMA/CD networks under finite population size. They measured throughput against the offered load and also studied the effect of the time taken to detect a collision on the throughput. Coyle studied the Ethernet under a finite population generating exponentially distributed inter-arrival times for packets [8, 9]. Due to the assumptions made in the analytical models, they sometimes provide incorrect/biased results. Takagi [30] showed that maximum throughput achievable by CSMA/CD is 60% when infact [4] implementation proved that for large packet size Ethernet throughput could be as high as 97% The Ethernet behavioral analysis is dependent on the functional requirements from the network and choosing an appropriate analytical model may be difficult. This has resulted in simulations being the prime source of analysis of the Ethernet.

Several simulation models have been presented for the Ethernet [1, 14, 19, 23, 22, 24, 36]. Many models represent the Ethernet as a point-to-point link with special characteristics. These assumptions in simulation can bias the results providing incorrect results. Tsui el al [36] models the Ethernet by dividing the link into sections of equal length, where each section is attached to at most one node. Other groups [24, 23] represented the Ethernet with a single server that kept count of number of the collisions seen by a packet and adjusted the packet delay accordingly. The REAL simulator [26] is based on a similar technique with a centralized master process to simulate CSMA/CD on point-to-point links. Armyros [2] developed a simulator for a equi-distant star topology of the Ethernet. Wang proposed a distributed simulation technique for complex Ethernet topologies [37].

The Ethernet performance has been evaluated using measurement studies [4, 12, 27, 29] by varying the packet lengths, network topologies and offered load. The Ethernet measurement studies indicate that the performance is high and very few packets are lost under normal offered load. In this paper we attempt to evaluate the amount of detail required to accurately simulate the Ethernet. We present two models for Ethernet simulation and perform measurement studies to validate our results.

3. Abstraction at different levels

We study the effect of abstraction at two layers in the network; the medium access control (MAC) layer and the transport layer. At the MAC layer, we propose two models of abstraction for studying the Ethernet, one a CSMA/CD model and the other a droptail model while at the transport layer, we consider a full TCP and a simple TCP model.

3.1. Medium Access Control

The proposed CSMA/CD and the droptail MAC simulation models are developed in ns [20], a discrete event driven simulator targeted at networking research. Each node in the network has its own buffer that stores packets before they are transmitted on the shared medium. Both MAC models in this paper focus on wired local area networks or the Ethernet. The CSMA/CD simulation model depicted in Figure 1 implements the complexities of the CSMA/CD multiple access protocol as specified by the IEEE 802.3 specification [7, 15]. The IEEE 802.3 specification proposes a 1-persistent Carrier Sense Multiple Access with Collision Detection (CSMA/CD) to control access of the shared transmission medium. End hosts monitor the carrier sense signal on the medium and defer to the passing traffic by delaying transmission of the data frame. When the medium is subsequently sensed idle, indicating the completion of the previous transmission, the end host continues to defer for an additional inter-frame spacing before initiating the transmission of the data frame. The inter-frame spacing provides recovery time for the CSMA/CD sublayer and the physical medium.

To handle collisions created due to transmissions from multiple end hosts, the specification additionally outlines a collision detection procedure. A transmitting end host should continuously monitor the signal on the medium to detect collisions. When a collision is detected, the transmitting end host propagates additional bits specified by the jam size on the medium to ensure collision detection at all end hosts on the local area network. The transmitting end host then attempts retransmission after waiting for a random time interval. On failure to retransmit, the end host doubles the waiting time interval, and attempts retransmission after a random period chosen from the new time interval. If the packet is not successfully transmitted after 16 attempts, the packet is dropped. The randomization of the delay after collision is also called truncated binary exponential backoff.

The CSMA/CD model depicted in Figure 1 is a detailed emulation of the IEEE 802.3 specification observed in physical networks. The nodes in the simulated network defer to the passing data frames and delay their transmission for an additional inter-framespacing once the medium is idle. When a collision is detected, the transmitting node enforces a jamming signal and performs a binary exponential backoff. After sixteen retransmission attempts, an error is reported and the frame is dropped. Although the CSMA/CD model is a careful implementation of the IEEE 802.3 specification, a few small mechanisms are not implemented due to limitations of the programming environment. The complete difference between the IEEE 802.3 specification and CSMA/CD model is outlined in Table 1. The droptail MAC model simplifies the shared access protocol and the contention mechanism. The model replaces the complex contention mechanism by a single shared drop tail queue as shown in Figure 2. All nodes on the network send data frames to the common queue, which in turn transmits the data frames onto the shared medium on a first-come-first-served basis. Each node at any time can have only a single frame in the shared queue, additional frames are stored in the individual buffers present in the node. The model thus eliminates the need to perform complex carrier sensing and collision detection mechanisms. The deference delay and binary exponential backoff delay experienced in the CSMA/CD model and the physical network is replaced with a queuing delay at the shared queue. Further, similar to drop of frames during high load in the IEEE 802.3 specification, frame loss will occur in the abstract model when the queue is full. Table 1 summarizes the difference between the proposed models and the IEEE 802.3 specification.

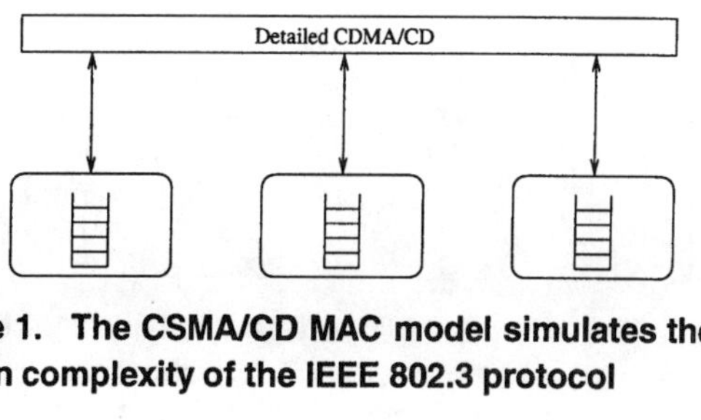

Figure 1. The CSMA/CD MAC model simulates the operation complexity of the IEEE 802.3 protocol

Table 1. Comparison: IEEE 802.3 specification, CSMA/CD and Droptail Ethernet simulation models

Feature	IEEE 802.3 Specification	CSMA/CD Ethernet Model	Droptail Ethernet Model
Deference Mechanism	Nodes defer to passing frames. Ensures at least one inter-frame spacing between frames. If carrier is sensed during the first $2/3^{rd}$ of the inter-frame spacing, reset inter-frame spacing timer.	Nodes defer to passing frames. Ensures at least one inter-frame spacing between frames. Does not reset timer.	A frame generated by a node, defers to all frames generated before it. All frames all queued in the shared queue and transmitted on the medium on a first-come-first-served basis.
Collision Detection and Enforcement	Collision is detected by the physical signaling unit. The collision signal is enforced on the medium by transmitting the additional bits called the jamming signal.	Collision is detected by a busy semaphore. The collision signal is enforced on the medium by transmitting the additional bits called the jamming signal.	No collisions occur since a shared queue ensures only one frame on the Ethernet.
Backoff and Retransmission	Uses truncated binary exponential backoff. A maximum of 16 retransmission attempts are made before reporting an error.	Uses truncated binary exponential backoff. A maximum of 16 retransmission attempts are made before reporting an error.	Since no collision occurs, a retransmission strategy is not needed.
Frame Size	Maximum: 1518 bytes Minimum 64 bytes Higher network layers modify frame if it does not fit the size specification via fragmentation and padding.	Print a warning message when frame size $>$ 1518 bytes. Adds padding if size $<$ 64 bytes	Print a warning message when frame size $>$ 1518 bytes. Adds padding if size $<$ 64 bytes.

3.2. Transport layer models

Simulation approximations can occur at multiple levels and hence it is important to study effect of abstractions at both the MAC level and network. Thus in this paper, in addition to the MAC models, we evaluate two transport layer TCP models; a simple TCP model and the full TCP model. The simple TCP model simulates all the details of the TCP congestion and error control behavior, however, the model does not simulate the connection establishment and tear down phases with SYN and FIN packets. Additionally during congestion and flow control, the simple model makes use of packet units (rather than byte units) for sequence numbers and acknowledgment numbers. This simple abstraction in TCP permits the transfer of data without initial connection setup and thus stores less state regarding the current source-destination transfer. On the other hand, the full TCP model is more detailed and simulates connections establishment and tear down phases using SYN and FIN packets. The full TCP model supports bidirectional data transfer and tracks sequence and acknowledgment numbers in packets. Although the simple TCP model is sufficient in many simulation scenarios where fidelity in the connection setup and teardown phases is not critical, the full TCP model is recommended when modeling a realistic TCP implementation. The connection establishment phase may be important in when trying to model short data transfers.

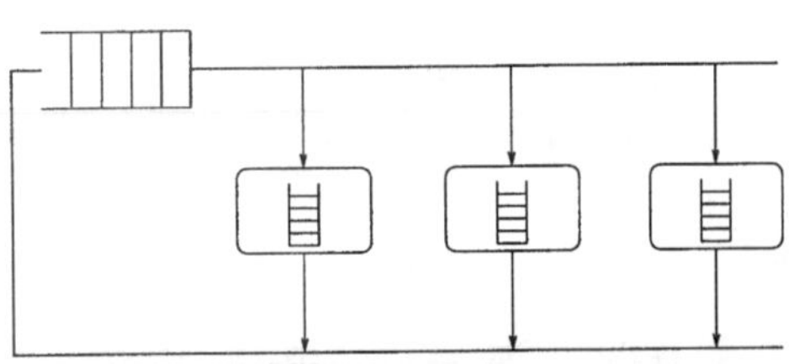

Figure 2. The droptail MAC model makes use of a shared queue to represent the contention mechanism

In this paper, we evaluate the effect of both layers of abstraction and validate our results with testbed measurements on both a 10Mbits/s and a 100Mbits/s local area network. The problem space exercised in the paper is summarized in Table 3.2. We describe the experimentation methodology in the next section.

4. Methodology

We evaluate the abstraction models proposed in Section 3 by comparing the results with testbed measurements. We outline the simulation and the testbed configuration next whereas the experimental results are presented in Section 5.

4.1. Simulation Environment

We study the effect of abstraction in CSMA/CD and droptail MAC models by comparing the throughput measurements obtained in simulation with measurements for the similar environment on a testbed. All measurements, both in simulation and the testbed, are gathered by making use of the topology described in Figure 3. The local area network consists of a single web server with multiple web clients.

We consider a physical network consisting of 10Mb/s and 100Mb/s Ethernet LANs, both in simulation and testbed experimentation. The Ethernet configuration parameters applied for the models are given in Table 3. We make use of the same bandwidth and propagation delay parameters for the droptail MAC model.

For our traffic workload, the number of web clients is progressively increased from 1 to 30. Network traffic is generated by a client node when it instantiates a web session with the server node. Every web session is made up of multiple pages where each web page consists of many web objects. The web session emulates user browsing behavior on the Internet, where a web page may contain multiple images (or objects) [18, 28]. In this paper, to reproduce similar web traffic on the testbed and in simulation, each web page consists of a single object. The web object size follows a cumulative distribution proposed by the Webstone benchmark [35] and is given in Table 4.1. The web object size is heavy-tailed where nearly 99% web pages are less then 50Kbytes and 0.1% of the pages are more than 5Mbytes. We believe this emulates the web page distributions observed on the Internet [10].

Each simulation experiment considers 10 minutes of simulation time. We vary three variables: network speed (10 or 100Mb/s), LAN model (a simple simulation model, a more detailed model, and a real testbed), and number of clients (from 1 to 30). We then evaluate the mean throughput and simulation time and simulation memory usage.

4.2. Testbed setup

To evaluate our simulation models we created a testbed environment for 10Mbit/s and 100Mbit/s LANs. We use the Webstone benchmark software [35] to record the throughput, using the same object size distribution as the simulation models (Table 4.1). The setup consists of one web server machine and five client machines in a private non-switched network and all measurements are made after 10minutes of run time. Every client machine can support multiple web clients, each capable of a distinct web session with the web server. The web sessions follow the same methodology outlined in Section 4.1. To make sure the limited number of client machines do not change the measurement results, we ensured that the client machines saturate the link and also observed the collision rate. The number of collisions stay fairly constant on adding a new machine. Hence, we believe that the above setup shall produce similar results as by an extended 30 machine LAN. In future we plan to extend the testbed to 30 clients to validate our belief. The 10Mbit/s experiments used a 200Mhz Pentium Pro, 128MB of physical memory machine running FreeBSDv4.3 and an Apache web server. The 100Mbit/s experiments used a Pentium III Xeon, 532MB of physical memory machine running FreeBSD v4.7 and an Apache web server. We monitored the server utilization during the experiments to determine if the bandwidth measurements were being affected

Table 2. Problem space exercised in simulation and testbed.

MAC layer model	Transport layer model			
	Simple TCP	*Full TCP*	*FreeBSD 4.3*	*FreeBSD 4.7*
CSMA/CD	X	X		
Droptail	X	X		
Testbed 10Mbit/s			X	
Testbed 100Mbit/s				X

Table 3. Configuration parameters: CSMA/CD model

Parameters	10Mbit	100Mbit
Bus Bandwidth	10Mbit/s	100Mbit/s
Max Propagation Delay	950ns	950ns
Jam time after Collision	3.2μs	0.32μs
Slot Size	51.2μs	5.12μs
Inter-frame Delay	9.6μs	0.96μs
Max Frame Size	1518 bytes	1518 bytes
Min Frame Size	64 bytes	64 bytes

Table 4. Web object distribution

Web Object Size	Access Probability	Cumulative Distribution
500B	0.35	0.35
5KB	0.50	0.85
50KB	0.14	0.99
500KB	0.009	0.999
5MB	0.001	1

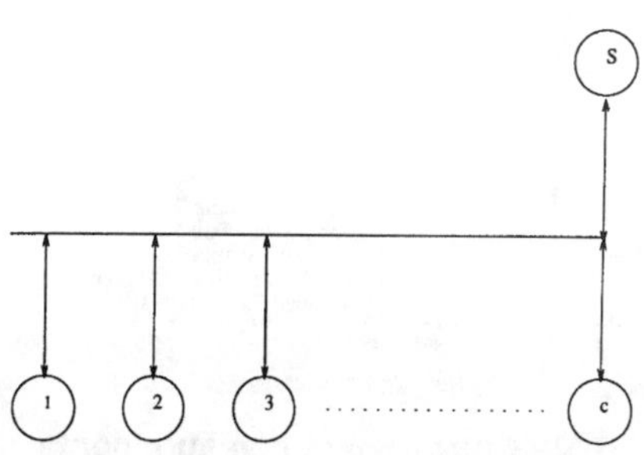

Figure 3. The Ethernet Simulation Topology

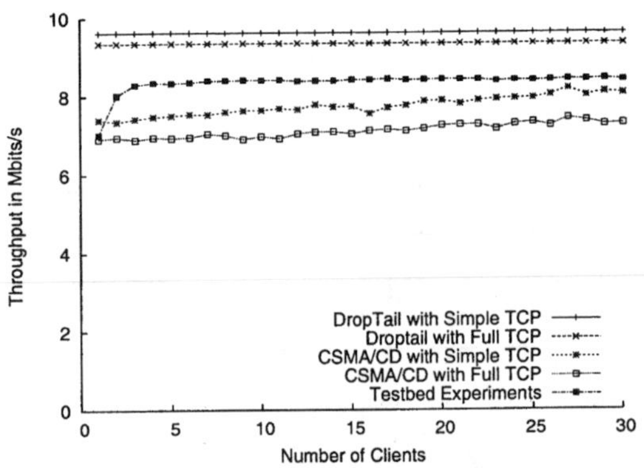

Figure 4. 10Mbit throughput against number of clients

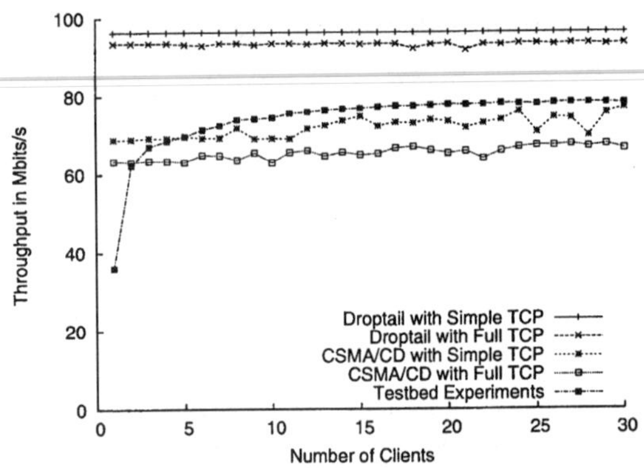

Figure 5. 100Mbit throughput against number of clients

by a bottleneck at the web server. The CPU utilization on the web server was always less than 60% indicating that the bandwidth in the experiments is limited by the network resources, not the server utilization. In the next section we present the analysis of our results.

5. Evaluation

Our first goal is to understand the relative accuracy of the MAC models as compared to each other and testbed experiments. We then consider the effect of TCP abstraction on accuracy. Finally, we evaluate the runtime and memory costs of detail in the simulation. We explore each of these issues in this section.

5.1. Effects of MAC Detail on Accuracy

To evaluate the relative accuracy of the simulation models, we measure and compare the throughput (the number of bytes transferred per unit time) obtained in each MAC model. Figure 4 shows observed throughput for the simulation and testbed measurements in a 10Mbit/s LAN and Figure 5 indicates the results for a 100Mbit/s LAN. We ran all experiments thrice and the variation in the throughput values was less than 2% and hence we did not plot error-bars.

We can make a number of observations from these two graphs. First, we observe that the throughput obtained in the simulation models of CSMA/CD closely follows the measurements on the testbed. Since this model is the most detailed and hence closely resembles the testbed environment, the above results validate the accuracy of the model. The results for both LAN capacities indicate that the CSMA/CD model measurements are close to testbed measurements but are slightly more conservative, with a 7% lower throughput. We believe the results in simulation are more conservative as the number of collisions in the simulation environment are higher. While the simulation model delay and back-off, it does not model jitter. In the real network, randomized jitter helps packets avoid collisions.

Next we observe that the droptail model has consistently higher throughput measurements at both LAN speeds. Although the queuing delay in the droptail model emulates the carrier sensing characteristic in CSMA/CD model, it does

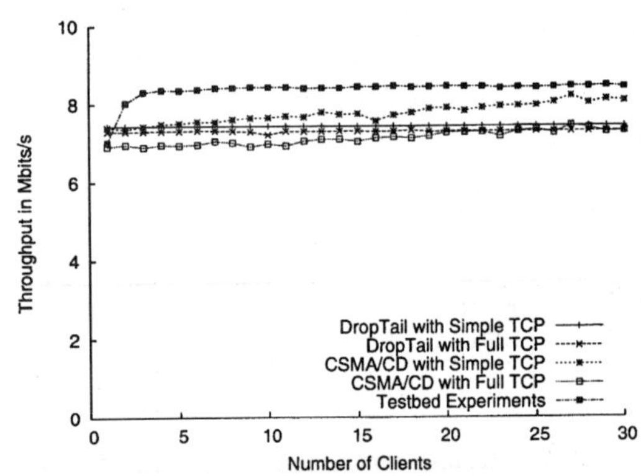

Figure 6. 10Mbit throughput measurements with 22% normalization of bandwidth for droptail model

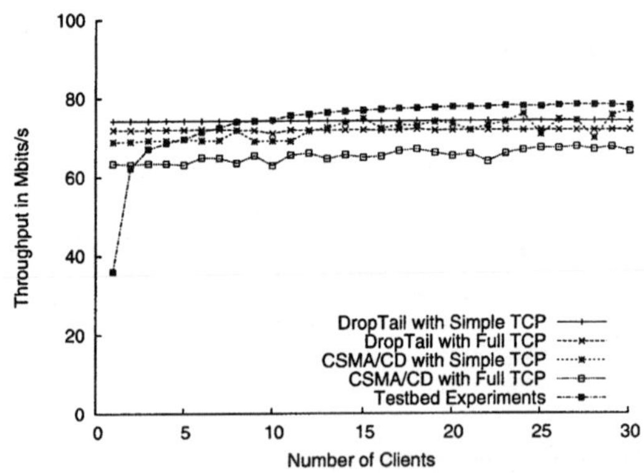

Figure 7. 100Mbit throughput measurements with 22% normalization of bandwidth for droptail model

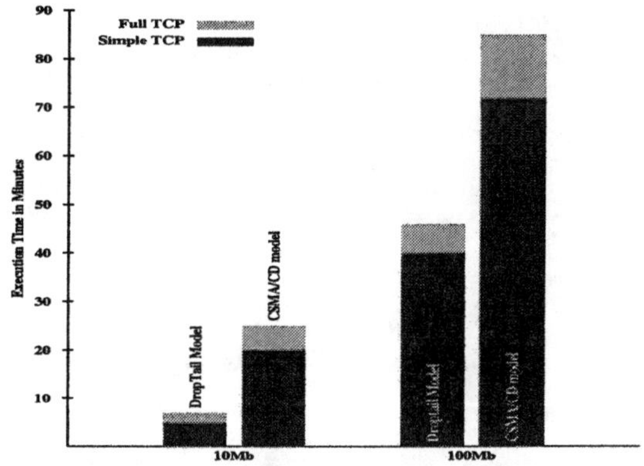

Figure 8. Real execution time corresponding to 10 minute Simulation time

not effectively capture the delay caused due to binary exponential back-off after a collision, and so it allows a higher utilization. Later, we discuss how the droptail model can be used in place of the CSMA/CD model to simulate the Ethernet. The throughput difference in the TCP models is discussed in the next section.

5.2. Effect of TCP abstraction

In addition to comparing MAC protocol detail, we considered two versions of TCP: ns's simpler one-way TCP, and full-TCP. The difference between these two TCP models is discussed in Section 3.2. We next compare the throughput results of simple and full TCP models. The Figures 4 and 5 indicate that the throughput measurements for simple TCP model are higher than the Full TCP model for both the droptail and the CSMA/CD models indicating that Ethernet performance is dependent on how the higher layers characterize the traffic. The cumulative distribution in Table 4.1 shows that about 85% of the generated web traffic consists of short duration flows that have fewer than 4 frames. Therefore connection establishment, tear down, and slow start mechanisms govern the data transfer and results in many small packets on the network. The lower throughput in the Full TCP model is due to the connection establishment and teardown phases absent in the simple TCP model.

5.3. Memory usage and Runtime measurements

A common motivation for abstraction is improved performance, so in addition to understanding the cost in accuracy we wanted to measure the differences in simulation runtime and memory usage. (The other common motivation of abstraction is simplicity of implementation; we do not consider that here because it is more difficult to quantify.) In this section, we compare the memory and runtime gains obtained by making simplifications in the MAC model.

The droptail simulation model is very easy to implement since it does not require collision detection, back-off and retransmission mechanisms. Figure 8 shows the execution time for the CSMA/CD and the droptail models for both 10 and 100Mb/s networks. Execution time shown in the figure represents the average computation time during three independent simulation runs. We observe that eliminating the detail in the MAC models reduces the execution time considerably. The droptail model is 75% faster than the detailed CSMA/CD model, and we observe that using Full TCP increases execution time by as much as 17-25%. We conclude that the much larger amount of abstraction in the MAC models results in a corresponding performance benefit. It is also important to note that the execution time difference increases by more than 15% on a 100Mbit network as compared to the same experiment scenario on a 10Mbit network. We might expect that CPU savings would scale linearly with increase in bit rates, but it does not, presumably due to constant factors.

Memory usage for 10Mbit MAC models ranged between 1O-12MB of RAM for all the simulation experiments. Similar results were observed for 100Mbit simulations.

5.4. Correcting Throughput with Abstract MAC Models

The above results indicate using an abstract MAC and TCP model will provide considerable savings in execution time and memory usage, although at some cost in accuracy. In our experiments, the models overestimated throughput by a constant amount (about 22%). This observation suggests that, when this constant can be determined, it can be applied as a correction factor to provide simulations that are both accurate and faster. Figures 6 and 7 indicate that the normalized throughput simulations do provide better results as compared to previous runs. With this correction factor throughput for droptail is similar to the detailed CSMA/CD model and the testbed. Thus the droptail model provides a reasonable analysis of Ethernet behavior if we normalize the bandwidth along with lower run-time and implementation costs.

If this approach is to be generalized to other simulations we need to understand the factors that affect the normalization factor. Is it a constant value or does it change as a function of network type, traffic load, or other factors in the scenario? For our scenarios we were able to determine normalization factors that were basically constant across varying workloads and network type. We are currently exploring what set of simulation scenarios have consistent normalization factors.

6. Conclusion

This paper presented a study highlighting different levels of abstraction on the Ethernet. We presented an abstract simulation model the eliminates the overhead of complex

CSMA/CD mechanism by using a shared queue. The abstract model provides significant savings in computational time requirements and allows quick exploration of protocol integrations without getting lost in the details of the model. Especially at high loads, abstraction provides a significant advantage by giving comparable results at lower computation time. We also studied the affect of TCP level abstraction on both the proposed Ethernet models.

However while using an abstraction care must be taken to understand the impact of the abstraction on the observed results. It is essential to employ some validation techniques to ensure their accuracy.

Acknowledgements

We would like to thank Joe Touch and Yu-shun Wang for providing the USC/ISI Postel Center (www.postel.org) resource for our testbed measurements. We would also like to thank all the anonymous reviewers for their helpful comments on the earlier versions of this paper.

References

[1] G. T. Almes and E. D. Lazowska. The behavior of ethernet-like computer communications networks. In *Proceedings of the 7th ACM Symposium on Operating Systems Principles (SOSP)*, pages 66–81, 1979.

[2] S. Armyros. On the behavior of ethernet: Are existing analytic models adequate? Masters Thesis.

[3] E. Arthurs and B.W.Stuck. A theoritical performance analysis of three bus transmission medium access methods. In *IEEE Infocom*, pages 128–138, Las Vegas, Nevada, USA, 1982.

[4] D. R. Boggs, J. C. Mogul, and C. A. Kent. Measured capacity of an ethernet: Myths and reality. In *Proceedings of the ACM SIGCOMM Conference '88*, pages 222–234, Stanford, California, Aug. 1988. ACM.

[5] W. Bux. Local area subnetworks - A performance comparison. In *IEEE Trans. Commun., COM-29(10):1465–1473*, 1981.

[6] A. Cerpa, N. Busek, and D. Estrin. SCALE: A tool for simple connectivity assessment in lossy environments. Technical Report 21, University of California, Los Angeles, Center for Embedded Networked Sensing, Sept. 2003.

[7] I. S. Committee. Ieee standards for local area networks: carrier sense multiple access with collision detection (csma). Technical Report ANSI/IEEE Std 802.3-1985, IEEE, 1985.

[8] E. J. Coyle and B. Liu. Finite population CSMA/CD networks. *IEEE Transactions on Computers*, COM-31(11):1247–1251, Nov. 1983.

[9] E. J. Coyle and B. Liu. A matrix representation of CSMA/CD networks. *IEEE International Conference on Communications: Integrating Communication for World Progress*, 1:53–64, 1985.

[10] M. Crovella, M. Taqqu, and A. Bestavros. Heavy-tailed probability distributions in the world wide web. In *A Practical Guide To Heavy Tails, chapter 1, Chapman and Hall,*, pages 3–26, New York, 1998.

[11] T. A. Gonsalves and F. A. Tobagi. On the performance effects of station location and access protocol parameters in Etherent networks. *IEEE Transactions on Computers*, 36(4):441, Apr. 1988.

[12] R. Gusella. A measurement study of diskless workstation traffic on an ethernet. *IEEE Trans. on Communications, Vol. 38, No. 9*, pages 1557–1568, Sept 1990.

[13] J. Heidemann, N. Bulusu, J. Elson, C. Intanagonwiwat, K. chan Lan, Y. Xu, W. Ye, D. Estrin, and R. Govindan. Effects of detail in wireless network simulation. In *Proceedings of the SCS Multiconference on Distributed Simulation*, pages 3–11, Phoenix, Arizona, USA, January 2001. USC/Information Sciences Institute, Society for Computer Simulation.

[14] H. Hughes and L. Li. Simulation model of an ethernet. In *Computer Performance, Vol. 3, No. 4*, pages 210–217, Dec. 1982.

[15] IEEE. Ieee std 802.3, 1998 edition. Technical Report ANSI/IEE Std. 802.3-1988, IEEE, 1998.

[16] L. Kleinrock and F. A. Tobagi. Packet switching in radio channels: part I carrier sense multiple-access modes and their throughput-delay characteristics. *IEEE trans. on commun.*, COM-23:1400–1416, 1975.

[17] S. S. Lam. Carrier Sense Multiple Access Protocol for local networks. *Computer Networks: The International Journal of Distributed Informatique*, 4(1):21–32, 1980.

[18] B. Mah. An empirical model of HTTP network traffic. In *Proceedings of the IEEE Infocom*, pages 592–600, Kobe, Japan, Apr. 1997. IEEE.

[19] P. Marino and A. Rio. Microprocessing and microprogramming, 1993.

[20] S. McCanne, V. Jacobson, and M. Vetterli. Receiver-driven layered multicast. In *Proceedings of the ACM SIGCOMM Conference '96*, pages 117–130, Stanford, CA, Aug. 1996. ACM.

[21] R. Metcalfe and D. R. Boggs. Ethernet: Distributed packet switching for local computer networks. *Communications of the ACM*, 19(7):395–404, July 1976.

[22] P. J. P. O'Reilly and J. L. H. Jr. An efficient simulation technique for performance studies of csma/cd local networks. *IEEE Journal on Selected Areas in Communications, Vol. SAC-2, No. 1*, pages 238–249, Jan. 1984.

[23] K. Prasad and R. Patel. Performance analysis of ETHERNET based on an event driven simulation algorithm. In *Proc. 13th Conference on Local Computer Networks*, pages 253–267, Minneapolis, Minn., 10-12 1988. IEEE Computer Society.

[24] K. Prasad and A. Singhal. Simulation of ethernet performance based on single server and single queue model. In *Proceedings of the 12th Conference on Local Computer Networks*, pages 74–85, Minneapolis, Minnesota, USA, Oct. 1987.

[25] T. S. Rappaport. *Wireless Communications, Principles and Practice*. Prentice-Hall, 1996.

[26] RealEditv1.0. http://www.cs.cornell.edu/skeshav/real/.

[27] J. F. Shoch and J. A. Hupp. Measured performance of an ethernet local network. *Communications of the ACM*, 23(12):711–721, 1980.

[28] F. Smith, F. H. Campos, K. Jeffay, and D. Ott. What tcp/ip protocol headers can tell us about the web. In *ACM SIGMETRICS 2001/Performance 2001*, pages 245–256, Cambridge, MA, 2001.

[29] W. Smith and R. Kain. Ethernet performance under actual and simulated loads. In *In 16th Conference on Local Computer Networks*, pages 569–581. IEEE Computer Society Press, 1991., 1991.

[30] H. Takagi and L. Kleinrock. Throughput analysis for persistent CSMA systems. *IEEE Transactions on Computers*, COM-33(7):627–638, July 1985.

[31] X. Tan, S. Jue, E. Lo, and R. Hardy. Transient performance of a csma system under temporary overload conditions. In *Proceedings of 15th Conference of Local Computer Networks*, 1990.

[32] S. Tasaka. Dynamic behavior of a CSMA-CD system with a finite population of buffered users. *IEEE Transactions on Communications*, COM-34(6):576–586, June 1986.

[33] F. Tobagi and N. Gonzalez-Cawley. On csma-cd local networks and voice communication. In *IEEE Infocom*, pages 122–127, Las Vegas, Nevada, USA, 1982.

[34] F. Tobagi and V. Hunt. Performance analysis of carrier sense multiple access with collision detection. In *Computer Networks, Vol. 4*, pages 245–259, October/November 1980.

[35] G. Trent and M. Sake. WebSTONE: The first generation in HTTP server benchmarking. http://www.mindcraft.com/WebStone/, Feb. 1995.

[36] L. Tsui and O. M. Ulgen. On modeling local area networks. In *SCS Winter Simulation Conference*, pages 842–849, 1988.

[37] J. Wang and S. Keshav. Efficient and accurate ethernet simulation. In *Proceedings on 24th International Conference in Local Area Networks*, pages 182–191, Oct. 1999.

[38] J. Zhao and R. Govindan. Understanding packet delivery performance in dense wireless sensor networks. In *Proceedings of the First ACM SenSys Conference*, page to appear, Los Angeles, CA, USA, Nov. 2003. ACM.

A Utility Model for Timely State Update in Distributed Wargame Simulations *

Suiping Zhou Stephen John Turner Wentong Cai
Hanfeng Zhao Xiaolin Pang
Parallel and Distributed Computing Center
School of Computer Engineering
Nanyang Technological Uninversity
Singapore 639798
{asspzhou,assjturner,aswtcai,ashfzhao,asxlpang}@ntu.edu.sg

Abstract

In distributed wargame simulations, the states of simulation entities need to be updated and sent to other simulation nodes in a timely manner, which may incur high overhead on the network. Thus, how to efficiently use the limited bandwidth of the network is very important to the performance of distributed wargame simulations. In this paper, a utility model is proposed to evaluate the relative importance of a simulation entity. In our proposed utility model, the utility of an entity is determined by the number of entities on which this entity may have influence and the distances between this entity and the entities within its area of influence. Based on the utility model, we may devise some flexible updating mechanisms which can utilize the bandwidth more efficiently. For example, the state updates of an important entity which may have great influence on the simulation could be sent to other nodes with a high frequency; on the other hand, the state updates of an entity with little importance may be sent to other simulation nodes with a low frequency. In this paper, we will focus on the utility computation of a simulation entity rather than the flexible state updating mechanisms for the simulation entities. Our proposed utility computation mechanism is general and can be easily implemented using the HLA services. Experimental results show that the utility computation mechanism incurs little overhead.

***Keywords**: Wargame Simulations, Distributed Simulation, Utility Model*

*This research was supported by a grant from the Defence Science and Technology Agency of Singapore under the Defence Innovative Research Programme.

1. Introduction

In distributed wargame simulations, the state of a simulation entity needs to be updated and sent to other simulation nodes in a timely manner, which may cause large communication overhead on the network if the number of entities involved is large. Thus, the limited network bandwidth needs to be used efficiently such that the inconsistency of the simulation will be minimized and the fidelity of the simulation can be maintained [1, 2, 3].

Some work has been done on how to efficiently use the network bandwidth in distributed simulations. For example, relevance filtering [4, 5, 6] and Dead Reckoning (DR) [7] are widely used in distributed simulations to reduce the number of state updates sent over the network. Though these techniques may considerably reduce the communication overhead of a distributed simulation, for large scale distributed wargame simulations in which tens of thousands of simulation entities interact with each other, the communication overhead may still be very high. To use the limited network bandwidth more efficiently, we may devise some flexible update mechanism such that an entity with higher importance will be updated more frequently, and an entity with lower importance may be updated less frequently. To this end, we propose a utility model in which the relative importance of a simulation entity is represented by the utility [8] of the entity. In our proposed model, the definition of the utility of a simulation entity takes into account the number of entities on which an entity may have influence and the distances between this entity and those entities which are within its area of influence, thus the utility model reflects how heavily an entity is "used" by other entities.

In this paper, we will focus on the computation of the utility of a simulation entity. A utility computation mechanism is developed based on the DDM (Data Distribution

Management) services in HLA (High Level Architecture) [9, 10]. The remainder of the paper is organized as follows. In Section 2, we present the utility model of a simulation entity. A mechanism to compute the utility of an entity is described in Section 3. Experiments are done in Section 4 to evaluate the overhead of the proposed mechanism. Finally, conclusions and future work are given in Section 5.

2. A Utility Model for Simulation Entities

2.1. A General Utility Model

For a simulation entity e in a distributed simulation, we have the following observations:

- If the state update of entity e has influence on a large number of entities in the simulation, then the state update of entity e may have great impact on the whole simulation. On the other hand, if the state update of entity e has influence on a small number of entities in the simulation, then the state update of entity e may have only little impact on the whole simulation. Thus, the number of entities on which entity e may have influence is an important factor in deciding the relative importance of a simulation entity.

- If entity e is close to some other entities, then the state update of entity e may have great impact on other entities (e.g., for collision detection). On the other hand, if entity e is far away from other entities, then the state update of entity e may have only little impact on other entities. Thus, the distance between an entity and other entities is another important factor in deciding the relative importance of the entity.

The relative importance of an entity could be used to decide the update frequency of the entity. For example, an entity with higher importance should be updated more frequently, and an entity with lower importance could be updated less frequently. Note that the relative importance of an entity is not the only factor in deciding the update frequency of the entity. We have developed some flexible update mechanisms where the update frequency of an entity is decided by its relative importance and its speed [11].

To evaluate the relative importance of a simulation entity, we first propose a general utility model based on utility theory, then in the next two subsections we will refine this utility model to take into consideration the above two factors in deciding the relative importance of a simulation entity.

Now suppose there are n entities in the simulation. These entities are classified into m different types denoted by $C_1, C_2, ..., C_m$ (such as tank, aircraft, etc.), and there are n_j entities of type C_j, where $j \in [1, m]$, and $\sum_{j=1}^{m} n_j = n$. Then, we have the following definition:

Definition 2.1 *The utility of a simulation entity e_i, where $i \in [1, n]$, is defined as*

$$U(e_i) = \sum_{j=1}^{m} \frac{n_j}{n} U_j(e_i) \qquad (1)$$

where $U_j(e_i) \in [0, 1]$ is the relative utility of entity e_i with respect to entity type C_j.

Obviously, the utility of an entity is a value between 0 and 1.

As can be seen from Definition 2.1, the relative utility $U_j(e_i)$ plays an important role in deciding the overall utility of entity e_i. In the next two subsections, we will give the definition of the relative utility of an entity based on the relative importance of the entity.

2.2. Relative Utility

To decide the relative importance of a simulation entity, we need to know the number of entities on which this entity may have influence. Let r_j denote the radius of the Area of Interest (AOI)[1] [5] of entity type C_j, for $j = 1, 2, ..., m$. Then, we define the area of influence of an entity as follows:

Definition 2.2 *The area of influence of an entity e_i with respect to entity type C_j, denoted as $\mathcal{I}_j(e_i)$, is the circular area centered around the position of e_i and with a radius of r_j, where $i = 1, 2, ..., n$, $j = 1, 2, ..., m$.*

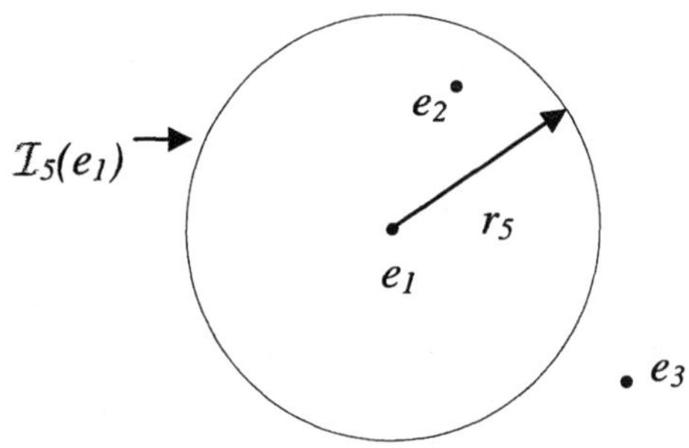

Figure 1. Area of influence of an entity

As an example, the area of influence of entity e_1 with respect to entity type C_5 is shown in Figure 1, where e_2 and e_3 are entities of type C_5. Since the distance between e_1 and e_2 is less than r_5, i.e., e_1 is within the area of interest of

[1] In this paper, we focus on the position of a simulation entity, and we assume that all entities of the same type have the same size of AOI.

e_2, the state updates of e_1 will have influence on e_2. On the other hand, the distance between e_1 and e_3 is greater than r_5, thus, the state updates of e_1 have no influence on e_3.

Let $N_j(e_i)$ denote the number of entities of type C_j which are within $\mathcal{I}_j(e_i)$, for $i = 1, 2, ..., n, j = 1, 2, ..., m$. We have the following definition:

Definition 2.3 *The relative utility of an entity e_i with respect to an entity type C_j is*

$$U_j(e_i) = \frac{N_j(e_i)}{n_j} \tag{2}$$

where $i = 1, 2, ..., n, j = 1, 2, ..., m$.

In the above definition, the relative utility of an entity e_i with respect to an entity type C_j is decided by the number of entities of type C_j that are within the area of influence of entity e_i with respect to entity type C_j.

2.3. A Refined Utility Model

In definition 2.3, we treat equally all the entities of type C_j that are within the area of influence of entity e_i with respect to type C_j. To consider the effect of the distances in deciding the relative importance of entity e_i with respect to type C_j, we further divide $\mathcal{I}_j(e_i)$ into multiple levels as shown in Figure 2.

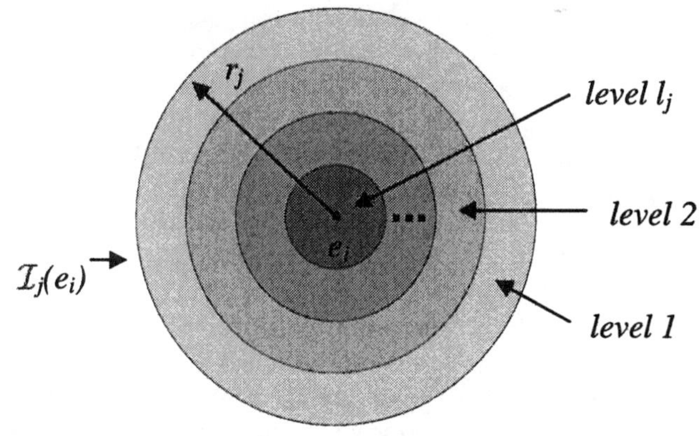

Figure 2. Multiple levels of area of influence

Suppose $\mathcal{I}_j(e_i)$ is divided into l_j levels as shown in Figure 2, and there are $N_j^{(1)}(e_i), N_j^{(2)}(e_i), ..., N_j^{(l_j)}(e_i)$ entities of type C_j within each level respectively. Considering the different distances between these entities and entity e_i, a refined utility model is given as follows:

Definition 2.4 *The utility of a simulation entity e_i, where $i \in [1, n]$, is defined as*

$$U(e_i) = \sum_{j=1}^{m} \frac{n_j}{n} U_j(e_i) \tag{3}$$

where

$$U_j(e_i) = \frac{1}{n_j} \sum_{k=1}^{l_j} w_j^{(k)} \cdot N_j^{(k)}(e_i) \tag{4}$$

with $\sum_{k=1}^{l_j} w_j^{(k)} = 1$, and $0 < w_j^{(1)} < w_j^{(2)} < \cdots < w_j^{(l_j)} < 1$

Remark 2.1 *In the above definition, different weights are given to different levels to reflect how close an entity is to other entities - the closer an entity is to other entities, the more important the state updates of this entity are to other entities.*

3. Utility Computation

It can be seen from Definition 2.4 that $N_j^{(k)}(e_i)$, i.e., the number of entities of type C_j which are within the k-th level of $\mathcal{I}_j(e_i)$, plays an important role in the computation of the utility of an entity e_i. Once $N_j^{(k)}(e_i)$ is known, $U(e_i)$ can be easily computed using (3) and (4). In this section, we develop a mechanism to compute $N_j^{(k)}(e_i)$ using some HLA services. In particular, the DDM services in HLA are used to associate a region with an attribute for update or subscription. Note that the utility of an entity represents the relative importance of an entity to other entities, and is used to decide how frequently the state updates of the entity need to be sent to other federates. Therefore, to compute $N_j^{(k)}(e_i)$, only the entities that are in other federates are considered.

The goal of the HLA DDM services is to limit the messages received by federates in large distributed federations to those messages of interest in order to reduce the traffic over the network. By specifying update regions and subscription regions, federates tell the RTI (Run Time Infrastructure) [9] of their data properties and requirements. A data connection will be established between a pair of federates only when an update region and a subscription region overlap.

We have the following observation:

Observation 3.1 *An entity e of type C_j is within the k-th level of the area of influence of entity e_i with respect to type C_j, if and only if e_i is within the k-th level of the area of interest of e.*

Based on Observation 3.1, we divide the area of interest of a type of entity into different levels. As can be seen from the following mechanism, compared with the approach of dividing the area of influence of a type of entity into different levels, the approach of dividing the area of interest will result in fewer number of update and subscription regions, and a federate does not need to know the AOIs of the entities in other federates using this approach.

Suppose there are m different types of entities in the simulation. The AOI of each type of entity is divided into l levels[2]. In addition to its normal attributes such as position and velocity, an entity e_i has l dummy attributes $d_k(e_i)$ associated with each level, $k = 1, 2, ..., l$.

When a federate starts, it calls the function *enableAttributeScopeAdvisorySwitch*() to instruct the LRC (Local RTI Component) to notify the federate of changing instance-attribute scope. Thus, whenever an instance-attribute comes into scope or goes out of scope, the LRC uses the *attributesInScope*() or *attributesOutOfScope*() callbacks to inform the federate [9]. Using these functions, we propose the following mechanism for a federate to compute $N_j^{(k)}(e_i)$ (assuming e_i is a simulation entity in this federate):

- When specifying update regions, the federate does the following (see Figure 3):
    1. Associates a point region defined by e_i's position with e_i's normal attributes (e.g., position, velocity, etc.);
    2. Associates the k-th level region of the e_i's AOI ($k = 1, 2, ..., l$) with the dummy attributes $d_k(e_i)$.
- When specifying subscription regions, a federate does the following (see Figure 3):
    1. Subscribes to the normal attributes of all entity types with e_i's AOI;
    2. Subscribes to the dummy attributes of all entity types with a point region defined by e_i's position.
- To get $N_j^{(k)}(e_i)$, the federate maintains a two-dimensional array CT of size m by l. The entry $CT[j][k]$ is used to keep the number of entities of type C_j that are within the k-th level of $\mathcal{I}_j(e_i)$, i.e., $CT[j][k] = N_j^{(k)}(e_i)$, where $j = 1, 2, ..., m$, $k = 1, 2, ..., l$. All entries of the array are initialized to 0 when the federate starts.
- When an entity of type C_j moves into a certain level of $\mathcal{I}_j(e_i)$, the LRC calls the function *attributesInScope*() in the federate ambassador. The function *attributesInScope*() is implemented as shown in Figure 4. The function does the following:
    1. Get the type index j of the entity using the object handle, and get the level index k using the attribute handle.
    2. Increase $CT[j][k]$ by 1.
- When an entity of type C_j moves out of a certain level of $\mathcal{I}_j(e_i)$, the LRC calls the function *attributesOutOfScope*() in the federate ambassador, which does the following:
    1. Get the type index j of the entity using the object handle, and get the level index k using the attribute handle.
    2. Decrease $CT[j][k]$ by 1.

[2]The AOIs of different types of entities may be divided into different numbers of levels. Here, we assume that all AOIs are divided into the same number of levels for simplicity.

It should be noted that the associated regions need to be modified as e_i moves. Thus, in addition to the computational overhead of functions $attributesInScope()$ and $attributesOutOfScope()$, the above mechanism also incurs some overhead when updating the associated regions.

4. Experiments

In this section, we investigate the overhead of the proposed utility computation mechanism. To this end, an HLA-based simulation scenario was developed and simulation experiments were performed.

4.1. Experiment Design

The simulation environment consists of two PCs connected by a 100Mbps LAN. There are two federates in the simulation. One federate running on one of the PCs simulates an aircraft, the other federate running on the other PC simulates a number of tanks. In the simulation, each tank is treated as an individual entity, though they may move in groups.

Since HLA only supports rectangular regions, in the simulation, the AOI of an entity (tank or aircraft) is represented by a square region. The AOI of a tank is set to a 200 unit by 200 unit square region centered around the tank, and the AOI of the aircraft is set to a 600 unit by 600 unit square region centered around the aircraft. To evaluate the overhead of the proposed mechanism, we focus on the utility computation for the aircraft. Thus the area of influence of the aircraft with respect to tanks is divided into multiple levels as shown in Figure 5. A point region is associated with a tank's position for updates, and the corresponding regions described in Section 3 are associated with a tank's dummy attributes. The aircraft subscribes a tank's position using the aircraft's AOI, and also subscribes a tank's dummy attributes with a point region defined by the aircraft's position.

Suppose there are 1000 tanks, and all tanks are initialized at position (-100, 0). The tanks are divided into 10 groups, with each group consisting of 100 tanks. The tanks move with constant speed of 1 unit per time step towards

```
/* Specify update regions */
for (each normal attribute of entity e_i) do{
   associate a point region with the attribute;
}
for (each dummy attribute of entity e_i) do{
   associate the k-th level region of e_i's AOI
   with the dummy attributes; /* k=1,2,...,l */
}

/* Specify subscription regions */
for (each entity type) do{
   subscribe to all the normal attributes with e_i's AOI region;
   subscribe to all dummy attributes with a point region;
}
```

Figure 3. Publish and subscribe object attributes

```
attributesInScope(RTI::ObjectHandle theObjectHandle,
const RTI::AttributeHandleSet& theAttributes){
   get the type index j of the entity using the object handle;
   get the level index k using the attribute handle in theAttributes;
   CT[j][k]++;
}

attributesOutOfScope(RTI::ObjectHandle theObjectHandle,
const RTI::AttributeHandleSet& theAttributes){
   get the type index j of the entity using the object handle;
   get the level index k using the attribute handle in theAttributes;
   CT[j][k]--;
}
```

Figure 4. Function *attributesInScope()* **and** *attributesOutOfScope()*

the aircraft which is stationary at position (0, 0). Different groups of tanks start to move at different time steps. At the start of the simulation, the first group of tanks starts to move, then another group of tanks starts to move at each of the following time steps. The simulation stops when the last group of tanks reaches position (100, 0). The utility of the aircraft is computed by the federate which simulates the aircraft. The total elapsed time of the simulation is recorded at the aircraft federate.

4.2. Results and Analysis

To evaluate the overhead of the utility computation mechanism, we record the elapsed time of the simulation without using the utility computation mechanism (denoted as T_1) and the elapsed time of the simulation using the utility computation mechanism (denoted as T_2). The overhead of the utility computation mechanism is defined as $\frac{T_2-T_1}{T_1}$.

In order to investigate how the overhead of the utility computation mechanism may change with the number of levels of the area of influence of the aircraft, simulation experiments were done with five different numbers of levels. Figure 6 shows the result of the experiments.

As can be seen from Figure 6, as the number of levels increases, the overhead increases slowly. In addition, we do not expect to have a very large number of levels in real applications. The computation in this experiment is very simple, e.g., within each time step, only a simple collision detection mechanism is used, and no 3D graphics computation is performed. Therefore, T_1 is very small. We expect the overhead of the utility computation mechanism to be very small for real applications where the computation is much more complex.

To investigate the effect of the number of entities on the overhead of the utility computation mechanism, the number of tanks is set to 100, 200, 500, 1000 and 2000 respectively

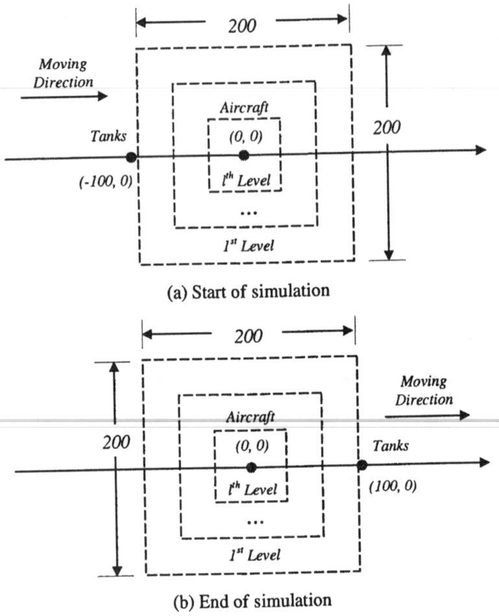

Figure 5. A simple simulation scenario

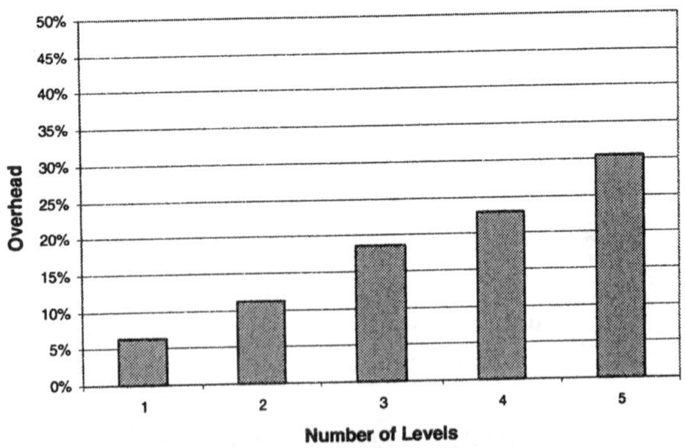

Figure 6. Impact of number of levels

in the following experiments. All tanks have the same AOI, and the number of levels is set to one in the experiments.

Figure 7 shows the result of the experiments. It can be seen that the overhead of the utility computation mechanism is small, and it decreases as the number of tanks increases. The reason for this is that the overhead of the utility computation mechanism does not increase as fast as the overhead of the collision detection mechanism as the number of tanks increases. Again, we expect the overhead to be very small for real applications where complex computation is involved.

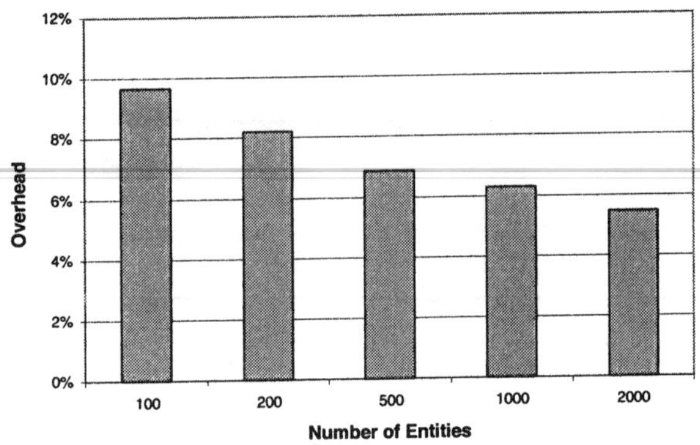

Figure 7. Impact of number of entities

5. Conclusions and Future Work

Distributed wargame simulations may cause high communication overhead on the network. Data inconsistency may occur if state updates of the simulation entities cannot be sent to other simulation nodes in a timely manner. Thus, how to efficiently utilize the limited network bandwidth is an important issue in distributed wargame simulations. In this paper, we propose a utility model to evaluate the relative importance of a simulation entity. Based on the utility model, flexible updating mechanisms can be designed to minimize the data inconsistency of the simulations. For example, the state updates of an important entity may be sent to other nodes more frequently, while the state updates of an unimportant entity may be sent to other nodes less frequently. We also propose a mechanism to compute the utility of an entity based on HLA services. Experimental results show that the proposed mechanism incurs little overhead.

In our future work, we will investigate a flexible updating mechanism based on the utility model. The flexible updating mechanism and the utility model will be implemented in a distributed wargame simulation to investigate the feasibility of using them in real wargame applications.

References

[1] V. Krishnawamy, M. Raynal, D. Bakken, and M. Ahamad, "Shared State Consistency for Time-Sensitive Distributed Applications", *Proc. of the International Conference on Distributed Computing Systems* (ICDCS 2001), April 2001, Phoenix, Arizona, USA, pp.606-614.

[2] F. Torres-Rojas, M. Ahamad, and M. Raynal, "Timed Consistency for Shared Distributed Objects", *Proc. of the 18th Annual ACM Symposium on Principles of Distributed Computing*, May 1999, Atlanta, GA, USA, pp.163-172.

[3] A. Ozaki, M. Furuichi, K. Takahashi, H. Matsukawa, "Design and Implementation of Parallel and Distributed Wargame Simulation System ", *IEICE/IEEE Joint Special Issue on Autonomous Decentralized Systems and Systems' Assurance*, vol.E84-D, no.10, 2001, pp.1376-1384.

[4] M. Bassiouni, M.-H. Chiu, M.Loper and M. Garnsey, "Relevance Filtering for Distributed Interactive Simulation", *Journal of Computer Systems Science and Engineering*, vol.13, no.1, January, 1998, pp.39-47.

[5] Katherine L. Morse, "Interest Management in Large-Scale Distributed Simulation", *Technical report #96-27*, Dept. of Information and Computer Science, Univ. of California at Irvine, 1996.

[6] S. J. Rak and Daniel J. Van Hook, "Evaluation of Grid-based Relevance Filtering for Multicast Group Assignment", *Proc. of 14th DIS workshop on Standards for the Interoperability of Distributed Simulation*, March 1996, Institute for Simulation and Training, Orlando, FL, USA, pp. 739-747.

[7] IEEE 1278, Standard for Information Technology - Protocols for Distributed Interactive Simulation Applications, 1993.

[8] L. G. Jones, A. J. Lattanze, "Using the Architecture Tradeoff Analysis Method to evaluate a Wargame Simulation System: A Case Study", *Technical Note CMU/SEI-2001-TN-022*, Sofeware Engineering Institute, Carnegie Mellon University, December 2001.

[9] U.S. Department of Defense, "High Level Architecture Interface Specification", Version 1.3, April 1998.

[10] DMSO, RTI 1.3-Next Generation Programmer's Guide (Version 5), 2002.

[11] S. P. Zhou, W. T. Cai, S. J. Turner, H. F. Zhao, and X. L. Pang, "Flexible State Update Mechanisms in Large Scale Distributed Wargame Simulations", *submitted to European Simulation Interoperability Workshop 2004*.

Session 6: Applications

A Component-based Simulation Layer for JAMES

Jan Himmelspach and Adelinde M. Uhrmacher
University of Rostock
18059 Rostock, Germany
{jh194, lin}@informatik.uni-rostock.de

Abstract

If a model shall be executed in a parallel, distributed instead of a sequential manner, typically the entire simulation engine has to be exchanged. To adapt the simulation layer more easily to the requirements of a concrete model to be run in a specific environment a component based simulation layer has been developed for JAMES. *A set of different simulator components demonstrates that a component-based design facilitates the exchange of simulators and their combination.*

1. Introduction

An efficient and effective execution of multi-agent systems faces different challenges. One simulation strategy will hardly suffice due to the diversity of multi-agent systems. Multi-agent systems might comprise thousands of light-weight reactive agents, a couple of deliberative agents, or a combination thereof. Since the execution time of deliberative components can hardly be foretold, conservative techniques that are based on lookaheads are not easily applicable. Multi-agent systems are characterized by dynamic patterns of composition and interaction. The costs introduced by saving states of the model, including information about added and deleted models and couplings, moving agents etc. hamper the use of optimistic strategies. In addition each single logical process executing an agent or part of an agent might consume a very different amount of wall clock time to advance in virtual time. The danger exists that most models of a simulation have run "optimistically" to "completion", before one agent has decided on its action. If the model comprises thousands of purely reactive agents the situation is again entirely different.

Particularly in testing software agents in virtual simulated environments, different types of simulators might be used, not for reasons of efficiency, but to exert a different degree of control on the experiment depending on the requirements of the software agent's development phase [13].

Thus, experimenting with agents requires a set of simulators that the user selects depending on the model and the available computing resources. Generally it is required that a change of simulation engines from sequential to parallel or vice versa should not induce a change in the model [8], nevertheless even a small change at the simulation engines level typically caused an exchange of entire simulation engines. A modular, component-based design of the simulation layer should facilitate adapting the simulation to the demands of a specific model to be run in a specific environment.

A component-based design of the simulation layer implies developing basic components that are extendable, exchangeable, and re-usable [6]. Therefore, common patterns referring to the properties and methods of object-classes and their interactions have to be identified [3][1]. The following summarizes our exploration into the world of components and patterns while re-designing the simulation layer of JAMES.

2. Background - Supported Modeling Formalism

JAMES has been developed based on the formalism DYN-DEVS. The model design resembles that of DEVS (Discrete Event System Specification) [14] extended by means of reflection which allows agents to adapt their composition, interaction, and behavior patterns. The model design distinguishes between *atomic* and *coupled models*. Coupled models are the means to develop complex models by hierarchical composition. A coupled model is a model consisting of different components and specifying the coupling of its components. Its interface to its environment is given by a set of external input and output events. The description of an atomic model embraces a set of input events, a state set, a set of output events, an internal, external, and confluent transition function, an output and time advance function. The internal transition function (`deltaInt`) dictates state transitions due to internal events, the time of which is determined by the time advance function. The external transition function (`deltaExt`) is triggered by external inputs which are defined as bags over simultaneously arriving input events. The confluent transition function (`deltaCon`) is invoked if internal and external event coincide. So executing DEVS models follows the scheme: activate all models having a tonie (time of next internal event) equal to the current simulation time and execute their lambda function. Afterwards these models have to determine whether there are any external inputs or not - if there are inputs the confluent, otherwise the internal transition function is executed. All models which have received an input but having a tonie different from the actual time execute the external transition function.

Reflective mechanisms empower the atomic model to change the composition and interaction structure of the model. Models are able to change their own behavior and interaction pattern, e.g. to commit suicide, to start migrating, to create new models and add migrating models within the embedding coupled model, and to alter their interaction structure with their environment.

To support the integration of external real time processes, e.g. planning systems, an atomic model class has been introduced that is equipped with a peripheral port and a time function. The former provides a port through which model and external process communicate, the latter enables the user to explicitly relate simulation time and resource consumption of the real-time process.

The simulation layer for DEVS-like models is traditionally structured into a tree of processors whose leaves are called simulators. They are responsible for executing the atomic models whereas the other processor nodes, the coordinators, are responsible for executing the coupled models [14].

3. The execution layer

In JAMES a series of different simulators have been implemented, e.g. [11, 12, 13]. The focus of these simulators has been on the parallel distributed simulation of multi-agent systems. The simulation of multi-agent systems typically comes in two forms:

(a) A dynamic system might be described as a multi-agent system.

E.g. in modeling the activities of the tryptophan operon in the cell as a multi-agent system, enzymes, DNA, and mRNA and repressors interact as autonomous reactive entities. Depending on the concentration of tryptophan and the state of the repressor, the repressor decides to move to the DNA and to block the operator inhibiting the production of mRNA and consequently of new enzymes [10]. Agents are used as a metaphor to describe and understand the dynamics within the cell.

(b) Simulation might be used to help developing agent software.

Zeigler proposed a continuation of using modeling and simulation throughout the entire software production process [4]. In JAMES we have concentrated so far on the testing of agents. As agent software is typically designed to run in dynamic and open environments, simulation seems a suitable method for systematically testing the software [13]. In this case, simulation of agents implies embedding agent software in virtual environments, i.e. a software-in-the-loop simulation.

In all simulators developed in JAMES, the support of variable structure models and an interaction with external computing resources has been paramount.

The new component-based simulation layer should reflect our previous experiences and support:

- Paced and unpaced simulators
  Most simulators in JAMES have been unpaced. However, for testing purposes paced variants of simulators might prove beneficial [13].

- Sequential and parallel simulators
  Depending on the existing computing infrastructure sequential simulators might be used or combined with parallel simulators to increase the efficiency of the simulation.

- Pure and "EPI" simulators
  Pure simulators are used if the entire system is modeled. "EPI" (External Process Interface) simulators are used to synchronize the externally running software and the virtual world supporting a software-in-the-loop simulation.

The same model can be run sequentially, or in parallel and in an unpaced or paced mode. However, "EPI" simulators depend on a specific class of models that contain peripheral ports and a time model which relates the consumed resources of the externally running software and simulation time. For a discussion of estimating the consumed resources in the context of agent-based simulation see [7].

In JAMES, models are equipped with the regular inports and outports to communicate with other models and with peripheral ports which can be employed to realize an interaction with external software, hardware, or users.

Let's take a look at how a component-based design supports the implementation of different simulators.

3.1. Using the template method for structuring the processors

Central to the execution of models in JAMES are the processors. However, whereas in earlier implementations each atomic model and coupled model had a processor of its own,

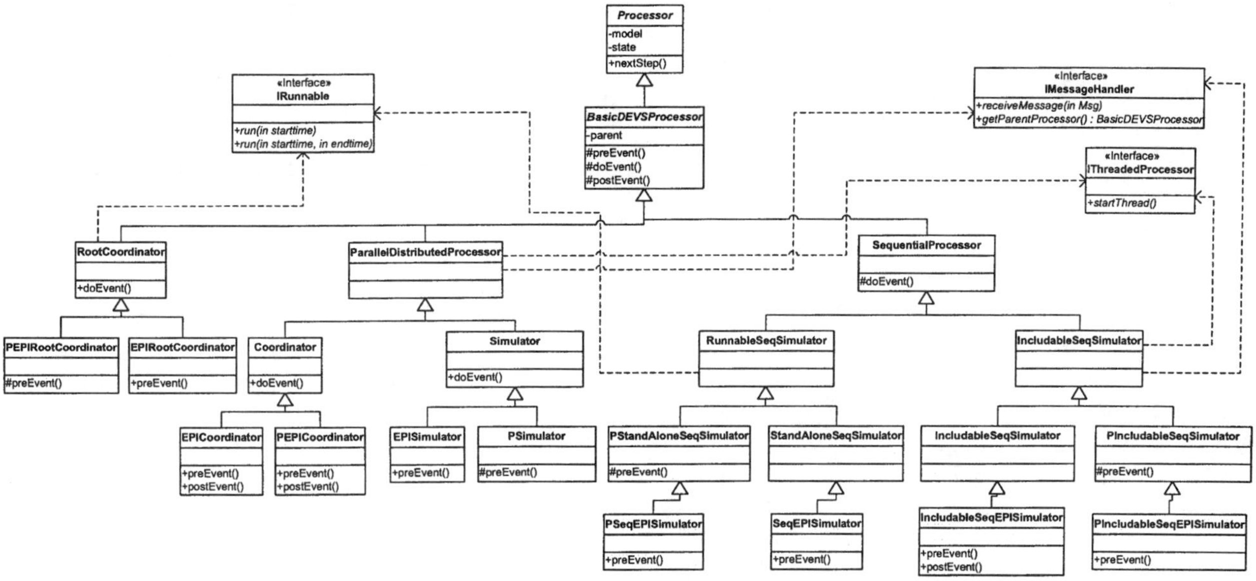

Figure 1. Class diagram of the processor inheritance hierarchy

this is no longer necessary in the new implementation. Entire model hierarchies or sub-hierarchies might be processed by one processor only.

To enable processors of different types to interact with each other and to combine them on demand for and possibly during simulation, all processors have to implement the common interface `IMessageHandler` (Figure 1).

By implementing the `IMessageHandler` interface, a processor ensures that it is capable of receiving * (internal event) - and *xy* (external event) - messages, that it will send an *xy* - message (output events) to the parent, and that it will inform the parent about its completion with a *done* - message. An epi-processor must additionally ensure that it is capable of handling epi-related messages as the guarantee request message. It is of no relevance, whether a processor executes concurrently or sequentially (actually the sequential processor `IncludableSeqSimulator` can be included in a hierarchy of parallel processors).

All simulation types follow the same pattern, i.e. the "template pattern" [3]. This pattern describes the idea of defining a skeleton for an algorithm and delegating the implementation of the single parts to descendants. The base processor class introduces the abstract method `nextStep` which is the method in which a simulation step has to be computed. In the `BasicDEVSProcessor`, this method is implemented as successively calling the `pre(pare)Event-`, `doEvent-`, and `postEvent-`method.

doEvent The necessity to implement the `doEvent` for all processor types is obvious. It describes the processing of situation-based and time-based events by invoking corresponding methods of the model, e.g. the lambda and delta internal or the confluent method. The `doEvent` method contains the core of the functionality needed for processing an event by a certain processor type and is never overwritten in a descendant class after is has been implemented once.

postEvent The `postEvent` is used to calculate and propagate relevant information to other processors, e.g. the time of next internal event. Thus, the implementation of the `postEvent` method is obligatory for all includable simulators.

preEvent The implementation of the `preEvent` is optional. E.g. in the case of a paced simulation it is used to delay the simulation for a certain time and in the case of (epi-processors) it is used to help to synchronize simulation and external processes.

3.2. Paced and unpaced simulation

In simulation, physical time, which is the time of the system being modeled, simulation time, which represents the physical time within the simulation, and wall-clock time, which is the time during which the simulation is executed, are distinguished. Whereas in unpaced mode the events are processed as fast as possible, in paced mode the simulation proceeds in synchrony with the wall clock time [2].

Paced simulations are particularly useful when the simulation interacts with external sources that are not under the control of the simulator [13]. In some cases the external source will be a user for whom the paced simulation provides a more realistic touch and feel of the simulation process. In other cases it might be agents that are started concurrently with the simulator and exchange messages asynchronously with the simulator[9].

```
01  wait until S2WC >= WC
```

Figure 2. Pseudo Code of the `preEvent`-method of a paced processor

Currently the only difference between paced and unpaced simulators is the implementation of the `preEvent` method, whose rather coarse and prototypical implementation is given in Figure 2. Whereas the coordinators are processing events as fast as possible, at the level of simulators the pre-event delays the processing of events and causes them to be executed at a time that corresponds to a certain wall clock time (`01`, figure 2). The relation between wall clock time and simulation time is specified in the function `S2WC` (SimTime2WallClockTime) which allows the simulation to be "scaled" to run faster or slower than wall clock time. The paced mode does not guarantee that the results of events are available at certain times. Particularly, in agent systems the computation time of events might vary significantly, and thus might temporally distort the realistic processing of events. One possibility to deal with this problem is to slow down the paced simulation. Otherwise the paced simulation will automatically proceed in an unpaced mode until the simulation and wall clock time matches again. Whereas for many applications this might be acceptable, for testing externally running agent software in paced mode, it is important to dynamically adjust the scaling factor during the simulation.

3.3. Parallel simulation

The algorithm used in the parallel processor is adapted from the one B.P. Zeigler describes in [14, 284 et sqq.]. In addition to * - and *done* - messages the algorithm introduces *y* - messages which are used for the transport of external events. Instead of distinguishing between different threads for handling the different types of messages in executing events in JAMES, in the new version one thread is responsible for executing an event at the level of coordinator and simulator respectively (Figure 5 and Figure 6). Thus, the new parallel simulation engine needs less than 50 % of the threads which increases the efficiency of simulating large models significantly.

The parallel simulator and parallel coordinator share the interface `IMessageHandler` and inherit the implementation or the `receiveMessage` method from the `ParallelDistributedProcessor`.

The implementation of the `preEvent` of the simulator processor will decide whether the parallel simulation will run in paced or unpaced mode. However, both coordinators and simulators are in need of implementing the `postEvent`.

For calculating the time of next event the simulators use

```
01  update tonie
02  send done message including tonie and
    variable structure request to parent
```

Figure 3. Pseudo Code of the `postEvent` method of the paced and unpaced parallel simulator

the time advance function (`01`, Figure 3). First the coordinator updates the time of next event of the imminent and influenced components (`01`, Figure 4). This set can have been changed by creating new components, deleting or migrating components. The coordinator sorts through its list of components to identify its minimal tonie (`04`).

```
01  for all updated lists of imminent or
    influenced models
02    update time of next event
03  end for
04  update tonie
05  send done message including tonie and
    variable structure request to parent
```

Figure 4. Pseudo Code of the `postEvent`- of the sequential includable processor and the parallel coordinator (paced and unpaced)

Both, coordinator and simulator send the *done* message including the time of next event and the information about structural changes that shall be executed on the next level of the hierarchy to the parent coordinator (`05`). Whereas structural changes are initiated at the level of atomic models, the execution of generating new models, removing or moving models is executed by the coordinator which updates the information at the level of the coupled model. If a requested change shall initiate the moving of an entire coupled model, the processor coordinating the coupled model has to be informed. Thus, a variable structure request can be propagated from the simulator via the coordinator to the next coordinator.

The parallel coordinator forwards an incoming * - message (`02`) to all imminent children (`04`). After that it expects to receive *xy* - messages from those children containing their outputs (`05`). The coordinator will extract all messages for its outports and collect them in a *xy* - message to be send to its parent (`06`). Afterwards he waits until he receives an *xy* - message from the parent, this time containing the values for its inports (`07`). The *xy* - message from the parent as well as the *xy* - messages from the children (if there are any) are recombined according to the external input couplings and internal couplings and are sent to the imminent and influenced children (`10`). After these children have processed the events they will return a *done* - message including the new tonie (`11`) and the variable structure change requests which are processed after all *done* - mes-

```
01 when receive * or xy message
02   if message is * message
03     receive * message
04     send * to imment children
05     wait for xy messages from those children
06     send xy message to parent
07     wait for xy message from parent
08   fi
09   receive xy message
10   send xy messages to all influenced and
     imminent children
11   wait for done messages from those children
12   execute structural change requests
13 end when
```

Figure 5. Pseudo Code of the `doEvent` of the parallel coordinator

sages are received (`12`).

```
01 when receive * or xy message
02   if message is * message
03     receive * message
04     lambda
05     send xy message to parent
06     wait for receive xy message
07     if isEmpty (xy message)
08       deltaInt
09     else
10       deltaCon
11     fi
12   else
13     receive xy message
14     deltaExt
15   fi
16 end when
```

Figure 6. Pseudo Code of the `doEvent` of the parallel simulator

If a simulator (which is a processor for an atomic model) receives an * - or *xy* - message it has to execute the delta methods of the model (Figure 6). If it receives a * - message (`02`) it first executes the model's lambda method (`04`) and sends the generated outputs in a *xy* - message to its parent (`05`). After that it will wait until it receives a *xy* - message from the parent (`06`). This message contains the values for the model's inports or a null event. If there are no inputs the model's delta internal method (`08`) or otherwise the delta confluent method is called (`10`). If the simulator has been activated by an incoming *xy* - message, the model's delta external method is executed (`14`).

3.4. Sequential simulation

The purpose of the sequential includable processor is to execute a hierarchy of models in a sequential manner on a host. This simulator can be integrated into a parallel execution to simulate entire branches of a model hierarchy. The `preEvent` decides whether the simulation shall proceed in paced mode. The `postEvent` is identical to the `postEvent` of the parallel and distributed coordinator. Only the calculation of the `doEvent` is different (Figure 7).

```
01 when receive * or xy message
02   if message is * message
03     receive * message
04     for all imminent models
05       execute lambda() and propagate to input
         ports of influenced models and output
         ports of the model's parental coupled
         model
06     end for
07     send xy message to parent
08     wait for xy message from parent
09   fi
10   receive xy message
11   for all models
12     propagate events from inports of the
       model's parental coupled model
13     if imminent model
14       if externalEventFromModel then
15         deltaCon()
16       else
17         deltaInt()
18       fi
19     fi
20     if not imminent but influenced model
21       deltaExt()
22     fi
23   end for
24   for all imminent or influenced models
25     collect structural changes
26   end for
27   execute structural change requests
28 end when
```

Figure 7. Pseudo Code of the `doEvent`- of a sequential includable processor

The sequential processor calculates all sub-models in a sequential order. Therefore the tree is first iterated from the leafs upwards to the root model, thereby for all imminent children the *lambda* function is executed. When all children of a particular coupled model have been computed the values on the outports are copied to the destinations (`05`). Afterwards the tree is traversed a second time, this time from the root to the leafs. Thereby the values on the inports of coupled models are copied to their destinations according to the external input couplings. For each imminent or influenced model the appropriate transition function is executed. Internally every model is represented by a "processor replacement" which holds the attributes which would have usually been stored in the processor of each model. These replacements are stored in a hash ordered list for reducing the accessing costs.

3.5. Software-in-the-loop simulation

To test software agents in virtual environments specific classes of processors and models have been designed. The models are equipped with peripheral ports. They are the means by which simulation and externally running agent interact. To transform the resource consumption of the agent software into simulation time, a time model function is used (e.g. $simtime = consumed_{time} * scale$). The processors that proved beneficial in executing several planning agents in a virtual environment are based on a conservative parallel distributed simulation which processes simulation and agents concurrently [12]. The simulation uses guarantees to avoid that the simulation runs too far ahead.

```
01  when receive guarantee request for time t
02    wait until consumedResources of external
      processes >= t or external process finished
03    if external process finished
04      determine finishedTime
05      update list of external processes
06    fi
07  end when
08  when receive * or xy message
09    if t = finishedTime
10      charge peripheral ports
11      update finishedTime
12    fi
13  end when
```

Figure 8. Pseudo Code of the `preEvent` method of the epi parallel simulator and the epi includable sequential simulator

The `preEvent` is responsible to handle the guarantee requests. It will wait until the time model applied to the resources consumed by the externally running software returns a simulation time greater or equal the required guarantee or until the external software process has been completed (`02`, Figure 8). Each completion of an external process schedules an internal event, the list of pending events is updated with the results of the completed external process being due at `timeFinished` (`04`) and the list of externally running software processes is updated (`05`).

If a simulator is activated by a * - or *xy* - message it first checks whether the current simulation time is a time at which peripheral results are scheduled (`09`).

```
01  update tonie
02  update busy flag
03  send done message including tonie,
    variable structure request,
    and busy flag to parent
```

Figure 9. Pseudo Code of the `postEvent` method of the unpaced epi parallel simulator

The `postEvent` looks also slightly different in the epi-simulator (Figure 9). The time of next event is now calculated as the minimum of `finishedTime` and regular tonie (`01`). If an external process has been started the parent coordinator has to be notified. Thus, the done message carries the tonie, variable structure requests, and a flag indicating that at least one external process is running. The `doEvent` method of the epi-simulator corresponds to the `doEvent` of the normal parallel simulator.

```
when guarantee message is received
  for all children having an external
  software running
    send guarantee request
  end for
end when
```

Figure 10. Pseudo Code of the `preEvent`- of the unpaced parallel epi coordinator

The `preEvent` of the epi coordinator is responsible for forwarding the guarantee requests to all components having an external process running (Figure 10).

The `doEvent` is the same as the `doEvent` of the normal parallel coordinator. In the case of a guarantee request, the `doEvent` will be invoked. However, as its code is only executed in case of receiving a * - or *xy* - message, the execution jumps directly to the `postEvent`.

```
01  for all updated lists of imminent or
    influenced models
02    update tonie
03    update busy flag
04  end for
05  update tonie
06  update busy flag
07  send done message including tonie,
    variable structure request,
    and busy flag to parent
```

Figure 11. Pseudo Code of the `postEvent`- of the parallel epi coordinator and the epi includable sequential simulator

The `postEvent` is similar to the `postEvent` of other coordinators (Figure 11). To know whether a component has an external process running, the done messages sent by the children are evaluated and the tonie and busy information about the children is updated. The information of time of next internal event, the variable structure requests, and in addition a flag that indicates that at least one component has an external process running is sent to the parent coordinator (`07`).

4. Summary

The motivation to re-design the simulation layer of JAMES in a component-based manner has been to facili-

Sim engine	par.	seq.	pac.	unpac.	pure	epi
1	x		x		x	
2	x			x	x	
3	x			x		x
4		x	x		x	
5		x		x	x	
6		x		x		x

Table 1. The different simulation engines

tate the construction of different simulation engines and the configuration of the simulation layer according to the user's needs.

Each execution layer for DEVS models embraces typically two types of processors (in addition to the root processor): coordinators and simulators. Each different type of execution requires new coordinators and simulators. By exploiting the template method and the inheritance of object-oriented programming, the effort in realizing processors for DEVS type models can be reduced significantly. Each processor calls successively the methods `preEvent`, `doEvent`, and `postEvent`, which are implemented or inherited to realize the different types of engines.

4.1. Realizing different types of engines

Whereas the component-based design of the simulation layer started with the requirement to have a parallel and a sequential simulator available, soon more variants have been added. This was eased by the usage of the template pattern. Three `doEvent` methods, three `preEvent` methods, and four `postEvent` methods suffice for the creation of at least six different types of simulation engines (table 1). Thereby, the sharing of `preEvent` and `postEvent` methods does not follow a general pattern. E.g. the paced variant of the sequential includable and the parallel simulator share the same `preEvent` method, whereas the unpaced variant of the sequential includable inherits the `preEvent` and the `postEvent` method of the unpaced parallel coordinator. The epi sequential includable simulator and the parallel simulator share the `preEvent` method, whereas the epi sequential simulator shares the `postEvent` with the epi parallel coordinator. Here sharing means that as long as single inheritance allows the same implementation is used, otherwise the same code has to be reimplemented (e.g. the code shown in Figure 2 has to be implemented twice: once for the paced parallel processors and once for the paced sequential processors).

Table 2 contains a summary of the usage of the pseudo code fragments described in this paper (the numbers in the table depict the Figure numbers of the corresponding pseudo code fragments, the processors in the

	Pre	Do	Post
`Coordinator`	-	5	4
`EPICoordinator`	10	5	11
`Simulator`	-	6	3
`PSimulator`	2	6	3
`EPISimulator`	8	6	9
`SequentialProcessor`	-	7	-
`IncludableSeqSimulator`	-	7	4
`PIncludableSeqSimulator`	2	7	4
`IncludableSeqEPISimulator`	8	7	11

Table 2. The usage of `preEvent`, `doEvent`, and `postEvent` among the processors

top half of the table process single models whereby the others process complete subtrees of a model). In this table the sequential non includable simulator is mentioned (`SequentialProcessor`) which has not been described here - this processor can process a complete model in a sequential manner. The sequential includable and sequential non includable share the same `doEvent` method (see Figure 1).

4.2. Combining different types of processors

By combining the `preEvent`, `doEvent` and `postEvent` methods a set of different simulators and coordinators can be realized which are used to design the six pure types of simulation engines of table 1. However, the design of the processors supports further combinations and thus "hybrid" forms of simulation engines.

The partitioning of the model and the selection of suitable processors is done by an instance of the abstract class `Partitioner`. It has been designed to split the model hierarchy into subhierarchies to execute them on different hosts, i.e. to support the distributed, parallel execution. For this purpose, the `getPartitions` method returns (depending on the model and the given resources) a partition that comprises a set of subhierarchies and factories for creating the processor trees.

Currently only one partitioner is realized, however, the system is designed to include other partitioners to support an experimentation with different partitioning algorithms [5]. Each sub tree that is not partitioned will typically be executed by a sequential simulator, i.e. the includable sequential simulator. Only after the partitioning of the model, processors are generated. The partition holds the information which type of processors shall execute the models. Therefore, different factories are included that shall generate the different processor trees on the hosts. However, which combination of processors is meaningful?

The includable sequential simulator can always be used

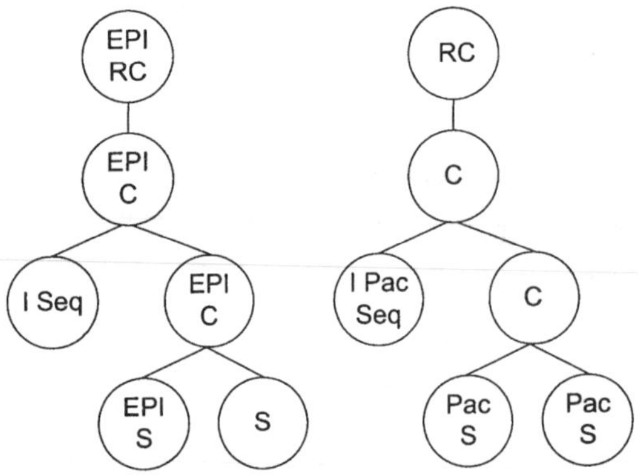

Figure 12. Examples for possible combinations

to simulate an entire branch of an otherwise concurrently proceeding simulation. In the paced variant only the simulators are currently delaying processing. A coordinator could easily execute certain components as fast as possible, whereas some components could delay the events shown to the user. However, as the delay of the paced simulators is realized in the `preEvent` method this would only make sense if the unpaced components do not depend on inputs from the paced one. Otherwise they would automatically be paced as well and the gain for processing possibly extensive events would be erased. Simulators that are designed to support software-in-the-loop applications can easily be combined with other processors. However it is necessary to ensure that all processors that are on the path towards the root are epi processors. Figure 12 shows two possible combinations.

4.3. Outlook

In our collection the paced epi simulator and coordinator is missing so far. Whereas we designed a first prototype of a paced epi variant [13], it has not been worked out in the template pattern yet. Also for the unpaced variant other simulators that support e.g. an optimistic parallel distributed simulation are planned. Different multi-agent systems are currently simulated, and more are still needed to explore the possibilities and limitations of combining the different types of simulators.

As the model changes its structure during simulation, so might the structure of processors. A dynamic reconfiguration of processors might prove beneficial. Given the modular design of the simulation layer, the realization of a dynamic reconfiguration including different types of processors should prove not too difficult. However, the benefit has to be shown in concrete applications. Whereas this value of a component-based simulator design has yet to be shown, one effect of the component-based approach is already apparent: its value in teaching the strategies of different simulation engines.

5. Acknowledgments

This research is supported by the DFG (German Research Foundation).

References

[1] G. Booch. *Object-oriented Analysis and Design. With Applications. Second Edition.* Addison-Wesley, Reading, MA, USA, 1993.

[2] R. Fujimoto. *Parallel and Distributed Simulation Systems.* John Wiley and Sons, 2000.

[3] E. Gamma, R. Helm, R. Johnson, and J. Vlissides. *Design Patterns: elements of reusable object-oriented software.* Addison-Wesley, Reading, MA, USA, 1994.

[4] X. Hu and B. Zeigler. An integrated modeling and simulation methodology for intelligent systems design and testing. In E. Messina and A. Meystel, editors, *Proc. of PERMIS, Gaithersburg*, 2002. Proceedings of the 2002 PerMIS Workshop.

[5] L. Li, H. Huang, and C. Tropper. DVS: An Object-Oriented Framework for Distributed Verilog simulation. In *17th Workshop on Parallel and Distributed Simulation*, pages 173–180, San Diego, 2003. IEEE Computer Society Press.

[6] H. Prähofer, J. Sametinger, and A. Stritzinger. Concepts and architecture of a simulation framework based on javabeans. *Future Generations Computer Systems*, 2000.

[7] P. F. Riley and G. F. Riley. SPADES - A Distributed Agent Simulation Environment with Software-in-the-Loop Execution. In *2003 Wintersimulation Conference*, 2003.

[8] R. Sargent. Requirements of a Modeling Paradigm. In *1992 Wintersimulation Conference*, pages 780–782, Arlington, VA, 1992.

[9] The RoboCup technical committee. Robocup-rescue simualtor manual version 0 revision 4. July 2000.

[10] A. Uhrmacher and D. Degenring. From Macro- to Multi-Level Models in Systems Biology. In *Proc. of the 3rd Workshop on Computation of Biochemical Pathways and Genetic Networks, Villa Bosch Heidelberg, October 6-7*, pages 29–36, Logos Verlag Berlin, 2003.

[11] A. Uhrmacher and K. Gugler. Distributed, Parallel Simulation of Multiple, Deliberative Agents. In *Parallel and Distributed Simulation Conference PADS'2000*, Bologna, 2000. IEEE Computer Society Press.

[12] A. Uhrmacher and M. Krahmer. A Conservative, Distributed Approach to Simulating Multi-Agent Systems. In E. Kerckhoffs and M. Snorek, editors, *Proc. European Multi-Simulation Conference*, pages 257–264, San Diego, 2001. SCS.

[13] A. Uhrmacher, M. Röhl, and J. Himmelspach. Unpaced and paced simulation for testing agents. In *Simulation in Industry, 15th European Simulation Symposium*, pages 71–80, Delft, 2003. SCS-European Publishing House.

[14] B. Zeigler, H. Praehofer, and T. Kim. *Theory of Modeling and Simulation.* Academic Press, London, 2000.

Optimistic Synchronization in HLA Based Distributed Simulation

Xiaoguang Wang Stephen John Turner
School of Computer Engineering
Nanyang Technological University
Singapore 639798
xgwang@pmail.ntu.edu.sg, ASSJTurner@ntu.edu.sg

Malcolm Yoke Hean Low Boon Ping Gan
Singapore Institute of Manufacturing Technology
71 Nanyang Drive
Singapore 638075
{yhlow, bpgan}@simtech.a-star.edu.sg

Abstract

With the wide use of Commercial Off-The-Shelf (COTS) simulation packages and the advent of the High Level Architecture (HLA) standard which supports interoperability and reusability, it is desirable to build distributed simulations by linking various types of simulation models developed using best-fit COTS packages. While almost all current work on integrating COTS packages and the HLA is based on conservative synchronization, it is worthwhile to investigate the optimistic synchronization approach. The optimistic approach can exploit parallelism and achieve promising performance in situations where causality errors may occur but in fact seldom occur. In our paper, we introduce a rollback controller using a middleware approach to handle the complex rollback procedure on behalf of the simulation model. To fully utilize the benefits of optimistic synchronization, we also introduce a novel time advance algorithm using the services provided by the HLA. A comparison of performance between the conservative and optimistic synchronization approaches based on a typical reference model is also provided.

1. Introduction

Distributed Simulation has become important as a strategic technology for linking various types of simulation components, even those that are geographically dispersed. These components interact and share information via the internet and give the appearance of a single model. Nowadays, instead of traditional programming languages, Commercial Off-The-Shelf (COTS) simulation packages are preferred as a means of developing simulation models with reduced risk and cost while increasing the functionality and capability of the system. These packages usually are designed for certain purposes and market niches. With the advent of the High Level Architecture (HLA) [1], it is desirable to glue together various simulation models (federates) built using best-fit COTS packages to generate an HLA-based distributed simulation (federation).

Much research work [2,3,4,5,6,7] has been done to integrate the COTS packages with the HLA in an explicit or implicit way from the modeler's point of view. While the explicit way needs the modeler to enhance the model with HLA functionality, the implicit approach means all HLA functionality is hidden from the modeler. A very important issue in distributed simulation is the time management mechanism. In general, synchronization algorithms can be divided into either conservative or optimistic approaches. Almost all of the current HLA-based COTS packages adopt the conservative synchronization approach. Compared to the conservative approach, the optimistic approach is generally more complex because of the need for state saving and rollback. However, the main constraint for the conservative approach is the need for lookahead to achieve good performance. Lookahead is a guarantee from a federate that it will not generate any external message with a time stamp smaller than its current time plus the value of lookahead. If the guarantee is zero, then the conservative protocols may perform poorly. Therefore, it is especially interesting to see whether established optimistic synchronization protocols can be integrated into existing simulation systems in a manner which does not require major user involvement [6].

While it is easy to implement the conservative approach using the HLA, the optimistic approach introduces more complications for COTS packages and simulation modelers. One complication is that the COTS packages must offer a technique for state saving and restoring the system state for recovering from possible

1087-4097/04 $20.00 © 2004 IEEE

causality errors. However, some COTS packages have provided such functionality. GPSS/H [8] offers the CHECKPOINT statement and Simplex3 [9] allows the user to schedule breaks within model experiments, both of which save the entire model state to hard disk. Some other COTS packages, e.g., Witness [10], have a replay service which also records the model state at runtime. Though the performance overhead of the state saving operations in these approaches is high, it is worth considering the optimistic approach since these techniques present the possibility of extensibility towards optimistic synchronization. The other complication is the burden of handling problems related to the rollback management. Even though the HLA offers some services for the optimistic approach, the rollback mechanisms provided by the RTI cover only event retractions. All the management of state saving and recovery in the federate should be implemented by the simulation modelers. To exploit the benefits of the optimistic approach and relieve the simulation developers from such a burden, we introduce a rollback controller using a middleware approach to realize the detailed implementation. Compared to the previous work done by Vardânega and Maziero [11], we use a novel time advance algorithm. We also compare the performance between the conservative and optimistic approaches using a typical model based on the reference models proposed by the High Level Architecture Commercial-Off-The-Shelf Simulation Package Interoperation Forum (HLA-CSPIF) [12].

This paper is organized as follows: Section 2 presents the HLA architecture and some services provided by the HLA to support the optimistic approach. Following that, the implementation of the rollback controller is described in Section 3. Section 4 discusses some problems in the current interface specification of the HLA and gives our proposed solution. Section 5 shows some experimental results and analysis. Conclusions and future work are given in Section 6.

2. The Optimistic Approach in HLA

The High Level Architecture (HLA) was developed by the U.S. Department of Defense (DoD) to facilitate interoperability and reusability. The standard provides a common technical framework for the integration of simulation models. It comprises three components: the HLA interface specification, federation rules, and the object model template (OMT). The interface specification, implemented by the Runtime Infrastructure (RTI), defines how federates interact with the federation, and with one another. In HLA terms, a federate is a simulation model while a federation is a collection of federates that form the entire simulation. Each federate defines the objects and interactions that are shared in its simulation object model (SOM). The responsibilities of federates and their relationship with the RTI are described by the federation rules.

In the HLA, both conservative and optimistic synchronization approaches are supported. In the optimistic approach, all events can be delivered to the federate without considering causality. So it is possible that another event containing a smaller time stamp will arrive later, possibly from a different federate. When such an event arrives, some incorrect computations must be rolled back. Performing rollback means restoring the current state to a previous "safe" state that has been recorded and canceling all the events scheduled by the incorrect computations. If the cancelled events have already been processed at other federates, those federates also need to roll back. Recursively applying this procedure will eventually erase the effects of the incorrect computation [13]. The HLA supports an optimistic federate by providing the following services to realize optimistic execution.

- *flushQueueRequest*(). Optimistic federates must be able to receive TSO (Time Stamp Order) messages before the RTI can guarantee that no smaller time stamped message will later be received in order to allow optimistic event processing. The *flushQueueRequest*() service forces the RTI to deliver all buffered events in the internal queue of the local RTI component.
- *retract*(). To ensure that optimistic federates are able to cancel previous incorrect events which have been sent out, the *retract*() service is provided to withdraw an update, interaction, or deletion previously scheduled by the federate. If the specified event is currently queued for delivery to a given remote federate, it is removed from its queue. If this event has been delivered to the federate, the appropriate callback *requestRetraction*() is invoked and the federate is responsible for rolling back its state as appropriate.
- Another important issue for optimistic federates is fossil collection. An optimistic federate must be able to compute a lower bound, called Global Virtual Time (GVT), on the logical time of any future rollback. Irrevocable operations occurring at a simulation time older than GVT can be performed, and storage carrying a time stamp older than GVT can be reclaimed. In the HLA the time granted by the RTI after a request to advance time can be used as the GVT value.

3. Implementation of Rollback Controller using a Middleware Approach

To relieve the simulation modeler from the burden of handling the complex details about the rollback procedure, we provide a middleware approach to extend the original services in the RTI APIs. All the services the federate calls will be intercepted by a *rollback controller* in the middleware, which implements the rollback procedure on behalf of the federate. The rollback controller is responsible for saving the states, restoring a "safe" state, retracting incorrectly scheduled events and handling the retractions received from other federates. It is important that all these processes are done as transparently as possible to the simulation modelers. They can still build their simulation federate as before, but instead of linking the RTI library to their simulation programs, the middleware library (extended RTI), known as RTI+ [14], is linked. Figure 3.1 shows the extended RTI architecture with the rollback controller.

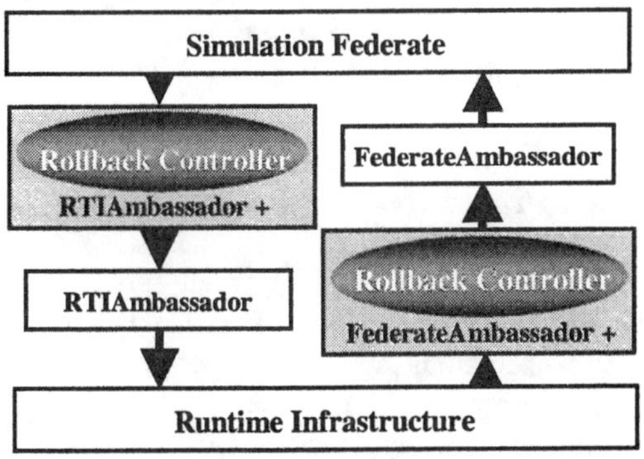

Figure 3.1: Rollback controller in middleware

The RTI+ provides all the RTI ambassador interfaces, and filters the federate ambassador callbacks through the *FederateAmbassador+* before passing them to the user's *FederateAmbassador*. The federate will continue to call the same methods of the *RTIAmbassador* class to interact with the RTI and it will receive RTI callbacks through the same *FederateAmbassador* class methods. However, some time management method calls related to the rollback procedure will be intercepted by the *RTIAmbassador+* and *FederateAmbassador+,* and then passed to the rollback controller. All the other methods are passed directly to the *RTIAmbassador* and *FederateAmbassador*. Using this approach, the federate can adopt an optimistic behavior without worrying about the handling of rollbacks.

3.1 The Structure of the Rollback Controller

Table 3.1: Abbreviation of RTI services

RTIAmbassador		FederateAmbassador	
FQR	*flushQueueRequest*	TAG	*timeAdvanceGrant*
NER	*nextEventRequest*	RAV	*reflectAttributeValues*
NERA	*nextEventRequestAvailable*	RI	*receiveInteraction*
UAV	*updateAttributeValues*	ROI	*removeObjectInstance*
SI	*sendInteraction*	RR	*requestRetraction*
DOI	*deleteObjectInstance*		

In the following description, the RTI services are abbreviated as shown in table 3.1. We first describe the structure of the rollback controller based on the optimistic time management introduced in [13]. Since the rollback controller is designed for the integration of COTS packages, the COTS packages' internal event queue (used to store the scheduled events) and external event queue (used to store the events received by the *FederateAmbassador*) cannot be accessed by the controller and should be saved as part of the federate's state. However, the controller will keep track of the events recently forwarded to the *FederateAmbassador* and when these events are forwarded. Therefore, the rollback controller class has the following attributes:

- A local virtual clock indicates the federate's current logical time t_c. The current time should be defined as the time stamp of the event being processed. To achieve this, a new service named "*processEvent*(t)" is provided in RTIAmbassador+, where t is the time stamp of the event to be processed.
- The rollback time t_{rb} stores the time stamp of the event which causes a local causality violation. A causality violation occurs when an event with time stamp less than t_c is received, or a previously processed event is retracted.
- A FederateState queue contains saved copies of the federate's recent states. In order to make rollback possible, the rollback controller must save the state of the federate from time to time. The state includes both the internal event queue and the external event queue. Each state in the FederateState queue is associated with a corresponding time t_s which is the current t_c when the state is saved.
- An InEvent queue contains all recently arrived messages sorted in order of their time stamps. Some of these messages have already been processed because no local causality error was detected at that time. Nevertheless, they are not discarded from the queue because it may be necessary to roll back and reprocess them. Each event in this queue is associated with a processed time t_p indicating when the event is forwarded to the federate.
- A nextEventIndicator points to the next event in the InEvent queue to be forwarded to the federate. Instead of forwarding all the received events from *FQR* to the federate, the rollback controller only forwards those events with the smallest time stamp. This can throttle the optimism and avoid the federate rolling back too many steps when a *RR* callback is received.
- An OutEvent queue contains copies of the messages the federate has recently sent, also kept in time stamp order. The rollback controller keeps track of all messages sent and their retraction handles. These messages are needed in case of rollback, in order to "unsend" them to other

remote federates. These outgoing messages act as the anti-messages in the optimistic mechanism. Each event in the OutEvent queue is associated with a scheduled time t_s indicating when the event is sent out to remote federates. When the rollback occurs, all those events in the OutEvent queue with scheduled time $t_s > t_{rb}$ should be retracted.

In addition to these attributes, the rollback controller class has some corresponding member functions to manage the FederateState queue, the InEvent queue and the OutEvent queue. Only the states or events with time stamp greater than or equal to GVT need to be retained.

3.2 State Checkpoint Mechanism

In order to restore some previous state when a rollback occurs, the rollback controller should keep periodic snapshots of the federate's internal state (state checkpoints). This requires the rollback controller to access the federate's state at any time. To provide that functionality, each federate should implement two callback methods that give controlled access to its internal state, to allow the rollback controller to save the current state or to restore a previous state: (1) *getState*(S_c), which returns the federate's current state S_c which is recorded at the current time t_c, (2) *setState*(S_p), which restores the federate's state to a previous state S_p. The rollback controller uses the *getState* method to add a new federate state into the FederateState queue and the *setState* method to restore a previous state from the FederateState queue, when a rollback occurs. Since we adopt a transparent approach for the user federate, the user federate need not consider the management of this state queue. What it should do is only record its current state and set the "safe" state from the rollback controller. An important issue to be addressed is when the rollback controller should call *getState*(S_c) or *setState*(S_p).

When the rollback controller invokes *getState*(S_c), it means a checkpoint should be recorded. The new state associated with the current time t_c is combined as a new record, which will be inserted into the state queue. The rollback controller currently uses the copy state-saving mechanism which means the whole state is recorded prior to the execution of each event. This can be realized when the federate calls the new service *processEvent*(t) in the *RTIAmbassador+*. In addition, the rollback controller also saves the state before forwarding the received events to the *FederateAmbassador*. Though forwarding the events will not change t_c, these states are saved to avoid the federate rolling back more steps than needed. When a RR is received, the federate only rolls back to the state before the event is forwarded, not a previous state recorded before processing events by the federate. To reduce the memory overhead, only the first state among those with the same t_c is saved. In the HLA, there are three major event types with time stamps that may be received by the federate: *RAV*, *RI* and *ROI*. These events should be managed separately by the rollback controller, to allow it to maintain control on all modifications performed on the federate state.

The rollback controller invokes *setState*(S_p) in the situation that a local causality error has occurred and the rollback operation must be invoked. A causality error can only be detected in TSO events *RAV*, *RI* and *ROI* or a *RR* event issued from other federates. In this case, the rollback controller searches through the Federate State queue to look for a state S_l with associated time stamp t_l satisfying this condition: $t_l \le t_{rb} < t_u$, where t_l and t_u are the adjacent time stamps of the Federate states. Then it calls *setState*(S_l) to restore the federate's state to a previous "safe" state. However, this "safe" state may not be really safe since another message older than t_l may possibly be received later and a state earlier than S_l must be restored.

3.3 Local Causality Violation Detection and Rollback Procedure

An optimistic federate will typically process messages containing a time stamp larger than GVT, giving rise to optimistic execution. Any number of messages may be processed before the RTI queue is again flushed. Such optimistic execution may incur a local causality violation and then trigger the rollback procedure. We describe these two processes as follows:

- Local causality violation detection
  As previously discussed, a causality error may be detected in the three types of TSO messages: *RAV*(t_r), *RI*(t_r) or *ROI*(t_r). When receiving such a TSO message the controller will first invoke *getState*(S_c) to record the federate's old state, and then compare the time stamp t_r with the current logical time t_c (the rollback controller is at the same simulation time as the federate it manages). If $t_r \ge t_c$, the message is considered as a safe message and stored in InEvent Queue. Otherwise, a local causality violation is detected. Besides these TSO messages, another message *RR* may trigger a rollback procedure. The rollback manger will search its InEvent Queue to find a received event with this event handle. If such an event is found but has not yet been processed, it will not cause a rollback and only an annihilation is needed. Otherwise, if it has been processed, the rollback procedure will be started. However, there is a possibility the anti-message (via a *RR*) arrives before the corresponding positive message. In this case, the information in the *RR* method will be stored and the corresponding positive message will be annihilated when it is received.

- Rollback procedure

  When the rollback procedure is triggered, the rollback time t_{rb} is set to the time stamp of the event causing the local causality error. The rollback controller should first "unsend" all the incorrect messages sent to other federates to reduce the effects of incorrect computations. So it searches its OutEvent queue and invokes the *retract()* method on the RTI to cancel all the incorrect events. The rollback controller stores all the received events in InEvent queue in time stamp order till a timeAdvanceGrant callback is made by the RTI. Before forwarding the grant time t_g to the federate, the rollback controller will: (1) search the Federate State queue and find the state S_l with time stamp $t_l \leq t_{rb} < t_u$, where t_l and t_u are the adjacent time stamps of the Federate states, invoke *setState*(S_l) to restore the federate to a previous "safe" state and set the time associated with S_l as current time t_c; (2) update the value of nextEventIndicator and forward the events with smallest time stamp to the federate (including those events *(RAV, RI, RO)* $_{old}$ that have been processed as shown in Figure 3.2); (3) discard all the events in OutEvent queue and the states in FederateState queue with time stamp larger than t_{rb} because they will not be needed for a future rollback procedure.

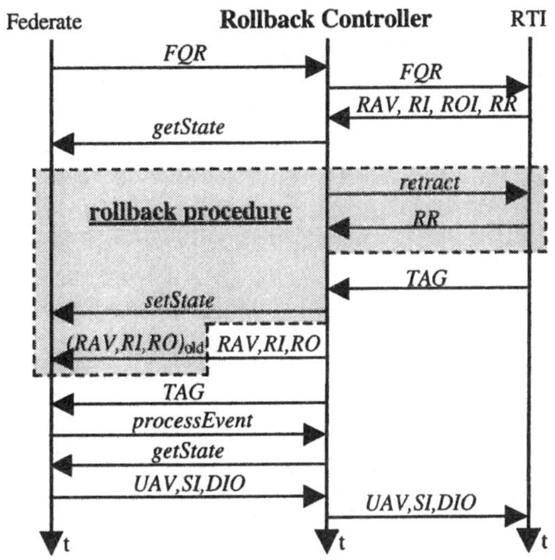

Figure 3.2: A typical optimistic federate simulation with rollback controller

Figure 3.2 shows a typical optimistic federate simulation with our rollback controller and the interactions between the federate, rollback controller and RTI. When the rollback controller detects that a causality violation occurs it interacts with the federate and RTI to execute the rollback procedure.

4. Problem in the Current Interface Specification and Solution

Optimistic federates must be able to compute the GVT as a lower bound on the logical time of any future roll back. GVT allows the optimistic federate to reclaim memory resources, and to perform operations such as I/O that cannot be rolled back. In the HLA, since the time t_g granted by the RTI after the federate issues a request to advance time is a guarantee that all the TSO messages with time stamps smaller than the grant time have been delivered, it can be used as the GVT value to process fossil collection [15]. Optimistic federates use the *FQR* service to receive the events, and then optimistically process those events. The time specified in this service provides local information for the RTI to compute t_g. Generally, the federate only needs to provide its next local event time as the specified cutoff time. However, an error in the current interface specification as implemented by DMSO RTI 1.3NG is observed in our experiments.

According to the RTI 1.3 specification [1], the grant time for *FQR(t)* is the minimum of the minimum-next-event time and the specified cutoff time *t*. The minimum-next-event time is calculated based on the smallest time stamp of all TSO events currently queued for delivery to the federate, without taking into account those which have been presented to the federate as a result of the flush. Thus, the federate may have received a TSO event and will then generate a new TSO event both with time stamp less than the grant time. This will incur an error indicating the time stamp is invalid. Some other RTI software, such as the Federated Distributed Simulation Kit (FDK) [16] have corrected this error, and it is also being corrected in the IEEE 1516 specification [17]. For current DMSO RTI 1.3NG, however, it is not safe to just use the next local event time to advance the time in *FQR* and an alternative way should be adopted to avoid the abnormal results.

Since we cannot know global information including the transient messages and the messages already in the buffer before the *FQR*, it is difficult to provide a safe time as the cutoff time for *FQR* other than using the last grant time. However, always using the last grant time will bring other problems for fossil collection; that is, without increasing GVT, fossil collection cannot be carried out.

In [12], the calls to the *FQR* method are intercepted by the rollback controller and executed in two phases. Initially the rollback controller uses a conservative approach, calling *NER* to receive the TSO messages from the RTI and then the federate's logical time is granted to t_f through the *TAG* callback. The time t_f can be considered as the GVT value and can be used to reclaim memory. After this conservative phase, the manager calls the *FQR* method. Using this approach, fossil collection can be processed safely. However, it will reduce the benefits of the optimistic approach since the conservative phase is interleaved with the optimistic phase every cycle.

We propose an algorithm to solve the current problem while trying to keep the characteristics of the optimistic approach. In the *RTIAmbassador+*, the *FQR* is extended in the middleware. The cutoff time the federate provides to the *FQR* is replaced by the last grant time in the *FQR* service. This value is always a safe guarantee for future events from this federate. But in addition, we will use *NERA* to advance GVT for fossil collection periodically. Based on this property, we name our time advance algorithm FPN (*FQR* and periodical *NERA*) and refer to the algorithm in [11] as NF (1 *NERA* followed by 1 *FQR*). Obviously one important issue is: when the *NERA* should be issued and how frequently this should be done.

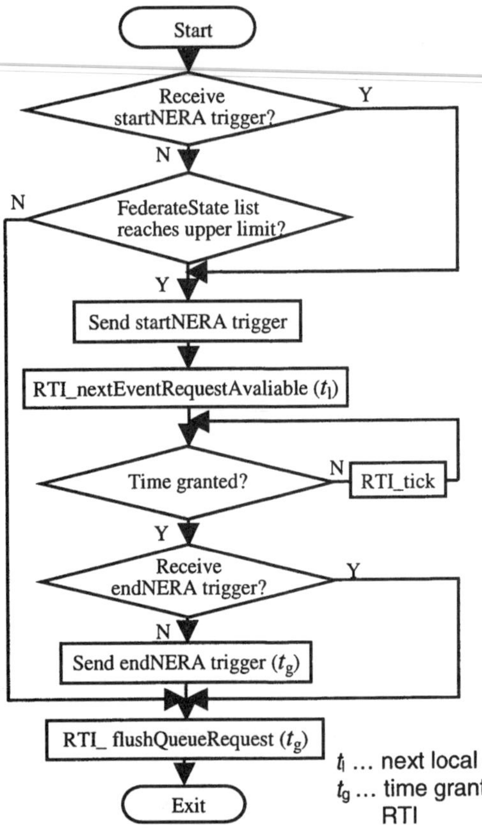

Figure 4.1: Extended FQR

Figure 4.1 shows the extended *FQR* in the *RTIAmbassador+*. For the users to construct optimistic federates, they still use the next local event time to issue a *FQR*. However, the rollback controller will process additional operations on behalf of the federate. We set an upper limit for the length of the FederateState queue based on the available memory. In each *FQR* procedure if this upper limit is reached, an *NERA* request with next local event time will be issued by the rollback controller. Before that, a startNERA trigger (via a RO interaction) is broadcast to all other optimistic federates in the federation. Each federate receiving such a signal will invoke an *NERA* request in its next request to advance time. The federate with the smallest next local event time will be granted its request by the RTI at once. To quickly free other federates from *NERA* block waiting for a *TAG* callback, an endNERA trigger (via a TSO interaction) is sent out to those blocking federates, which causes the RTI to send a *TAG* to those federates. After receiving the *TAG*, the rollback controller can use the new grant time to perform fossil collection. Using this algorithm, the time spent in the *NERA* request will be quite short and meanwhile the federation time will advance safely.

5. Experiment Design and Results

5.1 Experiment Design

The experiments are designed to test the proposed rollback controller and time advance algorithm, as well as to make a comparison between the conservative and optimistic synchronization approaches using the HLA. We use a model based on the bounded buffer distributed simulation reference model, one type of reference model introduced in [12]. This model could represent some practical real-world cases, not only in manufacturing simulation but also in other application areas such as the aviation model described in [18]. As shown in Figure 5.1, the federation is composed of two federates. Federate A generates entities in workstation W1, and sends them periodically via sink Si1 and source So2 into a bounded queue Q2 in federate B. When the queue becomes full, a message similar to the near zero lookahead (NZL) message in [18] is sent back to federate A, which causes federate A to block. At some later time, when the entity is processed in workstation W2, federate B clears a slot in Q2 and sends a second NZL message to federate A, which allows new entities to be transferred. Such NZL events are a constraint to conservatively synchronized simulations since the lookahead of federate B is set to near zero.

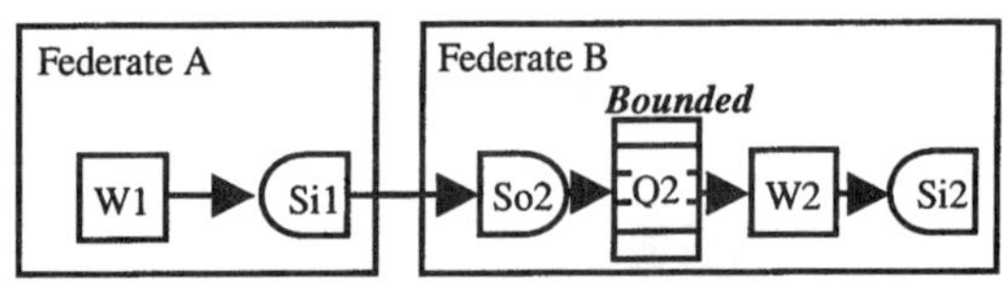

Figure 5.1: Bounded buffer distributed simulation reference model

The platform for our experiments is three DELL 2.2 GHz P4 1024 MB memory computers connected via 100Mbps Ethernet running Windows XP: one is used to run rtiexec (DMSO RTI1.3NG-V6) and the other two for the two separate federates. The execution time for federate A to run 1000 simulation loops is measured. In each loop federate A sends an entity and increments the simulation time by a random value between 100~190. In federate B the entities are processed in W2 where the simulation time for processing is constant and the whole simulation will be terminated after receiving the termination trigger from federate A.

5.2 Experimental Results and Analysis

Figure 5.2 shows the execution time versus the processing time in federate B for different queue lengths of Q2 in federate B. For the optimistic approach, we use two algorithms, NF and our new FPN, when issuing the request to advance time. Here we set the upper limit for the FederateState queue to 200, which means the *NERA* request will be issued when the length of the FederateState queue reaches 200.

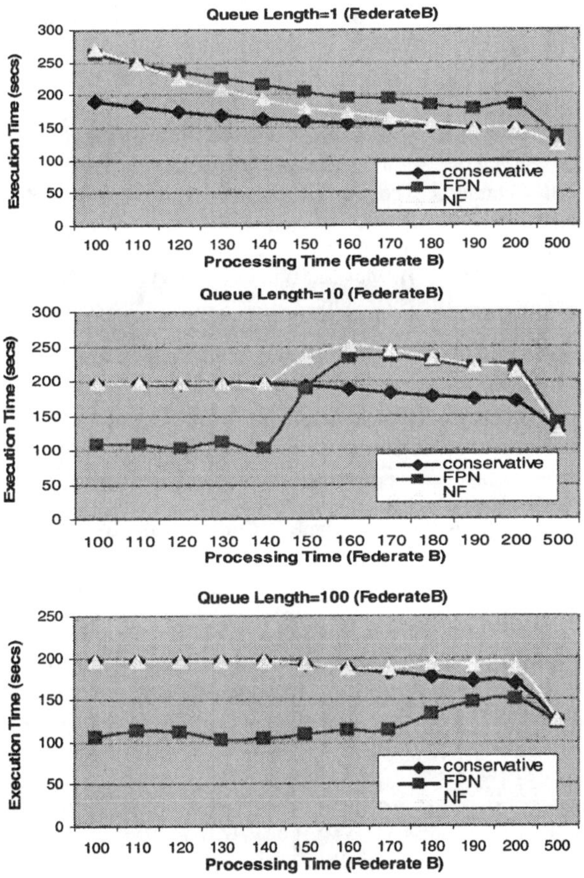

Figure 5.2: Execution time for conservative and optimistic synchronization approaches

As we can see, when the queue length is small, the conservative approach outperforms the optimistic approach. The reason is that the queue is almost always full and many NZL messages are issued, which incur many rollbacks in both federate A and federate B. However, with an increasing queue length, the performance of our optimistic synchronization algorithm FPN is better than the conservative approach. This improvement can be attributed to the fact that parallelism is fully exploited by the optimistic approach. In the conservative approach, near zero lookahead means the performance of the distributed simulation is similar to that of a sequential simulation. However, in the optimistic approach, the two federates can process the computations in parallel and achieve good performance in situations where the queue is seldom full. As shown in Figure 5.3, in some cases the number of rollbacks is very small, even zero, which will benefit the optimistic approach.

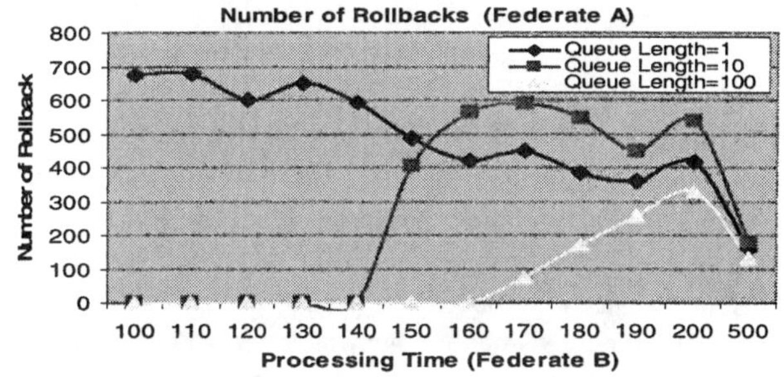

Figure 5.3: Number of rollbacks in federate A for different queue lengths in federate B using FPN

It is also observed that the performance of the optimistic approach with the NF algorithm is even worse than that of the conservative approach in many situations. It is due to the fact that this algorithm introduces some conservative elements to block the execution process while still having the optimistic overhead. The cost of the optimistic approach is mainly the cost of state saving, rollback and the anti-message overhead. That is why it is essential to utilize efficient algorithms to handle state saving, rollback and fossil collection.

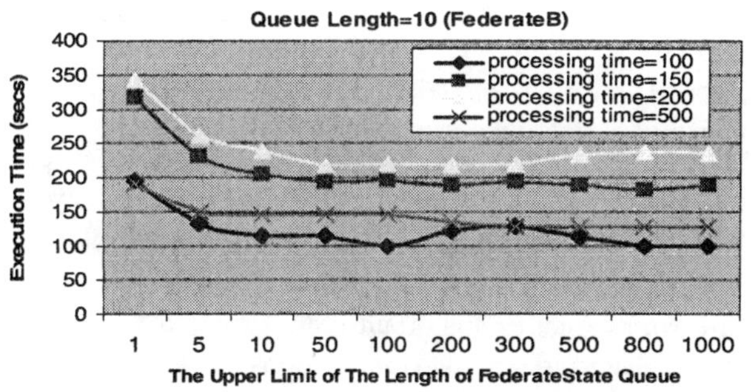

Figure 5.4: Execution time for optimistic approach with FPN algorithm

By varying the upper limit of the length of the FederateState queue, another set of experiments is conducted for the optimistic synchronization approach with our FPN algorithm. As shown in Figure 5.4, the performance is also related to this value. On one hand, the longer the *NERA* interval, the more optimistic the simulation. On the other hand, if the *NERA* interval is too long the fossil collection cannot be carried out, which will introduce more memory overhead. Therefore, this value should be selected based on the available memory resource. Short *NERA* intervals can also throttle the optimism to prevent the federate from executing too far ahead into feature, which can lead to inefficient execution. Therefore, this value should be selected based on the available memory resource and some specific properties of the simulation models.

6. Conclusions and Future Work

This paper investigates optimistic synchronization in HLA based distributed simulations. The experimental results show that the optimistic approach can achieve better performance than the conservative approach when lookahead is difficult to exploit or in situations where causality errors may occur but do not occur. In addition, although the optimistic approach introduces more overheads from the state saving and rollback procedure, they are not as heavy as expected. Especially when the computation time (real time) in the model is large, the extra time for the rollback procedure only takes up a very small portion of the total time. Since the proposed middleware could relieve the model developers from the burden introduced by the optimistic approach, the rollback controller could be embedded in the future integration of COTS packages and the HLA.

Further work is necessary in many areas. They include how to handle simultaneous events and what throttling mechanisms should be used. Besides, to reduce the cost of the optimistic approach, it is essential to utilize efficient algorithms to optimize the handling of state saving, rollback and fossil collection. The selection of appropriate algorithms is also closely related to the specific properties of the simulation models. However, to apply such application specific algorithms in a middleware approach is not simple, since the particular information of the models is transparent to the rollback manager. The investigation of simulation reference models and the most suitable synchronization algorithms will be part of our future work. Another important issue for building COTS package based distributed simulations is to design a friendly user interface, no matter which kind of synchronization approach is used.

References

[1] Defense Modeling and Simulation Office (DMSO), "High Level Architecture RTI 1.3NG Programmer's Guide, Version 5". February 2002.

[2] S. Straβburger, T.Schulze, U. Klein, and J.O. Henriksen, "Internet-based Simulation using Off-the-Shelf Simulation Tools and HLA", *Proc. 1998 Winter Simulation Conference*, Washington D.C., Dec. 13-16, 1998, pp. 1669-1676.

[3] G.D. Johnson, "Networked Simulation with HLA and MODSIMIII", *Proc. 1999 Winter Simulation Conference*, Dec. 5-8, 1999, pp. 1065-1070.

[4] B. Zeigler, G. Ball, H. Cho, J. Lee, H. Sarjoughian, "Implementation of the DEVS Formalism over the HLA/RTI: Problems and Solutions", *Proc. 1999 Spring Simulation Interoperability Workshop*, Orlando, March 1999, Number 99S-SIW-065.

[5] S. Pawletta, B. Lampe, W. Drewelow, T. Pawletta, "HLA-based Simulation within an Interactive Engineering Environment", *Proc. 4th International Workshop on Distributed Simulation and Real Time Applications (DS-RT 2000)*, San Francisco, California, USA, Aug. 24-26, 2000, pp. 97-102.

[6] S. Straβburger, "Distributed Simulation Based on the High Level Architecture in Civilian Application Domains". PhD Dissertation, University of Magdeburg, Germany, April 2001.

[7] H. Hibino, Y. Fukuda, "Manufacturing Adapter of Distributed Simulation Systems Using HLA", *Proc. 2002 Winter Simulation Conference*, San Diego, USA, Dec. 8-11, 2002, pp. 1099-1107.

[8] J.O. Henriksen, R.C. Crain, "GPSS/H Professional System Guide", *Wolverine Software Corporation*, 1995.

[9] B. Schmidt, "The Art of Modelling and Simulation: Introduction to the Simulation System Simplex3", *SCS-Europe Publishing House*, Ghent, 2000.

[10] P.L. Markt, M. H. Mayer, "Witness Simulation Software A Flexible Suite of Simulation Tools", *Proc. 1997 Winter Simulation Conference*, Georgia, USA, Dec. 7-10, 1997, pp. 711-717.

[11] F. Vardânega, C. Maziero, "A Generic Rollback Manager for Optimistic HLA Simulations". *Proc. 4th IEEE International Workshop on Distributed Simulation and Real-Time Applications (DS-RT 2000)*, San Francisco, California, USA, August 2000, pp. 79-85.

[12] High Level Architecture Commercial-Off-The-Shelf Simulation Package Interoperation Forum (HLA-CSPIF): http://www.cspif.com.

[13] D. Jefferson, "Virtual Time". *ACM Transactions on Programming Languages and Systems*, 1985, 7(3), pp. 404-425.

[14] B.P. Gan, Y.H. Low, J.H. Wei, X.G. Wang, S.J. Turner, W.T. Cai, "Synchronization and Management of Shared State in HLA-Based Distributed Simulation", *Proc. 2003 Winter Simulation Conference*, New Orleans, USA, Dec. 7-10, 2003, pp. 847-854.

[15] R.M. Fujimoto, "Time Management in the High Level Architecture", *Simulation*, Dec. 1998, 71(6), pp. 388 – 400.

[16] S.L. Ferenci, K.S. Perumalla, R.M. Fujimoto, "An Approach for Federating Parallel Simulators", *Proc. 14th Workshop on Parallel and Distributed Simulation (PADS 2000)*, May 28-31, 2000, Bologna, Italy, pp. 63-70.

[17] IEEE P 1516.1 "Standard for Modeling and Simulation (M&S) High Level Architecture (HLA) – Federate Interface Specification", April 1998.

[18] F. Wieland, "Parallel Simulation for Aviation Applications". *Proc. 1998 Winter Simulation Conference*, Washington, DC, Dec. 13-16, 1998, pp. 1191-1198.

Hybrid Performability Analysis of Logistic Networks

Falko Bause, Peter Buchholz, Markus Fischer, Peter Kemper
Informatik IV, Universität Dortmund, D-44221 Dortmund, Germany
{falko.bause, peter.buchholz, markus.fischer, peter.kemper}@udo.edu

Abstract

Resources in large logistic networks are occasionally unavailable or malfunctioning. This implies that perfomability becomes an issue for quantitative analysis of logistic networks. Different time scales between failures and normal operation often justify the decomposition of a performability model into a single availability model that considers failures and recovery of resources and a family of performance models whose individual instances depend on the state of resources. In this paper, we present an approach that simulates a set of performance models independently and in a distributed manner on a network of workstations. We propose to optimize the achievable quality of results for a given total amount of CPU time by minimizing the confidence intervals for performability measures. This is possible by an adaptive assignment of CPU time to simulate those models whose results have the largest impact on the width of confidence intervals.

1 Introduction

Quantitative analysis of a large logistic network is an important and challenging task during its development and operation. Key measures like throughput, sojourn times, cost of operation or usage of resources are usually computed by simulating a model of the system rather than performing experiments with the system itself. Among the many modeling formalisms known for dynamic systems, process-oriented notations are particularly useful in that application area. The ProC/B approach in [1] is one example of such a modeling formalism for logistic networks. The corresponding ProC/B toolset provides a variety of analysis techniques including simulation for the analysis of ProC/B models. Quantitative results of logistic networks or process chains depend on two parts, the load and the available resources to process that load. In practice, the perceived performance varies over time due to failure, malfunction, maintenance, repair and replacement of resources. In computer or communication systems, the concept performability [7] reflects these issues. A transfer of performability methods for computer and communication systems [4] towards logistic networks is not straightforward. The major difference is that the performance part of a performability model for a computer system is often adequately described by a product form queueing network but a model for a logistic network usually requires features that exceed what can be expressed by queueing networks. In consequence, the efficient algorithms employed for queueing network analysis of models of computer systems do not apply and simulation becomes the method of choice. On the other hand, there are similarities as well. For instance, normal operation and failure/repair actions typically perform on different time scales. In addition, the dependancy between performance of a system and availability is often only one-sided, i.e., the performance depends on availability of resources but not vice versa. These two observations lead us to a time scale decomposition approach where the availability part of a performability model is analyzed numerically as a continuous time Markov chain. The results of the availability analysis determine a family of performance models that are subsequently analyzed by simulation. We propose a distributed simulation on a network of workstations and describe how the work load is distributed in order to minimize confidence intervals of reward estimators.

The paper is stuctured as follows. Section 2 briefly introduces performability modeling and analysis of logistic networks. It proposes the decomposition approach and discusses issues of distributed simulation. In Section 3, we describe a case study. A model of warehouse is analyzed and we discuss benefits and limits of our approach.

2 Performability Models

From an application point of view, logistic networks handle orders that are issued by customers. Procurement of orders takes place by a single company or a network of companies that collaborate. A single company can consider its way of handling an order as a service that consists of a number of individual actions or steps that are either taken care of by own units (divisions, departments, groups, individual members of staff) or by some external partners (outsourcing). The notion of a service that is provided someone and requested by someone else serves the purpose of structuring

1087-4097/04 $20.00 © 2004 IEEE

a complex world. It gives a separation of concerns as well as a separation of resources and resource consumption.

The ProC/B formalism supports hierarchically structured models based on the notion of service in the aforegoing manner. The hierarchy is based on service calls (like function calls in a programming language) and inclusion of resource in the sense that a functional unit provides services whose detailed description resembles actions which in turn are performed as services of a (contained) resource. Basic resources for time consumption (an active resource like a server in a queueing network) and space consumption (a passive resource like a storage area) terminate this recursive description. Special source and sink nodes to produce or terminate service calls at the top level node of the hierarchy provide the load description. This process-oriented way of modeling has gained a lot of attention in logistic systems to identify inefficient organizational structures. The motivation for modeling logistic systems are manifold, for instance, there is interest in the identification of bottlenecks, in technical measures like utilization of resources, production lead times, the quality of service, the ability to meet deadlines. Furthermore, economic measures like an assignment of production costs to individual orders according to resource usage are of interest.

Obviously, the performance of real world systems varies due to failures of resources and delays due to the repair or replacement of faulty resources. This kind of dynamic behavior does not necessarily formalize well as a process. It is rather a behavior that a resource performs internally (and often independently from the state of its environment). Availability of resources is thus often modeled in a formalism like a Markov chain, a stochastic automaton or a GSPN.

If both aspects are present in a single model, we can study the performance degradation of a model due to failure of resources. Since performance and availability imply different types of dynamic behaviour, a model should reveal a structure that allows a partition into two distinct parts, one for performance aspects and one for availability aspects. In our case, this is accomplished by combining two different modeling formalims. In general, the timing behavior of both parts is mutually dependent. Trivially, the performance of a systems depends on the availability of resources. On the other hand, failure rates may depend on the load of a resource, a failure of one resource might cause a simultaneous failure of some other resource and repairs may be done by repairmen which are also shared resources. However, it is often the case, that there is only a one-sided dependancy present in a model, i.e., the performance model depends on the availability model, but not vice versa. This case is particularly advantageous for analysis and will be considered in the following.

We employ the ProC/B formalism to describe the performance part and GSPN for the availability part. It is straightforward to identify the number of available resources from the marking of the GSPN. In our case of a one-sided dependancy, the state of the availability model provides input parameters for the performance model.

2.1 Analysis Based on Decomposition

More formally, we consider a class of models that share state variables which describe the current configuration of resources - and one (the availability) submodel reads and writes those variables, while the other (the performance) submodel only reads that information. In order to distinguish the different degrees in the number of available resources, we define a set $\mathcal{C}$ of configurations, where a single configuration $c \in \mathcal{C}$ describes which resources are available and which are not. For realistic examples with resources of different types, the set $\mathcal{C}$ may contain up to several thousand configurations.

We assume that any measure that is of interest is formally described by a reward R [8] . Rewards can be used to express a wide variety of performance and performability measures including throughputs, sojourn times, rejections probabilities of orders or the filling of stocks. Let $E[R_c]$ be the first moment of the reward value if the performance model is in configuration c. Furthermore let p_c be the probability that the current configuration is c. The value

$$E[R] = \sum_{c \in \mathcal{C}} p_c E[R_c] \tag{1}$$

has to be computed.

The probabilities p_c are computed from the availability submodel. With our assumptions that the failure rates are independent of the state of the performance model, the probabilities can be computed with a high precision by numerical analysis of the Markov chain described by the GSPN.

In addition to this structural property, we observe different time scales for the dynamic behavior of performance and availability submodels. Note that, in a well designed system failure and repair rates are orders of magnitude smaller than service rates at resources. Usually the difference between service rates and failure rates is at least 3 to 4 orders of magnitude. This large difference has two implications. First of all, a model of the complete system, if it exists, cannot be analyzed using standard simulation. Since failures are rare events, a huge number of service events has to be simulated before the first failure occurs. To obtain statistically significant results for the performance of the system including failures and repairs, the number of necessary events would be much too large. However, the large difference between the rates also assures that between failures and repairs the performance model reaches quasi steady state such that independent simulation runs can be performed for the configurations of the performance model.

A time-scale decomposition of performability models is often considered in literature, however simulation is hardly used to compute an estimate of $E[R_c]$ for individual configurations c. It is more common to consider queueing networks for the performance submodel and perform product-form analysis for the price of hard restrictions on what can be expressed in the performance part. For modeling logistic networks, queueing networks are often too restricted to be of general use. Thus, the challenge of the simulative performance analysis is to analyze a large number of different performance models such that the confidence interval for $E[R]$ is sufficiently small. Before we consider this issue in depth, we discuss a side issue that is also of practical relevance. For many systems, a minimal number of resources must be available to be operational. Since the configurations determine the number of available resources, we need to ensure that only configurations that correspond to well-defined models are considered for simulative analysis. This is not trivial for complex models. It may require a functional pre-analysis of the configurations. Since the ProC/B toolset [1] allows a transformation of a performance model into a Petri Net (PN), we compose a PN that results from the performance model with the GSPN of the availability model and subsequently apply analysis techniques for PNs on the resulting net. Such functional techniques include model checking or invariant analysis. Currently, the composition of both PNs is performed manually useing features of the APNN toolbox [3] to manipulate hierarchical and compositional models. Let $\mathcal{C}^o \subseteq \mathcal{C}$ be the set of operational configurations among the set of configurations.

Performance models that are non-stationary form a second class of malfunctioning models. If a model is non-stationary, our assumption that the performance model reaches quasi steady state in each configuration is no longer justified. Since the detection of non-stationary behavior is not trivial, we assume in the sequel that all configurations of the performance model are stationary. This can always be achieved by limiting the number of processes in the system, as it is also done in practice whenever the number of arrivals exceeds the capacity of a logistic network.

We do not simulate a non-operational configuration c, nevertheless we need $E[R_c]$ in (1). If the requested reward describes the throughput of the system, then the reward in a non-operational configuration becomes 0. The determination of rewards that describe sojourn times or rejection probabilities is more complex. For those cases, we assume that no service occurs in a non-operational configuration and that all arrivals are rejected during a non-operational period. The latter assumption will only approximately match a real situation. It is justified, if the duration of a non-operational configuration is much longer than the interarrival time of new processes and the capacity is not too large. Let d_c be the mean duration of configuration $c \in \mathcal{C} \setminus \mathcal{C}^o$, which can be computed from the results of the numerical analysis of the availability model, and let λ_k be the mean arrival rate of processes of type k. If R describes the rejection rate of type k processes, then $R_c = d_c \cdot \lambda_k$ and if R describes the sojourn time, then $R_c = d_c$ because processes in the system have to wait the whole period. In this way rewards can be assigned to non-operational configurations. The assigned rewards are only approximations, but the approximation error tends to 0 for an increasing difference between service rates and failure/repair rates.

As sketched so far, the proposed approach can be considered as the solution of a Markov reward model where rewards of individual states are determined by simulation. This raises a number of interesting observations. For a given reward evaluation, we may want to design a system in a way that $E[R]$ obtains some optimal value which yields an optimization problem in order to change parameters of the availability model in a way that distribution of p_c over $\mathcal{C}$ increases (or decreases) the value of $E[R]$. As long as we assume that the behavior of the availability model is not directly influenced by the state of the performance model, this optimization can be done by modifying the availability model only and reusing the simulation results for the performance models. On the other hand, for a given $c \in \mathcal{C}$, we can adjust the quality of the simulation according to the relative importance of R_c for $E[R]$ as indicated by the value of p_c. The potential of this observation is considered in the following for distributed simulation on a workstation cluster.

2.2 Distributed Simulation

Simulation is used to determine an estimate $\bar{R}(n)$ for $E[R]$ where n denotes the number of sample points used for the estimate. Let S_n^2 be the sample variance of the estimator, then a confidence interval can be computed by

$$\bar{R}(n) \pm z_{1-\alpha/2}\sqrt{\frac{S_n^2}{n}}$$

for an n that is sufficiently large and where $z_{1-\alpha/2}$ is the $1-\alpha/2$ quantile of the normal distribution [6].

In our case, $E[R]$ is given as a weighted sum of $E[R_c]$ such that

$$\bar{R}(n) = \sum_{c\in\mathcal{C}^o} p_c \bar{R}_c(n) + \sum_{c\in\mathcal{C}\setminus\mathcal{C}^o} p_c R_c \,.$$

If the availability model is analyzed numerically, then the values for p_c are exact up to the numerical precision of the machine. Additionally, the values R_c are fixed for $c \in \mathcal{C} \setminus \mathcal{C}^o$. Thus, the variance of the estimator $\bar{R}(n)$ results from the variance of $\bar{R}_c(n)$ for $c \in \mathcal{C}^o$. If we assume that the sample values to determine $\bar{R}_c(n)$ are all independent we obtain for the sample variance of the estimator $\bar{R}(n)$

$$\bar{S}^2 = \sum_{c\in\mathcal{C}^o} p_c^2 \frac{S_c^2(n_c)}{n_c} \qquad (2)$$

where n_c is the number of sample values to determine $\bar{R}_c(n)$ and $S_c^2(n_c)$ is the estimator for the variance of R_c. The relation holds because for independent random variables X_i with variance $S^2(X_i)$, $S^2(\sum X_i) = \sum S^2(X_i)$ and $S^2(cX_i) = c^2 S^2(X_i)$ [6]. The confidence interval for $\bar{S}^2$ is computed as

$$\bar{R}(n) \pm z_{1-\alpha/2}\sqrt{\bar{S}^2}\ .$$

Since the simulation models are independent for different configurations of the performance model, an approach based on independent replications can be used [6] for the estimation of $\bar{R}_c(n)$. Different simulation runs can be distributed on different machines or processors and can be performed in parallel. We apply the approach in a workstation network and assume that M workstations are available. For simplification we assume that all workstations are identical, but the following approach can be easily extended to non-homogeneous machines. We further assume that we can start and stop a simulation run on some processor and obtain as a result of some run i for configuration c the values $n_{c,i}$, $R_{c,i}$ and $S_{c,i}^2(n_{c,i})$ for the number of observations, the estimated mean and variance, respectively. The variance $S_{c,i}^2(n_{c,i})$ can be estimated using some appropriate method for dependent observations like batch means, regenerative simulation or an autoregressive method [6].

We have defined a method to compute $\bar{R}(n)$ and its confidence interval from a simulation using M processors. We further assume that runs are performed in phases of length Δ. At the beginning of each phase on each workstation a simulation run is started which runs for Δ times units and produces results of the above form. We assume that T phases are simulated such that overall MT simulations runs are made. A schedule describes the assignment of simulation models to processors in the different phases. Since we assume identical processors, we only have to define which configurations are simulated in a phase and not the assignment of models to processors. Phases are numbered from 1 through T and $\mathcal{S}_t$ is the multiset of configurations which are simulated during phase t on some processor. $\mathcal{S}_t$ contains M elements, one model for each processor, and may contain the same elements several times since one configuration can be simulated on different processors in the same phase. A schedule is defined as

$$\mathcal{S} = \cup_{t=1}^{T} \mathcal{S}_t\ .$$

Let $occ_c(\mathcal{S})$ be the number of occurrence of c in $\mathcal{S}$ which describes the number of phases of length Δ in which configuration c has been simulated. Let $\bar{S}_c^2(a_c)$ be the estimator for the variance of $\bar{R}_c(n)$ if configuration c has been simulated for a_c intervals of length Δ. With this formalization we can define the optimization problem

$$\min_{\mathcal{S}} \left(\sum_{c\in\mathcal{C}^o} p_c^2 S(occ_c(\mathcal{S})) \right)$$

to find a schedule with a minimal variance of the estimator for $\bar{R}(n)$ and therefore also with the smallest confidence interval.

Of course, the computation of the optimal schedule requires knowledge of S_c^2 which is not available. Consequently, a schedule $\mathcal{S}_{t+1}$ is computed using the information which is available from the phases 1 through t. Let $a_c(t) = occ_c(\cup_{s=1}^{t}\mathcal{S}_s)$ and $\sigma_c(a_c(t)) = \sqrt{(\bar{S}_c^2(a_c(t))/a_c(t))}$. For the moment we assume $a_c(t) > 0$ for all $c \in \mathcal{C}^o$. Since $\bar{S}_c^2(a_c(t))$ is an unbiased estimator for S_c^2, $\sigma_c(t)$ is proportional to the width of the confidence interval for $\bar{R}_c(n)$ after t phases.

The gain of performing in phase $t+1$, i parallel runs of configuration c is proportional to the estimated reduction of the confidence interval width due to these simulation runs and is given by

$$g_c^i(t+1) = p_c^2\left(\sigma_c(a_c(t)+i) - \sigma_c(a_c(t))\right)\ .$$

Since we do not know $\sigma_c(a_c(t)+i)$ a priori we assume

$$S_c^2 = a_c(t)\left(\sigma_c(a_c(t))\right)^2 \Rightarrow \sigma_c(a_c(t)+i) = \sqrt{\frac{S_c^2}{(a_c(t)+i)}}$$

and

$$g_c^i(t+1) = p_c^2\sigma_c(a_c(t))\left(\sqrt{\frac{a_c(t)}{a_c(t)+i}} - 1\right)\ .$$

The following algorithm computes $\mathcal{S}_t$ from the available gains $g_c^i(t)$.

1. $\mathcal{S}_t = \emptyset$;
2. for ($m = 1$ to M) do
3. $\quad c = \min_c\left(g_c^{occ_c(\mathcal{S}_t)+1}(t) - g_c^{occ_c(\mathcal{S}_t)}(t)\right)$;
4. $\quad \mathcal{S}_t = \mathcal{S}_t \cup \{c\}$;

The only remaining point is the estimation of the initial values for $\sigma_c(.)$. One possibility is to run each configuration at least once at the beginning to obtain some result and start afterwards with the algorithm. If the number of configurations is huge, only some configurations are simulated and other configurations receive values of similar configurations which have been simulated. However, the latter approach introduces an additional approximation and usually requires the use of some form of a metamodel which goes beyond the goal of the current paper.

2.3 Tool Support

Performability analysis of realistic models of logistic networks requires adequate tool support. We propose the ProC/B toolset that provides a graphical user interface for the ProC/B formalism. Models are either mapped onto HIT-models [2] for a simulative analysis or onto Generalized Stochastic Petri Nets (GSPNs) for functional analysis based on invariant analysis or model checking, numerical analysis of the associated CTMC or simulation. HIT-models are supported by the tool HIT [2]; GSPN models are supported by the APNN toolbox [3]. The numerical analysis of the availability model is limited by the size of the resulting Markov chain; currently models in the order of $10^6 - 10^7$ states can be analyzed in the APNN toolbox.

3 Case Study: Warehouse

In this section, we analyze a model for the management of a warehouse at a manufacturing site for cars. The model contains three processes that describe the operational activities. The first process, denoted as `Truck_Arrival`, describes the supply and storage of sub-assemblies (engines etc.) and the return of buffered empties (boxes). The second process, labeled `In-Plant_Transport`, puts sub-assemblies (including their packages) on-demand into a second intermediate buffer that serves the actual production line. Finally, the third process, labeled `Demand`, describes the demand of the production line and moves freed shipping boxes back into the buffers. Since involved buffers have a finite capacity, certain activities remain blocked until sufficient inventory or free space becomes available. Fork-lifts access buffers for loading and unloading operations. They are statically assigned to specific buffers and exclusively-used to manipulate their inventory. Furthermore, fork-lifts are used to load and unload trucks that deliver sub-assemblies or take empties. Since the number of fork-lifts is limited (2 per buffer and 21 for trucks), processes may experience queuing and additional waiting times due to non-availability of requested fork-lifts. Fork-lifts occasionally fail and albeit the system remains operational, its overall performance degrades. Since failures happen rarely, the maintenance policy is as follows. A single worker is responsible for repairing fork-lifts on-site in case of a breakdown. In addition, an external company sends additional staff to perform regular maintenance checks in fixed time intervals to keep the number of breakdowns at an acceptable level. A maintenance check implies that all operational fork-lifts are not available for a short period of time, the maintenance interval.

In order to evaluate the impact of failures on performance measures we have created two models, a dependability model that captures the failure, maintenance and repair behavior of involved fork-lifts and a performance model that captures the three processes that the normal operation of the warehouse and measures lead times of the involved processes. Lead times are typically used to evaluate the performance of the system. Application experts are interested in the determination of optimal maintenance frequencies. Notice, exorbitant maintenance effort would prevent from failures (and non-availability), but this is at the expense of more frequent non-availability caused by maintenance interrupts. In the system, the time to failure of maintained fork-lifts is assumed to be the same as the time to failure of repaired fork-lifts.

In what follows, we briefly introduce a ProC/B performance model and a GSPN dependability model, cf. Fig. 1 and 2. Due to space limitation, we highlight only certain parts of the performance model and restrict ourselves to the `Truck_Arrival` process. The upper part of Figure 1 (separated by a dashed line) shows a flow-chart of activities (arrow-like hexagons) that make up the process of incoming trucks and their handling at the warehouse. The lower part gives the resources that are demanded by activities for their execution. Incoming trucks first go to an entrance office and experience a simple delay, then they register at this office. After registration, a specific storage area is selected (timeless activity) and the process forks into two subprocesses modeling the arrival of trucks (upper chain) and the arrival of requested fork-lifts (lower chain) at the loading ramp. Afterwards, the process performs unloading activities (represented by 5 arrow-like hexagons) and reaches a boolean branch. It is assumed, that only certain trucks carry sub-assemblies that need to be buffered. Therefore, in the upper branch the process puts the freight into the main store, proceeds to the empties store and unloads empties from the empties store by calling the service `unload`, whereas in the lower branch, the process immediately reaches a sink for finalization. Notice, the model is hierarchically structured and the description of services in terms of involved activities and demanded resources is delegated to the submodel and invisible from the calling activity denoted `Unload_Empties`.

We proceed in this section with a description of the GSPN model capturing the dependability aspects of the system under investigation. In our model we assume that the time to failure, the repair time and the maintenance time are all Erlang-2 distributed. Figure 2 shows a colored GSPN model of the described scenario. It consists of three parts:

- the upper part (subnet $p_7, \ldots, p_{10}, t_6, \ldots, t_8$) describes the maintenance process of all operational fork-lifts,
- the middle part (dotted box, subnet $p_{11}, \ldots, p_{13}, t_9, \ldots, t_{13}$) models the elapsed time between maintenance intervals, and
- the lower part (subnet $p_1, \ldots, p_6, t_1, \ldots, t_5$) describes operational fork-lifts, being subject to failures, and repair.

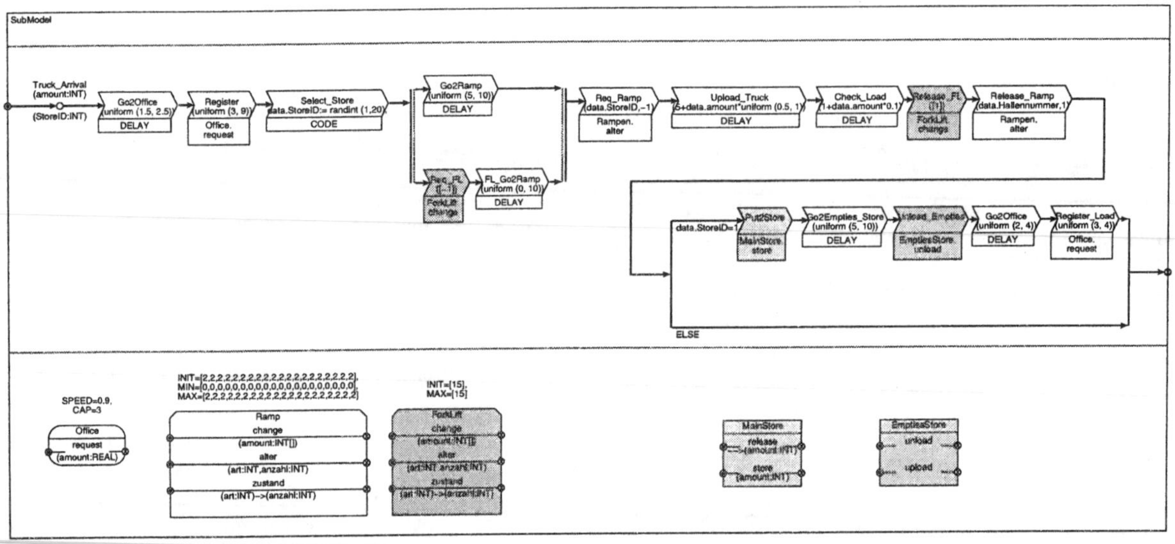

Figure 1. ProC/B performance model: `Truck_Arrival` process

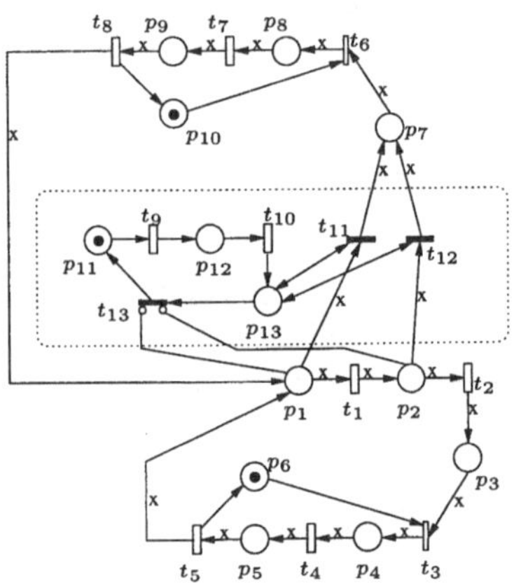

Figure 2. GSPN Dependability Model

Places $p_1, \ldots, p_5, p_7, \ldots p_9$ are colored places representing the four different types of fork-lifts and similarly transitions $t_1, \ldots, t_8, t_{11}, \ldots, t_{13}$ are colored transitions. All incidence functions are identity functions, indicated by a letter "x" in case of colored transitions, using the notation proposed in [5].

lower part: Places p_1 and p_2 model operational fork-lifts and transitions t_1 and t_2 represent the Erlang-2 distribution for the time to failure. A (colored) token at p_3 indicates that the corresponding fork-lift is broken an needs repair. After a negative exponentially distributed preparation delay the worker (p_6) starts repairing a fork-lift. Transitions t_4, t_5 model the Erlang-2 distributed repair time.

middle part: This part of the GSPN represents the fixed time interval between maintenance processes. We approximate this time interval by an Erlang-2 distribution (transitions t_9, t_{10}). The beginning of maintenance is indicated by a token at place p_{13}. While p_{13} is marked, transitions t_{11} and t_{12} empty the two places p_1 and p_2 thus "moving" all tokens to place p_7. Once the places p_1, p_2 have been emptied, transition t_{13} becomes enabled (note the inhibitor arcs from p_1, p_2) and the time interval between maintenance processes is restarted.

upper part: A token at place p_7 indicates a fork-lift waiting for maintenance. After a negative exponentially distributed preparation delay the mechanic starts with maintenance of the fork-lift, provided he is available (p_{10}). The time for maintenance is given by an Erlang-2 distribution represented by transitions t_7 and t_8. The fork-lift becomes available after maintenance at place p_1.

Since places p_1 and p_2 model the availability of operational fork-lifts we are interested in the probability $p_{i,x} := P[M(p_1)(x) + M(p_2)(x) = i]$ that i fork-lifts of type x are available. $p_{i,x}$ surely depends on the chosen parameters for timed transitions. In reality most of these parameters are determined by the type of fork-lift and are thus given. I.e. given the time to failure and repair and maintenance times, one might be interested to find an "optimal" duration between maintenance intervals. This results in the following optimization problem: Find a parameter λ (the firing rate for t_9 and t_{10} representing an Erlang-2 distribution) such that $p_{k,x}$ is maximal, where k denotes the number of existing fork-lifts of type x. In our model, we assume the fixed parameter setting of 20000 min for time to failure, 2000 min repair time and 80 min maintenance time.

Performability analysis comprises numerical analyzes of

parameterized dependability models and simulative analyzes of performance models. For the later we apply the proposed scheduling algorithm, see section 2.2, and compare its effectiveness with a conventional approach.

The GSPN dependability model is solved based on the underlying Markov chain with exactly $12,246,960$ states. Using numerical steady-state analysis techniques we can compute the probability mass function (pmf) of resource configurations (p_c values) within 80 minutes. The frequency of stipulated maintenances is regarded as a parameter of the dependability model. Therefore, we must perform numerical analysis for different dependability models and obtain a set of pmf's. Figure 3 shows the pmf restricted on $\mathcal{C}^0$ for different parameter settings.

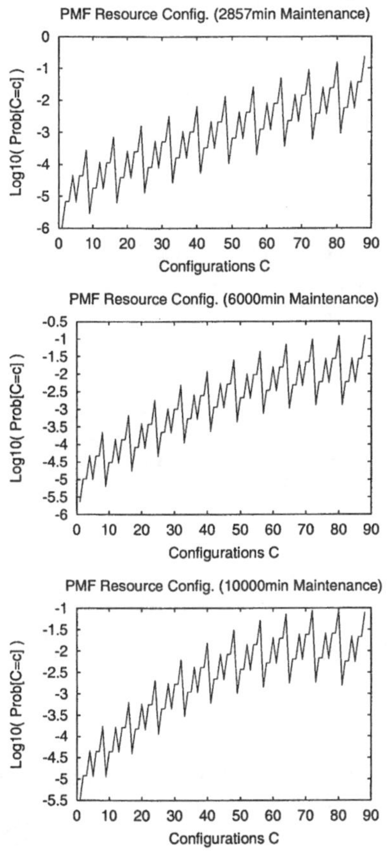

Figure 3. Pmf of resource configurations for different parameter values of the dependability model

The evaluation of the performance model requires to conduct independent simulation runs for each operational resource configuration $c \in \mathcal{C}^0$, see section 2.1. We vary the number of available fork-lifts and obtain 88 operational configurations in this particular setting. A particular simulation run determines estimates of quantities of interest (lead times of involved processes). First we consider a scenario with single simulation runs. Performance results thereby obtained based on runs that terminate at once if, either 90 percent confidence bands are attained of a width of at most 5 percent of the estimated means for all process lead times, or some maximum model time has elapsed. Totally, 88 single simulation runs need 17 hours of CPU time (measured on SUN Blade 100, Ultra Sparc IIe processor, 500 MHz). This solid stopping criterion ensures reliable results. However, the drawback is, that computational efforts for obtaining reliable performance results are by no means adapted to their relative importance (=p_c values) with respect to reliable performability results. Therefore, it is reasonable to replicate simulation runs using some adaptive control which makes use of p_c values and thus greedy reduces confidence intervals of performability quantities (see section 2.2). In our setting, the relative importance of configurations dramatically differs. Figure 3 reveals, that p_c values decreases exponentially for configurations with lower index (note the logarithmic scale). For our example, the controlled replication approach clearly outperforms its uncontrolled single run counterpart. The controlled version needs only 3-4 hours of CPU time (compared to 17 hours) in order to achieve confidence intervals that has been reached in the single run approach. Figure 4 shows the run-time behavior of the algorithm in terms of confidence intervals (percent) for performability measures (lead times of three basic processes) depending on dependability model parameters (8 settings). After 3-4 hours, charts fall below the mesh indicating confidence intervals of the single run approach. In order to gain a better understanding of the algorithms behavior we do not stop the execution at this point and proceed until 240 replications are conducted. 240 replications require 10-11 hours of CPU time and confidence intervals become fairly small ($\pm 0.1\%$), cf. Figure 4.

We conclude this section with performability results based on formula 1. Fig. 5 shows lead times of the three basic processes (`Truck Arrival`, `In-Plant Transport` and `Demand`) depending on the parameter setting of the dependability model. A time interval of about 5500 min between two maintenance inspections minimizes lead times of all processes. Lead times of processes are of interest by their own, however, their obvious interpretation necessitates deeper knowledge of the performance model.

4 Conclusions

This paper presents an approach for the performability analysis of large logistic networks by a combination of numerical analysis of a dependability model and simulative analysis of a possibly large set of performance models. From a simulation perspective it is particularly interesting

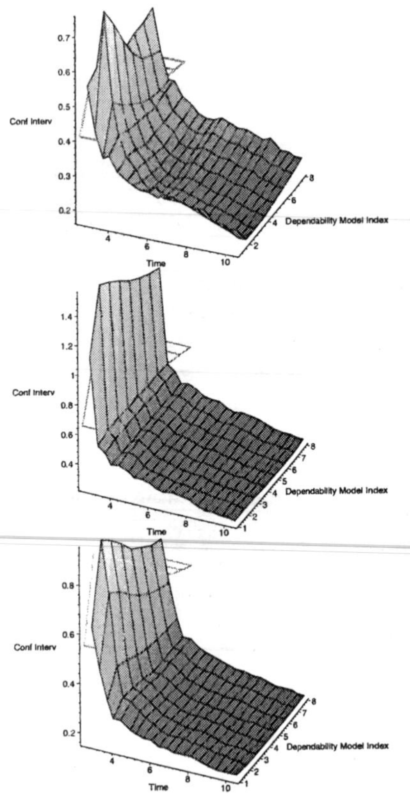

Figure 4. Run-time behavior of algorithm: confidence intervals (percent) of performability measures

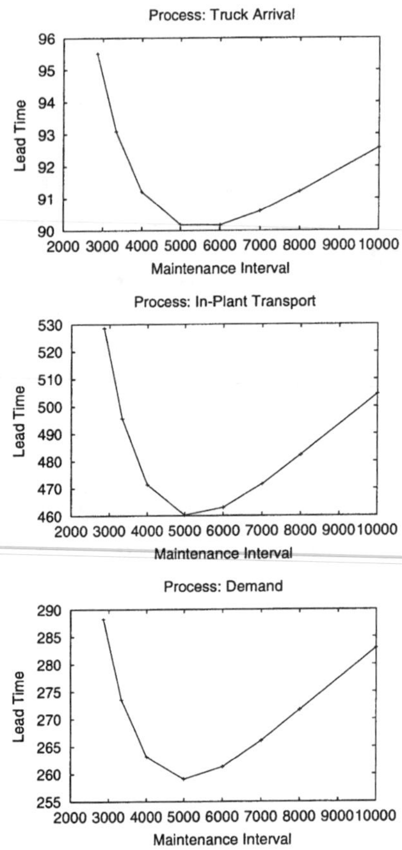

Figure 5. Performability Results: lead times of basic processes

how to distribute simulation time among the set of performance models to minimize the width the confidence intervals. The paper introduces an approach to perform simulation in phases and in parallel on a network of workstations. After every phase the available information is used to determine the subset of performance models which is simulated during the following phase to obtain a maximal gain measured in a maximal reduction of the confidence interval width.

References

[1] F. Bause, H. Beilner, M. Fischer, P. Kemper, and M. Völker. The Proc/B toolset for the modeling and analysis of process chains. In T. Field, P. G. Harrison, J. Bradley, and U. Harder, editors, *Computer Performance Evaluation Modeling Techniques and Tools*, pages 51–70. Springer LNCS 2324, 2002.

[2] H. Beilner, J. Mäter, and N. Weissenberg. Towards a performance modelling environment: news on HIT. In R. Puijanger, editor, *Proc. 4th Int. Conf. on Modelling Tools and Techniques for Computer Performance Evaluation.* Plenum Publishers, 1988.

[3] P. Buchholz, M. Fischer, P. Kemper, and C. Tepper. New features in the APNN toolbox. In P. Kemper, editor, *Tools of Aachen 2001 Int. Multiconference on Measurement, Modeling and Evaluation of Computer-Communication Systems*, pages 62–68. Universität Dortmund, Fachbereich Informatik, Forschungsbericht Nr. 760, 2001.

[4] B. R. Haverkort, R. Marie, G. Rubino, and K. Trivedi. *Performability Modelling*. Wiley, 2001.

[5] K. Jensen. *Coloured Petri Nets*. EATCS Monographs on Theoretical Computer Science. Springer, 1992.

[6] A. M. Law and W. D. Kelton. *Simulation modeling and analysis*. Wiley, 2000.

[7] J. F. Meyer. On evaluating the performability of degredable computer systems. *IEEE Transactions on Computers*, 29(8):720–731, 1980.

[8] W. H. Sanders and J. F. Meyer. A unified approach for specifying measures of performance, dependability and performability. In A. Avizienis and J. Laprie, editors, *Dependable Computing for Critical Applications*, Vol. 4 of Dependable Computing and Fault-Tolerant Systems. Springer, 1991.

Session 7:
Keynote

Component-based Distributed Simulations. The Way Forward?

Alexander Verbraeck
Delft University of Technology
Faculty of Technology, Policy and Management
Systems Engineering Section
P.O. Box 5015, 2600GA Delft, The Netherlands
a.verbraeck@tbm.tudelft.nl

Abstract

Parallel simulation and distributed simulation sometimes appear to be two different worlds. Where parallel simulation aims at increasing the speed of a single model by distributing it over more processors, distributed simulation looks at ways to link entire models or federates that run on different computers. In the case of distributed simulation, the models themselves are hard to distribute, and often they each run on one processor as a monolithic model. This paper advocates to build the more traditional simulation models in such a way, that they can be easily distributed. As simulationists, we can learn from component-based theory from the software engineering field to prepare our models for distribution, and parts of our models for reuse. The results of several projects show that componentizing simulation models can have many advantages. The results also show that it is not easy to create models in a componentized way, and that current methods for simulation model building should be adapted.

1. Parallel and distributed simulation

Parallel simulation and distributed simulation are related, but they also point to two very different motivations for wanting to distribute a model [15]. Parallel simulation aims at distributing a simulation model over a number of tightly coupled processors to speed up the run and/or spread the memory demand of the simulation execution. One of the major application areas is simulation of (tele)communication networks, which often need a lot of computer power to analyze [32], [33], [34].

The term 'distributed simulation' is often used to indicate that a number of stand-alone simulators or simulation models need to be integrated to enable joint execution. The major goal is to integrate the models from different sources into one larger model, without having to recode the model logic of each of the individual models. The HLA framework [24], developed under the guidance of DMSO and now an IEEE standard, has been the major architecture to use for distributed modeling. It has been noted, however, that distributed modeling is used mainly in the military field, and hardly in industry [44]. Nance and Sargent [28] describe the role and place of parallel simulation (p.167) and distributed simulation (p.168), and its limited use in the commercial field, and place these developments into a historical perspective. There is a limited number of studies described in literature about larger scale non-military applications of distributed simulation. Some of the notable exceptions are automobile factory simulations as described in [40] and [42], power grid simulations in [19], transport applications in [7] and [8], and enterprise simulations in [36]. So, slowly industry is increasing their use of distributed simulation. On the other hand, almost none of the existing commercial simulation software environments supports distributed modeling and simulation, nor do they support the HLA framework [43]. One of the few packages that did support HLA was the object oriented simulation language Modsim III [22], which is unfortunately not on the market anymore.

In the panel discussion described in [43], one of the major problems mentioned is the fact that common off-the-shelf simulation packages do not have the capabilities to interoperate. They usually *do* have possibilities to communicate, and wrappers are used to link one model to the other. This is in most cases not enough, and wrapping simulation environments can lead to unstable code and models that are hard to maintain, because the wrappers contain some logic of their own in addition to the model logic. Therefore, we should strive for simulation environments and simulation models that take the possibility to operate in a distributed mode as a starting point [20], [25], and look for ways to divide our simulation models into smaller parts, so it becomes easier to distribute individual models over more computers, or to group model parts in a different way than 'one model per computer'. Object orientation and component-based development immediately spring to mind as possible technologies to use when it comes to partitioning of software or models. Therefore, we will first briefly introduce the field of object-oriented development and

1087-4097/04 $20.00 © 2004 IEEE

component-based development, as we know it from the software-engineering field.

2. Object-oriented development

Object orientation in software development has always been a major promise for reuse and distribution. When programmed well, objects are 'closed' to the outside world due to their encapsulation [27], and access to the internal state of the object is only possible through selected 'public' methods. Object orientation is not only useful for software engineering, it can also be used in the simulation and modeling field. With the increased use of the Unified Modeling Language (see e.g. [35]), object orientation became more and more popular in the software engineering field, and also found its way to the modeling and simulation field. Many applications are developed in an object oriented way, although there are also claims of major problems with object orientation [26], [56].

Some simulation languages, such as Modsim III [22] and eM-Plant [17], [45] are based on the object-oriented paradigm. Actually, one of the earliest dedicated simulation languages, SIMULA, was fully object oriented [6], [13]. When it comes to simulation modeling, however, the object-oriented paradigm often falls short. Many of the applications of simulation are logistics simulations, where some kind of items (e.g., goods, persons, or vehicles) move through a number of processes that have limited capacity and that take some time. These processes with limited capacity are modeled as resources, which have attached queues for waiting entities when the required capacity of the resource is not available. The process interaction formalism, where the 'life cycle' of each entity type is described, is the most popular formalism for logistics simulations [4]. When modeling these logistics processes in an object-oriented way, we have to describe the 'active' servers rather than the 'passive' resources. The moving items are reduced to completely passive entities that just carry their information from one active server to the other. Model developers that 'see' the entities move from one server to the other find the object-oriented way of modeling difficult to use. Furthermore, the conceptual framework for most object-oriented simulations is the event scheduling formalism [4], rather than the process interaction formalism. Scheduling an event in the future is also more difficult to understand for a logistics person than describing the amount of time a process takes.

The developers of most of the commercially available simulation environments have tried to make a blend between object orientation and process interaction. Internally, the simulation software is built around event scheduling, allowing easy maintenance of the simulation software. For the model user, an entity / process view with queues and resources is presented for entering and changing the model. Languages like Arena [23] offer such a way of modeling, and even eM-Plant, which is an object-oriented simulation environment [45], has objects in its library that represent queues and processes 'through' and between which items can flow.

3. Component-based development

Object orientation does not guarantee reuse, nor does it guarantee that objects easily communicate with each other. The field of *component-based development* (CBD) has addressed this issue for the software-engineering world by aiming at reusable *building blocks* with a clearly defined *interface*. A research program at Delft University of Technology in the Netherlands called BETADE [52] has tried to transfer the ideas of components from the software world to other domains like modeling and simulation. We will use the word 'building block' rather than component for the applications in simulation and modeling, to distinguish it from the software components from the software engineering CBD field.

3.1. Definition of building blocks

What is a building block? Is it equal to an object or a component, and if not, what is the difference? The working definition that has been used in the BETADE research program is [52]:

> *A building block is a self-contained, interoperable, reusable and replaceable unit, encapsulating its internal structure and providing useful services or functionality to its environment through precisely defined interfaces. A building block may be customized in order to match the specific requirements of the environment in which it is 'plugged' or used.*

A clarification of the difference between a building block and components or other related terms is needed. In the area of automated transport systems, the representation of an automated guided vehicle will be a building block, as it is self-contained, interoperable, reusable and replaceable. It offers a clear service in the system, and for the system level, it hides its internal structure. In this example, an object will be a wheel: an essential, unique element of the solution of the transport problem, but not offering services on the system level. In this sense, the notion of *aggregation* or *composition* as we find in object orientation [21] and the Unified Modeling Language (UML), see e.g. [35], is clearly more important than the 'standard' object oriented software engineering concepts such as inheritance or polymorphism. Combining smaller elements into larger ones is the key.

The idea of components is derived from software-engineering environments (see e.g., [1], [2], [10], [11],

[16], [41], [55]), and builds upon the notion of distributed objects [14], [29]. However, the concept of a building block can also be used other environments, such as modeling and simulation. We state for the relationship between a building block and a component that a component is the implementation of a building block in a software environment. The interface (functionality) of the building block and the component are therefore different representations of the same thing.

This clear relationship between a component and a building block – from which the latter is clearly the broader notion – is supported by the following comments ([18], p.155): "A business component is the software implementation of an autonomous business concept (entity or process). It consists of all the software artifacts necessary to represent, implement, and deploy a given business concept as an autonomous, reusable element of a larger distributed information system. Important characteristics of the business component concept are its strong concepts of software artifact ownership, of black box/white box across the development lifecycle, of architectural viewpoints, of distribution tiers; and of its use as a unit of modularization, of deployment, of reuse, and of management."

3.2. Characteristics of building blocks

In this section, some properties of the building blocks are described. Building blocks are:

- self-contained (nearly independent of each other),
- interoperable (independent of underlying technology),
- reusable,
- replaceable,
- encapsulating their internal structure,
- providing useful services or functionality to their environment through precisely defined interfaces,
- customizable in order to match any specific requirements of the environment in which they are used (plugged).

In order to provide functionality, models are constructed by combining building blocks. More precisely stated, new – conceptual – building blocks can be formed by aggregation, which is combining lower level building blocks into new higher level building blocks. We embrace the object oriented paradigm and we want to be able to use the building blocks repetitively in our applications or models [9], [21]. Instances of building blocks will be combined to construct simulation models. The instantiation means that the attributes in the instance of the building block get a value in order to give the building block the exact functionality that the user wants within that application or model. Possibly, a number of attribute variables have a default value so the user does not have to worry about the values of all attributes of the building block.

3.3. Implementation of building blocks

The third aspect refers to the implementation aspects of a building block:

> *A building block is independent of its implementation and can therefore only described by its conceptual model and therefore by its function and interface with other building blocks. This means that independent of the implementation, a system consisting of a mixed implementation of different building blocks. For instance a combination of a simulation and a real-time application building block should function without problems.*

Even when humans fulfill certain activities, the system should remain functioning. So, building blocks go beyond software engineering or classical simulation studies. They can also be used to describe or design complex distributed business processes, such as the order handling at a bank.

3.4. Properties of building blocks

The following list of properties – inspired by [29] – of a building block can be given:

- *It can have different levels of granularity.* Building blocks can be composed of other building blocks and form so larger building blocks with more functionality. Building blocks have an extension that is dealt with in the former property.
- *It fulfils a clear function.* A building block is logically and physically cohesive, and thus denotes a meaningful structural and/or behavioral chunk of a larger system. It is not just some arbitrary grouping.
- *It has a well-specified interface.* A building block can only be manipulated through its interface. The functionality of the building block is addressed by its interface. In that way it is exposed to the outside world.
- *It exists in the context of a well-defined architecture.* A building block represents a fundamental building block upon which systems can be designed and composed. This definition is recursive: a system at one level of abstraction may simply be a building block at a higher level of abstraction.
- *It is nearly independent of other building blocks, but it rarely stands alone.* A given building block collaborates with other building blocks and in so doing assumes a specific architectural context. This architectural context is driven in large part by the implementation we chose.

- *It can be used in unpredictable combinations.* Building blocks can be used in ways that were totally unanticipated by the original developer. Typically, building blocks can be combined with other building blocks based on their interfaces.
- *It is an interoperable object.* A building block can be invoked as an object across address spaces, networks, languages, operating systems, and tools.
- *It may have several states.* A building block has some function, and by performing the function, its state may change from state, e.g. from passive to active.
- *It has limited domain specificity.* A building block is defined as being more or less generic.
- *It is a replaceable part of a system.* A building block is a substitute for any other building block, which realizes the same interfaces. This aspect helps during development, where parts of a system can be stubbed, sketched, and then replaced by mature, robust implementations. It also supports the evolution of a system, once deployed by making it possible to upgrade and evolve parts of the system independently.

4. A comparison with software components

In [10], a number of definitions are presented that were discussed on a workshop on Component Based Software Development (CBSD). They represent typical examples of the definitions found in the software industry:

1. A component is a nontrivial, nearly independent, and replaceable part of a system that fulfils a clear function in the context of a well-defined architecture. A component conforms to and provides the physical realization of a set of interfaces. (Philippe Krutchen, Rational Software);
2. A runtime software component is a dynamically bindable package of one or more programs managed as a unit and accessed through documented interfaces that can be discovered at runtime. (Gartner Group);
3. A software component is a unit of composition with contractually specified interfaces and explicit context dependencies only. A software component can be deployed independently and is subject to third-party composition. (Clemens Szyperski, Component Software);
4. A business component represents the software implementation of an "autonomous" business concept or business process. It consists of the software artifacts necessary to express, implement, and deploy the concept as a reusable element of a larger business system. (Wojtek Kozaczynski, SSA).

Key concepts in all these definitions is the (set of) interfaces as a means of characterizing components, and an architecture (structure) that provides the integration context for the components. The component must (be adaptable to) fit the integration context. A component can be either active or passive and a component can be seen as a black box or white box.

5. Component simulation 1: OLS

A first attempt at building block based development where building blocks can be easily interchanged, maintained, and replaced, has been carried out in a project called OLS, which is the Dutch acronym for Underground Logistic System. This research project is being carried out to survey the possibilities for underground logistic systems that use automated guided vehicles (AGVs) to transport goods on a large scale. One of the first practical applications that is being worked out is an underground logistic system called OLS Schiphol, between Amsterdam Airport Schiphol, the Flower Auction Aalsmeer, and a new high-speed rail terminal near Hoofddorp in the Netherlands. As usual in the design of a system like this, many design options were open at the start of the project. Because the number of options was so large, it was thought that a *library of easy to use simulation building blocks* would help to quickly create different versions of the system.

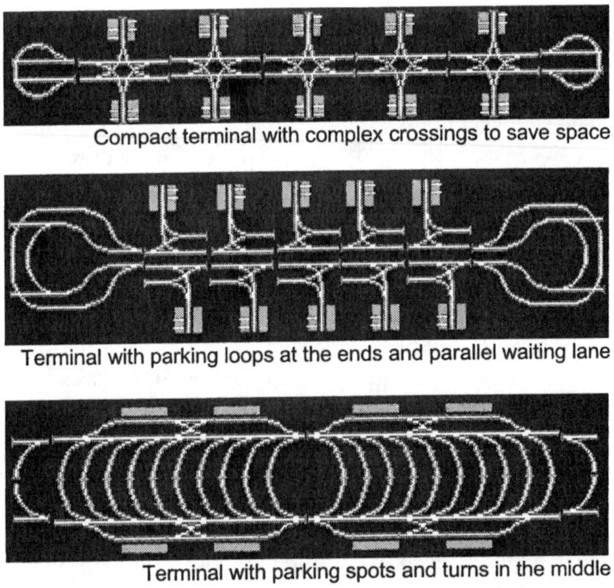

Figure 1. Three of the many developed OLS terminal designs, created from an eM-Plant library of simulation building blocks

After preliminary studies, several design choices were made for the OLS project. It was decided to partition the system into autonomous units as much as possible because of scalability and flexibility. Hierarchical building blocks were created (bottom-up) to be able to quickly make different infrastructure layouts [51]. After some attempts, it became apparent that infrastructure building blocks that contain information on the service they can provide, and that can function autonomous, are very easy to use. eM-Plant [45] served as the object-oriented simulation language in which the infrastructure (terminals, tracks, docks, parking areas, maintenance areas) was built; see Figure 1 for three of the many terminal examples.

For maintaining maximum flexibility in the terminals it was chosen to use free ranging AGVs. In that way, layout changes, dock changes, and problems with the unavailability of docks or passing halted vehicles, can be solved far easier than with AGVs that drive on fixed tracks. When looking at the control system of the AGV more accurately, two subsystems can be distinguished: the AGV driver and the AGV control. The driver takes care of controlling the motors, brakes, and steering servos. The AGV driver also processes signals from sensors on the AGV. The vehicles were also implemented in the simulation language eM-Plant, using building blocks for both the AGV driver and the AGV control. Because it was known that the objects would eventually be distributed, the AGV driver and the AGV control object were implemented as two different objects with a clear interface. From the start of the project, CORBA was used to define the interface between different building blocks in the OLS project [3], [30].

In a second phase of the project, the same object-oriented building blocks for the vehicle control were used as part of different simulation models on different computers. The purpose was to analyze and test the distribution of the objects to get a feeling for the problems that might occur with the communication when the actual AGV (i.e. the AGV driver object) resides on another physical location – in this case the on-board computer of the AGV – than the AGV control object. As part of this project, more building blocks of the simulation model were distributed over different models and/or computers.

The final step in this project was the replacement of the simulated AGV driver with the real AGV. As the interfaces between the building blocks remained the same, this was nothing more than taking out one building block, and replacing it with another building block [50].

In the OLS project, many (simulation and real-time control) experiments were carried out with the library of infrastructure elements, control blocks, AGVs, and docks. The flexible and easy to change building blocks in the eM-Plant simulation library that was designed for this project enabled fast changes whenever the project required so. It became clear that self-contained building blocks with clear interfaces that use asynchronous communication are key to success in flexible real-time vehicle control [37]. The robust communication between building blocks using CORBA gave almost no problems.

Suppose that the final control information system for OLS is implemented in a traditional language like C++ using the simulation model as an example for the implementation. Usually, testing control software is quite difficult, because the effects can be quite grave when the software is not functioning properly. In this case, however, it has been suggested to the OLS management to give the newly built control software exactly the same (CORBA) interface as the simulated control system. In that way, the control system can be tested in a simulated environment with the simulated vehicles. The clear interface and the open CORBA standard used between the vehicles and the control system allows for exchanging real and simulated information in a distributed setting on both sides. A major advantage is that a problem that occurs in a real control situation can be replayed in a simulation mode, and the simulations can also be used to test different solutions before they are implemented in the real system. In experiments that were carried out, fast software development iterations in the design have been used a number of times now. Often, changes in the system took only the replacement of one building block by an adapted version. Interfaces were almost never impacted. To give an example: the interface between the AGV control and the AGV driver remained constant during the experiments for more than two years. Only recently, a new definition for curves based on B-splines has been proposed, that will ask for two simple changes in the building block definitions on both sides. Again, because the building block interfaces have been defined well, it is immediately known where this interface change will have an impact and where not, and the changes that need to be made are well isolated from the rest of the complex control system.

Although the OLS project was originally not aimed at research on building blocks or on component based development, it has become apparent that libraries with self-contained building blocks with clear interfaces have an added value in projects where flexibility and maintain-ability are required to test many design options.

6. Components simulation 2: supply chains

A second application area for which a library of simulation model components has been developed and tested is the area of supply chains [38], [39]. Based on literature, a supply chain architecture has been developed, that was implemented in a library of simulation building blocks in the simulation languages Arena [23] and eM-Plant [45], and in the general programming language Java. When building a supply chain model with these simulation building blocks, entire organizations are placed in the model, for which the policies can be entered in a consistent way. This tremendously speeds up the model building process and the analysis of alternatives; as such a model is much simpler to build, maintain and operate than a model built in the standard simulation environment.

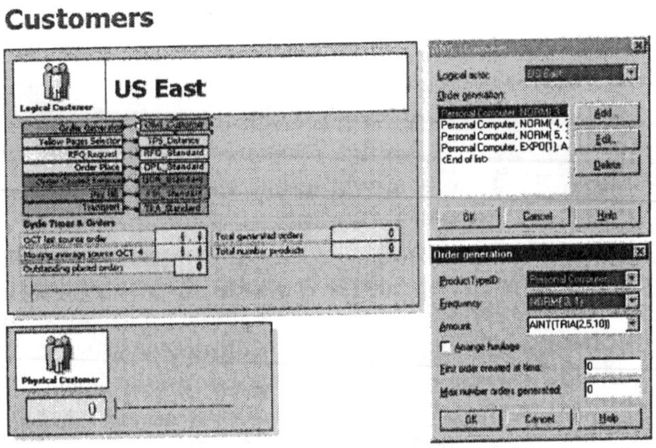

Figure 2. Customer simulation building block in Arena, when it has been dragged from the component library

In the customer or market simulation building block of Figure 2, the 'actor' that is entered in the simulation model by dragging a building block instance into the model is shown on the left hand side. In the building block, several policies can be seen in the rectangles, as well as automatically calculated performance indicators – in this case several counters and the order cycle time. The policies can be replaced with a rich set of policies from a policy library. Each policy has a number of properties, as can be seen in the right hand side of Figure 2. In this case, the order generation policy of the customer is opened, and it can be seen that the customer orders 'personal computers'. Four different orders are placed, each with its own order amount and interval. The properties of the top order are shown at the bottom right. Researching the effect of larger or more frequent orders from a certain market has been reduced to changing expressions or distribution parameters in policies. The policies themselves can also be easily replaced. Using building blocks like these saves the model builder a lot of time. The model also becomes much simpler to maintain, and the building blocks that are used have already been validated. Performance indicators have been built in to show the most important properties, and all animation functions have been defined. Several of the building blocks also show graphs and histograms of their most important indicators, such as the stock levels per product, the use of resources, and the financial situation. An example is shown in Figure 3, where the animation is shown for the 'bull-whip effect' in a simulation model with one market, five retailers, two distribution centers, one manufacturer, and three suppliers [49]. All graphs come from the building blocks that have been defined. The graphs at the bottom that show the demand for three types of organizations have been added by hand.

7. Discussion and conclusions

In addition to the two application areas described in sections 5 and 6, simulation component libraries have also been developed for airport applications [53], and for transportation applications in ports [7], [8]. In all four application projects, it turned out to be quite difficult to:

- *design* a good and consistent set of building blocks: especially the aggregation level and granularity were not easy to determine, see [47];
- *describe* the building blocks that have been created: there is no good language available for consistent component description, which supports the modeler's search process, see [5];
- *develop* the simulation model based on the building blocks: all simulation methods start from the assumption that models have to be built from scratch, and do not assume that there is a library of components available; development methods have to be changed, see [47];
- *teach* other persons than the simulation expert to use a set of building blocks: see [48];
- *make use of* standard simulation languages; although Arena and eM-Plant have been used in the two case-studies described more extensively here, preparing the models for distributed use turned out to be an extremely hard task, see [43].

Therefore, *the way forward* seems to be to research component-based development in relation to simulation and see where the two worlds can meet. Component-based simulation looks like a favorable method to join parallel and distributed simulation, and to carry distributed simulation into industry.

Acknowledgements

The research presented here has been carried out as part of the BETADE research program funded by TU Delft between 2000 and 2004. Parts of the paper have been described more extensively in [52] and build upon projects that have been carried out and published by the BETADE researchers. The author also wishes to thank TRAIL research school and Connekt for sponsoring the research described in the case studies. The concepts of this paper have also been sharpened during the extensive and interesting Dagstuhl seminar 04041 on component-based simulation in January 2004 [5].

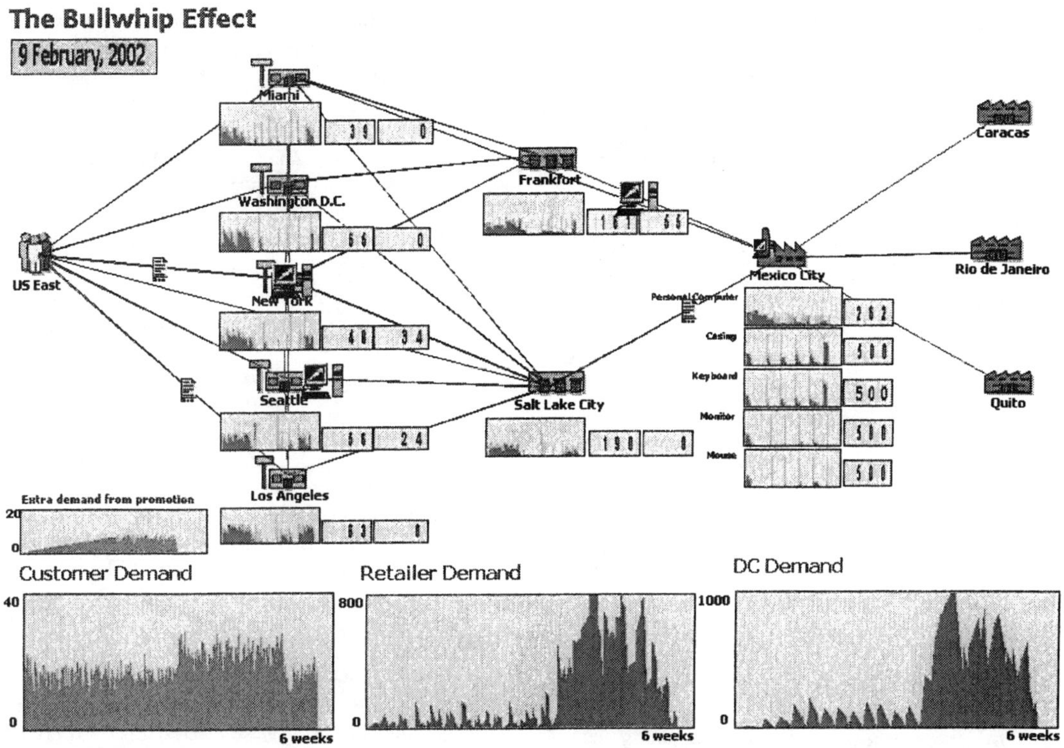

Figure 3. Example of almost automatically created output screen with the standard supply chain building blocks

8. References

[1] P. Allen, S. Frost. *Component-Based Development for Enterprise Systems*. Cambridge University Press, 1998.

[2] P. Allen. *Realizing e-Business with Components*. Pearson Education, 2001.

[3] S. Baker. *CORBA Distributed Objects*. ACM Press / Addison-Wesley, 1997.

[4] O. Balci, "The implementation of four conceptual frameworks for simulation modeling in high-level languages". In: *Proceedings of the 20th Winter Simulation Conference*. ACM Press, New York, 1988, pp. 287-295.

[5] F.J. Barros, A. Lehmann, P. Liggesmeyer, A. Verbraeck, B.P. Zeigler, *Dagstuhl Seminar on Component-based Modeling and Simulation*. http://www.dagstuhl.de/04041/

[6] G.M. Birtwistle, *Discrete Event Modelling on Simula*. Springer-Verlag, 1987.

[7] C.A. Boer, A. Verbraeck and H.P.M. Veeke. "Distributed Simulation of Complex Systems: Application in Container Handling. In: *Proceedings of the 2002 SISO European Simulation Interoperability Workshop*. SISO, Orlando, Florida., 2002.

[8] C.A. Boer, A. Verbraeck, A. de Waal, B. van Eck, and J. Seager. "Distributed e-Services for Road Container Transport Simulation". In: [54], pp. 541-550.

[9] G. Booch. *Object Oriented Design with Applications*. Benjamin / Cummings, 1991.

[10] A.W. Brown, K.C. Wallnau, "The current state of CBSE", in: *IEEE Software*, pp. 37-46, September/October 1998.

[11] A.W. Brown. *Large-scale Component-Based Development*. Prentice-Hall, 2000.

[12] S. Chick, P. J. Sánchez, D. Ferrin, and D. J. Morrice (eds.). *Proceedings of the 2003 Winter Simulation Conference*. IEEE, 2003.

[13] O.-J. Dahl and K. Nygaard, "Simula – an ALGOL based simulation language". In: *CACM* 9:9, 1966. pp. 671-678.

[14] P. Fingar, D. Read, J. Stikeleather. *Next Generation Computing: Distributed objects for business*. SIGS, 1996.

[15] R.M. Fujimoto, "Distributed Simulation Systems". In: [12], pp. 124-134.

[16] G.T. Heineman, W.T. Councill. *Component-Based Software Engineering – Putting the pieces together*. Addison-Wesley, 2001.

[17] M.U. Heinicke and A. Hickman, "Eliminate Bottlenecks with Integrated Analysis Tools in eM-Plant". In: J.A. Joines, R.R. Barton, K. Kang, and P.A. Fishwick, (eds.), *Proceedings of the 2000 Winter Simulation Conference*. ACM/IEEE, 2000, pp. 229-231.

[18] P. Herzum, O. Sims, *Business Component Factory – A comprehensive overview of component-based development for the enterprise*, Wiley / OMG Press, 2000.

[19] K.M. Hopkinson, K.P. Birman, R. Giovanini, D.V. Coury, EPOCHS: Integrated Commercial Off-The-Shelf Software for Agent-Based Electric Power and Communication Simulation. In: [12], pp. 1158-1166.

[20] P.H.M. Jacobs, N.A. Lang, A. Verbraeck. "D-SOL; A distributed Java based discrete event simulation architecture". In: [57], pp. 793-800.

[21] I. Jacobson, M. Ericsson, A. Jacobson. *The Object Advantage – Business process reengineering with object*

technology. New York: ACM Press / Addison Wesley, 1995.

[22] G. Johnson, "Networked Simulation with HLA and MODSIM III". In: P. Farrington, H. Nembhard, D. Sturrock. and G. Evans (eds.) *Proceedings of the 1999 Winter Simulation Conference*, ACM Press, New York, NY, pp. 1065-1070.

[23] W.D. Kelton, R.P. Sadowski, and D.T. Sturrock, *Simulation with Arena*. 3rd edition. McGraw-Hill, 2003.

[24] F. Kuhl, R. Weatherly, J. Dahmann, *Creating Computer Simulation Systems: An Introduction to the High Level Architecture*. Prentice Hall PTR, 1999.

[25] N.A. Lang, P.H.M. Jacobs, A. Verbraeck. "Distributed open simulation model development with DSOL services". In: [54], pp. 210-218.

[26] T. Love, *Object Lessons: Lessons Learned in Object-Oriented Development Projects*. Signature Sounds Recording, 1997.

[27] B. Meyer, *Object-Oriented Software Cconstruction*. Prentice Hall;, 2nd edition, 1997.

[28] R.E. Nance and R.G. Sargent. Perspectives on the Evolution of Simulation. *Operations Research*, Vol. 50, No. 1, 2002, pp 161-172.

[29] R. Orfali, D. Harkey, J. Edwards, *The Essential Distributed Objects Survival Guide*, John Wiley & Sons, 1996.

[30] R. Orfali, D. Harkey, *Client / Server Programming with Java and CORBA*, 2nd edition. John Wiley & Sons, 1998.

[31] S. Pllana and T. Fahringer, "UML based Modeling of Performance Oriented Parallel and Distributed Applications". In: [57], pp. 497-505.

[32] *Proceedings of the 2003 International Symposium on Performance Evaluation of Computer and Telecommunication Systems (SPECTS 2003)*. SCS, San Diego, 2003.

[33] *Proceedings of the 11th IEEE/ACM International Symposium on Modeling, Analysis and Simulation of Computer and Telecommunications Systems (MASCOTS 2003)*, IEEE/ACM, 2003.

[34] G.F. Riley and P.A. Wilsey (eds.), *Proceedings of the 17th Workshop on Parallel and Distributed Simulation (PADS2003), IEEE, Los Alamitos CA, 2003.*

[35] J. Rumbaugh, G. Booch, and I. Jacobson. *The Unified Software Development Process*, Addison-Wesley Publishing, 1999.

[36] S.M. Saad, T. Perera, and R. Wickramarachchi , "Simulation of Distributed Manufacturing Enterprises: A New Approach". In: [12], pp. 1167-1173.

[37] Y.A. Saanen, A. Verbraeck, J.C. Rijsenbrij, "The Application of Advanced Simulations for the Engineering of Logistic Control Systems". In: K. Mertins, M. Rabe (eds.). *The New Simulation in Production and Logistics – Prospects, Views and Attitudes. Proceedings 9. ASIM Fachtagung "Simulation in Produktion und Logistik"*. IPK, Berlin, 2000, pp. 217-231.

[38] J.F. Shapiro, *Modeling the Supply Chain*. Duxbury Press, 2000.

[39] D. Simchi-Levi, P. Kaminsky, E. Simchi-Levi, *Designing and Managing the Supply Chain: Concepts, Strategies, and Cases*. 2nd edition. McGraw-Hill/Irwin, 2003.

[40] S. Straßburger. *Distributed Simulation Based on the High Level Architecture in Civilian Application Domains*. SCS European Publishing House, Erlangen, Germany, 2001.

[41] C. Szyperski. *Component Software*, 2nd edition. Addison-Wesley Publishing, 2001.

[42] G. Tan, N. Zhao, and S.J.E. Taylor, "Automobile Manufacturing Supply Chain Simulation in the GRIDS Environment". In: [12], pp. 1149-1157.

[43] S.J.E. Taylor, B.P. Gan, S. Straßburger, and A. Verbraeck, "HLA-CSPIF Panel on Commercial Off-the-Shelf Distributed Simulation". In: [12], pp. 881-887.

[44] S.J.E. Taylor, *et al.* "Distributed Simulation and Industry: Potentials and Pitfalls". In: [57], pp. 688-694.

[45] Tecnomatix, *eM-Plant version 4.6 User Guide*. Tecnomatix, Stuttgart, 2000.

[46] E. Valentin, A. Verbraeck. "Simulation using building blocks". In: F.J. Barros, N. Giambiasi (Eds). *AIS'2002 - Proceedings of AI, Simulation and Planning in High Autonomy Systems*. SCS, 2002, pp. 65-72.

[47] E. Valentin, A. Verbraeck. "Guidelines for designing simulation building blocks". In: [57], pp. 563-571.

[48] E. Valentin, A. Verbraeck, H.G. Sol. "Advantages and Disadvantages of Building Blocks in Simulation Studies: A Laboratory Experiment with Simulation Experts". In: [54], pp. 141-148.

[49] R. Van der Hee, *Simulating and visualizing the real-time supply chain*. M.Sc. thesis, Delft University of Technology / University of Maryland, 2002.

[50] A. Verbraeck, C. Versteegt, "A bridge between the design and implementation of complex transportation systems - Linking simulation models and physical systems". In: D.P.F. Möller (Ed.), *ESS2000 - Simulation in Industry. 12th European Simulation Symposium*, SCS publications, Ghent, 2000. pp. 238-243.

[51] A. Verbraeck, Y.A. Saanen, E. Valentin. "Designing Effective Terminals and their Control Systems for the Underground Logistic System Schiphol". *Proceedings ISUFT 2000, 2nd International Symposium on Underground Freight Transportation by Capsule Pipelines and Other Tube / Tunnel Systems*. CD-Rom proceedings. Delft, 2000.

[52] A. Verbraeck, A.N.W. Dahanayake (eds.), *Building blocks for Effective Telematics Application Development and Evaluation*. Delft University of Technology, 2001.

[53] A. Verbraeck, E. Valentin. "Simulation Building Blocks for Airport Terminal Modeling". In: [57]. pp. 1199-1206.

[54] A. Verbraeck, V. Hlupic (eds.), *ESS'2003, Proceedings 15th European Simulation Symposium 2003 – Simulation in Industry*, SCS European Publishing House, Germany, 2003.

[55] K.C. Wallnau, S.A. Hissam, R.C. Seacord. *Building Systems from Commercial Components*. Addison-Wesley, 2002.

[56] B.F. Webster, *Pitfalls of Object Oriented Development*. Hungry Minds, Inc, 1995.

[57] E. Yücesan, C.-H. Chen, J.L. Snowdon, and J.M. Charnes, (eds.). *Proceedings of the 2002 Winter Simulation Conference*, IEEE, 2002.

Session 8:
Work In Progress

Session 9:
Network Simulation II

Conservative Synchronization of Large-Scale Network Simulations

Alfred Park Richard M. Fujimoto Kalyan S. Perumalla
College of Computing, Georgia Institute of Technology
Atlanta, Georgia, USA 30332-0280
{park,fujimoto,kalyan}@cc.gatech.edu

Abstract

Parallel discrete event simulation techniques have enabled the realization of large-scale models of communication networks containing millions of end hosts and routers. However, the performance of these parallel simulators could be severely degraded if proper synchronization algorithms are not utilized. In this paper, we compare the performance and scalability of synchronous and asynchronous algorithms for conservative parallel network simulation. We develop an analytical model to evaluate the efficiency and scalability of certain variations of the well-known null message algorithm, and present experimental data to verify the accuracy of this model. This analysis and initial performance measurements on parallel machines containing hundreds of processors suggest that for scenarios simulating scaled network models with constant number of input and output channels per logical process, an optimized null message algorithm offers better scalability than efficient global reduction based synchronous protocols.

1. Introduction

In conservative parallel discrete event simulation (PDES), an event cannot be processed unless it is safe to do so. Since all logical processes (LPs) do not have a consistent view of the state of the entire system, LPs must exchange information to determine when events are safe to process. This process of synchronizing LPs has been the subject of much past research [1].

Conservative synchronization algorithms can be broadly classified as asynchronous or synchronous. Asynchronous algorithms do not require global synchronizations. A well-known example is the null message algorithm for deadlock avoidance originally developed independently by Chandy and Misra [2] and Bryant [3]. Variants to the original Chandy-Misra-Bryant (CMB) null message algorithm to improve efficiency have been devised and evaluated [4-7]. On the other hand, synchronous algorithms use global synchronization and reduction computations to compute a Lower Bound on Timestamp (LBTS) of future messages that might be received by each LP, in order to determine when events are safe to process. A well-known example is the YAWNS protocol described in [8]. Other algorithms use techniques such as deadlock detection and recovery [9] and simulation time windows [10].

Although previous studies have evaluated the performance of conservative synchronization algorithms for inefficiencies and overhead (e.g., see [11-13]), the scale of these studies have been, for the most part, limited to modest sized configurations, with most using fewer than 100 processors. As the number of LPs that participate in a parallel and distributed simulation increase, performance conclusions based on small-scale simulation studies may not apply to a large-scale context and the appropriateness of a particular synchronization method can shift from one algorithm to another. Here, we address scalability concerns in order to compare an asynchronous CMB null message algorithm with a synchronous barrier algorithm for large-scale network simulations.

The paper is organized as follows. Related work is first discussed in the next section. A lazy null message algorithm and an associated analytical model are presented in section 3. Section 4 describes the simulation scenarios used for the experimental study, and presents comparison between analytical model predictions and measurements. Section 5 presents empirical data comparing the performance of CMB and global reduction algorithms for regular and irregular networks. Future work and conclusions follow in sections 6 and 7, respectively.

2. Related Work

While there has been much research comparing optimistic and conservative synchronization protocols, there has been comparatively little work devoted to comparing the performance of asynchronous and synchronous conservative synchronization algorithms for large numbers of processors. Bagrodia and Takai provide extensive performance comparisons of synchronous and asynchronous synchronization algorithms, but do not consider large numbers of processors [4]. Nicol describes scalability through analysis of model characteristics, partitioning, workload balance, and model complexity in a broad PDES context [14]. However, our work specifically analyzes the detailed costs associated with the operation of a lazy null message algorithm. Further, we show that better scalability can be achieved using CMB, compared to global reduction algorithms, in scaled network models with constant fan-in/fan-out. This is performed with an emphasis on quantitative results supporting our findings.

1087-4097/04 $20.00 © 2004 IEEE

Nicol and Liu [15] combine asynchronous channel scanning and synchronous global barrier algorithms with a good amount of experimental data examining fan-in/fan-out and lookahead up to 8 processors. We discuss performance implications on larger configurations, specifically comparing lazy null message-based and global reduction-based algorithms. These algorithms are applied to regular and irregular network models with varying load distributions and asymmetric lookahead values, on up to 128 processors. Nicol also presents models to provide a lower-bound on the performance of a synchronous global reduction algorithm that can apply to large numbers of LPs [16, 17]. Our analytic model differs from this work in its focus on scalability concerns for the CMB algorithm. While analyzers described in [18] illustrate speedup differences between synchronous and asynchronous algorithms, our focus lies in identifying detailed CMB performance characteristics, such as null message send frequency and overhead, and applied to analytical models for large-scale network simulation. Synchronization challenges are described by Naroska and Schwiegelshohn [19] for large number of processes. While their work focuses on VLSI design, we focus on network simulations. The work presented in [20] contains models that exclude lookahead values [21]. However, their approach requires extensive knowledge of various metrics and has no means to measure the effect of increasing scale.

3. Analytical Models for CMB

The impetus for utilizing an asynchronous rather than a synchronous algorithm is to avoid the potentially large amount of overhead in interrupting the simulation, calculating and distributing new LBTS values, and restarting the LPs. Synchronization based on the CMB algorithm depends upon null messages exchanged only between neighboring processors. The frequency and time stamp of these null messages dictate the behavior and performance of the simulation; this simple observation will drive the formulation of the analytical CMB model. We will iteratively build this model. The end result will be a model for the CMB null message algorithms that can approximate simulator performance in structured large-scale network simulations. In the following we assume the parallel simulator consists of a collection of LPs that communicate by exchanging messages.

3.1. Effect of Null Messages on Simulation Behavior

Lookahead is one of the most important factors to achieving good performance in conservative PDES. Each LP is allowed to process events without re-synchronizing with other LPs up to its LBTS value. In general, conservative PDES performs well when the difference between successive LBTS values is large relative to the simulation time between successive events, because each LP can process many events before it must re-synchronize with other processors.

In a traditional CMB algorithm, after an event is processed, null messages are sent to every output channel to neighboring LPs. It is well known that overly eager null message transmission schemes produce an excessive number of null messages, leading to other algorithms that improve CMB performance by sending null messages less often. However, a sufficient number of null messages must be sent in order to avoid deadlock. The frequency of null message sends can have a large effect on performance. As the number of null messages increases, the overhead to synchronize increases proportionately, and less useful work is accomplished each second of wallclock time. Lookahead, null message frequency, time advance conditions, and remote communication are all contributing factors in the analytical model characterizing the performance of algorithms based on null messages.

Here, we relax the constraints assumed in the original null message algorithm. Specifically, a LP need *not* send messages in time stamp order. We do assume that the communication channel delivers messages in the same order in which they were sent. These assumptions imply that all simulation time information for computing new LBTS values resides in the time stamps of null messages.

3.2. A Lazy CMB Null Message Algorithm

This variant of the CMB algorithm, which is traditionally referred to as *lazy CMB*, attempts to minimize the number of null messages by only sending them when absolutely necessary. Specifically, null messages are only sent when the LP reaches the end of its safe processing time, i.e., only when the LP must block. Failing to send null messages while in this blocked state could lead to deadlock situations.

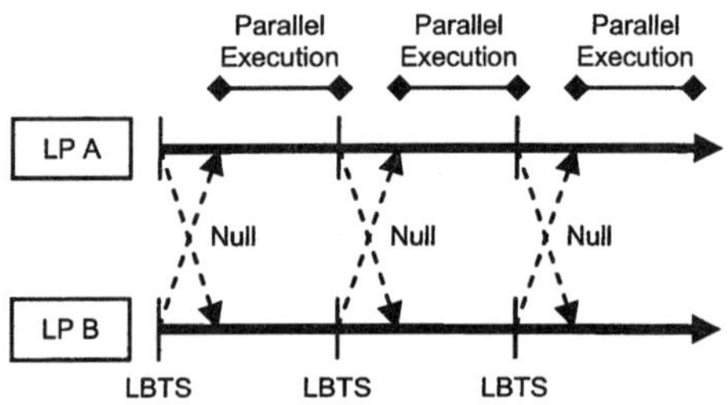

Figure 1. Execution Timeline of a Lazy CMB Algorithm

Figure 1 shows the progression of the simulation using the lazy CMB algorithm where each LP has the same lookahead. Note that "LBTS" in the figure represents when a new LBTS value is computed for time management. This lazy null message execution resembles that of a time-stepped simulation. With a minimal number of null messages exchanged between LPs, this scheme appears to be an efficient synchronization protocol. One can calculate the number of null messages N_Φ sent as:

$$N_\Phi = m \times n \times \left(\frac{s}{lookahead} \right) \qquad (1)$$

where m is the number of LPs, n is the number of output channels per LP, and s is the length of the run in simulation time. The number of execution windows (s divided by *lookahead*), gives the number of rounds or time-steps for which null messages are sent. Multiplying this result by the number of output channels yields the number of null messages sent each round. The product of this result and the total number of LPs gives the total number of null messages exchanged during the entire simulation. It is important to emphasize that formula 1 pertains to a CMB algorithm applied to a regular, structured network model. In other words, the lookahead of each LP is assumed to be the same.

In our sample simulation, let $m = 8$, $n = 2$, $s = 25$, and *lookahead* = 0.2 seconds. By formula 1, the total number of null messages would be 2,000. We can modify equation 1 to approximate the number of synchronization messages (N_Ψ) sent when a butterfly barrier is used (assuming that m is a multiple of 2):

$$N_\Psi = m \times \log_2 m \times \left(\frac{s}{lookahead} \right) \qquad (2)$$

The same simulation under a synchronous algorithm using global reductions through a butterfly barrier mechanism results in 3,000 synchronization messages from equation 2. More generally, if the number of output channels does not increase with the number of LPs, the number of null messages in CMB increases linearly with the number of LPs, yielding lower overhead than the approach using reductions.

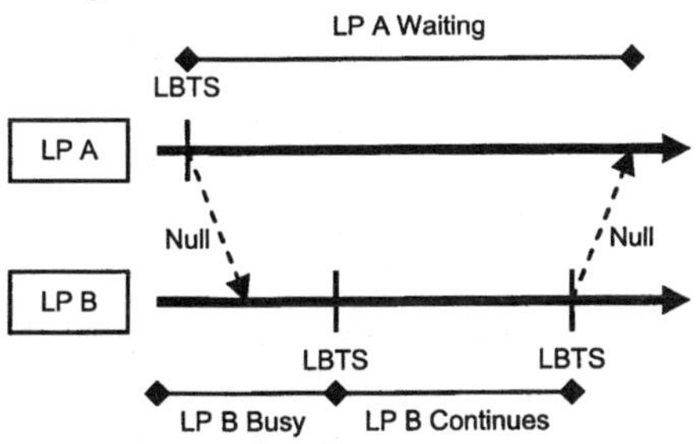

Figure 2. Blocking in a Lazy CMB Algorithm

It is important to note, however, that minimizing the number of null messages does not necessarily maximize performance. In particular, a modest load imbalance may lead to large waiting times that could be avoided by sending additional null messages. To see this, consider the example in figure 2, showing two LPs A & B with output channels between them. Here, LP A determines that it can no longer process events safely. LP A sends a null message to LP B and blocks. However, LP B is busy processing events within its own LBTS limit. Further, when LP B completes processing these events, it can process the null message from LP A, compute a new LBTS value, and begin processing events based on this new value, all *without* sending a null message to LP A. Because no new null message is sent to LP A, LP A will remain blocked. A null message will be sent to LP A only after LP B has finished processing these new events and is forced to block. Moreover, the delay to transmit this null message from LP A to LP B further increases the amount of time LP A remains blocked.

A solution to this problem is to have each LP send null messages more frequently. One must generate more null messages, but not so many that the system is burdened with an excessive amount. This is discussed next.

3.3. An Optimized Lazy Null Message Algorithm

One approach to generating additional null messages is to designate that each LP should send null messages every f units of simulation time advance, where f is less than the LP's lookahead (continuing to assume, for the moment, that all links have the same lookahead; we will relax this assumption later). By increasing the frequency of null messages sent to neighbors, potentially long blocking times can be avoided.

A second optimization to this approach is to eliminate null messages that carry no new useful information. For example, if two successive null messages carry the same time stamp it is clear there is no reason to send the second. Thus, we can cancel (suppress) any superfluous null messages that convey no new information, by not sending those messages at all.

To include these two changes, we can modify equation 1 to yield:

$$N_\Phi = m \times n \times \left(\frac{s}{f} \right)(1 - c) \qquad (3)$$

where c is the proportion of null messages cancelled and f is the frequency at which null messages are sent. Here, f is used in place of the lookahead value in equation 1. Due to the non-deterministic nature of the modified lazy null message algorithm, equation 3 provides only a lower-bound estimate on the number of null messages sent if lookahead is used for f. The quantity c cannot equal 1 nor can f equal 0 (which means all null messages are cancelled or no null messages are sent, respectively). If either of these conditions were true, then the deadlock avoidance guarantee of the CMB algorithm would be violated.

We now turn to the more general case of non-uniform lookahead on output channels. It is useful to construct an analytical model for which the simulation models are irregular. Here, we assume a lookahead value is assigned to each link.

In the case of different lookahead values for different LPs, formula 3 can be modified to yield:

$$N_\Phi = \sum_{j=1}^{m} \sum_{k=1}^{n} \frac{s}{f_{jk}} \left(1 - c_{jk}\right) \qquad (4)$$

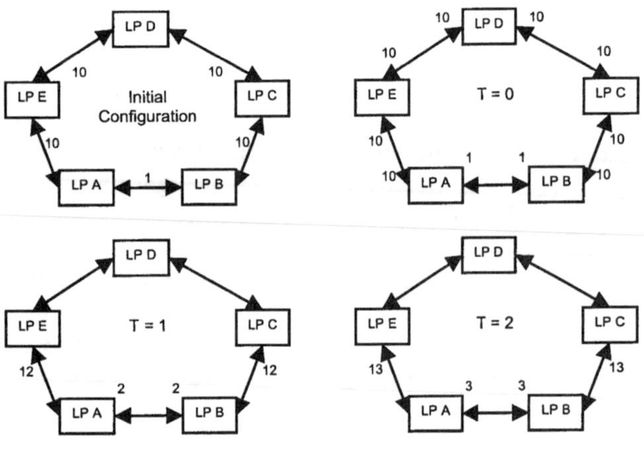

Figure 3. Example Illustrating the Operation of Null Message Exchange with Non-Uniform Lookahead

where f_{jk} represents either the minimum lookahead on the outgoing channel to LP jk or the frequency of null message sends. From a LP j, if there are multiple outgoing links to a neighboring LP x, they are consolidated into a single output channel with the lookahead assigned as the minimum of all outgoing links to x. In figure 3, a sample LP topology is constructed where the lookahead on all output links between LPs is 10, with the exception of the link between LP A and LP B. Although the lookahead is 10 between LPs A & E and LPs B & C, we can see that both LP C and LP E receive null message updates from LPs A & B at 1 time unit intervals. Therefore, the "localized effect" of non-uniform lookahead must be carefully considered before applying an estimate using equation 4. Equation 4 is applicable even in the case where all lookahead values are the same among all output channels, in which case the equation would then be equivalent to equation 3.

Equations 1-4 include lookahead and null message frequency to give an approximation on the number of null messages sent during the course of the simulation. As mentioned earlier, the number of null messages is useful, but it does not in itself offer an estimate on the efficiency of the synchronization algorithm. In addition to blocking, the type of communication (e.g. shared memory vs. Ethernet) and other related factors provide a better approximation on the overhead of a null message algorithm.

$$\alpha_{\Phi} = \frac{1}{a}\sum_{i=1}^{a}\ln\left[p_i w_i \times \frac{1}{m}\left(\sum_{j=1}^{m}\sum_{k=1}^{n}\frac{s}{f_{jk}}(1-c_{jk})\right)\right] \quad (5)$$

Equation 5 represents an overhead index for the lazy null message algorithm. Here a represents the number of different types of remote communication used in the simulation, p is the percentage and w is the weight given to a specific type of remote communication. The quantity w is a normalization factor for different communication media. For instance, if we had remote communication over both shared memory (w_1) and Ethernet (w_2), a possible normalization would be w_1=1 and w_2=10 to represent shared memory being faster by an order of magnitude compared to Ethernet. The natural logarithm is applied to represent the index as a monotonically increasing function of the product of the types of remote communication used and the average amount of null messages sent and received per LP.

Utilizing these equations, one could compute not only the number of null messages that would be sent over all LPs, but also the relative messaging overhead incurred with a particular null message algorithm or simulation scenario. This can be particularly useful when attempting to predict performance of a new scenario against an established baseline (e.g. scaled experiments).

3.4. Synchronizing Large-Scale Simulations

Equation 5 predicts that the overhead associated with these variations of the null message algorithm will remain relatively constant as a simulation scales, assuming the number of output channels for each LP does not increase with the number of LPs, and all other factors (such as relative amount of remote communication and lookahead) remain unchanged. On the other hand, synchronous time management algorithms have larger overheads as the simulation scales in the number of processors.

Notice that the only change from equation 1 to equation 2 is the substitution of $\log_2 m$ for n. For a synchronous time management algorithm, the number of synchronization messages increases at a rate of $m\log_2 m$, compared to a rate of m for CMB. In addition, this cost for synchronous algorithms does not include the penalty of jointly interrupting and restarting *all* LPs which increases linearly as the number of LPs increases, contributing to the overhead of time management for *every* LBTS computation. This claim will be discussed further with performance results in section 4.5.

4. Applying the Analytical Null Message Model to Predict Performance

Using the analytical model formulated in the previous section, we can forecast null message activity and overhead indices. These indicators can then be used to predict behavior and performance for different simulation models. We will first estimate null message activity and overhead and then verify our numbers through experimental measurements. For the following sections regarding experimental results, one LP corresponds to one physical processor (CPU).

4.1. Baseline Model

For our study, we used benchmarks developed at Dartmouth College as a set of baseline models for the network modeling and simulation community [22]. This baseline configuration was created to facilitate and demonstrate network simulator scalability.

Each portion of the network is referred to as a Campus Network (CN). Figure 4 shows the topology for the CN. Each CN consists of 4 servers, 30 routers, and 504 end hosts for a total of 538 nodes. The CN is comprised of 4 separate sub-networks. Net 0 consists of 3 routers, where node 0:0 is the gateway router for the CN. Net 1 is composed of 2 routers and 4 servers. Net 2 consists of 7 routers, 7 LAN routers, and 294 clients. Net 3 contains 4 routers, 5 LAN routers, and 210 clients.

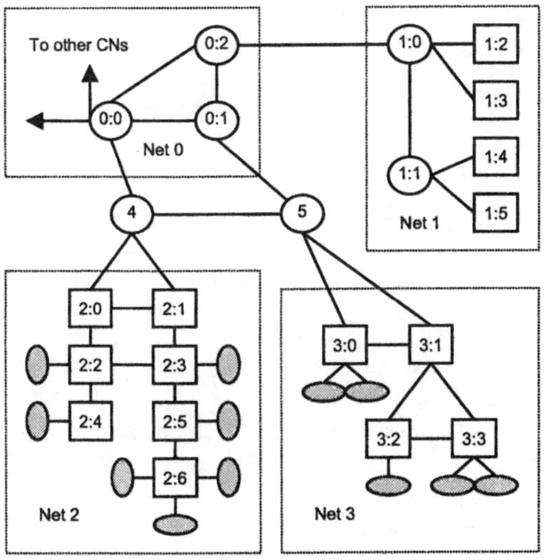

Figure 4. A Campus Network

All non-end host links have a bandwidth of 2Gb/s and have a propagation delay of 5ms with the exception of the Net 0 to Net 1 links, which have a delay of 1ms. End hosts are connected point-to-point with their respective LAN router and have links with 100Mb/s in bandwidth and have a delay of 1ms.

Multiple CNs may be instantiated and connected together to form a ring topology. This aspect of the network allows the baseline model to be easily scaled to arbitrarily large sizes. Multiple CNs are interconnected through a high latency 200ms "ring" link with 2Gb/s bandwidth via their Net 0 gateway router (node 0:0). The baseline model also contains chord links between CN i and CN $i + 4$ where $i \bmod 4$ is zero. A second set of chord links exist between CN i and CN $i + 10$ where $i \bmod 2$ is zero and i is less than half of the length of the ring. For our tests, we instantiated 7 CNs per LP, which is the maximum number of CNs representable within the total memory available per processor.

In our analysis and performance evaluation, we focus on pure TCP traffic transferred to and requested by end hosts from server nodes. We use a short transfer case of the baseline model, in which clients request 500,000 bytes from a Net 1 server. TCP sessions start at time selected from a uniform distribution over the interval from 0 and 10 seconds of simulation time. The baseline model specifies for TCP traffic to be requested from the neighboring CN that is one ring link hop away. This traffic model exercises only the ring links and no chord links, consequently, we have modified the traffic scenarios for some of our test cases to allow end hosts to request data from any Net 1 server in the ring network at random.

4.2. Scenarios

The baseline model was enhanced to test the effects of irregularity and asymmetry on time management performance. The modifications are intended to exercise irregularity of both traffic and topology. The five scenarios (see Table 1) represent five contrasting configurations, providing a range of benchmarks. Random server selection and varying propagation delay on ring and chord links were parameters that were modified to create scenarios used in the performance study.

Table 1. Benchmark Scenarios

Scenario	Traffic	Chord?	Special Properties
Baseline	Std.	No	None
Baseline-R	Rand.	No	None
Baseline-2ms	Rand.	No	Single 2ms ring link
Chord-R	Rand.	Yes	None
Chord-Asym	Rand.	Yes	Asym. Chord delays

Three scenarios were drafted where no chord links were used. The *Baseline* model consists of standard ring link delays and standard server selection. Traffic restrictions for *Baseline-R* are not limited to the next neighbor but any server in the ring network. *Baseline-2ms* is similar to the previous scenario, but has a single 2ms ring link that spans two LPs.

The other two scenarios contain chord links to add more paths to the network topology. *Chord-R* contains standard 200ms ring and chord delays with random server selection. *Chord-Asym* contains asymmetric, random chord delays from 10-50ms.

4.3. Software and Hardware Platforms

The Parallel/Distributed ns (*pdns*) [23] network simulator was used in the performance study. *pdns* is an HLA RTI-based network simulator that works by federating [24] sequential ns-2 simulators with additional syntax and functionality that allows individual ns-2 instances to communicate and send events to each other. *libSynk* [25, 26] was used as the underlying communications and time management library to manage the *pdns* instances. *libSynk* uses shared memory for communications within an SMP and TCP/IP for communication across SMPs. Optimizations to the RTI for efficient parallel simulation of networks [27] were included. The CMB null message algorithm was added to *libSynk* for the performance tests. The five benchmark scenarios were tested on two different hardware platforms:

Intel Pentium III Linux Cluster (P3) – Consists of 16 8-way 550MHz Pentium II Xeon SMP machines with 4GB RAM connected via Gigabit Ethernet. The operating system is Red Hat Linux 7.3 running a customized 2.4.18-27.7.xsmp kernel. *libSynk* and *pdns* (based on ns-2.26) were compiled using gcc-3.2.3 with compiler optimizations for the Intel Pentium III architecture.

Intel Itanium 2 Linux Cluster (IA64) – Consists of 30 2-way 900MHz Itanium 2 SMP machines with 6GB RAM connected via Gigabit Ethernet. The operating system is Red Hat Advanced Workstation 2.1 running a 2.4.18-e.31smp kernel. *libSynk* and *pdns* (based on ns-2.26) were compiled using Intel's ia-64 C/C++ compiler 7.1 (ecc).

Scalability tests for the *Baseline* model were conducted on the Pittsburgh Supercomputing Center's "Lemieux" *Compaq Alpha Tru64 Cluster* (PSC). The cluster has 750 4-way 1GHz Alpha ES45 SMP nodes with 4GB RAM connected via a Quadrics switch. *libSynk* and *pdns* (based on ns-2.1b9) were compiled using gcc-3.0.

4.4. Approximating Null Message Transmissions

Using the analytical model for CMB algorithms, the number of null messages sent can be estimated. Table 2 shows null message activity estimates for the *Baseline* scenario along with measurements from the parallel simulator. In this scenario, s=25, $lookahead$=0.2, f=(0.2/3), n=2, and c=0.5.

Table 2. Null Message Send Estimations

Number of CPUs	Approximation	Measurement
4	1,500	1,424
8	3,000	2,974
16	6,000	6,064
32	12,000	11,890
64	24,000	23,586
128	48,000	48,628
256	96,000	96,034
512	192,000	193,862

Table 2 shows that our analytical model predicts the null message counts quite accurately. The discrepancy between the approximation and simulation numbers are due to the estimation of the null frequency and null message cancellation rate. It is nearly impossible to predict the exact interaction between event processing and the effects on null message frequency and cancellations, yet the approximation is very close to the actual null message activity from simulation.

4.5. Approximating Null Message Overhead

Utilizing the previous estimation results for the number of null messages sent and equation 3 derived from the analytical model, it is possible to estimate the synchronization overhead incurred for each scenario.

Simply comparing the overhead index for a particular scenario to its corresponding run time performance (wallclock seconds) is inadequate. This is because the elapsed time to run a simulation does not gauge the amount of work performed by the network simulator. Instead, a new metric is defined: *Packet Transmissions per Second of wallclock time* (PTS). PTS is effectively the number of "packet hops" processed in a second of wallclock time where a "packet hop" represents the transmission of a packet from one node (a router or end node system) to another over a link in the network. The PTS metric will be used to determine work performed by the simulator, and is adequate to compare against the overhead index as the PTS rate is dependent upon time management overhead.

The overhead indices and PTS rates for 32 CPUs are shown in Table 3. For each of the scenarios, it is known that 28 CPUs (87.5%) send null messages through shared memory buffers and the remaining 4 CPUs (12.5%) communicate via TCP/IP over Ethernet. Using the values m=32, p_1=0.875, p_2=0.125, w_1=1, and w_2=10, the overhead index for the *Baseline* scenario is 6.25.

Table 3. Overhead Approximation

Scenario	Overhead Index	PTS
Baseline	6.25	1,512,410
Baseline-R	8.52	865,385
Baseline-2ms	10.54	621,008
Chord-R	9.43	699,848
Chord-Asym	12.21	684,630

Clearly, an inverse relationship between the overhead index and PTS metric exists. The lower the overhead costs for the null message algorithm, the higher the performance of the particular scenario. However, the *Baseline-2ms* and *Chord-Asym* models appear to exhibit conflicting results. The *Chord-Asym* model has a higher overhead index and still manages to have a higher PTS rate than the *Baseline-2ms* model. This anomaly illustrates that the overhead index measures only penalties associated with time management, not for other performance degrading parameters which are a result of the model itself. Although the overhead index does capture lookahead, it does not consider other factors such as load imbalance and the amount of remote communication due to event transmission. Nevertheless, the overhead index can be used as an approximation tool to predict time management efficiency and thus, simulator performance.

4.6. Scalability of the CMB Algorithm

In section 3.3, we stated that, provided all parameters for the scenario remain constant, the overhead due to the null message algorithm does not change as the simulation model increases in scale. We verify the same experimentally here for the *Baseline* scenario. Due to the dynamic nature of the other scenarios, it was impossible to keep other factors such as remote communication due to events and lookahead constant between scalability runs.

Table 4. Run times for the *Baseline* Scenario

Number of CPUs	Null Messages	Reductions
16	784	736
32	783	747
128	787	892

The run time using a CMB null message algorithm remains constant when the model is scaled from 16 to 128 processors as shown in Table 4. Execution times based on global reductions steadily increase from the 16 CPU to the 128 CPU case while remaining relatively constant for null messages. Figure 5 ("Red" denotes global reductions) shows the PTS rate for the two synchronization protocols used in the *Baseline* scenario.

Table 5. Large-Scale Run times for the *Baseline* Scenario

Number of CPUs	Null Messages	Reductions
64	420	508
128	414	523
256	420	563
512	436	620

Table 5 shows the runtimes of the *Baseline* scenario on the Compaq Alpha Tru64 cluster. The corresponding PTS rates are plotted in Figure 6. The run time performance of the baseline scenario using global reductions increases logarithmically as the model scales in the number of processors. In contrast, the null message algorithm performance exhibits a relatively constant run time performance up to 512 processors. These simulation results provide strong support to verify the overhead model and proposition put forth in section 3.3.

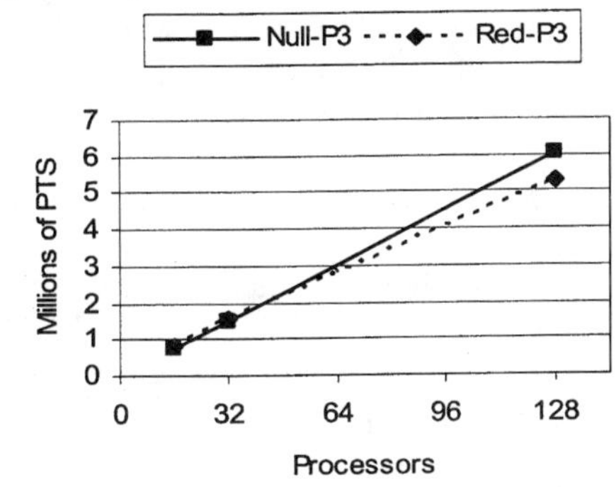

Figure 5. Effect of Scale on PTS Rate

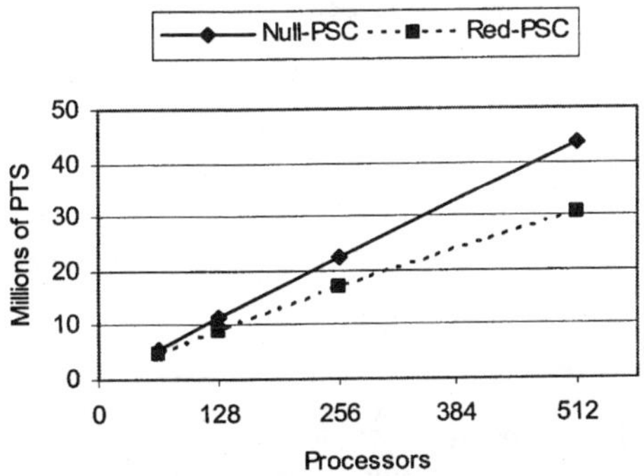

Figure 6. Large-Scale PTS Rate

The experimental results presented in this section have only investigated synchronization behavior of only a structured, regular network (e.g. *Baseline* model). In the next section, we will compare the performance of asynchronous and synchronous algorithms for network models of both regular and irregular structure.

5. Regular and Irregular Network Models

Due to the asynchronous nature of the null message algorithm, synchronization happens "locally" and remains constant even as the simulation model scales. This is the reason why CMB algorithms tend to scale better than schemes based on synchronous time management such as global reductions, if all other factors remain constant.

5.1. Simulation Performance of Structured, Regular Networks

First we examine the performance of synchronous and asynchronous time management in the context of relatively regular network models. The performance of the *Baseline* model on both the Intel Pentium III and Itanium 2 cluster is shown in Figure 7, which was discussed in the previous section.

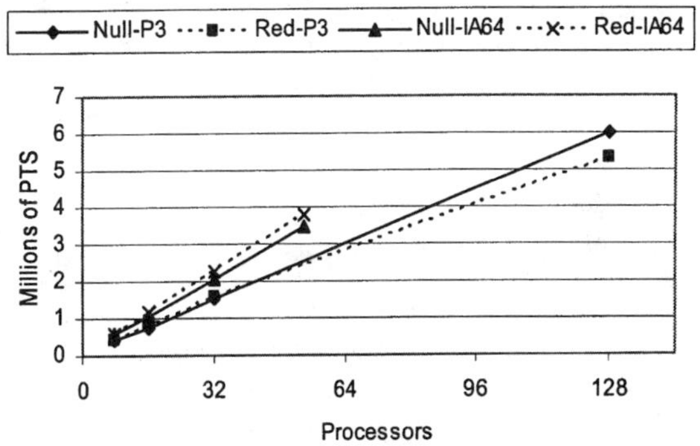

Figure 7. Performance of the *Baseline* Scenario

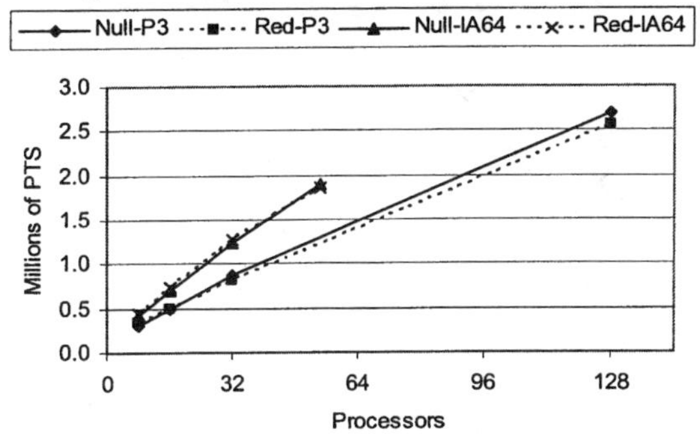

Figure 8. Performance of the *Baseline-R* Scenario

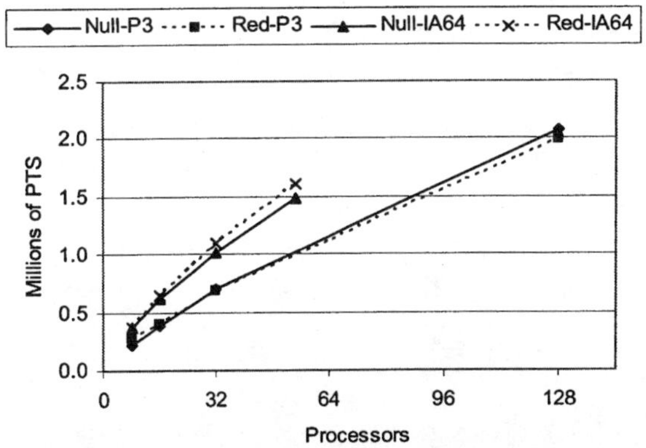

Figure 9. Performance of the *Chord-R* Scenario

The *Baseline-R* scenario is another network considered as a regular model with random server selection. Figure 8 illustrates that the trends of the *Baseline-R* scenario do not differ significantly from that of the *Baseline* model. The random Net 1 server selection pushes the performance asynchronous null message time management ahead of the global reduction algorithm at 16 CPUs for the P3 data and at 54 CPUs for the IA64 data.

The final regular network is the *Chord-R* scenario which is shown in figure 9. Although the addition of chords add asymmetry to the network, the structure and regularity of the network model is preserved by identical lookahead on all chord and ring links. Similar trends to the first two scenarios re-emerge in *Chord-R*.

These scalability runs thus far show that there exist only small gains in using one synchronization algorithm over the other in small- to medium-scale regular networks. However, simulation results suggest that the CMB algorithm with a constant number of output channels is more appropriate for large-scale simulations even in scenarios composed of nearly all consistent structure.

5.2. Simulation Performance of Asymmetric, Irregular Networks

The two irregular network scenarios, *Baseline-2ms* and *Chord-Asym* will highlight differences and deficiencies between synchronous and asynchronous time management algorithms.

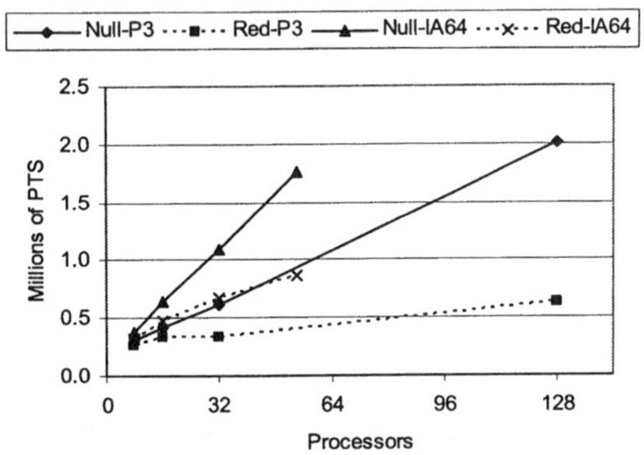

Figure 10. Performance of the *Baseline-2ms* Scenario

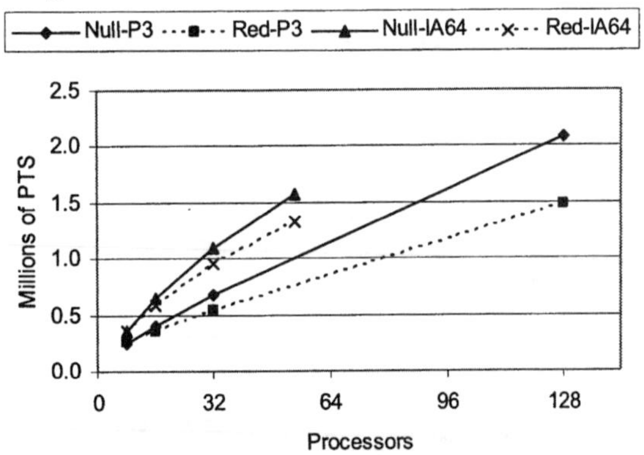

Figure 11. Performance of the *Chord-Asym* Scenario

Figure 10 shows a significant difference in PTS rate between the null message algorithm and global reductions for the *Baseline-2ms* network model. Moreover, the null message trends remain linear while the synchronous global reductions have constant or less than linear increases in PTS rates as the number of processors scale. This scenario shows the pathological case for global reductions, as the time management system must stop and synchronize the simulation every 2ms.

The *Chord-Asym* scenario shown in Figure 11 demonstrates the benefits of a null message algorithm in a typical irregular network. A null message algorithm can take advantage of the varying lookahead values for each output channel while a synchronous algorithm must interrupt execution of the simulation at intervals dictated by the global minimum lookahead.

6. Future Work

It is reasonable to assume that CMB allows simulations to scale to arbitrarily large sizes (assuming parameters discussed earlier are held constant), provided the software infrastructure supports very large scale simulation. Increasing the number of processors beyond 512 to test this conjecture would be the logical next step in furthering the scalability study. We have performed initial 1,024 CPU runs, which seem to indicate that CMB algorithm performs at expected levels extrapolated from table 5. Additional scenarios could be conceived to further test the suitability and adaptability of each type of synchronization algorithm, not only for network simulations, but for other applications as well. Other network simulators, such as *GTNetS* [28] could be used to gather additional data points in order to ascertain if similar improvements in performance is experienced across simulators.

Empirical data gathered on scalability tests over a heterogeneous mix of hardware consisting of varying network and platform (CPU, OS) components would be useful for simulation environments across different computational clusters. It would be interesting to see whether synchronous or asynchronous time management would prove to be the better option in these mixed environment cases.

7. Conclusions

We presented an analytical model for an asynchronous lazy null message algorithm for time management. The proposed equations can be used to approximate null message activity and a corresponding overhead index. In particular, the overhead index predicts that the optimized null message algorithm ensures no appreciable increase in overhead if the fan-in/fan-out of channels is held constant as the simulation scaled with the number of processors.

We also showed that a null message algorithm offers more flexibility for irregular and asymmetric network models. An optimized CMB algorithm can tailor synchronization messages according to output channel lookahead values to local neighbors only, in contrast to global communication in a synchronous time management system. These properties prove to be advantageous in large-scale network simulation.

Acknowledgments

Funding for this research was provided by DARPA Contract N66001-00-1-8934 and NSF Grant ANI-0136939. Large-scale computations designated as "PSC" were performed on the National Science Foundation Terascale Computing System at the Pittsburgh Supercomputing Center.

References

[1] R. M. Fujimoto, *Parallel and Distributed Simulation Systems*. New York: Wiley-Interscience, 2000.

[2] K. M. Chandy and J. Misra, "Distributed Simulation: A Case Study in Design and Verification of Distributed Programs," *IEEE Transactions on Software Engineering*, vol. 5, pp. 440-452, 1979.

[3] R. E. Bryant, "Simulation of Packet Communications Architecture Computer Systems," Massachusetts Institute of Technology. MIT-LCS-TR-188 MIT-LCS-TR-188, 1977.

[4] R. Bagrodia and M. Takai, "Performance evaluation of conservative algorithms in parallel simulation languages," *IEEE Transactions on Parallel and Distributed Systems*, vol. 11, pp. 395-411, 2000.

[5] W.-K. Su and C. L. Seitz, "Variants of the Chandy-Misra-Bryant Distributed Discrete-Event Simulation Algorithm," presented at the SCS Multiconference on Distributed Simulation '89, Miami, FL, 1989.

[6] J. Porras, V. Hara, J. Harju, and J. Ikonen, *Improving the Performance of the Chandy-Misra Parallel Simulation Algorithm in a Distributed Workstation Environment*. Arlington, VA, 1997.

[7] W. Cai and S. J. Turner, "An Algorithm for Reducing Null-Messages of the CMB Approach in Parallel Discrete Event Simulation," University of Exeter, 1995.

[8] D. M. Nicol, "The Cost of Conservative Synchronization in Parallel Discrete Event Simulations," *Journal of the ACM*, vol. 40, pp. 304-333, 1993.

[9] K. M. Chandy and J. Misra, "Asynchronous Distributed Simulation via a Sequence of Parallel Computations," *Communications of the ACM*, vol. 24, pp. 198-205, 1981.

[10] B. D. Lubachevsky, "Efficient Distributed Event-Drive Simulations of Multiple-Loop Networks," *Communications of the ACM*, vol. 32, pp. 111-123, 1989.

[11] Z. Xiao, B. Unger, R. Simmonds, and J. Cleary, "Scheduling Critical Channels in Conservative Parallel Discrete Event Simulation," presented at the 13th Workshop on Parallel and Distributed Simulation, Atlanta, GA, 1999.

[12] H. Y. Song, R. A. Meyer, and R. Bagrodia, "An Empricial Study of Conservative Scheduling," presented at the 14th Workshop on Parallel and Distributed Simulation, Bologna, Italy, 2000.

[13] M. L. Bailey and M. A. Pagels, "Measuring the Overhead in Conservative Parallel Simulations of Multicomputer Programs," presented at the 23rd Winter Simulation Conference, Phoenix, AZ, 1991.

[14] D. M. Nicol, "Scalability, Locality, Partitioning and Synchronization in PDES," presented at the 12th Workshop on Parallel and Distributed Simulation, Banff, Alberta, Canada, 1998.

[15] D. M. Nicol and J. Liu, "Composite Synchronization in Parallel Discrete-Event Simulation," *IEEE Transactions on Parallel and Distributed Systems*, vol. 13, pp. 433-446, 2002.

[16] D. M. Nicol, "Analysis of Synchronization in Massively Parallel Discrete-Event Simulation," presented at the 2nd ACM SIGPLAN, Seattle, WA, 1990.

[17] D. M. Nicol, C. Michael, and P. Inouye, "Efficient Aggregation of Multiple LP's in Distributed Memory Parallel Simulations," presented at the 21st Winter Simulation Conference, Washington, D.C., 1989.

[18] C.-C. Lim, Y.-H. Low, B.-P. Gan, S. Jain, W. Cai, W. J. Hsu, and S. Y. Huang, "Performance Prediction Tools for Parallel Discrete-Event Simulation," presented at the 13th Workshop on Parallel and Distributed Simulation, Atlanta, GA, 1999.

[19] E. Naroska and U. Schwiegelshohn, "Conservative Parallel Simulation of a Large Number of Processes," *Simulation*, vol. 72, pp. 150-162, 1999.

[20] J. Lemeire and E. Dirkx, "Performance Factors in Parallel Discrete Event Simulation," presented at the 15th European Simulation Multiconference, Prague, 2001.

[21] V. Jha and R. Bagrodia, "A Performance Evaluation Methodology for Parallel Simulation Protocols," presented at the 10th Workshop on Parallel and Distributed Simulation, Philadelphia, PA, 1996.

[22] "NMS Baseline Model. http://www.cs.dartmouth.edu/~nicol/NMS/baseline/."

[23] "pdns. http://www.cc.gatech.edu/computing/compass/pdns/."

[24] G. F. Riley, R. M. Fujimoto, and M. H. Ammar, "A Generic Framework for Parallelization of Network Simulations," presented at the 7th MASCOTS, College Park, MD, 1999.

[25] "libSynk. http://www.cc.gatech.edu/computing/pads/kalyan/libsynk.htm."

[26] R. M. Fujimoto, T. McLean, and K. S. Perumalla, "Design of High Performance RTI Software," presented at the 4th Workshop on Distributed Simulation and Real-Time Applications, San Francisco, CA, 2000.

[27] K. S. Perumalla, A. Park, R. M. Fujimoto, and G. F. Riley, "Scalable RTI-Based Parallel Simulation of Networks," presented at the 17th Workshop on Parallel and Distributed Simulation, San Diego, CA, 2003.

[28] G. F. Riley, "The Georgia Tech Network Simulator," presented at the ACM SIGCOMM '03, Karlsruhe, Germany, 2003.

Optimizing Parallel Execution of Detailed Wireless Network Simulation*

Zhengrong Ji, Junlan Zhou, Mineo Takai, Jay Martin, Rajive Bagrodia
University of California Los Angeles
Parallel Computing Laboratory
3809 Boelter Hall, Los Angeles, CA 90095-1596
{jizr,zjl,mineo,jmartin,rajive}@cs.ucla.edu

Abstract

With Parallel and Discrete Event Simulation (PDES) techniques, the runtime performance of detailed wireless network simulation can be improved significantly without compromising fidelity of the simulation results. However, modelling characteristics of wireless communications such as signal propagation and interference may severely hinder the potential speedup yielded by PDES. This paper proposes various optimization techniques to address three major concerns in achieving efficient parallel execution of wireless network simulation: i.e., (1) reducing communication and computation overhead of simulating signal propagation across multiple logical processes; (2) reducing synchronization overhead among logical processes; (3) minimizing event scheduling overhead within individual logical processes. These techniques have been implemented in a parallel version of GloMoSim and QualNet. The experimental results with mobile ad hoc networking scenarios demonstrate that the proposed optimization techniques can improve the performance of parallel wireless network simulation by up to an order of magnitude.

1. Introduction

Wireless communication is playing an increasingly important role in the design of contemporary digital communication systems. Rapid growth in both complexity and deployments of such wireless networks has created a need for simulation tools that can accurately predict the performance of next generation wireless network devices, protocols and deployed services. However, high fidelity simulation of wireless networks is computationally intensive, as it requires proper modeling of signal propagation and interference that can increase the number of events in the simulation as many as $O(N^2)$ where N is the number of network nodes. Its direct consequence is computational impracticality of high fidelity discrete-event simulation for even medium size wireless networks.

*This work is supported by the US Department of Defense/DARPA under Contract N66001-00-1-8937 "Maya: Next Generation Performance Prediction Tools for Global Networks".

With PDES techniques, the execution time of wireless network simulation can be reduced significantly without compromising fidelity of the simulation results. However, characteristics of wireless communications such as signal propagation and interference may severely hinder the potential speedup yielded by PDES. For instance, simulation of radio signal propagation requires scheduling of an event to every potential receiver, resulting in creation of a large number of signal arrival events. Although parallel execution can benefit from many of these events, it requires frequent communications and tight synchronization among logical processes (LP) in order to maintain causality of sequences of events. As a result, the runtime performance improvement by PDES is typically much less than the number of processors used for the execution.

To improve the runtime performance of parallel wireless network simulation, the following three concerns need to be addressed: (1) reduction of communication and computation overhead of simulating signal propagation across multiple LPs, (2) reduction of synchronization overhead among multiple LPs, and (3) minimization of event scheduling overhead within each LP.

This paper discusses each of the above three issues and proposes optimization techniques to substantially improve the runtime performance of wireless network simulation. These techniques have been implemented in a parallel version of GloMoSim and its commercial version QualNet [1]. The experimental results demonstrate that the proposed optimization techniques can improve the performance of parallel wireless network simulation by up to an order of magnitude.

The remainder of this paper is organized as follows: Section 2 describes related work on parallel simulation of wireless networks. Section 3 discusses simulation of signal propagation across multiple LPs and proposes effective techniques to reduce the associated communication overheads. Sections 4 and 5 respectively present techniques to extract greater lookahead to exploit additional parallelism among LPs, and reduce event scheduling overhead within each LP. Section 6 concludes the paper with future research directions.

2. Related Work

There have been several studies to parallelize the execution of network simulation [9, 10]. PDNS [9] is a parallelized version of ns-2, a commonly used simulator. PDNS can execute multiple instances of ns-2 via the Georgia Tech RTIKIT. Genesis [10] is another parallel simulator based on ns-2 and runs multiple instances of ns-2 in an iterative manner such that the network performance metrics collected in each instance converge. These simulators do not require modifications in the networking models for the parallel execution, but they can execute only wired network models in parallel; to our best knowledge, they have not been used for simulation of large wireless networks. SWAN [7, 8] is a parallel simulator for wireless mobile networks that employs a conservative synchronization algorithm. The study [7] shows that it can achieve good parallel performance by abstracting out parts of physical layer models and simplifying MAC state transitions.

GloMoSim [12] is a simulation tool designed for large scale mobile ad hoc networks with highly detailed physical layer propagation models. Built on top of PARSEC [3], it supports parallel execution of wireless network simulation. This paper uses GloMoSim and QualNet, the next generation of GloMoSim, as the base wireless network simulators because their model libraries include highly detailed physical layer models. The modeling differences of radio physical layer in ns-2 and GloMoSim, as well as the impact of such differences on the simulation results can be found in [11].

Many past studies on parallelizing wireless network simulation described above use abstract PHY layer models and neglect effects of signal interference. In those studies, radio signals weaker than the sensing threshold are not delivered to a node. These simplifications significantly reduce the number of events generated to simulate wireless communication. However, as demonstrated in [11] and [5], omitting such details could result in misleading experiment results and a simulator with such simplifications does not serve as a good analysis tool for wireless networking studies. In the studies presented in this paper, we take into consideration effects of signal interferences and carefully adopt a propagation limit, which is much larger than the sensing threshold used by previous studies. This propagation limit guarantees the aggregated interference power neglected at a receiver will not exceed the thermal noise level inside a receiver. Although it preserves the fidelity of wireless network simulation, this propagation limit produces limited performance gains and adds complexities to improving parallel runtime performance of the simulator. If this propagation limit is applied, performance improvements that can be achieved by the optimization techniques proposed in the past studies diminish. This motivates us to propose a number of novel optimization techniques, which can substantially improve the parallel performance of such detailed wireless network simulation without compromising fidelity of the simulation.

3. Reducing costs of simulating signal propagation across multiple LPs

3.1. Propagation limit

Due to the broadcast nature of radio transmissions, a radio signal transmitted towards a specific node can interfere with communications of many nearby network nodes and contribute to their noise level. To model interference, for each signal transmitted, two events (signal arrival and end events) will be scheduled to each of the nodes in a wireless network. Propagation limit is a known technique to reduce the complexity of modelling signal interference. With propagation limit, signal arrival or end events will be scheduled to a node only when the received power of the corresponding signal is above a certain threshold. However, although the power of each interference signal is not high enough to affect the node's behaviors, accumulation of such signals could cause a node to sense the channel to be busy thereby forcing the node to backoff from transmitting, or failing to receive a signal of interest due to poor SNR (Signal to Noise Ratio). Simulation ignoring this effect could produce unreliable results [11]. Thus it is important to gauge the impact of interference signals and apply a propagation limit with negligible impacts on accuracy of simulation results. In this study, we use a propagation limit of -111.0dBm, with which the aggregated power of the neglected interference signals is guaranteed to be less than the average thermal noise level of the receiver [5]. With this propagation limit, a radio signal can propagate up to 2.11km away from the transmitter with the two ray pathloss model.

3.2. Simulation of signal propagation across multiple LPs

In addition to reducing the cost of modelling signal interference, the propagation limit can also reduce the number of nodes to be scanned when used in combination with partitioning. A common approach to parallelize wireless network simulation is to divide the target network into multiple geographical areas of equal size, each represented by an LP. Each LP simulates the complete network stack of all nodes contained within its partition. To simulate signal propagation, when a node in a partition transmits a radio signal, the corresponding LP will send an event to each remote LP. Upon receiving the event, the remote LP will scan the list of nodes within its partition, and schedule signal arrival and end events for nodes at which the received signal power is above the propagation limit. It results in a large number of pathloss calculations which are computationally expensive and incurs high scanning cost. Since the terrain is geographically partitioned into grids, when a signal is transmitted by

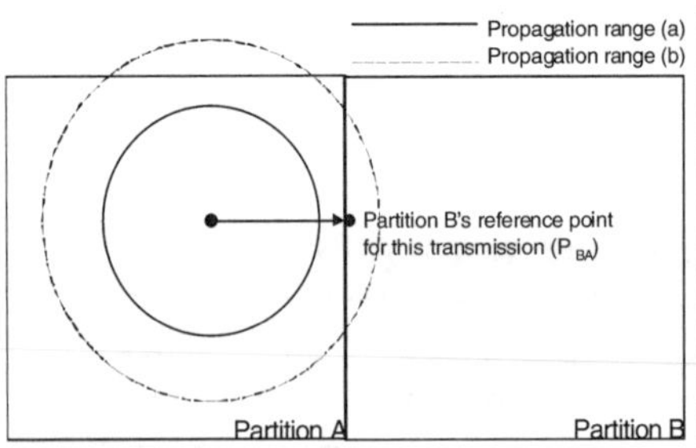

Figure 1: Effect of multiple partitions.

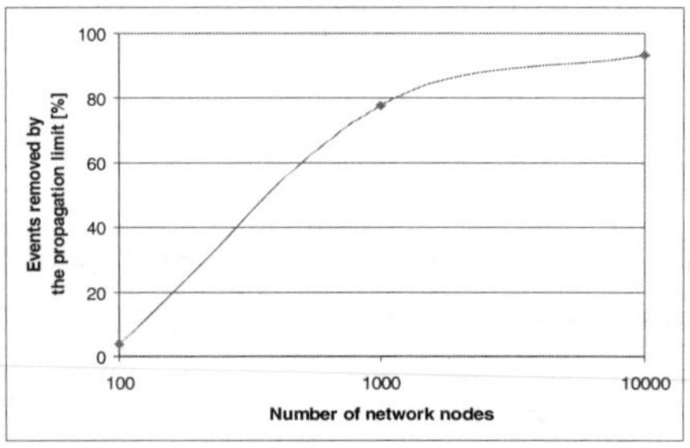

Figure 2: Effect of the propagation limit on the number of events.

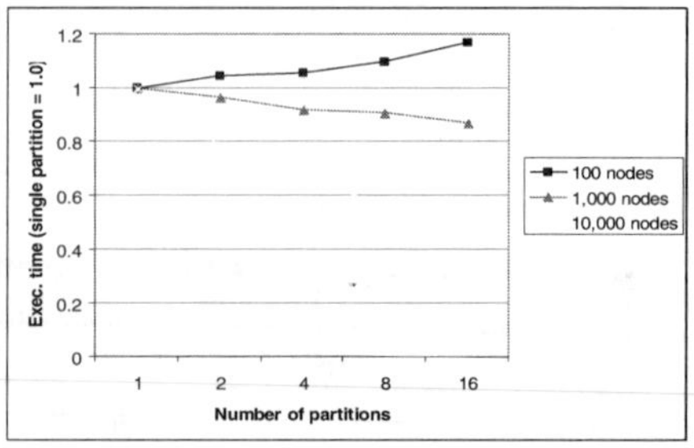

Figure 3: Execution time changes with multiple partitions.

a node within a partition, the corresponding LP can compute path loss values for the reference points of every remote partition. The reference point of a remote partition is chosen so that it yields the minimum path loss value for all locations in the remote partition. If the power of a signal received at the reference point in a remote partition is lower than the propagation limit, the remote partition will not receive a message of the signal transmission. For instance, consider a case with two partitions (A and B) where a node in Partition A transmits a signal as depicted in Figure 1. Depending on the radio power at the reference point in Partition B (PBA), Partition A may or may not schedule an inter-LP event for the signal transmitted. Assuming that each partition has equal number of nodes, the number of nodes scanned for the signal is reduced by half compared to the single partition case, if the signal is not reachable to PBA.

3.3. Performance evaluation

Figure 2 shows the reduction in the total number of events by applying the propagation limit. In this set of experiments, one LP is used to simulate the entire target network. Note that the number of events executed remains invariant with the number of LPs. Nodes in the target network are randomly placed on a flat terrain, at a density of 50,000m^2 per node. This placement results in terrain sizes of $2.23 \times 2.23 km^2$, $7.07 \times 7.07 km^2$ and $22.36 \times 22.36 km^2$ for 100, 1,000, and 10,000 node cases respectively. CBR (Constant Bit Rate) traffic at a rate of 20 packets per second is given to 15% of network nodes chosen randomly in the networks. LAR (Location Aided Routing protocol) scheme 1 [6] and IEEE 802.11 DCF are used for all the nodes in the network. As each signal needs to be propagated up to 2.11km with the propagation limit of -111dB and the two ray pathloss model, the effect of the propagation limit is very small for the 100-node case, while 94% of events are eliminated for the 10,000-node case. The percentage of reduction in execution time for single partition is almost identical to that of reduction in the total number of events executed. This result proves that although each radio signal needs to be propagated to a wide area, limiting the propagation of each signal has a significant impact on the runtime performance of simulation, particularly for large-scale networks.

Figure 3 shows the speedup of simulation execution with various numbers of partitions. To better quantify the total amount of reduction in computation and communication by the propagation limit, all partitions are executed on a single processor in this experiment, in which all event processing and node scanning are carried out. In the 100 node cases, the simulated terrain size ($2.23 \times 2.23 km^2$) is too small compared to the propagation range of the signal (2.11 km) and most signals can still travel across the entire terrain. Due to the overhead of context switching between LPs, simulation execution slows down a little as more partitions are created. In the larger network cases, the propagation limit significantly reduces the number of inter-LP events and nodes scanned. Compared to the sequential simulation execution without the propagation limit, speed-up of up to 6 and 20 times can be achieved (using 16 partitions) with the propagation limit for the 1000 and 10,000 node cases respectively.

To preserve the modeling fidelity, a conservative propagation limit is used in our studies. A large number of events are still generated at MAC and PHY layer, and simulation preserving such details at MAC and PHY layer has limited parallelism. In order to optimize parallel execution of such detailed wireless network simulation, there exist two other challenges as described in Section 1, i.e. reducing synchronization overhead among multiple LPs, and minimization of event scheduling overhead within each LP. This motivates us to propose a number of novel optimization techniques to be discussed in the next two sections.

4. Extracting greater lookahead

4.1. Synchronization protocol

Parallel simulation requires the use of a synchronization protocol among LPs to guarantee that causality errors are not introduced in the simulation results. An excellent overview of the problem of parallel discrete-event simulation and a comprehensive discussion of commonly used synchronization protocols can be found in [4]. In this paper, we use the synchronous conservative protocol. Each

LP defines its lookahead as the minimum duration (measured using the simulation clock) for which it will not send any messages on its outgoing links. Periodically, a global minimum of all LPs' simulation time plus their lookahead values will be computed, referred to as the ceiling of the next time window. The LPs can process all events within this time window safely without the need of additional synchronization.

When using this synchronous conservative protocol, as long as there is one LP with poor lookahead, other LPs can process only few events per global synchronization and cannot exploit great parallelism. Therefore, the ability of each LP to "look ahead" is important to the performance of parallel simulation. However, in wireless network simulation with detailed PHY and MAC layer models, nodes could transit from state to state very frequently due to fluctuation of channel conditions. On one hand, such state changes must be considered when extracting lookahead at a node so that no causality errors could occur. It adds complexity to extracting lookahead in wireless network simulation with detailed PHY and MAC layer models. On the other hand, exploiting characteristics of state changes of nodes being simulated with detailed PHY and MAC layer models could yield additional sources of lookahead that are absent in simulation with abstract PHY and MAC layer models. The following subsections discuss techniques of extracting lookahead in wireless network simulation with detailed PHY and MAC layer models, given that all nodes in a wireless network follow IEEE 802.11 standard [2], and present the performance improvement obtained by exploiting these sources.

4.2. Lookahead extraction

4.2.1 Lookahead at MAC layer

According to the 802.11 standard, all network nodes must perform virtual carrier sensing in addition to physical carrier sensing. A node has to wait for at least one type of inter frame space defined in the 802.11 standard before it starts to transmit a frame. Depending on the current status of the node's MAC or physical layer, simulation can determine the type of inter frame space to be used and use it as the minimum lookahead value. In addition to inter frame spaces, the duration of the current frame being received can also be added to the node's lookahead, as the node cannot initiate a transmission until the completion of the reception of current frame. A third source of lookahead at MAC layer is the backoff timer. According to the 802.11 standard, a node has to sense the channel before starting to transmit a packet (requested by the network layer). If the channel is busy, the node will go through a backoff procedure, of which the duration is uniformly distributed between zero and CW (Contention Window).

Table 1: Terrain Size for the High and Low Density Experiments

# nodes	# CBR sessions	High Density (20000m²/node) Terrain Size (m²)	High Density Partition Element Size (m²)	Low Density (50000m²/node) Terrain Size (m²)	Low Density Partition Element Size (m²)
100	15	1414x1414	354x354	2236x2236	559x559
1000	150	4472x4472	1118x1118	7071x7071	1768x1768
10000	1500	14142x14142	3536x3536	22360x22360	5590x5590

4.2.2 Lookahead at PHY layer

The simplest source of lookahead that can be extracted is the time defined for an 802.11 radio to transit from receiving to transmitting. This transition produces a delay between the time when the 802.11 MAC layer decides to transmit and the time when the transmitted signal is actually transmitted. This delay stated in the 802.11b spec is 5us, which is far too small to yield good parallel performance.

Fortunately, lookahead much larger than the radio transmitter turnaround delay can be extracted at the PHY layer using information of interference signals. As defined in the 802.11 standard, a node has to sense the channel before starting to transmit a packet. If the channel is busy, the node will back off. By looking at the current interfering signals (from far away transmissions) received at a node, simulation can predict the earliest possible time that the radio of the node will transit to "Idle State". Since the node cannot transmit when the channel is sensed busy, the duration when channel is busy can be used as a minimum lookahead of the specific node.

4.2.3 Lookahead from cross-interaction between PHY and MAC layer

An even larger lookahead can be extracted exploiting the cross interaction between the PHY and MAC layers. The backoff timer of a node pauses when the channel transits from idle to busy during the node's backoff period. The backoff timer will not resume until the channel becomes idle again and remains idle for a duration of DIFS. Before its backoff timer becomes zero, a node cannot transmit. Hence, if a node's backoff timer is paused, based on the list of interference signals received by the node, simulation can project the total duration of the channel being busy and predict the earliest possible time when the node can initiate a transmission. This duration can be used as a lookahead value of the node. This technique is illustrated in the Figure 4. The channel becomes busy at t_0 and t_2 (due to arrival of interference signals) and transits from busy to idle at t_1 and t_3 (due to end of interference signals). The backoff timer is T_{BO} at t_0 and $t_2 - t_1$ is shorter than DIFS. The backoff timer will not become zero until time $t_3 + T_{BO} + DIFS$. Therefore, the duration between the current simulation time and time $t_3 + T_{BO} + DIFS$ can be used as the lookahead value of the node. This technique and the one presented in the previous subsection to extract lookahead can only be done with detailed PHY layer models.

4.3. Performance evaluation

Table 1 summarizes the basic parameters that were used in the experiments. The nodes in the network were placed on a flat plane partitioned into grids. Only one node is placed in each grid cell, whose location is randomly chosen within the cell. A number of CBR sessions are set up between randomly selected source and destination nodes. The source and destinations for each session are chosen randomly to be between 1 to 8 grid squares away in both horizontal and vertical directions. Each CBR session generates 10 packets per second with a packet size of 512 bytes. The propagation limit radius for transmission is 2118m (4236m diameter) and the exclusionary "sensing" radius is 670m (1340m diameter). These test cases are executed using the synchronous protocol on a Sun Ultra Enterprise 6500 running at 336Mhz using 4, 8 and 16 CPUs.

The parallel speedup for the low density cases is shown in Figure 5. These speedup results are with respect to the best sequential implementation and thus are on top of the speedup already achieved with the techniques described in Section 3. The 100 node test cases achieve the maximum speedup of approximately 3.8 times on 16 CPUs with a performance plateau beyond 8 CPUs. The plateau occurs because when running on 16 CPUs, the small 100 node case has only on average 100/16 = 6.25 network nodes to simulate per CPU and synchronization costs begin to dominate the execution time of the model. This plateau contrasts with the observed improvements in the 1000 and 10000 node cases, where the parallel performance of the network model continues to improve from 8 to 16 CPUs, peaking at about 4.5 and 6 times speedup for the 1000 and 10,000 node models respectively .

Figure 5 also shows an anomalous crossing of the performance curves for the 100 and 1000 node test cases. The Figure 6 plots the probability density function (PDF) of time window size for test cases executed using 8 CPUs. For the 100 node case, the size of time windows spreads all the way up to the maximum lookahead value of around 250us, while in the 1000 node case, almost all time windows are below 75us. For the 10,000 node case, almost all windows are below 25us. There are two factors that affect the parallel speedup of simulation: the number of events executed per time window and size of time window. When the number of nodes in a target network increases, the number of events grows and size of time windows decreases as shown in Figure 6. Depending on which of these two factor dominates, the parallel speedup of simulation fluctuates as the size of target network increases.

The speedup for the high density experiments is shown in Figure 7. Compared to sequential simulation, parallel simulation of the same network scenarios achieves the maximum parallel speedup of 4, 5.8, and 4.6 for 100, 1000, and 10000 node cases respectively. The parallel performance of 10000 node case with high node density is worse than the corresponding low node density case. Figure 8 compares the PDF of ratio of the maximum over the average number of events per processor for 10k nodes cases with high and low node density. It indicates that the high density test case has a worse instantaneous load balance. As a result, less parallel speedup can be achieved compared to the corresponding low density case.

5. Reducing Intra-LP events

Although the runtime performance of parallel wireless network simulation is improved significantly by reducing scanning costs (see Section 3) and increasing parallelism (see Section 4), it is equally important to minimize the overhead within each LP. One observation made from the existing wireless network simulators is that in order to model the fluctuation of channel physical status (busy or idle) or interference signal power, each transmitter must schedule signal arrival and end events for every other node within the propagation range. Simulation will update changes to the aggregated power of signals or physical status whenever such an event occurs. These potential changes must be simulated in order to accurately model the wireless MAC/PHY device operations, such as evaluation of packet error and a backoff procedure. However, the high fidelity comes at the cost of scheduling a great number of signal arrival and end events, which incurs significant event scheduling overhead, especially when each LP is assigned many wireless nodes.

Clearly the simulation overhead at each LP will be greatly reduced if the scheduling for most of the signal arrival and end events can be avoided. To achieve this goal, the dependency between these events and the device operation of wireless nodes is investigated first. The only way a node interacts with other wireless nodes in the network simulation is via transmitting a signal. If it is ensured that all the incoming signals are processed in orderly fashion, the behavior of a node will remain the same, which also means that this node will causally affect other nodes in correct manner subsequently. Thus, the remaining goal is to ensure that eliminating arrival and end events of incoming signals does not alter the operation of a node.

There are three cases in which an incoming signal may alter a node's operation: first, the receiver could lock on to the signal and try to receive the corresponding packet; second, the receiver could fail to receive another packet due to high aggregated power of received interference signals; finally, the receiver could sense the channel busy while performing physical carrier sensing; In the first case, a signal arrival event must be scheduled because a transmitter cannot tell for certain if the packet will be locked on by

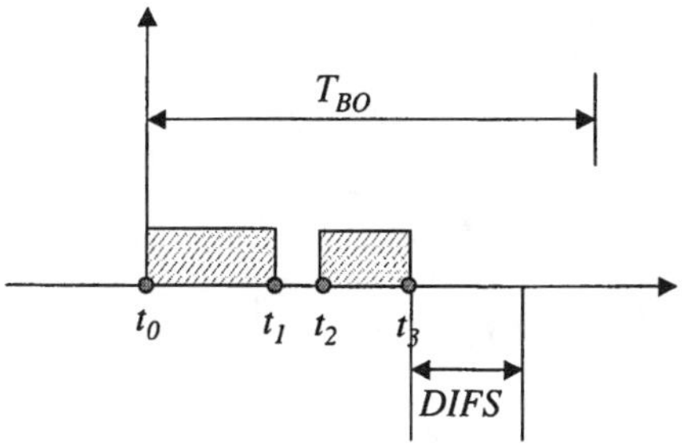

Figure 4: look extraction exploiting cross interaction PHY and MAC layer

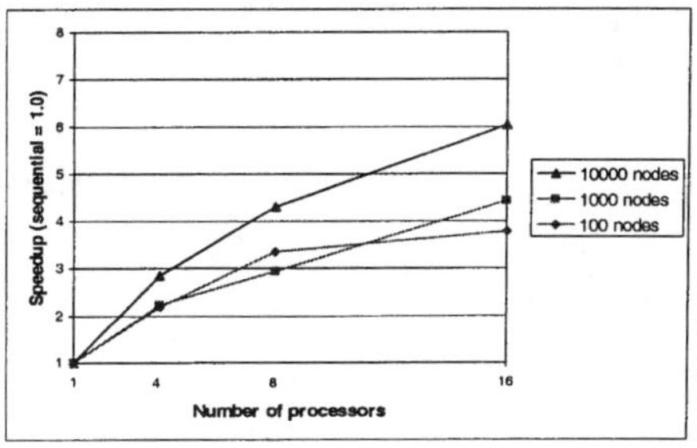

Figure 5: Lookahead extraction: low density test case.

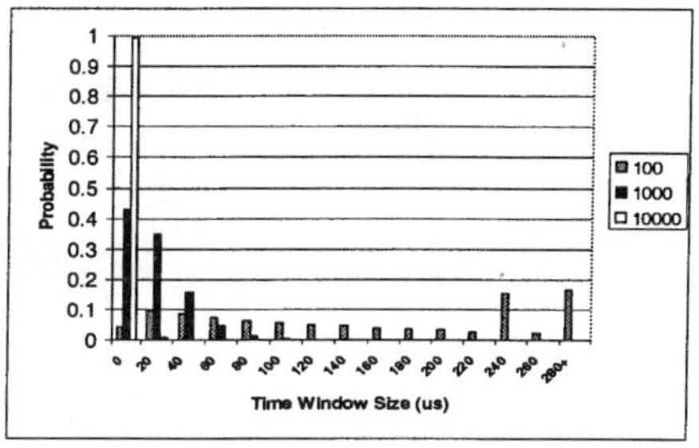

Figure 6: low density window size PDF.

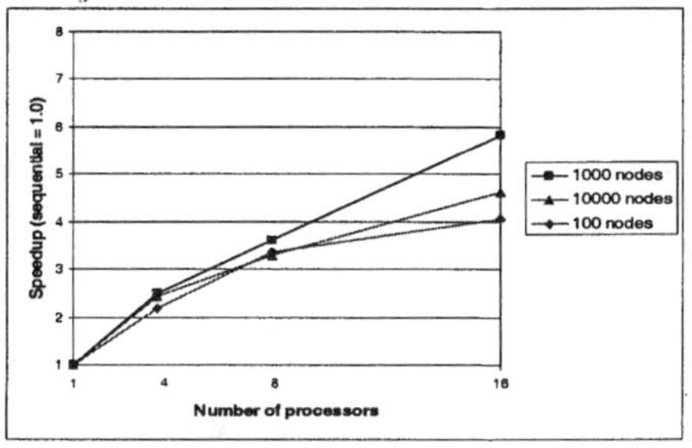

Figure 7: Lookahead extraction: high density test case.

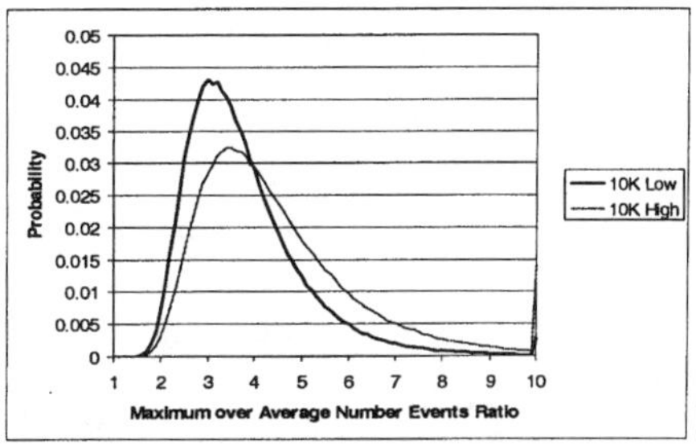

Figure 8: 10K Case: Maximum number events over the average per processor ratio PDF.

```
BOOL IsPacketDefinitelyNonReceivable(Packet p, Node s)
{
    IF (reception_power(p, s)<RECEIVING_THRESHOLD)
        Return TRUE;
    ELSE IF (CurrentStatus(s)==TRANSMITTING
            && TxEndTime(s)>ArrivalTime(p, s))
        Return TRUE;
    ELSE IF (CurrentStatus(s)==RECEIVING
            && RxEndTime(s)>ArrivalTime(p, s))
        Return TRUE;
    ELSE
        Return FALSE;
}
```

Figure 9: Routine to decide if a packet p is non-receivable at node s.

another node for reception until that actually happens. In the remainder of this section, we will propose solutions for the latter two situations to eliminate signal arrival and end events whose absences do not violate the causality constraints of the simulation, and we use the causal relationships among the events to illustrate how causality is preserved in those situations.

5.1. Eliminating events for non-receivable signals

A signal (or its corresponding packet) transmitted by a node is non-receivable by a neighbor if its arrival will NOT trigger the neighbor to lock on and receive the corresponding packet. A signal can be non-receivable to a neighbor in the following cases. First, the signal strength is below the neighbor's receiving energy threshold and cannot be detected by the neighbor's radio. Second, the neighbor is either transmitting its own packet or receiving another packet when the signal arrives. Figure 9 illustrates how a transmitter decides whether the signal is non-receivable to other nodes. Note that non-receivable signals can only affect the neighbor's successful reception of another packet or its channel status (idle or busy) (the latter two of the three ways mentioned earlier). We argue that the signal arrival and end events for non-receivable signals can be completely eliminated without affecting the correctness of the simulation by using the following approach. The decision of whether a packet is definitely non-receivable at each node is made at the beginning of its transmission. The signal will be appended to the signal history of every node regardless of whether it generates signal arrival and end events for that node. Each signal recorded in signal history contains information such as signal arrival and end time, received signal power etc. The next two subsections describe this approach in more detail.

5.2. Non-receivable signals vs. evaluation of packet reception

Figure 10 illustrates the happen-before causal relationships among the signal transmission beginning (end) incident, and the signal arrival (end) incident (corresponding to a non-receivable packet), as well as the end of reception for some other packet at the receiver. As one can see, a packet transmission happens strictly before its signal arrives at the receiver, due to nonzero propagation delay. The other signals that affect the packet reception must arrive before the end of the packet reception period, which means that their corresponding packet transmission incidents must have happened before the end of packet reception at the receiver.

It is intuitive that as long as the history of other interference signals overlapping with the packet reception is known (i.e. all causal events happened before are known) at the end of the packet reception, the success (or failure) evaluation to the packet reception can be bulk-processed at the end of the packet reception without violating the causality constraints. This is because that one can simply reproduce those processings according to the order in which the sig-

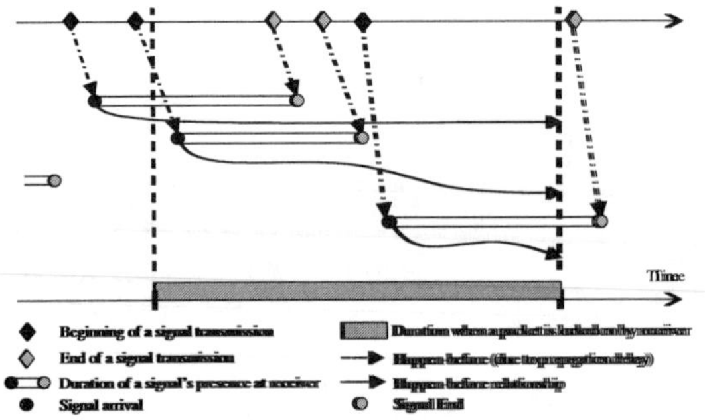

Figure 10: Causal orders of signal arrival/end events with reference to the end of packet reception.

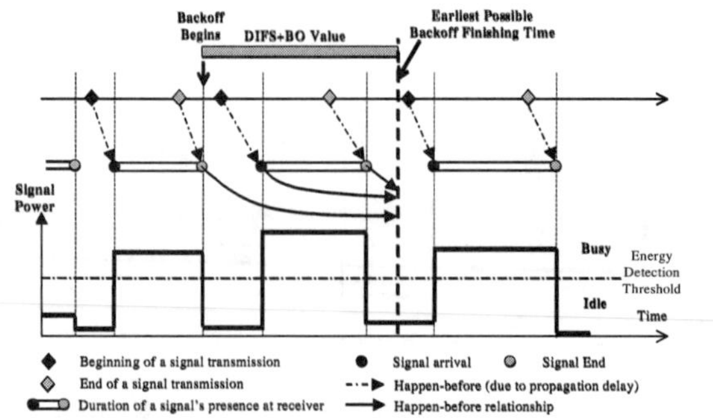

Figure 11: Causal orders of signal arrival/end events with reference to the deterministic lower bound of backoff finishing time.

nals arrive and end. Note that signals ended before the end of the packet reception can be removed from the signal history.

5.3. Non-receivable signals vs. timer operation

Besides changing the fate of a packet being received at a node, non-receivable signals can also affect the physical status (idle or busy) at the node, which may in turn affect when the node can transmit its own packet. Using the 802.11 DCF as an example, the following describes how the DIFS/EIFS and Backoff (BO) timers are implemented in existing wireless network simulators. When a node has a packet to transmit and the channel is determined to be idle at the same time, a timeout event will be scheduled to occur after the DIFS/EIFS duration. If the channel becomes busy (triggered by signal arrival event) before the DIFS/EIFS duration expires, the timer will be cancelled by deleting the timeout event. Otherwise, when the timeout event is processed, the node knows that the channel is idle for a DIFS/EIFS period and randomly picks a BO value to continue backoff similarly. When the BO timer is suspended before it expires, the old timeout event is deleted. A new timeout event will be scheduled with remaining BO duration plus additional DIFS/EIFS when backoff is resumed. When a BO timeout event is processed, the BO counter finally reaches zero, and the node is allowed to transmit the packet. Backoff is also scheduled when a node successfully receives an ACK for its data packet.

Based on the above description, we can see that the incident, in which the DIFS/EIFS or BO timer reaches zero, will potentially trigger the node to transmit a packet. Thus, it is important to study the causality among arrival/end events of non-receivable signals and actual incident of packet transmission at a node. Figure 11 illustrates the causal relationships with an example that a node will backoff after it senses the channel to be busy (The example would be equivalent to no backoff if BO is 0). Though it is non-decidable when exactly backoff finishes, we can find a deterministic bound on the earliest time that the backoff will end by assuming that the channel will always be idle from the moment the backoff procedure starts. An event can be scheduled for that time. When the event is processed, similar to the previous subsection, all the signals that arrived previously will be available in the signal history. Thus, retroactively, simulation can decide exactly how much the BO value should have been decreased. Since there is always an idle DIFS/EIFS period before BO value starts to decrement, it is easier for the simulation to restart the backoff process from the most recent busy to idle transition point with the readjusted BO value. It is as if we are inserting additional checkpoints between the time when backoff first starts and the time when the BO value finally reaches zero. As the causal effects of non-receivable signals on backoff process are still maintained by checkpointing at the next deterministic backoff timeout bound, the correctness of the simulation is unaffected. Note that during the backoff process, it is possible that a node receives packets from other nodes. The beginning and end of the packet reception are two special checkpoints for the above timer operation simulation as well, having priority over the ordinary checkpoint described above. Old signals will also be removed from the signal history at the checkpoints. Due to space constraints, a formal correctness proof of the above event reduction method will not be given here. However, it is important to know that simulation results are exactly the same with or without this optimization.

5.4. Performance evaluation

Experiments have been conducted to evaluate the impacts of the above optimization technique on the runtime performance of the parallel simulation. Note that the baseline simulator for comparison here has incorporated optimizations in both Section 3 and 4. In the first set of experiments, the node density is fixed to one node per 200x200 square meters, while the total number of nodes in the modeled wireless network is varied from 400 up to 3200. Nodes in the network use LAR as their routing protocol. 15% randomly chosen nodes have a CBR session of 20 packets per second and 512 bytes per packet to another randomly se-

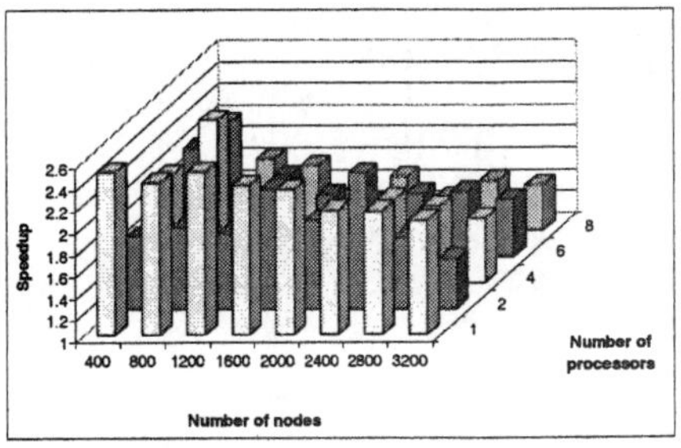

Figure 12: Reducing intra-LP events: varied network size.

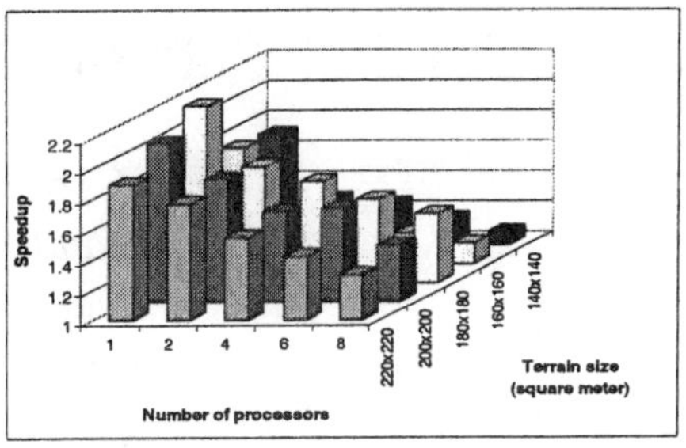

Figure 13: Reducing intra-LP events: varied node density (3200 nodes).

lected receiver approximately within two hops of distance. This setting isolates scalability problem of LAR in large-scale network scenarios, which is not of interest to this paper. Figure 12 shows the relative speedup achieved with the optimization technique described earlier in this section. For networks with 400 to 3200 nodes, the achieved speed-up ranges from 1.3 to 2.6. In the second set of experiments, the number of nodes in the network is fixed at 3200 while node density is varied from one node per $140 \times 140m^2$ to one node per $220 \times 220m^2$. As the number of partitions (processors) increases, the additional speedup achieved via reducing event scheduling overhead drops slightly. It suggests that as the number of partitions increases, other overhead, such as synchronization among LPs becomes dominant in overall simulation execution time. As a result, effect of reducing event scheduling overhead becomes less significant.

Figure 13 shows the relative speedup achieved with the optimization technique described in this section. The achieved speedup decreases as the node density increases because more nodes fall in the reception range of a signal transmitted. Although the event scheduling overhead is reduced, the complexity of the bulk-processing is increased at both packet reception evaluation and timer checkpoints for high node density cases. In the ranges of the node density and the number of partitions used by the experiment, additional speedup from 1.09 up to 2.2 is achieved.

6. Conclusion

Explosive growth of wireless communication technology spurs a growing demand for detailed simulation tools that accurately predicate performance of wireless devices, protocols, and services. However, detailed simulation of wireless networks is computationally expensive. Speed-up achieved with parallel execution of wireless network simulation might be hindered by complexities of wireless networks. This paper has presented a number of optimization techniques to improve the parallel performance of detailed wireless network simulation. First, a propagation limit is introduced to reduce the cost of simulating signal propagation across multiple LPs. Experimental results show that the maximum speed-up of 20 times can be achieved with this optimization technique for the 10,000 node cases. Second, various sources of lookahead are identified to reduce synchronization overhead among LPs. With the above optimization, parallel simulation can achieve a speedup of up to 6 times with respect to sequential simulation for the 10,000 node cases. The last optimization technique eliminates events scheduled for non-receivable signals within each LP. An average speedup of 1.8 times can be achieved with this optimization technique for a network of 3200 nodes. Unlike many past studies, the optimization techniques take into account the details of the PHY and MAC layers for fidelity of wireless network simulation while exploiting the characteristics of such details to improve parallel performance of the simulation.

References

[1] Qualnet. *www.qualnet.com.*

[2] International Standard ISO/IEC 8802-11. *ANSI/IEEE Standard 802.11*, 1999.

[3] R. Bagrodia, R. Meyer, and et al. Parsec: Parallel simulation environment for complex systems. *IEEE Computer*, 31(10):77 – 85, Oct 1998.

[4] R. Fujimoto. *Parallel and Distributed Simulation Systems.* Wiley-Interscience, Dec, 1999.

[5] Z. Ji, J. Zhou, M. Takai, and R. Bagrodia. Scalable simulation of large-scale wireless networks with bounded inaccuracies. In submission.

[6] Y. B. Ko and N. H. Vaidya. Location-aided routing (LAR) in mobile ad hoc networks. In *Proceedings of ACM/MOBICOM'98*, pages 66–75, Oct 1998.

[7] J. Liu and D. Nicol. Lookahead revisited in wireless network simulations. In *Proceedings of PADS'02*, May 2002.

[8] J. Liu, L. Perrone, D. Nicol, M. Liljenstam, C. Elliott, and D. Pearson. Simulation modeling of large-scale ad-hoc sensor networks. In *European Simulation Interoperability Workshop 2001*, 2001.

[9] G. F. Riley, R. M. Fujimoto, and M. H. Ammar. A generic framework for parallelization of network simulations. In *Proceedings of the Seventh International Symposium on Modelling, Analysis, and Simulation of Computer and Telecommunication Systems (MASCOTS)*, Oct 1999.

[10] B. K. Szymanski, A. Saifee, and et al. Genesis: A system for large-scale parallel network simulation. In *Proceedings of PADS'02*, May 2002.

[11] M. Takai, J. Martin, and R. Bagrodia. Effects of wireless physical layer modeling in mobile ad hoc networks. In *Proceedings of ACM/MOBIHOC'01*, pages 87–94, Oct 2001.

[12] X. Zeng, R. Bagrodia, and M. Gerla. Glomosim: a library for parallel simulation of large-scale wireless networks. In *Proceedings of PADS'98*, May 1998.

Space–Parallel Network Simulations using Ghosts *

George F. Riley[1]
Talal M. Jaafar[1]
Richard M. Fujimoto[2]
Mostafa H. Ammar[2]

[1]Department of Electrical and Computer Engineering
Georgia Institute of Technology
Atlanta, GA 30332-0250
{riley,jaafar}@ece.gatech.edu

[2]College of Computing
Georgia Institute of Technology
Atlanta, GA 30332-0280
{fujimoto,ammar}@cc.gatech.edu

Abstract

We discuss an approach for creating a federated network simulation that eases the burdens on the simulator user that typically arise from more traditional methods for defining space–parallel simulations. Previous approaches have difficulties that arise from the need for global topology knowledge when forwarding simulated packets between the federates. In all but the simplest cases, proper packet forwarding decisions between federates requires routing tables of size $O(mn)$ (m is the number of nodes modeled in a particular simulator instance, and n is the total number of network nodes in the entire topology) in order to determine how packets should be routed between federates. Further, the benefits of the well–known NIx-Vector routing approach cannot be fully achieved without global knowledge of the overall topology. We seek to overcome these difficulties by utilizing a topology partitioning methodology that uses *Ghost Nodes*. A *ghost node* is a simulator object in a federate that represents a simulated network node that is spatially assigned to some other federate, and thus that other federate is responsible for maintaining all state associated with the node. However, ghost nodes do retain topology connectivity information with other nodes, allowing all federate in a space–parallel simulation to obtain a global picture of the network topology. We show with experimental results that the memory overhead associated with the ghosts is minimal relative to the overall memory footprint of the simulation.

1 Introduction

One approach to creating simulation models for large–scale topologies in network simulations is to use a space–parallel partitioning methodology, coupled with distributed simulation methods. In a space–parallel network simulation, the model for the entire simulated network is divided logically into k sub–models, where k is the number of federates in the distributed simulation. With this approach, each federate is responsible for approximately $1/k^{th}$ of the entire topology model, and instantiates simulation objects to represent its own portion of the network elements in the complete topology. Since a given federate has no responsibility for the remaining $(k-1)/k$ portion of network elements, no simulation objects are created and thus the federate has no knowledge about the remaining topology. This approach is fairly easy to implement, and is the method used by existing space–parallel distributed network simulators such as *Parallel/Distributed ns* (*pdns*) and the *Georgia Tech Network Simulator* (*GTNetS*) [1, 2]. Further, this method has very good scalability, since each federate need only be concerned with its own network elements, and thus only allocates simulator memory for a fraction of the entire set of network elements. However, as we shall show this approach introduces a number of difficulties that must be addressed in order to insure correct packet forwarding between the federates.

Our solution to these difficulties is to introduce the notion of a *Ghost Node*. A ghost node is a simulator object that acts as a placeholder for nodes that are assigned to other federates. The ghost node object has none of the complex and memory intensive state needed for real nodes (such as queues, routing tables, port maps, and applications). Rather, a ghost node simply contains topology connectivity information about links and neighbors. Thus, using ghosts, a federate is afforded a global picture of the simulated topology, without the memory overhead of maintaining unneeded state for the ghosts.

The remainder of this paper is organized as follows. Section 2 discusses the space–parallel approach for distributed network simulation, and shows some of the difficulties associated with these traditional approaches. Section 3 gives the basic design of our *Georgia Tech Network Simulator* with emphasis on the ghost node implementation. Section 4 discusses related work. Section 5 presents memory usage statistics comparing our ghost node approach to more traditional routing table approaches. Finally, section 6 describes conclusions from this work.

*This work is supported in part by NSF under contract numbers ANI-9977544, ANI-0136969, ANI-0240477, ECS-0225417, and DARPA under contract number N66002-00-1-8934.

1087-4097/04 $20.00

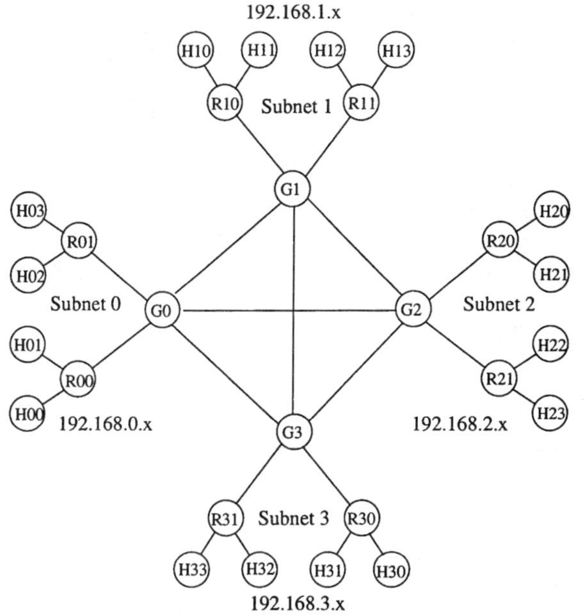

Figure 1: Simple Space–Parallel Topology

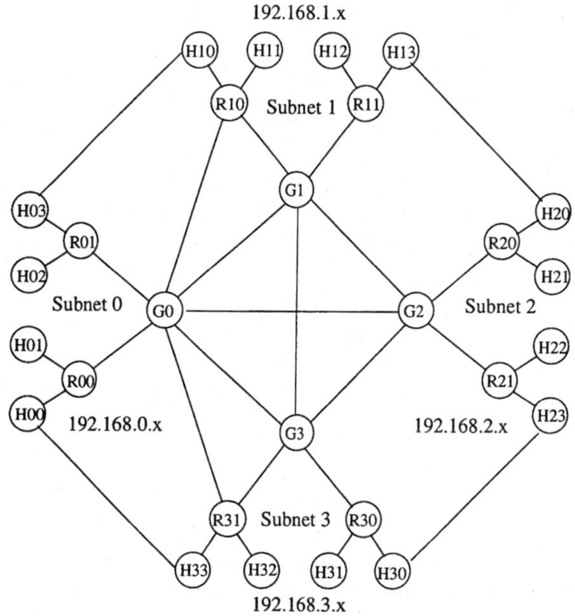

Figure 2: Difficult Space–Parallel Topology

2 Space–Parallel Simulations

To illustrate the concepts and issues regarding space–parallel network simulations, we will present two simple examples. Consider the simple topology shown in figure 1, consisting of four subnetworks. Each subnetwork has four hosts, two intermediate routers, and one gateway router. Each of the four gateway routers is connected to each of the other three gateway routers, forming a fully connected mesh. All of the simulated nodes for a subnetwork have a common 24 bit network address prefix, such as 192.168.0.x for subnetwork 0 as shown.

Now suppose that, due to resource constraints in our simulation environment, we cannot model more than seven network nodes in a given simulator instance without running out of memory on the computing platform in use. Clearly, such limited resources are not realistic, but are used here for illustrative purposes. Even with these resource constraints, we can still create a simulation of the four subnetwork topology by using space–parallel distributed simulation. We create four different simulator instances, each running on a separate hardware platform. Each of the four simulator instances instantiates models for the seven nodes in a single subnetwork. For example, simulator 0 would model the seven nodes in subnetwork 0, simulator 1 would model the seven nodes in subnetwork 1, etc. Our simulation environment must have some way to describe simulated links between federates (such as the link from $G0$ to $G1$). Links that span federate boundaries are called *remote links*, or *rlinks*. Issues such as time management and event distribution between federates can easily be solved using one of several available *Runtime Infrastructure* packages, such as the Georgia Tech *Federated Simulation Developers Kit* (*FDK*)[3], or the *DMSO RTI*[4]. The end result is that we are able to model twenty–eight network nodes, using four instances of a simulator that can only model seven nodes each, using the space–parallel methodology. The following paragraphs discuss some of the issues that arise when determining correct packet routing in this type of simulation.

Default Routes. In this simple example, the routing of packets between federates is nearly trivial. Suppose host $H00$ sends a packet to host $H23$. Simulator 0 can easily determine that the destination node ($H23$) is not modeled locally[1]. Since in this example the destination node is defined and managed on simulator 2, simulator 0 must make a routing decision based on incomplete knowledge of the overall topology. In this case however, gateway node $G0$ is the only way that packets can leave or enter subnet 0 (and hence simulator 0), $H00$ simply forwards the packet to node $G0$ (through node $R00$) for further processing. In *pdns* and *GTNetS* this is known as a *Default Route*, and works well when there is a single simulated node responsible for all packets in and out of a simulator's topology view.

Inter–Federate Route Aggregation. Route aggregation is a method used in Internet routers to reduce routing table size. If all of the routing table entries for a set of destination addresses are identical, and the destination set has a common *address prefix*, then this entire set of routes can be stored with a single entry.

Using route aggregation, once the packet arrives at gateway node $G0$, the routing decision is again easy and takes little memory. Although gateway node $G0$ has three *rlinks*, the routing decision can easily be made based on the destination *IP Address*. The *rlink* from $G0$ to $G1$ is the correct path for any *IP Address* starting with `192.168.1`, since all nodes with that prefix are defined in simulator 1. Thus, using route aggregation, only three routing table entries (one for each *rlink*) are sufficient for simulator 0 to make correct routing decisions in all cases. Both *pdns* and *GTNetS* provide commands to specify this type of aggregated routing entries for the remote links. In this simple case, assuming the use of NIx-Vector routing within each federate, we need routing state in each of the gateway nodes of size $O(f)$, where f is the number of federates in the distributed simulation.

[1]Details of how this is done are dependent on the implementation, but not important for this discussion

Since f is rarely more than a few hundred, this can be expected to be quite memory efficient.

A More Complicated Example. It appears from the above discussion that the problem of inter–federate routing in space–parallel network simulations is easily solved. However, consider the slightly modified topology shown in figure 2. This topology is nearly identical to the previous example, excepting the addition of two more intra–subnet links, connecting certain hosts to hosts in a neighboring subnet, and two extra links from gateway node $G0$ to neighboring interior routers. With this topology, the simplifying assumptions observed for the previous example no longer hold, and inter–federate routing of packets becomes much more difficult to manage.

First, the notion of the *default route*, indicating that all packets not destined to a local *IP Address* should be routed to a common gateway, can no longer be used. Thus, each node in each simulator will need a routing table (potentially with $O(n)$ entries, n being the total number of nodes in the simulation) to select which inter–federate gateway node is the best path to remote nodes.

Secondly, the clean and simple route aggregation method that worked nicely on the previous example may no longer work. Now, gateway node $G0$ has four *rlinks*, two to subnet 1 and two to subnet 3. The assignment of the *IP Addresses* to nodes in subnets 1 and 3 will affect how well the route aggregation will work for the *rlink* routing entries. In the best case, we can still use a single aggregate entry for each *rlink*, but in the worst case we need routing entries for *every node* in subnets 1 and 3 in the routing table for $G0$. The end result of both of these problems together is that we still need routing state of size $O(mn)$, where m is the number of nodes managed in each federate, and n is the total number of nodes in the global topology. We point out that the $O(mn)$ memory requirement is worst case, and in practice we still expect some saving from route aggregation.

Using NIx-Vector Routing. An efficient source–routing methodology called NIx-Vector routing is discussed in [5]. With this method, a route between a source and a destination is calculated only when needed, and is cached at the source for later re–use. Further, the calculated path from the source to the destination is stored *in the packet* using the compact NIx-Vector format, which allows intermediate routing decisions to be made without the use of routing tables. However, this approach requires a global picture of the topology from the source to the destination. Clearly, in the space–parallel methodology, this global topology knowledge is not available. However, we can provide additional routing information at the *rlinks* which allows a partial NIx-Vector to be calculated within a federate.

Suppose host $H00$ is sending a packet to host $H13$. Since host $H13$ is managed by simulator 1, simulator 0 lacks global knowledge of the topology to calculate a NIx-Vector to $H13$. However, if each *rlink* in simulator 0 has routing information specifying *which addresses are reachable from this link*, and *how many hops to each*, a NIx-Vector that routes the packet to the appropriate gateway can be calculated using a modified *Breadth First Search* (*BFS*) algorithm. In our example, the *rlink* from $G0$ to $G1$ will have a routing entry indicating it can reach $H13$ in three hops, and the *rlink* from $H03$ to $H10$ will indicate it can reach $H13$ in five hops. The modified *BFS* algorithm will calculate that the shortest path from $H00$ to $H13$ should use the *rlink* from $G0$ to $G1$, and calculates a NIx-Vector from $H00$ to $G1$ (the last hop is the *rlink* from $G0$ to $G1$).

This method has some of the benefits of NIx-Vector routing, in that no routing tables are needed at any node excepting those with *rlinks* to other federates. The memory requirements are still $O(kn)$ (k is the number of inter–federate *rlinks*, and n is the total number of nodes in the simulation). Further, in all cases except the simplest topologies, the calculation of these inter–federate routes can be time consuming. For example, we computed inter–federate routes for the million–node *MILNET* topology defined by Liljenstam et. al[6]. The off–line computation took 4 hours on a 866Mhz desktop processor, resulted in more than 5 million inter–federate routes, and required over 500MB of disk space to store the computed routing information.

Using Pre–Computed Routes. An easy approach to intra–federate routing is to use *Pre–Computed Routes*. In this approach, an off–line program creates a complete picture of the simulated topology, using a simplified and memory efficient representation of the topology. Once this complete topology model is created, a complete set of routing information can be computed for all nodes, giving paths to all other nodes. An advantage of this approach is that the time–consuming route computation step can be performed once, and used repeatedly in the simulation runs. The obvious disadvantage of this method is the $O(n^2)$ memory requirements for the all–pairs routing tables. For example, if the entire topology consists of one million nodes, the resulting pre–computed routing tables would consist of 10^{12} entries, consuming unreasonably large amounts of disk space and memory. This approach is used by the distributed memory Dartmouth *SSF* (*DaSSF*) simulator[7] described in [8].

Using Routing Protocols. Another approach to inter–federate and intra–federating routing in network simulations is the use of simulated *Routing Protocols* within the simulation. For example, we could include a model of the widely–used *Border Gateway Protocol* (*BGP*) on each node with inter–subnet connections. In the example in figure 2, this would be nodes $G0$, $G1$, $G2$, $G3$, $H00$, $H03$, $H10$, $R10$, $H13$, $H20$, $H23$, $H30$, $R31$, and $H33$. Further, we could use an *Interior Routing Protocol*, such as *EIGRP*[9, 10] or *OSPF*[11] on interior routers within a subnetwork (such as nodes $R00$, $R01$, $R11$, $R20$, $R21$, and $R30$ in our example). This approach is used by the *SSFNet* simulator[12, 13], and results in an easy to use space–parallel simulation. Additionally, this method inherently deals with dynamic topology changes, such as reacting to link or node failures. When creating the simulated topology, the user need not be concerned about routing information, since the routing protocols will compute the best routes using routing message exchanges between federates. Further, these routing protocols use route aggregation techniques to reduce the size of the resulting routing tables as much as possible. However, this approach still requires simulator memory to hold the routing tables calculated by the routing protocol, which in the worst case is still $O(mn)$.

```
#include "simulator.h"
#include "node.h"
#include "linkp2p.h"

int main()
{ // Simple sequential simulation
  Simulator s; // Sequential simulation
  Node* n1 = new Node(); // Node 1
  Node* n2 = new Node(); // Node 2
  // Define a link object
  Linkp2p link(Rate("1Mb"),
               Time("10ms"));
  // Add the link from n1 to n2
  n1->AddDuplexLink(n2, link,
      IPAddr("192.168.1.1"), Mask(32),
      IPAddr("192.168.1.2"), Mask(32));
```

Figure 3: Simple Sequential Script

```
#include "simulator.h"
#include "node.h"
#include "linkp2p.h"

int main(int argc, char** argv)
{ // Simple distributed simulation
  // Get instance id from arguments
  int myId = atol(argv[1]);
  Simulator s(myId); // Distributed sim
  // n1 is managed by simulator 0
  Node* n1 = new Node(0); // Node 1
  // n2 is managed by simulator 1
  Node* n2 = new Node(1); // Node 2
  // Define a link object
  Linkp2p link(Rate("1Mb"),
               Time("10ms"));
  // Add the link from n1 to n2
  n1->AddDuplexLink(n2, link,
      IPAddr("192.168.1.1"), Mask(32),
      IPAddr("192.168.1.2"), Mask(32));
```

Figure 4: Distributed Simulation Script

3 Ghost Nodes in *GTNetS*

In this section, we discuss the basic design of the space–parallel distributed simulation support in *GTNetS*, with particular attention to the ghost node approach. A *GTNetS* network simulation is created by writing a C++ main program, that instantiates objects representing the network topology (nodes, links, queues, etc.), the data flows and applications (web servers, web browsers, FTP clients, etc.). Also each *GTNetS* simulation instantiates a single `Simulator` object that controls the simulation (maintains the pending event list and schedules events).

GTNetS supports both sequential, single–process simulations as well as space–parallel distributed simulations. We expect that the majority of *GTNetS* simulations will use sequential execution, so we wanted to make the distinction between sequential and distributed as simple as possible. To this end, we simply provided two versions of the object constructor for the `Simulator` object, one with no parameters and one with a single *Distributed Simulation Identifier* parameter. For sequential simulations, the default constructor without arguments is specified by the user, in which case none of the distributed simulation support functions are called, and the complete topology is assumed present in the single address space. See figure 3 for a simple code snippet. The remainder of this section will focus on the distributed simulation methods.

To specify a distributed simulation, the `Simulator` object is instantiated with a single integer argument, assigning an instance identifier to this simulator that is unique within the federated simulation. If there are to be k federates in the distributed simulation, the instance identifier is in the range of $0\ldots(k-1)$. When the `Simulator` object is constructed in this manner, *GTNetS* will call the necessary distributed simulation support functions in the *RTI*, such as initialization functions, data distribution management, and time management requests. Further, the instance identifier is used to determine if node objects are to be *real* nodes or *ghost* nodes, as discussed in the following paragraphs.

The next action needed in the distributed simulation script is to identify, for every node in the topology, which simulator instance is responsible for that node object. This is accomplished by providing a node object constructor with a single argument which specifies an instance identifier. If the specified instance identifier matches that specified on the `Simulator` object constructor, then this simulator is responsible for the node object, and a *real* node object is created. Otherwise, a *ghost* object is created.

See figure 4 for a simple code snippet showing a distributed simulation instance. Note that the only differences (other than command line argument processing) are the `myId` parameter passed to the `Simulator` constructor, and the single integer arguments passed to the `Node` object constructors. In this simple example, one simulator process would be initiated with the command line argument "0", and the second would be initiated with the command line argument "1". Notice that when node objects `n1` and `n2` are created, the `Node` constructor is called with the arguments 0 and 1 respectively, indicating that node `n1` is to be modeled on simulator 0, and `n2` is to be modeled on simulator 1. In simulator 0, node `n1` is a *real* node and `n2` is a *ghost*. In simulator 1, node `n1` is a *ghost* node and `n2` is a *real*.

There are two important points to be seen from this simple example. First, there is little difference from the users' perspective between the sequential simulation and the distributed simulation. The only differences are the presence of the *instance id* parameter on the `Simulator` constructor, and the *responsible instance id* parameter on the `Node` constructor. Excepting a few other minor differences discussed later, the remainder of the script is identical. Secondly, each simulation instance runs *exactly the same script*. Using this method, we don't need to create a different *GTNetS* main program for each simulator in the distributed simulation. Each federate runs the same program, differentiated with command line parameters.

Ghost Node Implementation. From the above discussion, it is clear that in *GTNetS* the Node objects come in two flavors, *real* nodes and *ghost* nodes. Equally clear is that the *API* for the two node types (ie. the set of member functions available to object owners) must be identical or nearly identical. If this were not the case, there would be many conditional checks in the simulation script to take different action depending on the *real* or *ghost* status of the nodes. Note for example the call to AddDuplexLink for Node object n1 in the above example. While the actions taken in this method are different for *real* and *ghost* nodes, the *API* is the same. In fact, all Node methods are identical for *real* nodes and *ghost* nodes. Finally, the *ghost* node implementation must be memory efficient, utilizing as little state as possible. If this were not the case, the advantage of exploiting multiple processors to simulate larger networks would be lost, since the entire topology is required on every federate.

We achieve these goals by using a simple one–level method indirection. The basic Node object has all the *API* methods needed by *GTNetS* to manage nodes, but only has a single *Implementation Pointer* state variable. This implementation pointer points to an object that is a subclass of class NodeImpl. The NodeImpl class defines the required set of methods needed for nodes, but only has state common to *ghost* nodes and *real* nodes. The only common state between *ghost* nodes and *real* nodes is the *IP Address* and a vector of *Interfaces*. In this context, the word *Interface* refers to a simulation model of a hardware link interface (such as a *NIC* card) in a router or end system. Finally, there are two classes that are subclasses of NodeImpl, namely NodeReal and NodeGhost. Objects of class NodeReal have all the state associated with *real* nodes, such as port maps, routing information, animation size and color, and location information.

When a node is created in a distributed simulation, the Node constructor checks whether the system identifier specified in the constructor argument matches that specified in the Simulator constructor. If so, this node is real, and a new object of class NodeReal is created and pointed to by the implementation pointer. If the system identifiers do not match, the node is a ghost, and a new object of class NodeGhost is created.

We mentioned previously that both real and ghost nodes maintain a list of *Interfaces* that model the link interfaces in nodes and routers. This seems at first glance to be inefficient in terms of memory usage, since these interfaces have a substantial amount of state (for example a packet queue) that is not necessary for ghost nodes. We solve this problem by defining two Interface subclasses, InterfaceReal (which has the state needed to model an interface), and InterfaceGhost (which does not). When a new Interface object is needed by a node object, real nodes create a real interface, and ghost nodes create a ghost interface. Similarly, we use real and ghost Link objects for the same purpose. The key point is that the *API* is common across real and ghost objects, such that any owner of these objects can call the defined methods without regard to whether the object is real or a ghost.

Using this technique of real and ghost objects, each simulator in the distributed simulation has a complete picture of the simulated topology, and can compute NIx-Vector routing information from any source to any destination. We show in the next section that the overhead incurred by ghost objects is small compared to the overall memory footprint of the simulation.

```
int main(int argc, char** argv)
{ // Simple distributed simulation
  // Get instance id from arguments
  int myId = atol(argv[1]);
  Simulator s(myId); // Distributed sim
  // n1 is managed by simulator 0
  Node* n1 = new Node(0); // Node 1
  // n2 is managed by simulator 1
  Node* n2 = new Node(1); // Node 2
  // Add WebServer application to n1
  WebServer* svr = n1->AddApplication(
        TCPServer());
  if (svr) {
    // Application added
    svr->EnableGCache();
  }
  // Add WebBrowser to n2
  WebBrowser* br = n2->AddApplication(
        WebBrowser( ... ));
  if (br) {
    // Added, configure and start
     br->ConcurrentConnections(4);
     br->Start(0.1);
  }
```

Figure 5: Adding Applications

There is one case where the behavior of a ghost node and a real node can require the simulator user to be aware of whether the node is real or not. All of the previous discussion has focused exclusively on the topology generation part of the simulation script. In a network simulation, we also need to define the flow of data between the nodes in the topology. In *GTNetS* this data flow is defined using *Application* objects. *GTNetS* presently has defined application models for thirteen different application behaviors, including web browsers, web servers, Gnutella clients, and others. However, we do not use the concept of ghost applications. Since applications are added to nodes using the AddApplication method for node objects, a simpler method is to design ghost nodes to ignore any request to add an application. Since the semantics of the AddApplication method are that it returns a pointer to the newly added application object, the design is that ghost nodes simply return a *NULL* pointer instead. The user simulation scripts simply check for a *NULL* return from the AddApplication call, and if so skips further application initialization. See figure 5 for a code snippet illustrating this point. While the script does not directly determine whether an application is being added to a ghost node or a real node, it detects the *NULL* return to differentiate between the actions performed by the two node types.

Consistent Topology View. It is apparent that, for the ghost node approach to work properly, all federates must have a consistent view of the global topology being modeled. While this seems easy to achieve, there are two instances that can cause problems with this requirement.

First is the use of randomly generated topologies, using

a tool such as the *Georgia Tech Internet Topology Modeler (GTITM)*[14]. In our *GTNetS* simulator, a single *C++* object can represent an arbitrarily large network, generated randomly based on the *GTITM* technique. Thus, different federates could randomly generate different topologies, thus violating our consistent view constraint. In this case, care must be taken to insure the random number generators are seeded in a deterministic way, to insure each federate generates identical random topologies.

The second issue is the modeling of link or node failures in a network. If a given federate has a *real* node representation of a given network node, and generates a random node failure event, other federates must be made aware of this failure. Although not implemented in our simulator, it is straightforward to use state update events between federates to achieve these notifications. Further, these state update events need *not* be sent between federates with zero simulation time advance, since node and link failures cannot be detected in a network any faster than packets can flow through the network. It is well known that zero time update events between federates leads to poor performance.

The design of *GTNetS* leads to an easy to use, and low overhead way to manage a space–parallel network simulation. The ghost nodes give the simulation the necessary topology information to calculate NIx-Vector routing information, while at the same time use little memory.

4 Related Work

There are several network simulation tools available that use a space–parallel approach to distributed simulation. *Parallel/Distributed ns (pdns)* by Riley[15, 16] (based on the venerable *ns2*[17] simulator), and has used the space–parallel approach from its inception. The *SSFNet* simulator was initially designed for parallel simulation in a multi-threaded shared–memory environment, but has since been adapted by Liu and Nicol[8] to the support distributed memory platforms. The Dartmouth *SSF (DASSF)* simulator[7] also has been adapted for a distributed simulation with a space–parallel methodology. Wu et. al[18] report some limited success in adapting the commercial *OPNet* simulator[19] to operate in a distributed environment, using a space–parallel approach.

The concept of using limited state objects as place–holders for remote objects is not new. In the Distributed Interactive Simulation (*DIS*) community, tools such as SIMNet[20] often use dead reckoning or other approximation methods to estimate the state of objects that are managed in remote federates. In a battlefield simulation for example, a federate may report the position and velocity of a tank object at a particular point in time. Other federates will maintain the tank's location by assuming a constant velocity until informed otherwise. Ferenci[21] discusses the use of *Proxy Objects* in distributed simulations, which are conceptually similar to our ghosts. However, Ferenci's proxy objects exist primarily to facilitate inter–federate message routing, and do not in fact represent any global state. Additionally, Ferenci discusses his approach in the context of optimistic simulations, where we deal exclusively in the conservative environment.

To our knowledge, we are the first to apply the limited–state object method to represent the global topology information in space–parallel network simulations.

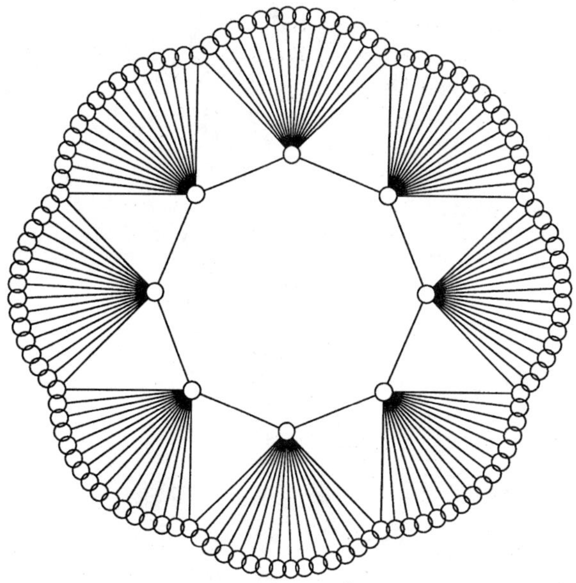

Figure 6: Simple Star/Ring Topology

5 Experimental Results

To demonstrate the effectiveness of the ghost node approach, we ran three sets of experiments to measure the memory usage of the space–parallel network simulations, using both the traditional approach with manually specified inter–federate routing and our new ghost node approach. The first set of experiments uses a simple topology similar to that shown in figure 6. This topology consists of k subnetworks (k is eight in the figure shown), each with n nodes arranged in a star topology (n is sixteen in the example). Each of the subnetworks is connected to its neighbors, forming a ring. This topology was chosen since it is the best possible case for the traditional approach. Each of the leaf nodes in the star subnetwork can use the simple *default route* method to reach the single gateway node. At each gateway, the *route aggregation* method can easily and efficiently specify which addresses are reachable on each of the *rlinks*.

The simple topology was run on eight federates, with varying numbers of leaf nodes per subnetwork. The experiments were performed using both the traditional approach and the ghost node approach. One hundred and fifty *TCP* flow endpoints were assigned to leaf nodes, and 1MB transfers we simulated. The memory usage and execution time of each simulation is shown in table 1. Since in this experiment, all federates model an identical subnetwork, results are only shown for federate zero. As can be seen, the memory footprint for the ghost node approach is only slightly larger than the traditional method. For the 120,008 node case (the largest we performed), there were 15,001 real nodes and 105,007 ghosts. The ghosts required a total of 19 MB of memory, representing 16 percent of the total memory footprint.

Interestingly, the overall execution time for the ghost node approach is less than the traditional approach. Using ghosts, we pay a one–time cost for the calculation of the NIx-Vector, but gain an $O(1)$ routing decision at each hop in the path. Without NIx-Vectors, the routing at gateway nodes and hubs requires an $O(k)$ computation (k is the number of *IP Addresss* assigned to the node) to determine if the packet has arrived at the destina-

Table 1: Star Topology Memory Usage

Node Count			Memory MB		Execution Time (sec)	
Star Size	Total Nodes	Ghost Nodes	No Ghosts	Ghosts	No Ghosts	Ghosts
1,501	12,008	10,507	45	47	156	150
3,501	28,008	24,507	53	57	188	152
7,501	60,008	53,507	68	77	271	150
15,001	120,008	105,007	95	114	331	228

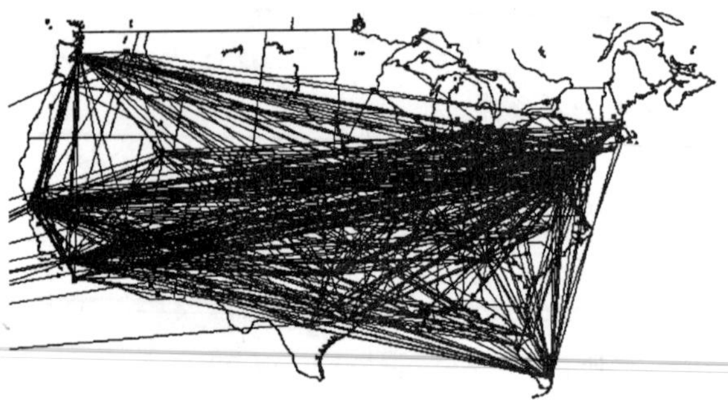

Figure 7: Milnet Topology

tion. We are looking into a less burdensome way to make this decision, to reduce this to $O(\lg k)$.

The second set of experiments are nearly identical to the previous one, excepting the use of a star size of 7,500 and the addition of more data flows. The data flows were composed of three hundred TCP clients (10MB of data each), six TCP servers, two thousand web browsers (requesting random web objects), and two hundred webservers. The simulation time was five hundred seconds. On average, the memory used by each federate was 71MB using the traditional approach, comparing to 80MB using the ghost node approach. The execution time was higher using the traditional approach as expected; 1,215sec compared to 1,111sec using the ghost node approach.

The last set of experiments used a large and complex topology known as the *MILNet* defined by Liljenstam et. al[6]. This topology consists of a backbone network containing over three thousand routers and eleven thousand links, that roughly models the backbone network for United States military bases. Connected to the backbone are 163 subnetworks of various sizes from five hundred to nine thousand nodes each. The entire network exceeds one million nodes. A graphical representation of the *MILNet* backbone is shown in figure 7.

The results from the *MILNet* experiments are shown in table 2. The *MILNet* topology was divided between 8 federates, with federate zero modeling the high–speed backbone and the other federates modeling approximately equal parts of the remaining nodes. In the traditional (Non–Ghost) approach, we used an off–line routing computation program that required more than 4 hours of CPU time and computed more than 5 million inter–federate routes. This routing information was then used to populate the inter–federate routing information in the remote links. In contrast, the ghost node approach uses the on–demand NIx-Vector routing method and thus no precomputation is needed. The results show that the memory used for ghosts considerable, but in most cases a small fraction of the total memory usage. The exception is for federate zero, which models only 3,070 of the high–speed backbone routers of *MILNet*. This federate has more than a million ghosts, using 143MB of memory, which is 66 percent of the total. In all other federates, the ghosts take between 100MB and 150MB, accounting for around 16 percent of the total.

Interestingly, the initialization time for the ghost node simulation is less than half of that of the traditional method. In this experiment, the entire topology is specified in a large *XML* file, which must be read in its entirety by both approaches. However, the traditional approach also requires the population of the inter–federate routing information. As mentioned, this information consists of over 5 million individual routes, which take considerable time to read and process, as evident by the larger initialization times.

6 Conclusions and Future Work

We have shown that the ghost node approach is a viable method to achieve efficient and easy–to–use space–parallel network simulations. The memory required for the ghosts is non–zero, but small relative to the overall memory footprint of a large–scale network simulation. Using ghost nodes, no precomputation of routing information is needed and the memory–efficient NIx-Vector routing method can be used. The implementation of ghost nodes in *GTNetS* allows the same simulation script to be used for all federates, with simple command line parameters identifying node mapping.

Even with the ghost node approach, simulation user must still specify the mapping of node objects to federates. In all but the simplest cases, determining a suitable and efficient mapping is challenging and requires considerable analysis of the traffic patterns between the simulated network elements. Liu and Chien[22] describe an automated method to partition networks which they used in their *MicroGrid*[23] emulation tool. These results seem promising, and we are investigating their applicability to our ghost node approach for space–parallel network simulation.

References

[1] G. F. Riley, "The Georgia Tech Network Simulator," in *Proceedings of the ACM SIGCOMM workshop on Models, methods and tools for reproducible network research*, pp. 5–12, ACM Press, 2003.

Table 2: MILNet Memory Usage

Federate	Nodes			Memory (MB)		Initialization (Sec)	
	Real	Ghost	Total	No Ghosts	Ghosts	No Ghosts	Ghosts
0	3,070	1,095,558	1,098,628	73	216	692	299
1	181,268	917,360	1,098,628	704	833	699	299
2	144,769	953,859	1,098,628	568	699	696	299
3	141,421	957,207	1,098,628	557	688	695	299
4	150,060	948,568	1,098,628	588	720	699	299
5	151,465	947,163	1,098,628	593	724	697	299
6	171,224	927,404	1,098,628	671	798	705	299
7	155,351	943,277	1,098,628	606	737	698	299

[2] G. F. Riley, "The Georgia Tech Network Simulator." Software on-line: http://www.ece.gatech.edu/ research/ labs/ MANIACS/ gtnets.htm, 2003.

[3] R. Fujimoto, S. Ferenci, M. Loper, T. McLean, K. Perumalla, G. Riley, and I. Tacic, "Fdk users guide." Georgia Institute of Technology, March 2001.

[4] S. T. Bachinsky, L. Mellon, G. H. Tarbox, and R. M. Fujimoto, "Rti 2.0 architecture," in *Proceedings of the 1998 Spring Simulation Interoperability Workshop (SIW'98)*, Mar 1998.

[5] G. F. Riley, M. H. Ammar, and R. M. Fujimoto, "Stateless routing in network simulations," in *Proceedings of the Eighth International Symposium on Modeling, Analysis and Simulation of Computer and Telecommunication Systems*, August 2000.

[6] M. Liljenstam, J. Liu, and D. M. Nicol, "Development of an internet backbone topology for large–scale network simulations," in *Proceedings of the 2003 Winter Simulation Conference (WSC'03)*, Dec 2003.

[7] J. Liu and D. M. Nicol, "DaSSF 3.1 user's manual," April 2001.

[8] J. Liu and D. Nicol, "Learning not to share," in *16th Workshop on Parallel and Distributed Simulation*, 2002.

[9] B. Albrightson, J. J. Garcia-Luna-Aceves, and J. Boyle, "EIGRP – a fast routing protocol based on distance vectors," in *Proceedings of Networld/Interop*, May 1994.

[10] J. J. Garcia-Luna-Aceves, "Loop–free routing using diffusing computations," *IEEE/ACM Transactions on Networking*, vol. 1, Feb 1993.

[11] J. Moy, "Internet RFC2328: Ospf version 2." Network Working Group, April 1998.

[12] J. H. Cowie, D. M. Nicol, and A. T. Ogielski, "Modeling the global internet," *Computing in Science and Engineering*, January 1999.

[13] J. Cowie, H. Liu, J. Liu, D. Nicol, and A. Ogielski, "Towards realistic million-node internet simulations," in *International Conference on Parallel and Distributed Processing Techniques and Applications*, June 1999.

[14] E. W. Zegura, K. Calvert, and S. Bhattacharjee, "How to model an internetwork," in *Proceedings of IEEE Infocom 96*, 1996.

[15] G. F. Riley, R. M. Fujimoto, and M. H. Ammar, "A Generic Framework for Parallelization of Network Simulations," in *Proceedings of Seventh International Symposium on Modeling, Analysis and Simulation of Computer and Telecommunication Systems (MASCOTS'99)*, October 1999.

[16] G. F. Riley, R. M. Fujimoto, and M. H. Ammar, "Parallel/Distributed ns." Software on-line: www.cc.gatech.edu/ computing/ compass/ pdns/ index.html, 2000. Georgia Institute of Technology.

[17] S. McCanne and S. Floyd, "The LBNL network simulator." Software on-line: http://www.isi.edu/nsnam, 1997. Lawrence Berkeley Laboratory.

[18] H. Wu, R. Fujimoto, and G. Riley, "Experiences parallelizing a commercial network simulator," in *Proceedings of the Winter Simulation Conference*, Dec 2001.

[19] S. Bertolotti and L. Dunand, "Opnet 2.4: an environment for communication network modeling and simulation," in *Proceedings of the European Simulation Symposium*, October 1993.

[20] D. C. Miller and J. A. Thorpe, "SIMNET: The advent of simulator networking," *Proceedings of the IEEE*, vol. 83, pp. 1114–1123, Aug 1995.

[21] S. Ferenci, K. Perumalla, and R. Fujimoto, "An approach to federating parallel simulators," in *14th Workshop on Parallel and Distributed Simulation*, May 2000.

[22] X. Liu and A. A. Chien, "Traffic–based load balance for scalable network emulation," in *Proceedings of the ACM Conference on High Performance Computing and Networking*, November 2003.

[23] H. Song, D. Jakobsen, R. Bhagwan, X. Zhang, K. Taura, and A. Chien, "The MicroGrid: a scientific tool for modeling computational grids," in *IEEE Supercomputing Conference (SC'2000)*, November 2000.

Session 10:
Emerging Methods

Space Uncertain Simulation Events: some Concepts and an Application to Optimistic Synchronization

Francesco Quaglia and Roberto Beraldi
Dipartimento di Informatica e Sistemistica
Università di Roma "La Sapienza"
Via Salaria 113, 00198 Roma, Italy

Abstract

The notion of temporal uncertainty, expressed as the possibility for an event to occur in an interval of simulation time, rather than at a specific instant, has been recently proposed and exploited in order to enhance the performance of parallel/distributed simulation systems. In this paper we propose the concept of "spatial uncertainty" expressed as the possibility for a simulation event to occur in one of a set of points within the simulated system space. How to handle/exploit space uncertain events in an optimistic simulation system is discussed. Also, experimental results for optimistic simulations of a Personal Communication System (PCS) modeled with space uncertain events are reported. These results show the ability of spatial uncertainty to increase the performance of the parallel simulation system by providing a more flexible approach to synchronization.

1 Introduction

Increasing the performance of a parallel/distributed simulation system, whether it be based on conservative or optimistic synchronization, is still a core issue to address. To this purpose, the notion of temporal uncertainty of simulation events [6] has been recently proposed and exploited, especially in the context of federated simulation systems. Basically, a time uncertain simulation event is an event for which we do not define a precise timestamp for its occurrence. Instead, we admit an interval of simulation time within which it eventually occurs. The advantage of temporal uncertainty derives from the fact that the execution of events at any Logical Process (LP) is ordered on the basis simulation time intervals, rather than precise timestamps, with any two events considered as concurrent in case the corresponding intervals overlap and they are not causally dependent on each other. This increases the flexibility of synchronization since concurrent events lead to the admission of multiple correct event execution orders at an LP. In the context of optimistic synchronization, this allows reducing the amount of rollback in the parallel execution [2], in the case of conservative synchronization it allows overcoming problems due to poor lookahead in the simulation model [6, 11].

Actually, temporal uncertainty has its justification in the fact that any simulation is only an approximation of the simulated system. Therefore there are some aspects that might not be directly captured by the simulation model; we call this phenomenon as *discrepancy*. Assigning an uncertainty to the occurrence time of a simulation event is a way to express the existence of the discrepancy. As an example, consider a wireless communication system simulation, where the service area is partitioned into cells. Typically, the simulation model assigns to each cell a defined geometric shape in a way that there is no overlapping between cells (e.g. cells are modeled as non-overlapping hexagons). On the other hand, real wireless systems have cells that overlap, thus giving rise to portions of the coverage area that are served by multiple base stations. This implies that, in the real system, the hand-off procedure of a mobile that switches between cells can occur when the mobile is in any point of the overlapped portion of the coverage area. This peculiarity, not explicitly captured by the simulation model, is some way expressed by assigning a temporal uncertainty to the occurrence time of the hand-off event in the simulation model.

In this paper we present the concept of *spatial uncertainty* that expresses the possibility for a simulation event to occur in a spatial region of the simulated system, rather than in a precise point. As for the case of temporal uncertainty, spatial uncertainty is a mean to express the previously mentioned discrepancy phenomenon, which might appear in specific simulation applications. To make clear the latter assertion, consider again the example above regarding the wireless system simulation, where cells are modeled as non-overlapping hexagons. Consider a mobile within a cell, say cell A, that moves outside this cell, thus giving rise to a hand-off event in the simulation. Also, suppose, as shown in Figure 1.a, that an exact point p is defined for the hand-off just around a corner of cell A. In this case the simulation model only admits the possibility for the mobile to enter cell B. However, in the real system we might have overlapping between cells B and C around point p therefore either cell might accept the mobile and serve it. This discrepancy can be captured, and expressed, by assigning to the hand-off event a spatial region, say the segment L in Figure 1.b, thus re-introducing in the simulation model the possibility that either cell B or cell C accepts the mobile as it could occur in the real system.

Similarly to temporal uncertainty, spatial uncertainty can provide a mean to improve the run-time behavior of parallel/distributed simulation systems. Specifically, the possibility for an event to occur in any point within a spatial region means that multiple LPs in the parallel/distributed simulation system, i.e. all those LPs modeling a portion of that

1087-4097/04 $20.00 © 2004 IEEE

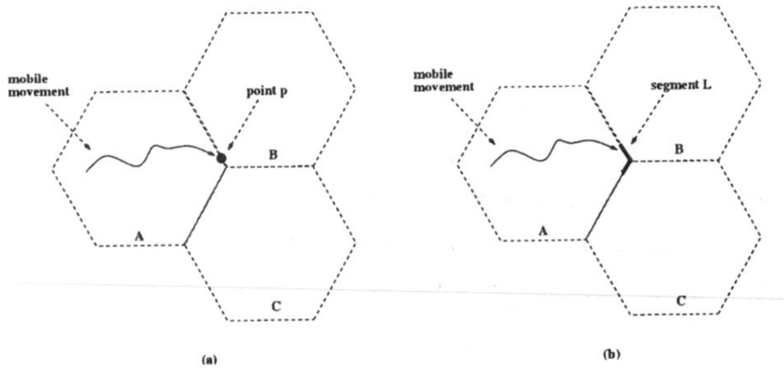

Figure 1. Hand-off in a Point p (a) or on a Segment Region L (b).

spatial region, might take care of the execution of that event. Therefore, the decision on which LP should really execute that event can be taken at run-time in a way to improve specific performance metrics for the parallel/distributed simulation system. This aspect, together with mechanisms for handling space uncertain events, will be explored in this paper for the case of optimistic simulation. Then we also report the results of an experimental study on optimistic simulations of a Personal Communication System (PCS) based on spatial uncertainty, thus providing a quantification of the performance benefits that can be achieved just through the exploitation of such a kind of uncertainty.

The remainder of this paper is structured as follows. In Section 2 we present a simple, pragmatical model for space uncertain events and provide indications on how to map the model on parallel simulation methodology. Section 3 presents a discussion on how to exploit spatial uncertainty in optimistic synchronization, and describes additional mechanisms required by an optimistic simulator to handle the uncertainty. The results for the experiments with the PCS application are reported in Section 4.

2 Spatial Uncertainty in Parallel Simulation

In this paper we are interested in spatial uncertainty as a mean to improve the run-time behavior of a parallel/distributed simulation system. In particular, we focus on the reduction of the wall-clock time on a whole run for an optimistically synchronized parallel simulator. For this reason we provide in this section the description of an event model with spatial uncertainty that well fits the requirements of parallel/distributed simulation methodology. However, we argue that the notion of spatial uncertainty might be also exploited in other ways that we reserve for future work. As an example, a space uncertain event might give rise to multiple different outcomes depending on the decision we take on the final position for the occurrence of the event. Therefore, we might associate with each space uncertain event a decision point that enables cloning of the simulation [8]. This might allow fast exploration of multiple execution paths due to sharing of portions of the computation on different paths, independently of whether the simulator executes sequentially or concurrently.

The remainder of this section is structured as follows. We first introduce the event model expressing spatial uncertainty as an extension of a classical event model for parallel simulation, then we provide hints on the correctness of the execution of a simulation model with space uncertain events.

2.1 A Model for Space Uncertain Events

A discrete event simulation model is classically viewed as a set $S = \{s_1, s_2, \ldots, s_n\}$ of state variables, also referred to as *state of the simulation model*, and a sequence of state changes, also referred to as events, occurring at discrete points (timestamps) in simulation time.

In parallel discrete event simulation, the state S is partitioned into disjoint subsets of state variables S_j (with $j \in [1, m]$) such that $S = \bigcup_{\forall j \in [1,m]} S_j$. The peculiarity of such a partitioning is that each event, namely each state transition, involves a single subset S_j. Therefore, the state transition function associated with a given event takes as input values only the variables within S_j and updates only those same variables. In practice, this is implemented by assigning the management of each subset S_j of state variables to a specific LP, namely LP_j, which is entirely responsible for the execution of the state transition function associated with the event. We can model such a classical approach by associating with each event e the tuple $\tau(e) = [timestamp, content, position]$, where $timestamp$ is the simulation time for the event occurrence, $content$ is its content (which determines the state transition function to be invoked), and $position$ is a value in the interval $[1, m]$. The latter value represents the index of the subset of state variables involved in the state transition associated with the event, therefore the state variables involved in the transition due to the event e are only those in $S_{\tau(e).position}$ ([1]).

The notion of spatial uncertainty we propose is based on an extension of the previous classical perspective, and deals with the partitioning of the simulation model state S into the previously mentioned disjoint subsets S_j. Specifically, we associate with the event e a tuple $\tau(e) = [timestamp, content, \Pi]$, where the first two elements have the same meaning as above, while Π is a non-empty set of values, all different from each other, belonging to the interval $[1, m]$. Π specifies multiple possibilities as respect to the subset of state variables that are involved in the state transition associated with the event e. Therefore, it expresses uncertainty on where, within the state of the simulation model, the event e will have an effect. In practice this means that we have multiple LPs that can take care of the execution of the event e, which expresses the fact that the state transition associated with the event e can involve one of a set of distinct parts of the system under investigation.

A special instance occurs when $|\tau(e).\Pi| = 1$. In this case we obtain that the event e has no degree of uncertainty since, as respect to the partitioning of the state S, we exactly know which is the subset of state variables where the state transition function associated with $\tau(e).content$ needs to be applied. This also shows how the classical approach with no spatial uncertainty can be seen as a special case of a simulation with space uncertain events, namely the case in which the set Π has cardinality one for all the events.

[1] We use the notation $\tau(e).x$ to indicate the value of element x within the tuple associated with the event e.

2.2 Correctness Criteria with Spatial Uncertainty

When dealing with parallel simulation, we need to address the problem of correctness for the model execution, i.e. the synchronization problem. This is because concurrency is admitted for the execution of events acting on distinct subsets of state variables S_j (i.e. distinct LPs) and the execution of an event acting on a given subset can schedule events destined for other subsets, therefore we have dependencies among state transitions occurring on different subsets of state variables.

For the case of no spatial uncertainty, we say that the simulation model execution is correct if, for each pair of events e and e' such that $\tau(e).position = \tau(e').position$ and $\tau(e).timestamp < \tau(e').timestamp$, then the state transition function associated with $\tau(e).content$ is executed before the one associated with $\tau(e').content$. This is reflected by the classical perspective according to which the execution of events at each LP in non-decreasing timestamp order is a sufficient condition for the correctness of the simulation model execution, i.e. the correctness of simulation results. We want to exploit this same perspective for the case of simulation models with spatial uncertainty. In other words, we want to define a property of the model execution such that timestamp ordering is preserved at each LP. A natural way to approach such an issue is to define a property based on the positions we admit for each event and on how the admitted positions combine for distinct events within the model execution itself.

Before proceeding, let us introduce an additional, simple notation: we denote as $location(e)$ the value belonging to $\tau(e).\Pi$ that identifies where, within the simulation model state S, the state transition function associated with $\tau(e).content$ really acts. In other words, $S_{location(e)}$ identifies the subset of state variables really involved in the execution of that transition function while the model execution proceeds. Hence, $LP_{location(e)}$ is the LP that really takes care of the execution of this event.

We can now envisage the following property, we call ACceptability ($\mathcal{AC}$), for the model execution:

Property 2.1 - ACceptability ($\mathcal{AC}$).
Model execution is acceptable if, for each pair of events e and e′ such that $(\tau(e).\Pi \cap \tau(e').\Pi \neq \emptyset) \wedge (\tau(e).timestamp < \tau(e').timestamp)$*, at least one of the following two conditions holds: (1) the state transition function associated with* $\tau(e).content$ *is executed before the state transition function associated with* $\tau(e').content$*; (2)* $location(e) \neq location(e')$.

In other words, property $\mathcal{AC}$ asserts that, given any pair of events e and e' having the potential to work on a same subset S_x of state variables within the state of the simulation model, we accept to process them with no ordering constraint among each other in case we are able to select distinct locations for them while the model execution proceeds. Trivially, in any acceptable model execution, for each subset of state variables S_x, events eventually located on this subset are all executed in non-decreasing timestamp order, which translates in that each LP_x is guaranteed to execute its events in non-decreasing timestamp order. Therefore the $\mathcal{AC}$ property can be seen as a criterion that expresses correctness of the model execution in the same classical terms that characterize simulations with events having no spatial uncertainty. At the same time, any parallel/distributed simulation system built to ensure the $\mathcal{AC}$ property could take advantage from higher flexibility while synchronizing the LPs. Specifically, the flexibility might come out by proper specification of the function $location(e)$ determining which LP really takes care of the execution of the event e. In the next section we discuss a scheme, layered on top of classical optimistic synchronization, to build simulation systems providing acceptability in the model executions as expressed by Property 2.1.

3 Optimistic Synchronization with Space Uncertain Events

We focus on the classical approach to parallel/distributed simulation, where LPs exchange messages to notify each other about newly scheduled events. In this context we are interested in the relation between the optimistic approach to synchronization, as designed for events with no spatial uncertainty [9], and the notion of acceptable model execution in the sense of Property 2.1. More precisely, we aim at extending basic mechanisms underlying the optimistic approach to synchronization to embed within the simulation system the ability to achieve, in an efficient way, an acceptable model execution. The first step towards this direction is to properly define an algorithm specifying the function $location()$, namely an algorithm that establishes how to determine final positions for the events. To this purpose, we introduce an algorithm called Rollback If No Additional Chance (RINAC). It specifies the function $location()$ in the attempt to keep low the occurrence of rollback. The last part of this section is devoted to the management of cancellation of events when considering that their location is established through RINAC. As we shall discuss, this issue will be tackled through a proper Multicast Cancellation scheme (MC).

3.1 Rollback If No Additional Chance

When we need to define an algorithm specifying the function $location()$ in a way to provide an optimistic simulation system supporting the $\mathcal{AC}$ property, several different approaches might be devised. As a first example, upon the scheduling of the event e by a given LP, say LP_x, it might be possible to collect information, e.g. via polling/reply messages, on the current simulation clock value for all the LPs in the set $\phi = \{LP_j | j \in \tau(e).\Pi\}$. Then LP_x might address the event e to the LP in the set ϕ, say LP_y, having simulation clock lower than $\tau(e).timestamp$, if any. In such a case, unless the simulation clock of LP_y oversteps $\tau(e).timestamp$ due to processing of other events before the notification message for e finally arrives at LP_y, the event e can be processed by LP_y in timestamp order, thus not causing violation of the $\mathcal{AC}$ property ([2]). This avoids the need for rollback procedures to recover acceptability in the model execution. Another approach would be to let all the LPs in the set ϕ to execute an explicit coordination algorithm, e.g. via rounds of messages, to resolve the location

[2]This is because, there is no event e' different from e, with $\tau(e').timestamp > \tau(e).timestamp$, such that $location(e') = location(e)$ and the state transition function associated with $\tau(e').content$ is executed before the one associated with $\tau(e).content$.

```
Behavior of LP_i upon the receipt of a notification
  message m[e, visited]:
  1. if ((local simulation clock ≤ τ(e).timestamp ) ∨
         (visited = τ(e).Π − {i}))
  2.       accept the event e for processing;
  3. else
  4.       visited = visited ∪ {i};
  5.       select x ∈ τ(e).Π − visited;
  6.       forward m[e, visited] to LP_x;
```

Figure 2. The RINAC Algorithm.

for the event e, again with the aim to address the event e itself to an LP that can process it in timestamp order. On the other hand, the overhead due either to polling/reply messages sent/collected by LP_x or to the explicit coordination algorithm among the LPs in ϕ might be excessive, thus giving rise to a simulation system unable to really exploit spatial uncertainty for performance purposes.

We are interested in this paper in the definition of an algorithm specifying the function $location()$, which can be implemented with minimal overhead. More precisely, we neither want to collect information about current simulation clocks of the LPs, nor want to execute an explicit coordination algorithm. Instead, our proposal is based on a forwarding mechanism according to which an LP that receives a notification message for an event e accepts the event in case its simulation clock is lower than the event timestamp. Otherwise it rejects the event, and the notification message is forwarded to another LP among the possible destinations for that event. This is done in the hope that the next destination LP is able to maintain acceptability in the model execution without the need for rollback procedures. To avoid cycles of forwarding, that might lead to a situation in which no LP eventually accepts the event (thus the event itself is not eventually executed), forwarding can be done only among the set of LPs not yet visited by the notification message. If all the possible destination LPs have been visited, the LP lastly visited in the forwarding scheme cannot reject the event, even in case the event timestamp is lower than the current simulation clock of that LP. Therefore, we need to execute rollback on that LP to recover acceptability in the model execution since there is no more chance to visit another LP in the forwarding scheme. Hence the name RINAC (Rollback-If-No-Additional-Chance) for the algorithm we propose to specify the function $location()$.

The pseudo-code for RINAC is shown in Figure 2. Actually, to support RINAC we assume each notification message m for a given event also carries a set of values, called $visited$, initially empty, that contains the identifiers of all the LPs that have already been visited during the forwarding scheme. By line 1 of the algorithm, LP_i accepts to process the event in case no rollback needs to be executed or it is the last LP visited through the forwarding scheme. Otherwise it updates the $visited$ set to include its identifier, namely the value i (see line 4), selects a not yet visited LP among the possible destinations for the event (see line 5) and then forwards the notification message to that LP.

We argue that the cost of managing RINAC is definitely lower than the cost of collecting information on current simulation clock values, or executing explicit coordination. On the other hand, as respect to those approaches, RINAC might increase the time required to explore all the possible destination LPs on time for the event to be addressed to any of them and processed in timestamp order. This is because possible destinations are explored serially through the forwarding of the event notification message. Such an additional delay in the exploration of the possible destinations might cause non-minimal rollback length since we are actually delaying acceptance of the event, with possible execution of rollback, until we become aware that there is no chance to process the event in timestamp order at any LP among the possible destinations. Anyway this phenomenon is expected to have a limited impact each time the set $\tau(e).\Pi$ has relatively low cardinality. Also, non-minimal rollback length might be anyway acceptable if we are able to keep low the frequency of rollback occurrence by carefully locating the events among the LPs, which is exactly the aim of RINAC. Overall, RINAC represents a tradeoff between the cost of management of spatial uncertainty and advantages from its exploitation.

We also note that RINAC might be particularly effective in case the simulation system makes use of the so called kernel approach to implement core functionalities. Specifically, when using this approach, the LPs are typically executed as application level threads, and each processor runs an instance of a dispatcher thread (DT) that controls and schedules a set of LPs for event execution according to a given algorithm, e.g. Smallest-Timestamp-First [10]. DT has control on the event queues of those LPs, on their current simulation clock values, and so on. In this case, upon the arrival of an event notification message at DT, the RINAC algorithm is used to verify whether the condition in line 1 holds for the destination LP. If the condition does not hold and forwarding of the notification message is required towards another LP belonging to the set controlled by that same DT, then the message does not really need to be re-sent since it is already buffered within a memory area accessible by DT itself. This reduces the real number of message send operations performed to explore the set of possible destinations for a given event.

There is a final observation we would like to bring to the reader's attention. As already pointed out in Section 2.2, the function $location(e)$ identifies the LP that finally executes the event e. This means that the value of $location(e)$ might theoretically be considered as not definitely determined until an LP really executes the event e. In practice, RINAC determines the value of $location(e)$ by definitely establishing which LP accepts to eventually process the event e, with no possibility to switch to another LP even in case the event e remains unprocessed for a while. In other words, with no loss of correctness, we are studying the case in which the final position for the event is established prior to the event is really executed. It is established just upon the acceptance of the event, for future processing, at a given LP. We reserve for future work investigations on the possibility to keep the establishment of the location provisional until the event execution really occurs, which might further increase flexibility in the synchronization scheme.

Behavior of LP_x when cancelling the event e:
1. $\forall i \in \tau(e).\Pi$
2. send $m^-[e]$ to LP_i;

Figure 3. Multicast Cancellation.

3.2 Multicast Cancellation

When the location of events is established through RINAC, we need to consider an adequate scheme for cancelling a scheduled event e due to rollback. Specifically, the main problem in the cancellation issue is that, when LP_x needs to cancel an event e it has previously scheduled, it might have no knowledge on the identity of the LP that finally accepted the event e for processing. Therefore it has no knowledge on where to send the antimessage for the event e. As for the algorithm specifying the function $location()$, we do not want LP_x to collect information about the final location for the even e prior to sending the antimessage. This is due to both the overhead for information collection and the fact that this approach might excessively delay the send operation of the antimessage itself. Therefore, we have devised a cancellation scheme called Multicast Cancellation (MC), according to which LP_x multicasts the antimessage for the event e to all the LPs defined as potential locations for the event e.

The pseudo-code for MC is shown in Figure 3, where the notation m^- is used to specify we are sending an antimessage, i.e. a negative message. With MC we expect to promptly catch and annihilate the event e that needs to be cancelled, this is because all the possible destinations are notified about the need for cancellation at once. Therefore we do favor the potential to annihilate the event e prior it is really executed. On the other hand, with this scheme we need to send $|\tau(e).\Pi|$ antimessages for each event e to be cancelled. However, we argue that the communication overhead due to multicasting can be kept low in any case the cardinality of $\tau(e).\Pi$ is relatively low. Also, the number of real send operations might be reduced in case proper solutions for multicasting can be included within the simulation system. This might be the case of the kernel based approach mentioned in the previous section, since sending a set of antimessages to LPs controlled by the same dispatcher thread (DT) could actually be implemented by sending a single antimessage to that DT, indicating the identities of all the receivers. Also, if the communication layer provides facilities for efficiently multicasting information, then MC could actually be implemented through a multicast send operation with adequate specification of the multicast group. We note that MC simply specifies where to send the antimessages in case we deal with spatial uncertainty resolved through RINAC. However it does not indicate when the send operation should occur. This means that MC can be coupled with either lazy or aggressive policies for the definition of the time instant for the send operation of antimessages [7].

Actually when dealing with MC, there is the possibility that the antimessage $m^-[e]$ arrives at the LP, say LP_y, that finally accepts the event e before the arrival of the corresponding positive message $m[e, visited]$. This is because the message $m[e, visited]$ can be delivered to LP_y through the forwarding scheme after the delivery of $m^-[e]$. However, this is not a problem since classical optimistic synchronization admits the possibility for an antimessage to arrive before the corresponding message (e.g. for example due to non-FIFO message delivery between LPs). In this case the antimessage is simply kept within a queue of pending antimessages. It will eventually annihilate the corresponding message upon its arrival.

The real problem with MC is that the event e is accepted by a single LP, while all the LPs that are potential destinations for the event e receive the antimessage $m^-[e]$. Therefore we obtain annihilation between m and m^- on a single LP, while on all the other LPs the antimessage $m^-[e]$ remains pending. This creates problems in case the event e, after being cancelled, is re-scheduled. In this case there is the possibility that a new instance of the message $m[e, visited]$ arrives at an LP that accepts the event, but that holds a copy of a pending antimessage $m^-[e]$. In this case, the new instance of the event e is cancelled via an antimessage destined for cancellation of the previous instance. Therefore we obtain that the event disappears from the system, which obviously means incorrect execution of the simulation model. To avoid this problem we can piggyback on each notification message for an event e a serial number, established by the LP that scheduled the event e, which uniquely identifies that message, i.e. that instance of the event, in the system . At the same time, all the antimessages multicasted for catching a given message should carry that same serial number, so that annihilation occurs only in case the serial numbers on m and m^- coincide at the LP that accepted the event. With this solution we avoid cancelling an event via an antimessage destined for cancellation of a previous instance of that same event, thus no event disappears in the system.

We note that an antimessage $m^-[e]$ remaining pending at an LP due to the fact that the event carried by the corresponding message $m[e, visited]$ is not accepted/delivered by/to that LP, can be eventually discarded just while executing fossil collection procedures. Specifically, upon computation of Global Virtual Time (GVT), $m^-[e]$ can be discarded in case the GVT value is larger than $\tau(e).timestamp$. Therefore the storage usage due to pending antimessages that will not eventually match with the corresponding positive message can be run-time controlled via classical fossil collection mechanisms.

4 An Experimental Study

In this section we report the results of an experimental study carried out using a Personal Communication System (PCS) simulation application as a test-bed. In this study, we would like to verify whether spatial uncertainty, exploited through RINAC, is able to really provide a more flexible approach to synchronization, with respect to classical optimistic synchronization, thus giving rise to better run-time behavior of the simulation system. On the other hand, we also would like to observe whether the simulation model with space uncertain events provides performance indices for the PCS system (e.g. call-block frequency) that exhibit no significant error with respect to the values that can be obtained in case of no uncertainty in the model when considering the same amount of events simulated by the simulation system. In other words, we would like to observe the impact of spatial uncertainty on the accuracy of the simulation results that are produced. The remainder of this section is organized as follows. We first provide details on the testing environment we have used. Then we present the simulation model and the performance metrics we have selected. Finally, we report the obtained results.

4.1 Testing Environment

The experiments were all performed on a myrinet cluster of 4 Pentium III 866 MHz (256 Mbytes RAM). All the PCs of the cluster run LINUX (kernel version 2.2.15) and are equipped with M3M-PCI64C myrinet cards employing LANai 9 technology. CCL v3.0 [12] has been used to support message passing. Message exchange among LPs hosted by the same machine does not involve operations of the CCL layer. We make use of the kernel approach to implement the core functionalities of the simulation system, therefore each LP is implemented as an application-level thread and there is an instance of an optimistic simulation engine, namely the dispatcher thread (DT), on each machine. DT manages the local event list (resulting as the logical collection of the event lists of the local LPs) and schedules LPs for event execution according to the standard Smallest-Timestamp-First algorithm [10]. Dynamic memory allocation/release based on standard `malloc()/free()` calls is adopted for the entries of the event lists. Checkpointing is performed for any LP before the execution of each new event by exploiting functionalities provided by CCL. GVT calculation and fossil collection are executed periodically. Finally, antimessages are sent on an aggressive basis. Also, in case of MC, one antimessage for each potential receiver LP of the event to be cancelled is sent, therefore no specific optimization has been implemented while supporting this type of cancellation.

4.2 Simulation Model

In a PCS system, base stations provide communication services to mobile units. In our simulation model the service area is partitioned into cells, each modeled by a distinct LP. A cell represents a receiver/transmitter having some fixed number of channels allocated to it. The model is call-initiated [5] since it only simulates the behavior of a mobile unit during conversation, i.e. the movement of a mobile unit is not tracked unless the unit itself is in conversation. Therefore, the model is organized around two entities, namely cells and calls. Call requests arrive to each cell according to an exponential distribution [3, 4, 5] with inter-arrival time t_{int} seconds. All the calls initiated within a given cell are originated by the LP associated with that cell, therefore no external call generator is used. The state vector of any LP records statistics, information about busy channels and, for each channel, information about features of the mobile unit involved in the ongoing call (e.g. scheduled call termination time, call initiation time, class of the mobile unit etc.), if any. As a result, the size of the state vector depends on the amount of channels associated with the cell. We have selected a model with 100 channels per cell, which gives rise to LP state vector size of about 4 Kbytes.

There are three types of events, namely hand-off, due to mobile unit cell switch, call termination and call arrival. A call termination simply involves the release of the associated channel, whose identifier is maintained into the event compound structure, and statistics update. A call arrival checks if there is at least an available channel. In the negative instance, the incoming call is simply counted as a block, otherwise an available channel is allocated for the call. When a hand-off occurs between adjacent cells, the hand-off event at the cell left by the mobile involves the release of the channel and statistics update. Similarly, the hand-off event at the destination cell checks for channel availability, and allocates an available channel, if any, for the call. If there is no available channel, then the call is simply cut off (dropped). In our model there are two distinct classes of mobile units. Both of them are characterized by residence time within a cell which follows an exponential distribution [3], with mean 3 minutes (fast movement units) and 30 minutes (slow movement units), respectively. The average holding time for each call associated with both fast and slow movement units is 2 minutes. When a call arrives at a cell, the type (slow or fast) of the mobile unit associated with the incoming call is selected from a uniform distribution, therefore any call is equally likely to be destined to a fast or a slow movement mobile unit.

Cells are modeled as hexagons, therefore all the cells, except bordering cells of the coverage area, have six neighbors. In the experimental study we have varied the model size (i.e. the amount of cells, namely the amount of LPs) between 16 and 256, with even distribution of the LPs on the 4 machines of the cluster. Variation of the model size allows us to observe the simulation system behavior while varying the degree of parallelism in the model execution which, in its turn, typically gives rise to different rollback patterns. We have set the expected call inter-arrival time per cell t_{int} to 1.4 seconds, thus obtaining channel utilization factor of about 85%.

In this simulation model, a single type of events can be scheduled among distinct LPs, namely the hand-off events. Specifically, when the mobile involved in conversation switches out from a cell, the corresponding LP schedules a hand-off event for the destination cell. We use a classical random walk model for mobility [1], which means each mobile can switch out from a cell in any point along the border of the cell. However, on top of random walk we build an uncertainty segment that establishes a spatial region for the hand-off. More precisely, we establish through random walk the median point of a segment L that represents the whole spatial region where the hand-off can occur. We have varied the length of the segment L between 0% and 95% of the length of a single side of the hexagonal cell. The case of 0% means that the length of L is null, therefore we obtain an exact point for the hand-off, just defined according to classical random walk; in other words, we have a simulation model with no spatial uncertainty since the destination cell (i.e. the destination LP) for the hand-off is precisely defined. Instead, for non-null values of the length of L we have a model in which there might be uncertainty on the destination cell for the hand-off. Specifically, there might be two possible destinations. Obviously, the larger L, the higher the likelihood that the hand-off is uncertain in space

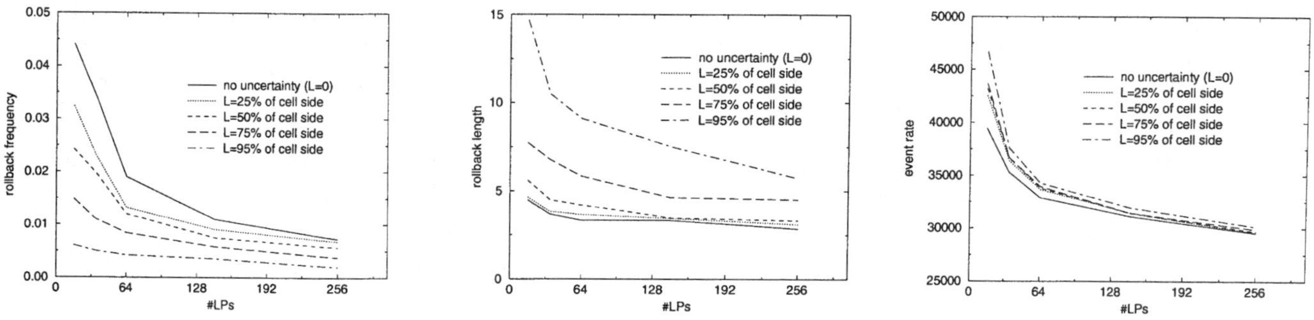

Figure 4. Performance of the Simulation System.

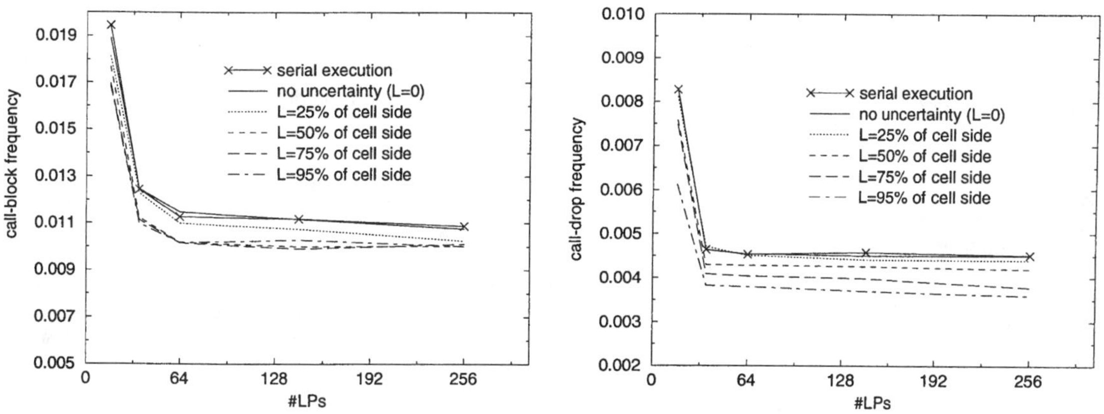

Figure 5. Statistics Related to the PCS.

due to the fact that two different cells might accept the mobile. Therefore, increasing L actually means studying the system behavior while the amount of uncertain events increases. Actually, the upper value for L we consider, i.e. 95% of the length of the side of the hexagonal cell, originates a situation in which a hand-off event has two possible destinations with probability 0.95. In other words, for that value of L, the large majority of hand-off events are space uncertain. As a final preliminary observation, each time the hand-off has two possible destinations due to the fact that the segment L covers a portion of the border that is adjacent to two different cells, then the first LP visited by the forwarding scheme in RINAC is the one associated with the cell touched by the median point of the segment L.

4.3 Performance Metrics

As already pointed out, when dealing with spatial uncertainty we are interested in considering two different effects. One is the possible improvement in the run-time behavior of the simulation system (in our case through RINAC), the other one is the effect of the uncertainty on proper statistics related to the simulated system, namely the PCS. We consider both these effects.

As respect to performance metrics for the simulation system, we report measures related to the event rate, classically evaluated as the amount of committed simulation events per second, which is an indicator of the speed of the model execution. We also report values related to the rollback frequency (classically evaluated as the ratio between the number of rollbacks and the number of executed simulation events) and the rollback length (classically evaluated as the average number or rolled back events at each rollback occurrence), which are indicators of the amount of rollback experienced during the execution. Specifically, the amount of rollback is typically expressed as the product pr between the rollback frequency and rollback length, and this product measures the probability for whichever executed event to be eventually rolled back. The quantity $1 - pr$ is a metric referred to as the efficiency of the simulation model execution. It indicates the probability to carry out productive simulation work, i.e. to execute events that are not eventually rolled back. We report data related to rollback frequency and rollback length just because we want to observe whether possible variations in the execution speed due to spatial uncertainty derive from variations in the rollback pattern (e.g. a reduction in the amount of rollback). As respect to proper statistics of the PCS, we report observed values for both the frequency of call-block and the frequency of call-drop, which are two classical parameters characterizing any PCS. Each reported value is computed as the average over 5 runs, all done with different seeds for the pseudo-random generation. At least 2×10^6 simulation events have been committed in each run.

4.4 Results

The obtained results related to the performance of the simulation system are reported in Figure 4. By the plots we obtain that spatial uncertainty exploited through RINAC is able to strongly reduce the frequency of rollback occurrence as compared to the case of no spatial uncertainty, i.e. the case of $L = 0$ ([3]). Also, a greater reduction of the rollback frequency is observed in case of larger values for L. This is an expected behavior when considering that larger values for L mean higher likelihood for the hand-off event to be addressable to two distinct LPs. Therefore, increasing L actually means increasing the percentage of hand-off events that can be forwarded to the second chance LP through RINAC in case they cannot be accepted by the first chance LP without the need for rollback. As an extreme, when $L = 95\%$ of the length of the cell side, we have a reduction of the frequency of rollback on the order of up to 86%. On the other hand, we note that the reduction of the rollback frequency is non-negligible (it is between 26% and 44%) even for lower values of L, namely values between 25% and 50% of the length of the cell side.

As already discussed in Section 3.1, RINAC might delay the execution of rollback procedures in case no LP along the forwarding chain is encountered, which has simulation clock lower than the event timestamp. This delay, in its turn, might increase the length of rollback. However, this phenomenon does not seem to appear in the results. Specifically, the execution with spatial uncertainty exploited through RINAC does not exhibit significant increase of the rollback length for values of L up to 50% of the cell side. It exhibits increase of the rollback length only in case of very large values of L, namely 75%-95% of the length of the cell side. By this phenomenon we argue that the increase in the rollback length for this particular application is not primarily related to delay in the execution of rollback procedures possibly caused by the forwarding scheme underlying RINAC. Instead, it should be mainly due to the fact that when L is largely increased we get a very strong reduction of the rollback frequency, which means the simulation execution is becoming more "asynchronous". Therefore simulation clocks at LPs on different processors might slightly diverge, which, as expected, tends to negatively impact the rollback length. However, the increase in the rollback length is less relevant as respect to the reduction we obtain in the rollback frequency. Therefore, even for very large values of L, the amount of rollback in the execution gets lower than the one achieved with no spatial uncertainty. Direct effect of the combination of results for the rollback frequency and the rollback length is an increase in the execution speed, namely in the event rate, when spatial uncertainty is exploited. This increase is more evident for the case of larger values of L (due to the much larger reduction of the rollback frequency as compared to lower values), and when considering higher degree of parallelism in the model execution, namely a lower amount of LPs. Specifically, when the number of LPs is 16, we get an increase in the execution speed between 10% and 20%. This gain tends to decrease while increasing the number of LPs. However, we would like to note that the reduction of the gain in the execution speed when the number of LPs is increased (while keeping the same size of the underlying computing system) is not a flaw of RINAC. Instead, it is due to the fact that reducing the degree of parallelism leads to an execution with very low amount of rollback even in case of no uncertainty and classical optimistic synchronization, therefore the improvements in the run-time behavior achievable through spatial uncertainty and RINAC are necessarily limited.

Figure 5 reports statistics related to the PCS system. Actually, we have also reported the call-block and call-drop frequencies estimated through serial executions of this same simulation model. By the results we get that statistics obtained with values of L up to 50% of the length of the cell side are very close to those achieved with serial execution or with parallel execution with no spatial uncertainty (i.e. the case of parallel execution with $L = 0$). Specifically, call-block and call-drop frequencies obtained with L set up to 50% of the length of the cell side differ by no more than 10% from the values obtained with serial execution or parallel execution with no uncertainty. On the other hand, for larger values of L, those parameters show values that remain within the 20% of those achieved with serial execution or parallel execution with no uncertainty.

5 Summary

In this paper we have presented the notion of spatial uncertainty of simulation events, with an application to optimistic parallel/distributed simulation. As we have shown, spatial uncertainty allows more flexible synchronization, with consequent improvement in the run-time behavior of the simulation system. We have also shown that the numerical results obtained for a PCS simulation application with space uncertain events are relatively close to those obtained with no uncertainty when considering the same amount of committed simulation events.

References

[1] I. F. Akyildiz, Y. B. Lin, W. R. Lai, and R. J. Chen. A new random walk model for PCS networks. *IEEE Journal on Selected Areas in Communications*, 18(7):1254–1260, 2000.

[2] R. Beraldi and L. Nigro. A Time Warp based on temporal uncertainty. *Trans. of the Society for Modeling And Simulation*, 18(2):60–72, 2001.

[3] A. Boukerche, S. K. Das, A. Fabbri, and O. Yildz. Exploiting model independence for parallel PCS network simulation. In *Proceedings of the 13th Workshop on Parallel and Distributed Simulation*, pages 166–173. IEEE Computer Society, May 1999.

[4] C. D. Carothers, D. Bauer, and S. Pearce. ROSS: a high performance modular Time Warp system. In *Proceedings of the 14th Workshop on Parallel and Distributed Simulation*, pages 53–60. IEEE Computer Society, May 2000.

[5] C. D. Carothers, R. M. Fujimoto, and Y. B. Lin. A case study in simulating PCS networks using Time Warp. In *Proceedings of the 9th Workshop on Parallel and Distributed Simulation*, pages 87–94. IEEE Computer Society, June 1995.

[6] R. M. Fujimoto. Exploiting temporal uncertainty in parallel and distributed simulation. In *Proceedings of the 13th Workshop on Parallel and Distributed Simulation*, pages 46–53. IEEE Computer Society, May 1999.

[7] A. Gafni. Space management and cancellation mechanisms for Time Warp. *Tech. Rep. TR-85-341, University of Southern California, Los Angeles (Ca,USA)*, 1985.

[8] M. Hybinette and R. M. Fujimoto. Cloning parallel simulations. *ACM Trans. on Modeling and Computer Simulation*, 11(4):307–407, Oct. 2001.

[9] D. R. Jefferson. Virtual time. *ACM Trans. on Programming Languages and System*, 7(3):404–425, July 1985.

[10] Y. B. Lin and E. D. Lazowska. Processor scheduling for Time Warp parallel simulation. In *Advances in Parallel and Distributed Simulation*, pages 11–14, 1991.

[11] M. L. Loper and R. M. Fujimoto. Pre-sampling as an approach for exploiting temporal uncertainty. In *Proceedings of the 14th Workshop on Parallel and Distributed Simulation*, pages 157–164. IEEE Computer Society, May 2000.

[12] F. Quaglia and A. Santoro. CCL v3.0: Multiprogrammed semi-asynchronous checkpoints. In *Proceedings of the 17th Workshop on Parallel and Distributed Simulation*, pages 21–30. IEEE Computer Society, 2003.

[3]Recall that $L = 0$ means we have an exact point for the hand-off of the mobile. Therefore the destination cell, that is the destination LP, for the hand-off event is precisely defined.

Exploiting Symmetry for Partitioning Models in Parallel Discrete Event Simulation

Jan Lemeire[1], Bart Smets[1], Philippe Cara[2], Erik Dirkx[1]
[1]*Parallel Systems lab,* [2]*Department of Mathematics*
Vrije Universiteit Brussel (VUB)
Brussels, Belgium
Email: {jlemeire,bsmets,pcara,erik.dirkx}@vub.ac.be

Abstract

We investigated the benefit of exploiting the symmetries of graphs for partitioning. We represent the model to be simulated by a weighted graph. Graph symmetries are studied in the theory of permutation groups and can be calculated in polynomial time with the nauty algorithm [15]. We designed an algorithm to extract useful symmetries from the automorphism group, which can be used to create partitions derived from the graph's structure. Our approach is focused on composite graphs, for which identical subgraphs reoccur in the graph. If these identical subgraphs can be mapped onto each other by symmetries, the subgraphs are replaced by equivalent multivertices, resulting in a 'natural' aggregation of vertices. This approach is applied to parallel simulation of a detailed IP-switch with a conservative synchronous algorithm. The experimental results show that even for good partitions, global and temporal load imbalances are inevitable.

1. Introduction

We study the problem of finding good model partitions for Parallel Discrete Event Simulation (PDES). This problem is equivalent to graph partitioning, where the model is represented by a weighted graph. The weight of an edge represents its amount of communication and the weight of a node its amount of computation. Graph partitioning is an important problem that has extensive applications in many other areas, including scientific computing, VLSI design, data mining and grid applications. The goal is to partition the vertices of a graph in roughly p equal parts to balance the graph, such that it minimizes the number of edges connecting vertices in different parts. These are the edge-cuts, representing the communication between the different parts.

We investigated how symmetries can be used to partition the graph. This work started with the work Bart Smets [16]. Naturally, symmetry is not guaranteed and symmetric partitions are no guarantee for efficient partitions. However, models in PDES, like network or electronic components, are often highly structured. They often consist of reoccurring *components* with more communication inside the components then between them. These structural properties of the model result in what we called *composite graphs* and can be exploited to get an 'natural' partition.

1.1. Parallel Discrete Event Simulation

In *discrete event simulation,* the device under study is modeled by interconnected *logical processes,* in which state changes happen at discrete times by *events.*

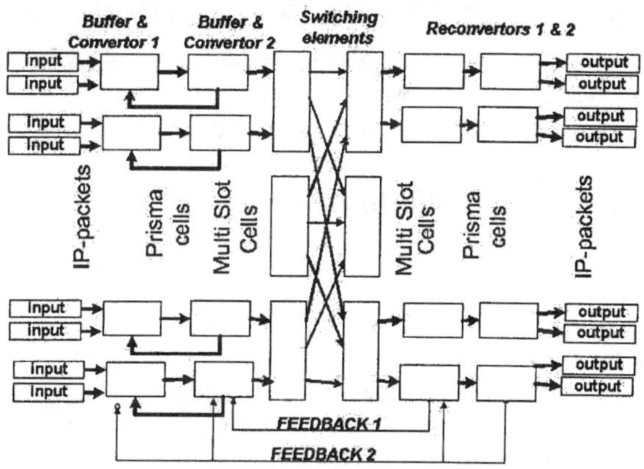

Figure 1. IP-switch model

Figure 1 shows the model of a detailed IP-switch [8], in which the IP-packets are first converted into prisma cells, then into multi-slot cells before going through the switching elements. After this, the original IP-packets are reconstructed and sent to the output. Feedback signals try to prevent packet loss due to congestion in the switching elements. Packets are therefore buffered into the input stages. The switch contains 32 inputs, resulting in more than 4000 processes.

In *Parallel Discrete Event Simulation* (PDES) [5,6] the model is partitioned among the available processors and simulated with a parallel algorithm that synchronises the

1087-4097/04 $20.00 © 2004 IEEE

different partitions. We will explain our approach with the simplified model of the switch (Figure 2), whereas the experimental results are gathered from the simulation of the detailed model.

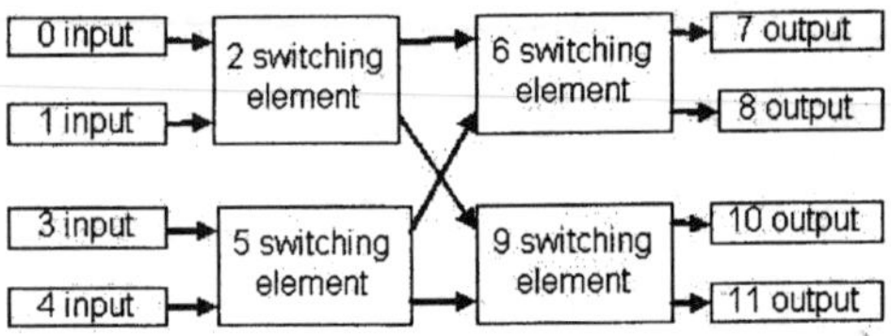

Figure 2. Simplified switch model

1.2. Related Work

The partitioning task is known to be NP-complete in general [7]. However, when the graph exhibits certain regularities, good partitions can be found in polynomial time. An example is METIS [13], a multilevel coarsening algorithm, in which highly interconnected nodes are successively grouped (step 1) to become a much smaller graph with lower partitioning complexity. After partitioning of the aggregated graph (step 2), the partitions are gradually refined when the multivertices are expanded to reconstruct the original graph (step 3). In [14], the assumptions on the graph for the success of the algorithm are analyzed.

Graph partitioning is defined in section 2 and graph symmetries in section 3. Section 4 discusses the symmetry tree that is used in section 5 for partitioning. Finally, section 6 shows the experimental results.

2. Graph Partitioning

A graph contains the relational information of an object. It is defined as a structure $G=<V, E>$ in which V is a finite set of *vertices* (or *nodes*) and $E \subset V \times V$ is a finite set of *edges* (unordered pairs or ordered pairs for a directed graph). Two vertices u and v are called *adjacent* if $(u,v) \in E$. A *weighted graph* associates a number $|v|$ to each vertex and a number $|e|$ to each edge.

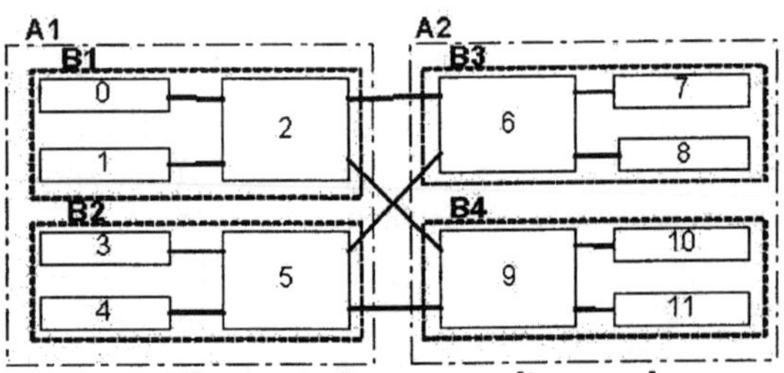

Figure 3. A composite graph

We define a *composite graph* is a graph that is composed of subgraphs that occur multiple times in the graph. Identical subgraphs can then be replaced by a single *multivertex*. Structured models often contain such subgraphs, as shown in Figure 3, in which nodes can be replaced by the multivertices A_1, B_1, etc. In fact, the vertices of Figure 3 are on their turn composed out of subgraphs of the detailed IP switch model of Figure 1. Furthermore, each process of Figure 1 can again be described in more detail, as shown in Figure 4, which is the detailed description of the buffer&convertor1 process of Figure 1. This is called the *level of abstraction* of the model. We study the graphs for which these subgraphs are symmetric. Note that we are now working with undirected graphs, since the direction of the communication is irrelevant for the partitioning.

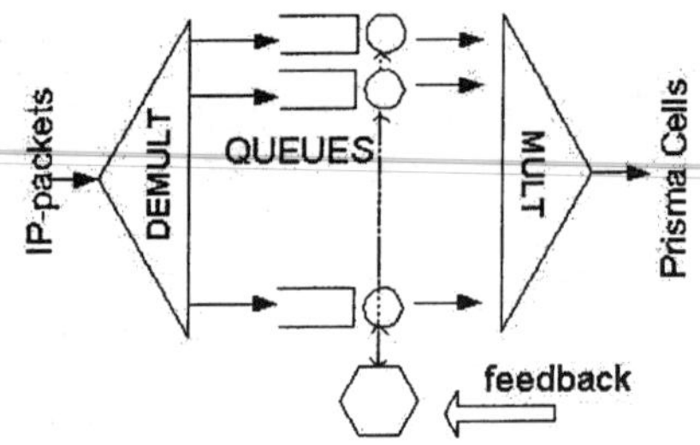

Figure 4. The buffer&convertor1 process in detail

Graph partitioning is defined as follow: given a graph $G=<V,E>$, partition V into p disjoint subsets V_1 ... V_p such that the following objectives are optimized:

1. The sum of the weights $|v|$ of all v of V_i for each i $(1...p)$ is the same.
2. The sum of the weights of the cut edges (edges for which the nodes belong to a different partition) is minimized.

3. Graph Symmetries

Symmetries are investigated in mathematics by Group Theory [12]. A *symmetry* of an object is defined as a transformation that leaves the essential features of the object unchanged [10]. The set of all symmetries of an object form a *group*. This means that symmetries can be composed, an identity transformation exists and each transformation has an inverse transformation.

A *graph symmetry* is a permutation f of the vertex set V that preserves adjacency:

$$\forall v_1, v_2 \in V : (v_1, v_2) \in E \Leftrightarrow (f(v_1), f(v_2)) \in E \quad (1)$$

The group of all such permutations together with composition is called the automorphism group *Aut(G)* of the graph [3]. A permutation is a bijective transformation. It can be described with the *cyclic notation*. For example, the permutation (a_1, a_2, a_3) carries a_1 to a_2, a_2 to a_3 and a_3 to a_1. The permutation $(a_1, a_2)(b_1, b_2)$ carries a_1 to a_2, a_2 to

a_1 and simultaneously b_1 to b_2 and b_2 to b_1. Some of the symmetries of the graph of Figure 2 are:

(0, 1)
(3, 4)
(0, 3) (1, 4) (2, 5)
(7 8)
(10 11)
(7 10)(8 11)(6 9)
(0 7)(1 8)(2 6)(3 10)(4 11)(5 9)

Note that all other symmetries can be composed out of these, therefore they are called a set of *generators* for *Aut(G)*.

An efficient and widely used algorithm for finding the symmetries in a graph is *nauty* [15, see also http://cs.anu.edu.au/~bdm/nauty]. The average performance is polynomial, with a degree no bigger than 4 and in practice less than 3 [15]. A handy tool for finding and manipulating graph symmetries, using the nauty algorithm, is GAP [http://www.gap-system.org].

We will analyze the symmetries in composite graphs. Note that reoccurring multivertices are called *isomorphic* subgraphs in group theory. We define a *multivertex symmetry* as a permutation that maps multivertices onto each other and preserves adjacency of these. It is clear that the multivertices of Figure 3 are symmetric. These multivertex symmetries are interesting for optimizing the partitioning task. Therefore we have to extract them from *Aut(G)* and describe them into a practicable representation.

4. The Composite Symmetry Tree

We represent the composite graph by a hierarchical tree of reoccurring multivertices, where each multivertex is refined in the next level. Figure 5 shows the composite symmetry tree of the switch in Figure 2. At each level, equivalent multivertices are represented by the same symbol, they are mutually interchangeable by a symmetry.

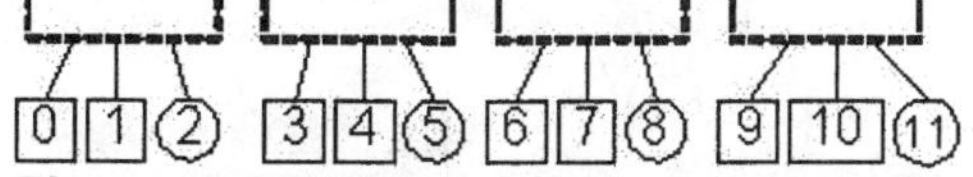

Figure 5. The composite symmetry tree of the simplified switch model

In the work of Smets [16], the definition of the tree is extended for *ring symmetries*. This is represented by connecting the nodes which are neighbors in the ring transformation.

4.1. Additional Definitions

For the construction of the tree, we need some concepts from the theory of permutation groups [9]. The *orbit* of a vertex $v \in V$ is defined as: $orb(v) = \{g(v): g \in Aut(G)\}$, the set of all vertices on which v can be mapped by the automorphisms of the graph. If a vertex $v' \in orb(v)$, then v is also an element of the $orb(v')$. In this way, the orbits partition the vertices of the graph into disjoint subsets (Figure 6).

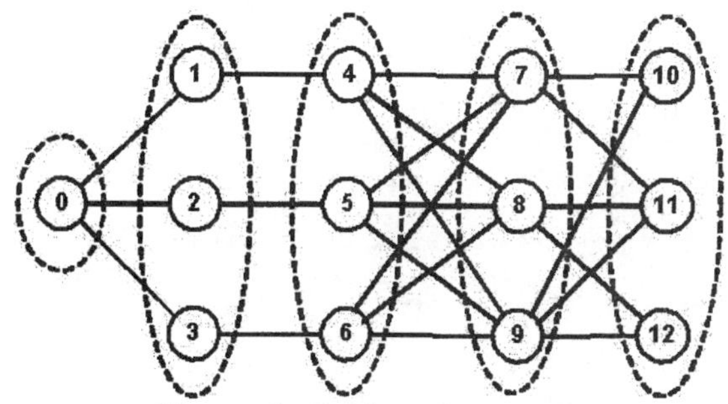

Figure 6. Orbits of a graph

The *stabilizer* of a subset *V'* of *V*, are the symmetries that keep all elements of *V'* unchanged:

$$Aut(G)_{V'} = \{g \in Aut(G) \mid \forall v \in V': g(v) = v)\} \quad (2)$$

A *block of imprimitivity* is a set of vertices $B \subseteq V$ for which:

$$\forall g, g' \in Aut(G): g.B = g'.B \;\; or \;\; g.B \cap g'.B = 0 \quad (3)$$

A block of imprimitivity is completely mapped onto itself by the symmetries *or* onto a disjoint set of vertices. The other set will necessarily also be blocks of imprimitivity. A *maximal block of imprimitivity* of a vertex set *V'* is an imprimitivity block $B \subset V'$ of maximal size, but non-trivial (*B*=*V'*). These concepts can be calculated by GAP/nauty.

4.2. Construction Algorithm

The intuitively defined symmetric components are clearly blocks of imprimitivity. We will however only aggregate vertices if an objective choice exists and if the number of connections between the different multivertices is low.

The principle of the algorithm is to aggregate vertices of different orbits. For the graph of Figure 6, the goal is to aggregate the vertices 1 and 4 into a multivertex, that is isomorphic to multivertices {2,5} and {3,6}. However, we will only group vertices that are adjacent to exactly one vertex of another orbit. In other cases, when all or multiple vertices of one orbit are connected to the same vertex, aggregation makes no sense. When all vertices are interconnected, as for 2, 5 and 8 with 0, and {4,5,6} with {7,8,9} in Figure 6, both orbits can permute independently and there is no objective reason to group vertices. If only some, but more than one, vertices are adjacent, as for the vertices of orbit {7,8,9} with orbit {10,11,12} in Figure 6, vertices of both orbits cannot transform independently. By permuting some of the vertices of one orbit, some of the other should also permute. Then, there are multiple equivalent choices in grouping the vertices of the different orbits. Moreover, grouping such vertices would cause a lot of communication between the multivertices. Hence, we will also not aggregate vertices in such cases.

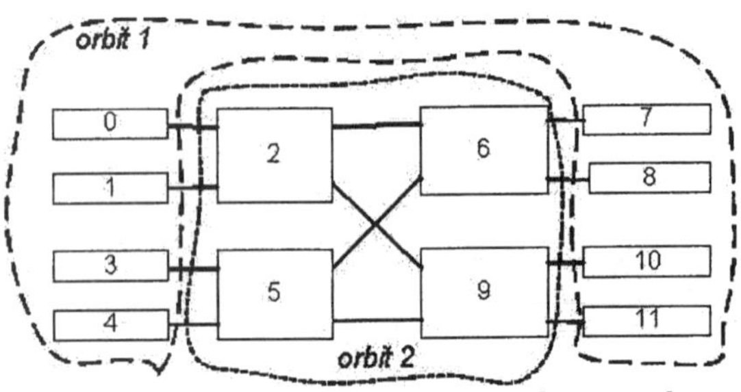

Figure 7. Orbits of a composite graph

For complex composite graphs, a 'hierarchy' can be identified inside orbits, as in Figure 7. To apply the aggregation method, we should start with grouping the *maximal imprimitivity blocks* of the orbits, shown in Figure 8. By applying the above algorithm, block *1a* can be aggregated with block *2a*, and block *1b* with *2b*. They form the top-level components A_1 and A_2 of the symmetry tree of Figure 5.

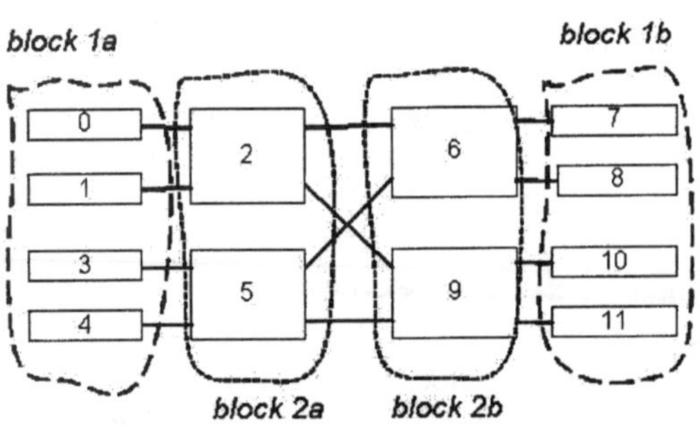

Figure 8. Maximal blocks of imprimitivity of the orbits

The symmetry tree is recursively built in a top-down way. For deeper investigation of the symmetries of a multivertex, all other multivertices are *stabilized*. The new automorphism group $Aut'(G)_{V'}$ is then used to find the subcomponents with the same aggregation method. Since components are isomorphic, all subcomponents found in one component also appear in the other components. Applied onto the graph of the switch (Figure 3), the symmetric supervertices A_1 and A_2 can be refined into B_1, B_2, B_3 and B_4. This gives us the desired symmetry tree of Figure 5.

4.3. Performance

The experimental performance results on a 1.8GHz Pentium 4 processor are shown in Table 1. We compared the processing time of the algorithm for a random graph, the simplified switch of Figure 2 and the detailed switch of Figure 1, for a varying number of vertices.

Table 1. Processing time (in *seconds*) of symmetry tree construction in function of the number of vertices

#vertices	1000	2000	3000	4000
Random graph	0.014	0.091	0.165	0.242
Simplified switch	9.35	132	480	1331
Detailed switch	8.87	116	413	983

It is known that nauty quickly detects that graphs have few symmetries, namely in polynomial time of degree 2 [15]. This is confirmed by the experiments that give a quadratic processing time for a random graph without symmetries. For the simplified and detailed switch we get a third degree polynomial dependency.

5. Exploiting the Symmetry Tree for Partitioning

With the Composite Symmetry Tree, proposals for graph partitions can easily be extracted. The simplified switch can be partitioned along 2 axes, as shown in Figures 9 and 10. A switch with more inputs will have axes parallel with Ax 2 and partitioning along these axes will give good results.

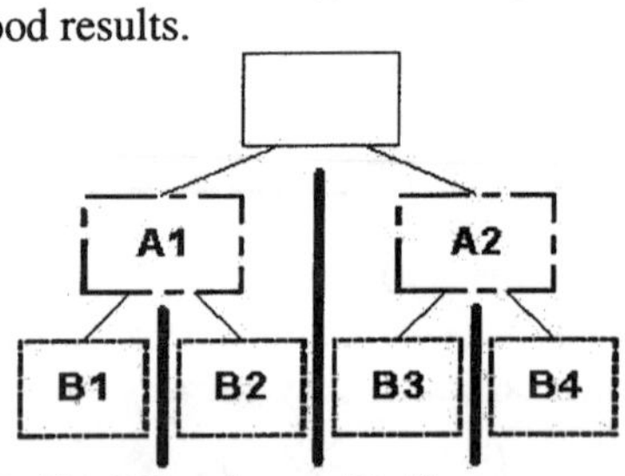

Figure 9. Partitioning with the symmetry tree

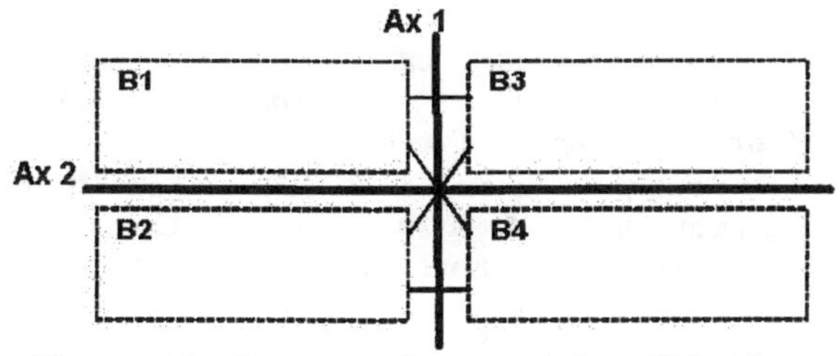

Figure 10. The resulting model partitioning

The partitions result from the structure of the graph, so it is a kind of 'natural' partitioning. The symmetries guarantee an equal distribution of the workload and by construction, the communication is minimized.

Note that the approach resembles the aggregation method of METIS and is a kind of 'natural' aggregation of the vertices according to symmetries.

6. Simulation of IP Switch

The illustrating experiment is the simulation of the detailed IP-switch [8] of Figure 1 on a cluster of 8 Pentium II processors of 333MHz connected by a 100Mb/s non-blocking switch. For parallel simulation, we use a conservative synchronous algorithm [1], based on the time window algorithms [5]. It consists of cycles of independent simulation on each processor, alternated with synchronization between the different processors by communicating the events traveling through the cut-edges. The cycle length or window size equals the *lookahead*.

Table 2. Experimental results for the parallel overheads

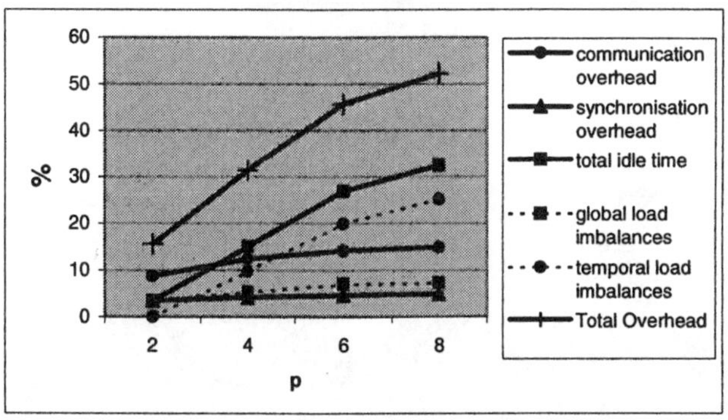

The switch has 32 in- and output channels and is fed with random TCP/IP traffic according to a normal distribution. It puts an average load of 62% on the switching elements. It is partitioned along the horizontal symmetry axes (parallel with Ax 2 in Figure 10). The experimental results in function of the number of processors are shown in Table 2. The values for the speedups are 1.7 for *p*=2, 3.0 for *p=4*, 4.1 for *p=6* and 5.2 for *p*=8.

The parallel simulation time with 6 processors of 1s real time was 1683s, resulting in a speedup of 4.06. The total overhead of 45.6% of the parallel runtime was mainly caused by communication overhead overlapping with computation (14.1%) and load imbalances (26.9%). The synchronization overhead of our algorithm only took 4.6% of the parallel runtime. The relatively high communication overhead is caused by the packets traveling through the edge-cuts. This intercommunication is unavoidable. On the other hand, the high load imbalances suggest a bad partitioning, but this is not the case. The total idle time T_{idle} is measured as the sum over all cycles that the processors have to wait for the slowest processor, since the simulation happens synchronously in cycles:

$$T_{idle} = T_{gli} + T_{tli} = p. \sum_{k \in cycles} (SimT^k_{\max} - SimT^k_{avg}) \quad (4)$$

where $SimT^k$ is the simulation time of cycle *k,* the maximal and average respectively. We identify 2 different types of load imbalances that cause idling: the *global* and *temporal load imbalances*. The global load imbalance T_{gli} is caused by unequal total simulation time *TotalSimT* between the processors:

$$T_{gli} = p.(TotalSimT_{\max} - TotalSimT_{avg}) \quad (5)$$

The temporal load imbalances T_{tli} on the other hand, are caused by fluctuations of the load imbalances between the different cycles and can be calculated as follow:

$$T_{tli} = T_{idle} - T_{gli} \quad (6)$$

The slowest processor that causes the idle time at each synchronization point can differ from cycle to cycle. The resulting global load imbalance, which is an average of the load imbalance over all cycles, can thus be low (here: 7%), whereas temporal fluctuations are generating a much higher idling of the processors (here:19.9%).

Since our model is completely symmetric, with the same average, but stochastic, load in each of the symmetric components, no better partitioning is available. However, the deviation from the average load leads to a global imbalance and load fluctuations generate high temporal imbalances as an effect of using a synchronous parallel simulation algorithm. Table 2 shows how the temporal imbalances increase rapidly with the number of processors and cause the main limitation on the growth of the speedup.

7. Conclusions

We argued that if a graph has symmetries, these should be exploited for partitioning. We constructed an algorithm that uses the theory of permutation groups to find *multivertex symmetries* in composite graphs. These useful symmetries are represented in a *symmetry tree*, from which proposals for partitions can easily be constructed. The application of this approach to our highly structured models yields promising results.

We want to extend the algorithm to other types of symmetries and to quasi-symmetries. Moreover, symmetrical properties are useful in reducing the complexity of algorithms in general and should be reflected in the visualization of such models and their graphs.

8. References

[1] W. Brissinck, "Tuneable Granularity Parallel Discrete Simulation." *PhD thesis*, Vrije Universiteit Brussel, Brussels, May 1999.

[2] R.E. Bryant, "Simulation of Packet Communications Architecture Computer Systems." *Technical Report* MIT-LCS-TR-188, Massachusetts Institute of Technology, 1977.

[3] Peter J. Cameron, "Automorphisms of Graphs", Queen Mary University of London, 2001.

[4] K.M. Chandy and J. Misra, "Distributed Simulation: A Case Study in Design and Verification of Distributed Programs", *IEEE Trans. on Softw. Eng.* SE-5, 5 , 440-452, Sept 1997.

[5] A. Ferscha, "Parallel and Distributed Simulation of Discrete Event Systems", *Handbook of Parallel and Distributed Computing,* McGraw-Hill, 1995.

[6] R.M. Fujimoto, "Parallel Discrete Event Simulation", *Communications of the ACM*, 33, pp 29-53, Oct 1990.

[7] M. Garey, D. Johnson and L. Stockmeyer, "Some simplified NP-complete graph problems", *Theoretical Computer Science*, 1976.

[8] S. Geudens, "Quantitative Study of a Highly Formant Network Switch with Distributed Simulation", *Master Thesis*, Vrije Universiteit Brussel, Brussels, 2000.

[9] M. Jr. Hall, "The Theory of Groups", Macmillan, New York, 1976.

[10] R. Howlett, "Aspects of Symmetry", *Lecture Notes*, Sydney (http://www.maths.usyd.edu.au:8000/u/bobh/2gwhole.pdf).

[11] G. Israel and M. Wilhelm, "Groups and Their Graphs", The Mathematical Asociation of America,1965

[12] John F. Humphreys, "A Course in Group Theory", Oxford University Press, 1996.

[13] G. Karypis and V. Kumar, "A Fast and High Quality Multilevel Scheme for Partitioning Irregular Graphs", *Technical Report* 95-035, Dept. Computer Science, Univ. Minnesota, Minneapolis, Minnesota, 1995.

[14] G. Karypis and V. Kumar, "Analysis of Multilevel Graph Partitioning". *Proceedings of Supercomputing'95*, San Diego, 1995.

[15] B. McKay, "Practical Graph Isomorphism", *Congressus Numerantium* 30, 45-87, 1981.

[16] B. Smets, "Symmetrie-onderzoek van Graffen", *Master thesis*, Vrije Universiteit Brussel, Brussels, 2003.

Time-Parallel Simulation with Approximative State Matching

Tobias Kiesling[1], Siegfried Pohl[2]
Fakultät für Informatik[1], *ITIS e.V.*[2]
Universität der Bundeswehr München
85577 Neubiberg, Germany
{kiesling,pohl}@informatik.unibw-muenchen.de

Abstract

Time-parallel simulation offers the potential of massive parallelization of a simulation application, due to the amount of achievable parallelism not being restricted by the decomposability of the state space of a simulation model. Unfortunately, the potential speedup of a time-parallel simulation highly depends on the ability to match final and initial states of adjacent time intervals. Depending on the properties of the underlying simulation model, it might be feasible to accept a simulation iteration, even if the states of adjacent time intervals do not match exactly. This leads to the concept of approximative state matching in time-parallel simulation, which is introduced in this paper. Experiments with a prototypical implementation of a simple simulation model show encouraging results in terms of simulation speedup and introduced error.

1. Introduction

In traditional parallel discrete-event simulation [2] the set of state variables of a simulation model is decomposed into subsets. Each of these is assigned to a logical process that manages the corresponding part of the global state. The drawbacks of this approach are the introduction of an overhead for the synchronization between logical processes and the limited amount of achievable parallelism, which is restricted by the number of state variables and the decomposability of states in the model. Time-parallel simulation takes a different approach by partitioning the time axis of an intended simulation execution and performing the simulation of the resulting time intervals in parallel [1]. Afterwards, the results of all intervals are combined to create the overall simulation result. This has the potential for massive parallelism, as the maximum number of logical processes is determined by the number of possible time intervals, which is only restricted by the granularity of the time representation in the simulation implementation.

However, without further mechanisms, the final and initial states of adjacent time intervals do not necessarily coincide at the interval boundaries, leading to incorrect state changes. A straightforward approach to handle this problem is to reexecute the simulations of those intervals that started from an initial state inconsistent with the final state of the previous interval. Of course, the effective speedup of the parallel simulation quickly decreases with every additional simulation run of the same time interval.

Several different methods for reducing the cost of achieving state consistency between time intervals have been proposed. [7] introduces the notion of regeneration points which are states that keep reoccuring throughout a simulation execution. If these points are known a priori, a number of simulations can be executed concurrently, starting from a regeneration point and continuing until the regeneration point is reached again. Afterwards, the traces of the parallel simulations are concatenated to get a correct trace of the simulation over the whole time period. [6] uses fix-up computations to correct the simulations of those time intervals that are known to have started from incorrect states. For the specific application of simulating cache accesses presented in [6], it is possible to perform these computations without completely repeating the simulation of the incorrect time intervals. [5] reduces the problem of simulation of certain kinds of queuing networks to recurrence relations that can be solved on massively parallel computers.

The approaches mentioned above guarantee correct results in the sense that the states of adjacent time intervals always match at the interval boundary (resp., are corrected, if they do not match). The alternative approach proposed in this paper is to allow a deviation of states at the interval boundary according to predefined rules. An obvious drawback of this approach is the error introduced by the approximate state matching. It must be considered that this error might even invalidate simulation results. However, for many simulation models (e. g. queuing networks), small errors in state changes occuring infrequently do not signifi-

1087-4097/04 $20.00 © 2004 IEEE

cantly influence simulation results.

[12] utilizes the concept of unmatched sets to weaken the state-match problem. There, two system states partially match, if a subset of the state variables match. The *unmatched set* comprises the rest of the variables. The efficiency of a time-parallel simulation execution can be raised by artificially fixing the unmatched variables (of a simulation iteration), in order to remove them from the unmatched set. [12] further elaborates on two sophisticated algorithms for the simulation of G/G/1/K and G/D/1/K queues.

There are also approaches in traditional space-parallel simulation which accept an error introduced by the simulation algorithm in order to reduce the overhead for synchronization between processes, e. g. [8] [10] [11] [3].

The challenge of the approach introduced here is to determine the rules for the allowed deviation of states for a given simulation model, such that the efficiency of the parallel simulation is maximized, while the introduced error stays below an acceptable level.

The rest of the paper is organized as follows. Section 2 presents the concept of approximative state matching in time-parallel simulation. A prototypical implementation is discussed in Section 3. Section 4 contains the results of experiments conducted for a simple simulation model. Finally, Section 5 concludes the work.

2. Time-parallel simulation with approximative state matching

As already outlined in the last section, time-parallel simulation is a parallel simulation approach, which is not restricted by the decomposability of the simulation model. However, the state-match problem, i. e. the problem of inconsistent final and initial states of adjacent time intervals, renders time-parallel simulation for many models almost useless. This is especially true for classes of models which exhibit complex states. Therefore, the concept of approximate state matching is proposed here as an efficient solution to the problem.

2.1. Time-parallel simulation

According to [4], a discrete event simulation essentially consists of the *state variables*, which establish the state space, the *event list*, which contains the events to happen in the future of the simulation, and the *simulation clock*.

To conduct a discrete event simulation in a parallel or distributed way, one possibility is to decompose the space-time diagram depicted in Figure 1 horizontally, in order to partition the set of state variables.

In time-parallel simulation, the space-time diagram is partitioned vertically, i. e. every logical process manages all state variables, but only for a limited time interval.

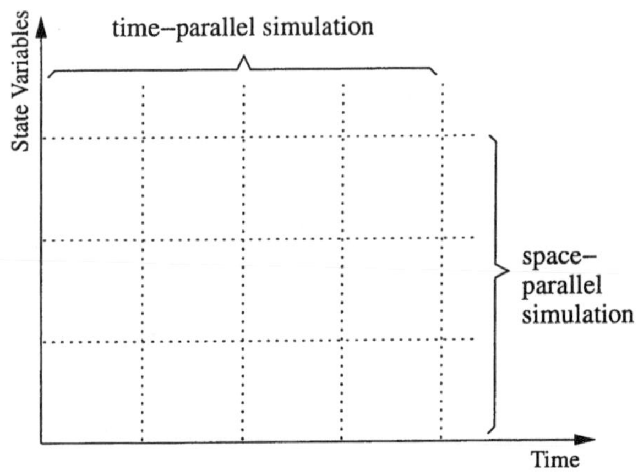

Figure 1. Space-time diagram of a simulation

Let $T := [0,t]$ be the interval of the whole simulation time. T is partitioned into the *time intervals*

$$
\begin{aligned}
T_1 &:= [t_1, t_2], \\
&\vdots \\
T_m &:= [t_m, t_{m+1}],
\end{aligned}
$$

with $t_1 = 0$ and $t_2, \ldots, t_m \in (0,t)$ and $t_{m+1} = t$, such that every point in the simulated time is contained in some interval and the intervals overlap only at the interval boundaries, which are the times $t_2, \ldots, t_m$.

For performing the simulations of time intervals in parallel, each interval has to start the simulation from some *initial state* $\hat{s}$. At the beginning of the simulation only the initial state of T_1 is known. For every other interval T_k, with $k \in \{2, \ldots m\}$, the initial state $\hat{s}_k$ has to be guessed. After the simulation of an interval T_k has been executed, the *final state* $\check{s}_k$ of T_k is known. As the simulations of different intervals are supposed to be executed in parallel, there is no guarantee that the final and initial states of adjacent intervals match, i. e. it is possible that $\check{s}_{k-1} \neq \hat{s}_k$ for interval T_k. This property of time-parallel simulation is known as the *state-match problem* [4].

Every time-parallel simulation algorithm must assure that the state-match problem is solved in order to perform a correct simulation of the whole simulation time. A straightforward approach is to reexecute the simulation of each time interval whose initial state deviates from the final state of the previous interval. However, without a successful strategy of guessing initial states, the repeated simulation of intervals leads to a degeneration of the efficiency.

2.2. Approximative state matching

In many cases, where final and initial states of adjacent time intervals deviate by a marginal amount, it might be feasible to accept the simulation of an interval even if this produces incorrect simulation results.

Allowed deviation The *allowed deviation* $\mathcal{AD}(s)$ of the state s is a subset of the state space $\mathcal{S}$, such that changing the state of the simulation from s to $s' \in \mathcal{AD}(s)$ is accepted, even if it does not correspond to a valid state change defined in the model.

Reasonable implementations of $\mathcal{AD}(s)$ can only be defined for a particular model, e. g. in a simulation of a G/G/1 queue, abrupt changes in the number of jobs waiting to be served can be accepted, as long as they do not influence the results of the simulation significantly. For a given model, $\mathcal{AD}(s)$ can be determined analytically or empirically, or it can already be defined by the modeler.

Approximative state matching The function $\mathcal{AD}$ is used to implement the concept of approximative state matching. Instead of performing an exact match of final and initial states at the time-interval boundaries of a time-parallel simulation, a simulation run of an interval T_k is accepted if the initial state of T_k is within the allowed deviation of the final state of interval T_{k-1}, i. e. $\hat{s}_k \in \mathcal{AD}(\check{s}_{k-1})$.

In Figure 2 the scenario is explained in detail: a simulation execution of time interval T_k started with an initial state $\hat{s}_k$. When the simulation of the previous interval T_{k-1} completes, it is found that $\hat{s}_k$ is an incorrect state, since it does not exactly match the final state $\check{s}_{k-1}$ of the simulation of T_{k-1}. Nevertheless, the simulation of T_k is accepted, due to $\hat{s}_k \in \mathcal{AD}(\check{s}_{k-1})$.

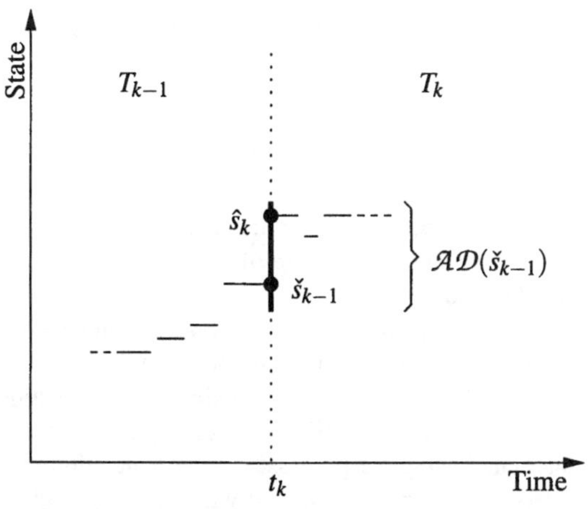

Figure 2. Approximative state matching

A simple algorithm for a time parallel simulation with approximative state matching is given in Figure 3. As the algorithm describes a parallel simulation approach, a notation inspired by the Occam programming language [9] is used to denote parallel execution of statements. The designator

for all <list> **do in parallel** <statement> **end for**

indicates that the enclosed statement is executed in parallel for every element in <list>.

Input: $T_1, \ldots, T_m, \hat{s}_1, \ldots \hat{s}_m$
Output: $\check{s}_m$
$S := \{1, \ldots, m\}$
repeat
  for all $k \in S$ **do in parallel**
    simulate time interval T_k with initial state $\hat{s}_k$
  end for
  $S := \{k \in \{2, \ldots, m\} \mid \hat{s}_k \notin \mathcal{AD}(\check{s}_{k-1})\}$
  for all $k \in S$ **do**
    $\hat{s}_k := \check{s}_{k-1}$
  end for
until $S = \emptyset$

Figure 3. Iterative time-parallel simulation algorithm

In the algorithm presented in Figure 3, parallel simulation of the time intervals is performed in iterations until the initial state of every interval is within the allowed deviation of the final state of the previous interval. Intervals to be simulated during a simulation iteration are recorded by a set S. After each iteration, S is set to those intervals, whose initial states do not approximately match the final states of the previous intervals. The initial states of intervals in S are reset to the final states of the previous intervals and the simulations of intervals in S are reexecuted.

Note that the overhead of this parallel simulation algorithm is determined by the search for intervals where $\hat{s}_k \notin \mathcal{AD}(\check{s}_{k-1})$, which can be implemented in an efficient way.

The algorithm directly shows the importance of the allowed deviation for the efficiency of the algorithm. The average number of repetitions of the simulations can be minimized by lowering the probability of $\hat{s}_k \notin \mathcal{AD}(\check{s}_{k-1})$. At worst, $\mathcal{AD}(\check{s}_{k-1}) = \check{s}_{k-1}$, in which case the algorithm is identical to the simple time-parallel simulation without approximate state matching. At best, with $\mathcal{S}$ representing the state space, $\mathcal{AD}(\check{s}_{k-1}) = \mathcal{S}$ is the trivial case where only one parallel run of the simulation is needed.

However, the increase in efficiency comes at the cost of an error that is introduced with the approximative state matching. Depending on the properties of the simulations, an incorrect initial state of a time interval T_k might propagate through the intervals T_{k+1} to T_m and influence the results of the whole simulation. If the simulated model has recurring states that keep occuring throughout a simulation execution, chances are good that an error does not propagate too far, influencing simulation results only marginally, or not at all. Therefore, the viability of the approach of approximate state matching depends on the specificities of the underlying model.

2.3. Regeneration points

The approach introduced above uses approximation with fix-up computations to solve the state-match problem. However, the allowed deviation function can also be used with the regeneration-point-based approach of [7].

As introduced in Section 1, a regeneration point is a state that keeps reocurring during a simulation execution. If this state is known a priori, time-parallel simulation can be performed by executing a number of simulations in parallel that start with an initial state that is the identified regeneration point and continue simulation until the regeneration point is reencountered. After the simulation, the sequences of states of all parallel simulations can be concatenated to a correct overall sequence of states.

In many practical cases, the identification of regeneration points is a hard problem. Instead of an exact match of the current state with the regeneration point, an approximate match can be performed by checking whether the regeneration point is contained within the allowed deviation of the current state (or if the current state is in the allowed deviation of the regeneration point, which is equivalent). This technique can be utilized to ease the determination of regeneration points.

A similar approach, that is a special case of the allowed deviation function, has been proposed by [13]. There, the concept of partial state matching is used, where states can be matched successfully if a pre-defined subset of the set of state variables matches. The rest of the state variables are allowed to have arbitrary values. The allowed deviation function proposed here for approximate state matching is a more general approach, where a finer granularity for state match decisions is possible, leading to a better control of the introduced error.

3. Implementation

The approach outlined in the last section was implemented in order to gain a first impression of its viability. Here, an overview of the implementation is presented and some interesting implementation issues are discussed. The results of experiments with the developed prototype for a simple simulation model are presented in the next section.

3.1. System overview

In order to implement the parallel simulation of time intervals in the algorithm of Figure 3, every interval is assigned to a *logical process* for simulation. Note that the number of processes n is independent of the number of time intervals m, although increasing n beyond m is not reasonable, as the maximally achievable parallelism is determined by m.

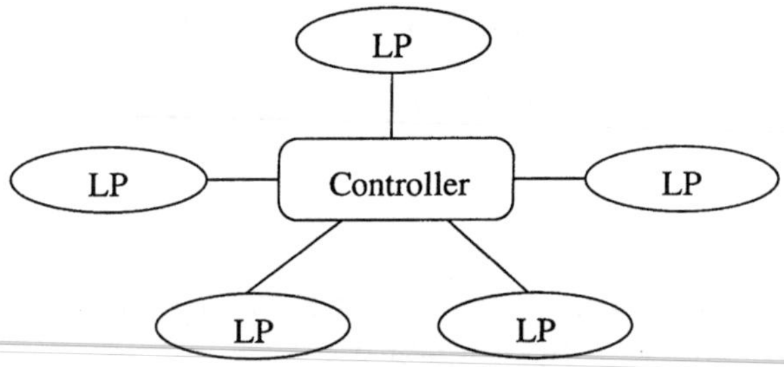

Figure 4. System structure

The basic structure of the simulation system is shown in Figure 4. The logical processes (LPs) are responsible for performing the simulations of particular time intervals. They are mainly sequential simulations that can be controlled over a network interface. The controller manages the whole simulation execution by assigning simulation tasks to the logical processes.

The communication between controller and logical processes is simple:

- the processes register with the controller,
- the controller assigns simulation tasks to the processes,
- the processes report simulation results to the controller, and
- the controller sends termination messages to the processes on completion of the simulation.

For these tasks, a simple communication protocol has been defined and implemented on top of TCP/IP for usage in a distributed simulation.

Before starting a simulation, the controller initializes a given number of time intervals and collects the logical processes that wish to participate in the simulation execution. A simulation run consists of the repeating simulation of time intervals by logical processes. The simulation ends if all intervals have been simulated with an acceptable deviation between their initial state and the final state of the previous interval.

3.2. Assignment of time intervals

In general, the assignment of intervals to logical processes can either be static, i. e. a fixed set of intervals is assigned to each process, or dynamic, i. e. the assignment is determined during runtime. Dynamic scheduling incurs an overhead for the administration of the time intervals, but it has the potential to reduce the idling of logical processes if a considerable amount of idle times is likely to occur.

In a system with m logical processes where the simulation time is partitioned into the same number m of intervals, consider the case where all of the initial states of the first $m-1$ time intervals can be accepted after the first simulation iteration, but the simulation of the remaining time interval has to be reexecuted due to an unacceptable deviation of states. Another iteration is necessary, where $m-1$ logical processes are idle. The longer the execution time for the simulation of one time interval, the more idle time is introduced. Here, the idle times can be considerably reduced by increasing the number of time intervals (as increasing the number of time intervals reduces the length of each interval, and thus the execution time needed to simulate one interval). As has been discussed in [14], the usage of a small number of intervals leads to an unbalanced processor load and consequently to a reduced efficiency of the overall simulation.

The amount of idle times of processors can be further reduced by breaking up the strictly iterative approach of the algorithm in Figure 3. However, this requires the introduction of a complex management of time intervals.

In the prototypical implementation, every time interval is in one of five possible states: `RUN` indicates that the simulation for the interval is currently run by a process, `READY` denotes an interval ready to be simulated, an interval that is `DONE` does not have to be simulated any more, and `WAIT` signifies an interval that has been simulated, but that is still waiting for a state change in the previous interval. A state diagram defining the time-interval management is shown in Figure 5.

Upon initialization, every time interval is in state `READY`, which is only left when the interval is scheduled for execution by a logical process, changing its state to `RUN`. When a logical process finishes execution of an interval T_n, the event `FINISH(n)` is sent to the state machines of all intervals, possibly resulting in further state changes. A time interval T_n that receives a `FINISH(n)` event in state `RUN`, checks whether its starting state is in the allowed deviation of the final state of the previous interval (this is indicated in the state diagram by the function call `accept(n-1)`). If the two states do not match approximately, the interval returns to the state `READY`. If the difference in simulation states is acceptable, the interval either enters the `DONE` state if the previous interval is also `DONE` (this is checked by the function call `done(n-1)`), or enters the `WAIT` state to wait for the previous time interval. A waiting interval T_n reenters the `READY` state if the simulation of T_{n-1} is finished and the difference in simulation states is not acceptable. A time interval's state changes from `WAIT` to `DONE` if any earlier interval is finished, the difference in simulation states is acceptable, and the previous interval T_{n-1} is `DONE`. This state change is only correct, if a `FINISH(n)` event is sent to intervals in increasing order of interval indices, i. e. time interval T_{k-1} processes the event before interval T_k for all $k \leq n$.

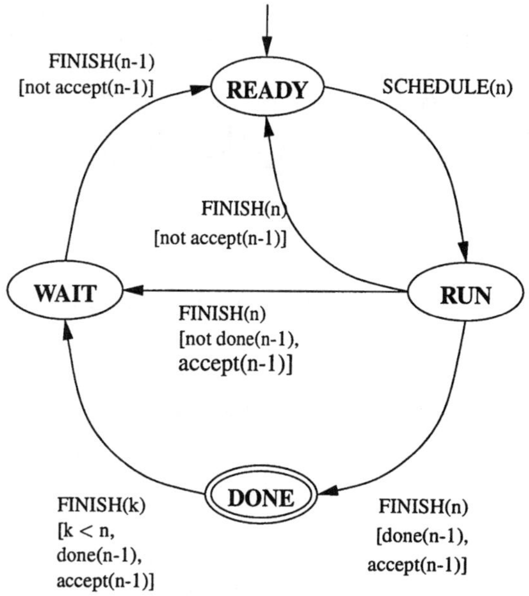

Figure 5. State diagram for time interval T_n

The state diagram in Figure 5 shows that time intervals T_k with $k > n$ are dependent on earlier intervals but not vice versa. Therefore, scheduling of intervals to processes, performed by the controller, uses the simple approach of always selecting the interval in state `READY` with the lowest index. This guarantees that simulation of intervals in the `WAIT` state can be resumed as early as possible.

3.3. Simulation example

Figure 6 depicts a sample run of the simulation system where the messages exchanged between the controller and two logical processes LP_1 and LP_2 are shown. The time axis of the simulation is separated into three intervals T_1, T_2, T_3. The sample shows the situation where the result of a simulation run for T_2 is known, but it cannot yet be decided, if this simulation run can be accepted, as the result of the simulation of T_1 is not known yet. Time interval T_2 has to be frozen, until the results of T_1 are known. If there are still intervals left to be simulated (T_3 in the example), the logical process that just finished execution does not have to remain idle, but can execute a remaining time interval.

Further, in the sample run of Figure 6, when the first simulation run of T_2 is rejected after the results of T_1 are known, T_2 is resimulated by LP_1. The decision for rejection of a simulation run for a specific time interval depends on the allowed deviation defined for a particular model.

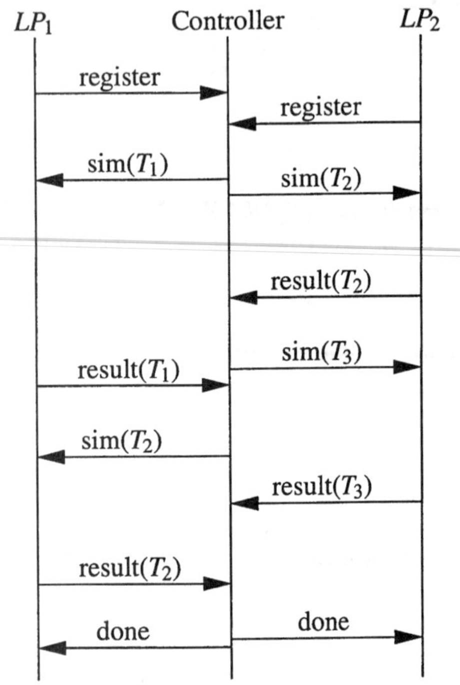

Figure 6. Sample run of the system

The example shows that the approach chosen here is fully dynamic. As already mentioned before, this incurs an overhead for process management, but has the advantage that process idle time can be minimized as long as there are intervals to simulate.

4. Experimental results

The prototype described in the last section was adapted for the simulation of an M/M/1 queue. The state $s_t = (j_t, A_T, D_t)$ of the simulation at a given time t consists of the number of present jobs j_t and the time of the next arrival A_t, as well as the next departure D_t if a job is present. In order to perform approximate matching of states at time-interval boundaries, the allowed deviation is defined as:

$$\mathcal{AD}(j_t, A_T, D_t) := \{(j'_t, A'_t, D'_t) \in \mathcal{S} : |j_t - j'_t| \leq \delta\},$$

where $\mathcal{S}$ is the state space of the simulation. Note, that $\mathcal{AD}(s)$ is a function of the number of jobs present in the system, i. e. any deviations of the next arrival and departure times are accepted. This is reasonable, because as long as the ratio of number of intervals to mean number of arrivals in an interval is sufficiently low, the statistical error introduced by the allowed deviation is determined by the difference in job numbers. The allowed deviation still depends on the parameter δ, which can be varied for a higher or lower approximation in the state matching.

Experiments were conducted as a distributed simulation on a network of workstations with 4 and 8 logical processes, each running on a different processing node. The runtime of the simulation was measured and compared to the runtime of a sequential simulator in order to measure the speedup of the parallel simulation. The influence of the allowed deviation on the speedup of the simulation was measured by varying the parameter δ. Further, the server load is known to have a great influence on the achievable speedup. This is due to the fact that it is rather easy to guess the correct number of jobs present in the system at a given time if the server load is low (in particular, the number of jobs was always guessed to be 0, which is more likely to be correct if the server load is low). As the server load increases, the variance of present jobs increases, leading to a lower probability that a guessed state is correct. Finally, also the influence of the number of time intervals on the speedup was measured for a different number of intervals.

In order to be able to measure the introduced error, the maximum number of present jobs and the average waiting time were recorded during the simulation execution. However, no definite trend in the deviation of the parallel simulation results from the sequential simulation results could be observed, even for higher values of δ. This is due to the rather small number of errors introduced and the specificities of an M/M/1 queue with server loads below 1. Because of the stable nature of such a system, the number of present jobs eventually drops to zero. Therefore, an error introduced at some time does not propagate far in simulation time. This locality of errors results in an only marginal influence of a single error on global simulation statistics. A serious distortion of simulation results could only be introduced by a high number of local errors. However, the maximum number of local errors is determined by the number of time intervals, which did not exceed 100 in the conducted experiments.

Figures 7-10 show the average speedup that could be achieved for various parameter combinations. The results presented here are averages of the results of ten repetitions for every parameter combination. Figure 7 shows the speedup for 4 logical processes and 100 time intervals. The speedup was measured for different server loads and allowed deviations. As suspected, the efficiency of the

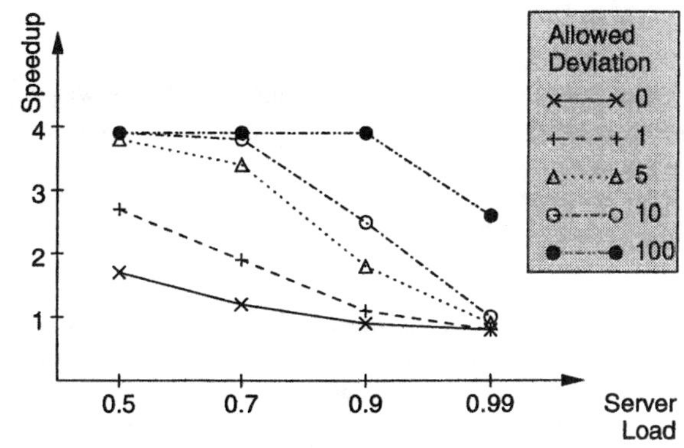

Figure 7. 4 processors and 100 time intervals

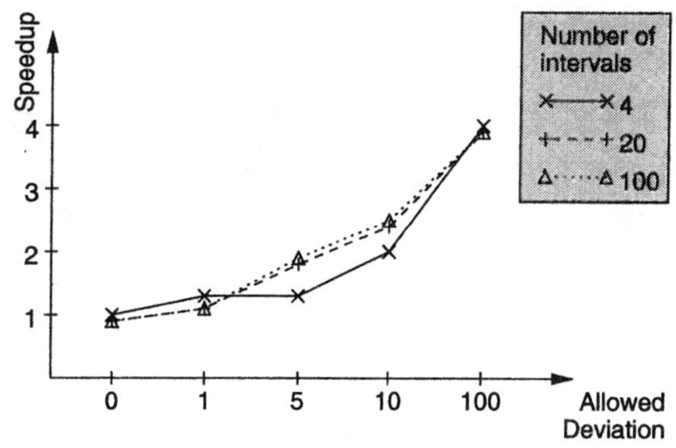

Figure 9. 4 processors and 0.9 load

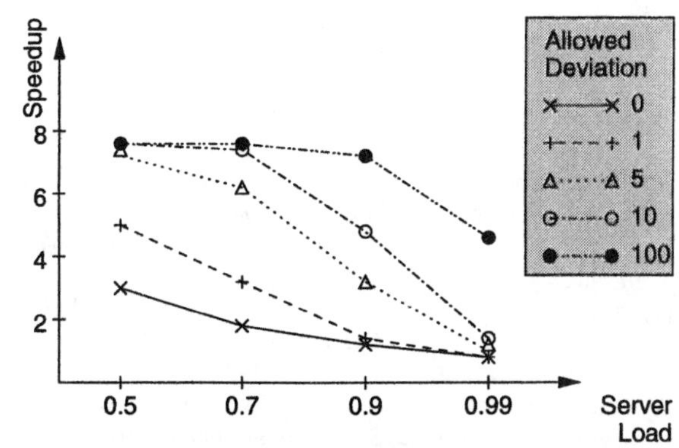

Figure 8. 8 processors and 100 time intervals

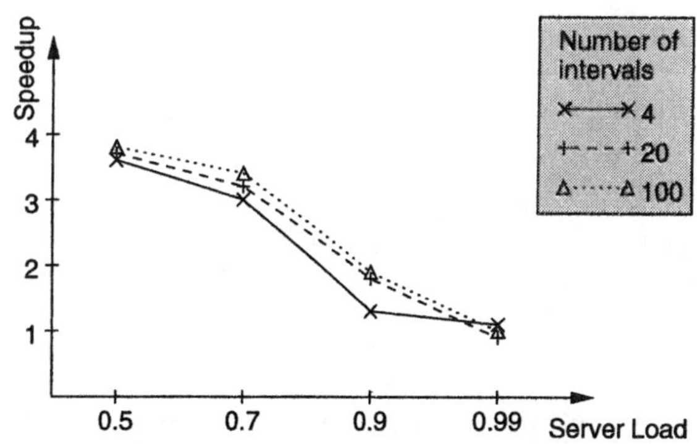

Figure 10. 8 processors and deviation 5

simulation decreases with a higher server load. However, even for high loads, an appropriate allowed deviation partly compensates the loss of speedup. For lower server loads, it is interesting to note the significant increase in speedup even with the introduction of the allowed deviation with a marginal value of $\delta = 1$. Note also that with a reasonably high allowed deviation, it is possible to approach the maximal speedup of 4, which indicates the low overhead of the simulation algorithm.

Figure 8 shows the results for 8 logical processes and 100 time intervals. These results are very similar to those for 4 processes. However, it can be noticed that the overall speedup slightly drops for 8 processors, which is due to higher communication overhead in the simulation system.

Figures 9 and 10 show the influence of the number of time intervals on the speedup. In Figure 9, this influence is compared for various allowed deviations and a server load of 0.9. For small allowed deviations, almost all of the time intervals have to be simulated more than once, wherefore the processes are busy regardless of the number of intervals. The same is true for large allowed deviations, where most of the intervals are simulated exactly once. However, for modest allowed deviations, with a small number of time intervals, the idle time of processors reaches a significant level. In this case, a higher number of intervals leads to a significant increase in speedup, whereas for very small and very high allowed deviations, the overhead of a higher number of intervals results in a slightly worse speedup compared to a small number of intervals. Figure 10 shows similar results for different server loads and an allowed deviation of 5. With high and low server loads, idle times of processors are low regardless of the number of intervals. Only for modest server loads, a higher number of intervals is beneficial for the speedup.

For the simple example of an M/M/1 queue, even with a high server load, the parameters that control the parallel simulation execution can be tuned to obtain a maximal speedup with a minimal amount of introduced error.

5. Conclusion

This work introduces the approach of approximative state matching in time-parallel simulation. An important characteristic of time-parallel simulation is the state match problem: if the simulation of a time interval starts from an initial state that is inconsistent with the final state of the previous interval, the whole simulation is incorrect. Instead of an exact solution to the problem, approximative state matching is a heuristic approach that accepts deviations in final and initial states of adjacent intervals at the cost of a deviation of simulation results from the correct values.

Time-parallel simulation with approximate state matching is a general parallel simulation approach that can be applied to any simulation model. The challenge in applying approximative state matching is to find an allowed deviation of states that maximizes the speedup of the simulation, while keeping the introduced error below an acceptable level. More work is required to gain understanding of the allowed deviation of complex states in contrast to the rather simple state of an M/M/1 queue.

The experimental results in Section 4 show that approximative state matching can reasonably be applied to the simulation of an M/M/1 queue. It would be desirable to research the application of approximative state matching to other, more realistic models. In particular, the use of approximation for practical purposes has already been mentioned in [6] for the simulation of computer caches with the LRU replacement policy, which is the dominant policy in computer caching systems. In other areas (e. g. web caching), more complex replacement strategies are used, where approximate state matching might reasonably be applied.

The fact that no error could be observed in the simulation results of the experiments is due to the low ratio of the number of time intervals to the overall simulation time. The total number of incorrect state changes leading to the introduction of an error is bounded by the number of intervals. Hence, the introduced error directly depends on the partitioning of the time axis. Analytical examination of the introduced error could stimulate further understanding of the influence of simulation parameters on the error.

With the help of approximative state matching in time-parallel simulation, the extended parallelization of appropriate simulation models is viable. Together with the approach of dynamic scheduling used by the prototypical implementation presented in this paper, it should be possible to construct a simulation system that can be executed efficiently on unreliable and/or high-latency networks with a very high number of processing nodes.

Acknowledgments

The authors would like to thank the PADS working group of ITIS e.V. for discussions which led to the ideas in this work.

References

[1] K. Chandy and R. Sherman. Space-Time and Simulation. In *Proceedings of the SCS Multiconference on Distributed Simulation*, pages 53–57, 1989.

[2] R. M. Fujimoto. Parallel Discrete Event Simulation. *Communications of the ACM*, 33(10):30–53, 1990.

[3] R. M. Fujimoto. Exploiting temporal uncertainty in parallel and distributed simulations. In *Proceedings of the 13th Workshop on Parallel and Distributed Simulation*, pages 46–53, 1999.

[4] R. M. Fujimoto. *Parallel and Distributed Simulation Systems*. John Wiley & Sons, Inc., 2000.

[5] A. G. Greenberg, B. D. Lubachevsky, and I. Mitrani. Algorithms for Unboundedly Parallel Simulations. *ACM Transactions on Computer Systems*, 9(3):201–221, 1991.

[6] P. Heidelberger and H. S. Stone. Parallel Trace-Driven Cache Simulation by Time Partitioning. In *Proceedings of the 1990 Winter Simulation Conference*, pages 734–737, 1990.

[7] Y. Lin and E. Lazowska. A Time-Division Algorithm for Parallel Simulation. *ACM Transactions on Modeling and Computer Simulation*, 1(1):73–83, 1991.

[8] P. Martini, M. Rümekasten, and J. Tölle. Tolerant Synchronization for Distributed Simulations of Interconnected Computer Networks. In *Proceedings of the 11th Workshop on Parallel and Distributed Simulation*, pages 138–141, 1997.

[9] D. Pountain and D. May. *A Tutorial Introduction to Occam Programming*. BSP Professional Books, 1987.

[10] D. M. Rao, N. V. Thondugulam, R. Radhakrishnan, and P. A. Wilsey. Unsynchronized Parallel Discrete Event Simulation. In *Proceedings of the 1998 Winter Simulation Conference*, pages 1563–1570, 1998.

[11] N. V. Thondugulam, D. M. Rao, R. Radhakrishnan, and P. A. Wilsey. Relaxing Causal Constraints in PDES. In *Proceedings of the 13th International Parallel Processing Symposium (IPPS/SPDP '99)*, pages 696–700, 1999.

[12] J. J. Wang and M. Abrams. Approximate Time-Parallel Simulation of Queueing Systems with Losses. In *Proceedings of the 1992 Winter Simulation Conference*, pages 700–708, 1992.

[13] J. J. Wang and M. Abrams. Determining Initial States for Time-Parallel Simulation. In *Proceedings of the 7th Workshop on Parallel and Distributed Simulation*, pages 19–26, 1993.

[14] H. Wu, R. M. Fujimoto, and M. Ammar. Time-Parallel Trace-Driven Simulation of CSMA/CD. In *Proceedings of the 17th Workshop on Parallel and Distributed Simulation*, pages 105–114, 2003.

Steering Committee
A. S. Elmaghraby
Univ. of Louisville, USA
R. M. Fujimoto (Honorary)
Georgia Inst. of Tech., USA
P. S. Magnusson
Virtutech Corp., USA
G. Riley
Georgia Inst. of Tech., USA
S. J. E. Taylor
Brunel Univ., UK
S. J. Turner (Chair)
Nanyang Tech. Univ., Singapore
B. W. Unger
Univ. of Calgary, Canada

General Chair
D. M. Nicol
Univ. of Illinois (UIUC), USA

Program Co-Chairs
C. D. Carothers
Rensselaer Polytech, USA
S. J. Turner
Nanyang Tech. Univ., Singapore

Program Committee Members
A. Boukerche
Univ. of Ottawa, Canada
D. Degroot
TechsUs Inc., USA
L. Donatiello
Univ. of Bologna, Italy
A. S. Elmaghraby
Univ. of Louisville, USA
R. M. Fujimoto
Georgia Inst. of Tech., USA
A. Lehmann
Univ. der Bundeswehr, Germany
M. Liljenstam
Univ. of Illinois (UIUC) USA
J. Liu
Univ. of Illinois (UIUC), USA
J. Luethi
FHS KufsteinTirol, Austria
A. L. M. Thom McLean
Georgia Inst. of Tech., USA
E. H. Page
U.S. Army, USA
K. Perumalla
Georgia Inst. of Tech., USA
F. Quaglia
Univ. of Rome, Italy
G. Riley
Georgia Inst. of Tech., USA
R. Simmonds
Univ. of Calgary, Canada
E. G. Sirer
Cornell, USA
B. K. Szymanski
Rensselaer Polytech, USA
G. Tackett
U.S. Army, USA
M. Takai
UCLA, USA
S. J. E. Taylor
Brunel Univ., UK
C. Tropper
McGill Univ., Canada
A. Uhrmacher
Univ. of Rostock, Germany
B. Unger
Univ. of Calgary, Canada
F. P. Wieland
The MITRE Corp, USA
P. A. Wilsey
Univ. of Cincinnati, USA

CALL FOR PAPERS - PADS 2005

19th ACM/IEEE/SCS Workshop on Principles of Advanced and Distributed Simulation (PADS 2005)

June 1 – 3, 2005, Monterey, California, USA

PADS has a New Name & Expanded Scope! The steering committee for the Workshop on Principles of Advanced and Distributed Simulation (PADS 2005) (formerly called *Parallel and Distributed Simulation*) continues the **expanded scope** for PADS in 2005. In addition to the traditional focus on parallel and distributed simulation methods and applications, the workshop now includes all aspects of simulation technology. The steering and program committees look forward to a number of high-quality paper submissions in the following areas.

- The construction of simulation engines using advanced computer science technology.
- Techniques for constructing scalable simulations.
- Advanced modeling techniques that allow solution of previously difficult or impossible problem domains.
- Simulation visualization techniques.
- Algorithms and methods for parallel or distributed simulation, including synchronization, scheduling, memory management, and load balancing.
- Applications of large–scale or distributed simulation methods.
- Distributed interactive simulation and distributed virtual environments.
- Tools, and techniques for interoperability of simulations, and emulations of real systems.
- Mechanisms for efficient design of experiments.

Sponsors: ACM Special Interest Group on Simulation (SIGSIM), IEEE Computer Society Technical Committee on Simulation (IEEE-TCSIM), and Society for Modeling and Simulation International (SCS).

Important Dates: Send submissions to the Program Co- Chairs no later than **October 22nd, 2004**. Electronic submission of postscript or PDF is highly encouraged, using the URL given below. Notification of acceptance will be made by **December 15th, 2004**. Camera ready copies must be submitted by **February 15th, 2005**.

Submissions: Papers must be written in English and should not exceed 5000 words. Papers must be unpublished and must not be submitted for publication elsewhere. Each submission must be accompanied by the following information: a short abstract, a complete list of authors and their affiliations, a contact person for correspondence, post and email addresses. All submissions will be reviewed using a double-blind review process, i.e., the identity of authors, and referees will not be revealed to each other. To ensure blind reviewing, authors' names and affiliations should not appear in the paper, bibliographic references should be modified so as not to reveal the identities of the authors.

Selected articles from PADS 2005 will be considered for extension and publication within a Special Issue of *SCS Simulation.*

General Chair
David M. Nicol
Univ. of Illinois Urbana-Champaign
`nicol@crhc.uiuc.edu`

Program Co–Chairs

Christopher D. Carothers
Rensselaer Polytechnic Institute
`chrisc@cs.rpi.edu`

Stephen J. Turner
Nanyang Tech. Univ., Singapore
`ASSJTurner@ntu.edu.sg`

Conference URL: Refer to the conference web page at:
`http://www.pads-workshop.org/pads2005`
for paper submission instructions and up–to–date information.

Notes

Author Index

Notes

Notes

Notes

Notes

IEEE COMPUTER SOCIETY

IEEE

IEEE Computer Society Publications

The world-renowned IEEE Computer Society publishes, promotes, and distributes a wide variety of authoritative computer science and engineering texts. These books are available from most retail outlets. Visit the CS Store at *http://computer.org* for a list of products.

IEEE Computer Society Proceedings

The IEEE Computer Society also produces and actively promotes the proceedings of more than 160 acclaimed international conferences each year in multimedia formats that include hard and soft-cover books, CD-ROMs, videos, and on-line publications.

For information on the IEEE Computer Society proceedings, please e-mail to csbooks@computer.org or write to Proceedings, IEEE Computer Society, P.O. Box 3014, 10662 Los Vaqueros Circle, Los Alamitos, CA 90720-1314. Telephone +1-714-821-8380. Fax +1-714-761-1784.

Additional information regarding the Computer Society, conferences and proceedings, CD-ROMs, videos, and books can also be accessed from our web site at *http://computer.org/cspress*

Revised: 20 February 2004